# Praise for *Future Families*

"Ross Parke's wonderful book arrives in a time intensified (again), with widely clashing views about what ideal families should be like. Parke provides a detailed and engaging account of the diversity of contemporary families, laying waste along the way to many widely-held myths about what is healthy for parents and children that have dominated current discussions without paying attention to the evidence. This book will serve as the new go-to reference source for family scholars and their students in the social sciences and humanities. It will also be required reading for (open-minded) political decision-makers and family-service providers who are concerned with how we allocate resources for families, especially in these times of economic distress."

Carolyn and Philip Cowan, *Professors Emeriti of Psychology,*
*University of California, Berkeley*

"*Future Families: Diverse Forms, Rich Possibilities* is the best introduction to the topic of family diversity that I have seen to date. A succinct but remarkably comprehensive treatment of the topic of family diversity."

Frank Furstenberg, *The Zellerbach Family Professor of Sociology,*
*University of Pennsylvania*

"This is the most important book on the family to have been written in the 21st Century. It is unsurpassed in terms of its sensitive and erudite consideration of the key questions raised by contemporary family forms and the extent to which these questions can be answered by empirical research. It brings the topic alive by including real-world examples and discussion of the social and psychological implications of Future Families – a 'must-read' for everyone with an interest in family life today."

Susan Golombok, *Professor of Psychology and Director of The Centre*
*for Family Research, University of Cambridge*

"Even Tolstoy, who thought 'all happy families resemble one another', could not have imagined the diversity of forms those happy families take, but Ross Parke has. In this innovative book he provides context, understanding, and the scientific basis for appreciating differences in numbers of parents, gender of parents, and sources of children. His scholarship will inform professionals, parents, policymakers, students, and faculty about the continuing changes in modern family structure and life."

Arnold Sameroff, *Professor Emeritus of Psychology,*
*University of Michigan*

# Future Families

*Diverse Forms, Rich Possibilities*

Ross D. Parke

University of California–Riverside

**WILEY** Blackwell

This edition first published 2013
© 2013 John Wiley & Sons, Inc

*Registered Office*
John Wiley & Sons, Ltd, The Atrium, Southern Gate, Chichester, West Sussex, PO19 8SQ, UK

*Editorial Offices*
350 Main Street, Malden, MA 02148-5020, USA
9600 Garsington Road, Oxford, OX4 2DQ, UK
The Atrium, Southern Gate, Chichester, West Sussex, PO19 8SQ, UK

For details of our global editorial offices, for customer services, and for information about how
to apply for permission to reuse the copyright material in this book please see our website at
www.wiley.com/wiley-blackwell.

The right of Ross D. Parke to be identified as the author of this work has been asserted in accordance
with the UK Copyright, Designs and Patents Act 1988.

*Library of Congress Cataloging-in-Publication Data*

Parke, Ross D.
Future families: diverse forms, rich possibilities/Ross D. Parke.
    pages  cm
  Includes bibliographical references and index.
  ISBN 978-0-470-67445-1 (cloth) – ISBN 978-0-470-67449-9 (pbk.)   1. Families.   I. Title.
  HQ728.P28 2013
  306.85–dc23
                                        2013012093

A catalogue record for this book is available from the British Library.

Cover image: Cover photograph courtesy of Heather Camerio.
Cover design by Design Deluxe.

Set in 10/12.5pt Galliard by SPi Publisher Services, Pondicherry, India
Printed in Malaysia by Ho Printing (M) Sdn Bhd

1   2013

# Contents

# Preface

Like many books, this one has been percolating during many years of reading, research, and writing and has been advanced most of all by discussions with colleagues and students. The book brings together my varied interests in new family forms and is based on my own and others' research on fathers, same-gender parents, new reproductive technologies, immigrant families, cross-cultural insights about family forms, and the implications of these issues for children's social and emotional development.

I have been studying families since the 1960s when I began this journey with observations of fathers and newborns. I thought that in a decade or so parental roles would shift and men and women would be equal partners in parenting. Although the revolution never happened, there has been a gradual steady evolution in the way that parents organize their family roles and responsibilities. This book chronicles these shifts, but this was only the beginning. The very definition of family has been changing and the concept of the ideal or perfect family has been challenged by a variety of shifts. Instead of the two-parent nuclear family rearing their biological offspring, the traditional family form has been moved off center stage by a wide range of other family forms. Single mothers and single fathers have become more common, either as a result of divorce or by design. Stepfamilies have emerged as a more prevalent family form in the aftermath of the rise in divorce rates. Even marriage itself has declined as more couples have chosen to cohabit instead of marrying, with children often being part of the cohabitating household.

Who can become parents has shifted through advances in assisted reproductive technologies. This has allowed previously infertile couples or individuals to achieve their goal of parenthood, as well as providing an alternative pathway to parenthood for same-sex couples. The increased prevalence of same-sex parents as a family form, combined with the mounting evidence that children reared in these family contexts are well adjusted, has led discussions away from a focus on the gender of parents and the necessity of opposite-sex parents as the family unit to a focus on parenting processes. One of the central messages of this book is that family process trumps family form. Shifts in social science away from our Western-centric bias has led to a reexamination of other cultures and their historical reminder that our myopic focus on the Western ideal family form of two opposite-sex parents and their biological children is found less often in past cultures. Instead, in many other cultures cooperative community-based models of parenting in which parental caregiving and supervisory responsibilities are shared with kin and nonkin are common. Similar models of cooperative caregiving are found among African American families as well as among recent waves of immigrant families from Central and South America and Asia. The lessons that can be learned from these groups can usefully inform our contemporary dialogues about the effects of new family forms on children by highlighting the fact that children can thrive in a variety of family forms, especially if there is sufficient community support for all forms of families. In response to recent suggestions that parenting may be detrimental to one's mental health, especially happiness and life satisfaction, we address this issue by showing that caregiving is, in fact, not only good for children but good for the adult providers as well. The policy implications of these shifts in family forms are addressed with the goal of achieving more equitable social policies for all family forms and not just the ideal family form, which is the narrow template that guides many of our current policies. Suggestions are offered for overcoming the barriers that limit our acceptance of new family forms since increased acceptance of these family forms can potentially benefit children's socioemotional development.

The book brings together a set of issues that are often treated independently but that share the common thread of challenging our notion of an ideal family form. Moreover, the book goes beyond mere description to examine the implications of these forms for children's development. For example, books on a variety of specific family issues such as child care, working mothers, shifting parental roles, same-sex parents, cultural and ethnic issues, and the assisted reproductive technologies have appeared in recent years, but they often fail to assess the implications of these changes for children's development.

In addition, many earlier books treat the changing family issues as separate and independent rather than as a unified set of social changes. Often, they offer a variety of perspectives of the individual authors without the benefit of any overarching theme or argument that links the disparate but related changes in families. In addition, they are often written from the perspective of a single discipline and therefore fail to capture the richness of the issues that do, indeed, cut across disciplinary boundaries. As a corrective, the scope of this book is interdisciplinary and draws from work in many areas beyond my own field of developmental psychology, including sociology, cross-cultural scholarship, ethnic studies, anthropology, history, legal studies, economics, neuroscience, and even architecture and design. As is being increasingly recognized, families are too important and too complex to be left in the hands of a single discipline.

The book is best thought of as a stimulus to new conversations about our conception of families and an exploration of the implications of changing family forms for children's social and emotional development. The goal is to generate dialogue about our cultural definition of families and to argue for a broadened view of families beyond some imagined ideal form. A related goal is to build a new scholarly agenda to guide future research on families by identifying new avenues for future researchers and policy makers. However, it would be mistaken to assume that scholars or politicians own these issues. Many of the topics addressed here are being debated and discussed not only in seminar rooms and in political caucuses but among ordinary but concerned individuals around water coolers, in parental playgroups, and over lunch across the nation. Although the book will be thoroughly grounded in the empirical literature from a variety of disciplines, my goal is to make the book accessible to a wider general audience of individuals who are interested in social trends in families and the implications of these trends for our children. To appeal to a general readership, I limited the use of jargon (or carefully define technical terms when needed), while providing qualitative material in the form of quotes from real families to draw readers into the narrative and to illustrate the quantitative findings. So the hope is that parents and others concerned about the changing nature of families in our society will profit from this book as well.

# Acknowledgments

A host of individuals have contributed to this book. I owe a great deal to the students and colleagues who have shared in my research program on families and shared their ideas and insights at the University of Wisconsin, the Fels Research Institute, the University of Cincinnati College of Medicine, the University of Illinois, and, for the past 20 years, at the University of California, Riverside (UCR). Scott Coltrane, my sociologist colleague, has been an integral part of this journey and shared my interests in fathers, changing family roles, and immigrant families as part of our collaborative work at the Center for Family Studies at UCR. The Center for Society and Ideas at UCR provided an opportunity for an interdisciplinary seminar on the implications of the new reproductive technologies on families. Robin DiMatteo, a health psychologist, Christine Gailey, an anthropologist and women's studies scholar, Scott Coltrane, a family sociologist, and myself, a developmental psychologist, formed this group, and our deliberations and writing informed chapter five on assisted reproductive technologies (ART). In addition, several individuals have offered scholarly material as well as helpful critiques of drafts of this book. My long time colleagues and friends, Carolyn and Philip Cowan, provided detailed feedback on the whole book as did Scott Coltrane. Several individuals provided helpful comments on portions of the book, including Susan Golombok, Charlotte Patterson, Patricia East, Mary Gauvain, Bonnie Leadbeater, Ernestine Avila, Tanya Ann Nieri, Raymond Buriel, Melinda Leidy, and Michele Adams. Les Whitbeck, Melissa Walls, and Brian Armenta shared their work on North American indigenous families. Sonya Lyubomirsky sent me her recent work on the effects of being a caregiver on psychological well-being. Marc Bornstein shared new material on the neurological preparedness of adults for caregiving. Charlotte Patterson directed me to the most recent work on same sex-parent families. Susan Golombok alerted me to the latest studies on families using assisted reproductive technologies. Several anonymous reviewers provided me with helpful and cogent feedback. Heather Vogel provided assistance with the bibliography. Alison Clarke-Stewart, my wife, collaborator, and best friend, encouraged me to write this book even though it moved me out of my comfort zone while discouraging me from taking on easier and safer projects. Her editing and formatting expertise are unrivaled as is her support and critique of my ideas.

Finally, thanks to the Wiley Blackwell editorial team for their support and guidance. Matt Bennett recognized the value of the book and offered the book contract, while Danielle Descoteaux oversaw the book after Matt departed. Her support and responsiveness to my many queries are greatly appreciated. Karen Shield guided the production phase of the book, N. Yassar Arafat oversaw with great care the copyediting phase of the book, and Olivia Evans and her team designed a cover that nicely captured the themes of the book.

# About the Author

Ross D. Parke was Distinguished Professor of Psychology and Director of the Center for Family Studies at the University of California, Riverside. He also taught at the University of Illinois at Urbana-Champaign and at the University of Wisconsin. He is Past President of the Society for Research in Child Development, from which he received the Distinguished Scientific Contribution to Child Development Award, and of the Developmental Psychology Division of the American Psychological Association, from which he received the G. Stanley Hall Award for his contributions to developmental psychology. He has served as editor of the *Journal of Family Psychology* and *Developmental Psychology* and was associate editor of *Child Development*. He is the author of *Fatherhood*, coauthor of *Throwaway Dads: The Myths and Barriers That Keep Men from Being the Fathers They Want to Be* and *Social Development*, and coeditor of *Family–Peer Relationships: In Search of the Linkages; Children in Time and Place; Exploring Family Relationships with Other Social Contexts;* and *Strengthening Couple Relationships for Optimal Child Development*. He obtained his PhD from the University of Waterloo, Ontario, Canada, and his work has focused on early social relationships in infancy and childhood, the effects of punishment, aggression, child abuse, fathers' roles in child development, links between family and peer social systems, ethnic variations in families, and the effects of new reproductive technologies on families. He is highly regarded as a textbook author with seven editions of *Child Psychology: A Contemporary Viewpoint* to his credit.

# 1
# Challenges to the Ideal Family Form

*Family is not a static institution but one that is constantly being reworked, reshaped, reimagined and reenacted in complex and dynamic ways* (Abbie Goldberg, 2010)

As Michael Sandel (2004) argued in his provocative essay, "The case against perfection," as a society we are concerned about achieving perfection in many spheres of our lives, including ideal physical beauty enhanced through the use of surgery and drugs, athletic perfection created by performance enhancing substances, and "designer" babies produced through the application of new reproductive technologies. This concept of the pursuit of perfection can be extended to contemporary views of families as well. Just as our society has developed notions of perfect thighs, ideal faces, and endorsement-worthy athletes, it has developed a cultural image of a perfect or ideal family. Every society and historical era invents and legitimates a particular version of the family in terms of the identity of members, their rights and responsibilities toward each other and their children (Coltrane & Collins, 2001). In our own society, the concept of an "ideal" family form incorporates the traditional ideas about Dad as breadwinner and Mom as homemaker living with their children in a safe suburban setting surrounded by a manicured lawn and a white picket fence. The cultural embodiment of this "ideal" family is the nuclear family form consisting of two heterosexual parents who conceive and rear their biological children, and is the template against which other family forms are judged. According to a national survey in Canada, 80% of Canadians believe two married, heterosexual parents and their children constitute a family (Ipsos Reid Poll, September, 2010). Similar views prevail in the United States as well. Consider a US report *Counted Out: Same-Sex Relations and American's Definitions of Family* by sociologist Brian Powell and his colleagues (2010) which also found that the most agreed-upon definition of a family was a husband, a wife, and their children. Fewer agreed that single-parent families, married couples without children, or cohabitating couples with children constituted a family.

*Future Families: Diverse Forms, Rich Possibilities*, First Edition. Ross D. Parke.
© 2013 John Wiley & Sons, Inc. Published 2013 by John Wiley & Sons, Inc.

Perhaps this notion has its roots in our distant past as anthropologist Meredith Small has noted:

> There's something 'right' about a nuclear family, or so we think. Family, we're taught by culture and religion, 'should' be composed of a mother, father and at least two kids, preferably one of each sex. That ideal was recently underscored by finding a 4600-year-old mass grave in Germany containing thirteen individuals, many of them children. Poignantly, some adults were buried facing each other, with their arms entwined. But even more poignant, scientists from the University of Bristol and University of Adelaide used DNA analysis to link one couple with their two children, the oldest evidence of a nuclear family. This report tugs at our heart strings because it fits with what our culture has embraced as the definition of a family. As such, those bodies laid to rest together seem to confirm that the nuclear family is an ancient, and therefore evolutionarily selected, 'natural' human grouping (Small, December, 2008).

In spite of the fact that the heterosexual nuclear family is currently conceived of as both normative and ideal, and may have existed in ancient times, it is also true that it has been neither normative nor ideal in other times in human history. Even in our own contemporary society this particular family form is fast becoming less prevalent and coexists with a wide variety of other family forms. My goal of this book is to explore these other forms, which, in reality, reflect how many families in Western cultures live, and to explore not only the viability of these forms as contexts in which children are raised but to discuss their possible advantages as well. By fully embracing a range of family forms rather than presuming a single form is ideal, we can better align our social policies to support a diversity of child rearing environments. Both adults and children will benefit from our heightened appreciation of this rich array of family forms.

As a guide to the concept of the "ideal" family form that will be a recurring theme throughout the book, turn to Table 1.1 for a schematic summary of the contrasting ways in which the nuclear family form and other family forms differ from each other.

**Table 1.1**  Assumptions Underlying the "Ideal" Family Form versus Alternative Family Forms

| *"Ideal" family form* | *Alternative family forms* |
| --- | --- |
| Two parents | One parent, no parents, or multiple parents |
| Married | Cohabiting, planning to marry, staying single, or divorced |
| Heterosexual | Homosexual, bisexual, nonsexual, transsexual |
| Two biological parents | One or more social parent(s) through artificial insemination, surrogacy, adoption, foster care, or kinship (relative headed household) |
| Coresident | Part-time resident, shared custody, visitation access to children |
| One (male) breadwinner | Dual earner couple, job cycling in/out reverse role families (female as breadwinner; male as primary caregiver) |
| Child care only by parents | Childcare by parents and/or relatives, siblings, staff in child care centers or family day care homes, neighbors, members of childcare cooperatives, members of a collective community |

# The Myth of the Historical Baseline

In spite of the current cultural endorsement of the nuclear family as the ideal family form, this has not always been the predominant family form or the ideal family form. We have constantly reinvented the ideal family form in response to changing historical circumstances. So why has this particular form emerged as the ideal family form today? Why has the nuclear family captured such attention and found so many champions? Part of the reason is that although change has characterized families over time, we have chosen a period in our history that we imagine or recall as being a particularly good period for families and then used this era as the baseline for comparisons with the contemporary state of the family. However, selection of a particular period in the past is a tricky business and typically misleading since it ignores the dynamic and changing nature of family forms. In fact, at numerous times in our past, many families failed to conform to the "ideal" family form even if at first glance they appeared to support it. Here is an example of how we can be led astray. It turns out that anthropologist Meredith Small's discovery of support for the nuclear family in the mass grave in Germany was not clear-cut. Focusing attention on only the four related bodies that conformed to our ideal notion of the nuclear family and ignoring the other nine unrelated bodies is biased. As Small herself argued:

> The presence of the other nine individuals underscores the fact that our ideas of the 'ideal' family are narrow, and just plain inaccurate. The thirteen bodies in that German grave are there not because they are a family per se, but because they were important to each other, connected in some way, either economically or emotionally, because that's really what people do (Small, December 5, 2008).

Consider also the alternatives to the ideal family form that characterized families during the past two centuries in the United States. As legal historian Stephan Sugarman (2008) observed,

> During times of slavery in America, slave couples were forbidden to marry. While slaves who were fathers worked, they were plainly not in the paid labor force, and mothers who were slaves were hardly allowed to remain at home to care for their young. Even for white families, it has been recognized for ages that the 'ideal' was not always possible. Sometimes the man of the house died young, say, in a farming or industrial accident, leaving his wife and children behind. Sometimes the mother died, perhaps in childbirth, and was survived by her husband and children. Widowers generally were expected to remarry, if possible, thereby creating a new stepfamily with the parents still playing traditional roles. Widowed mothers were encouraged to remarry as well, although this was understood to be less likely to occur. Moreover, in earlier days in America, when so many people were recent immigrants, a large share of the population was poor, and vast numbers lived on farms or were employed in factories. In those families, many women worked at jobs beyond childrearing at home. In addition, multigenerational living arrangements were common, with sons or daughters bringing their spouses into the family home to live with those who would become the grandparents of their children. Furthermore, as sharp downturns frequently struck the economy, there were many desperately poor families with no regularly employed members. And in some eras these families were consigned to live in communal 'poorhouses' or 'workhouses,' rather than their own homes. Additionally, even putting joblessness aside, throughout the first half of the twentieth century, candid observers recognized that considerable deviance from the preferred

societal norm was the reality. Some fathers simply abandoned their families, leaving their wives and children in miserable conditions. Some couples divorced, often to the considerable detriment of wives and children. Some unmarried women became mothers and sometimes lived with men who may or may not have been the fathers of their children (pp. 232–233).

Clearly, the concept of the nuclear family as a cultural ideal or a common family form is not supported by the historical record. Instead it is a relatively recent ideal that is centered in the 1950s. As Sugarman further observed:

> By the 1950s, American law and policy, largely centered on a single vision of the 'ideal' family, composed of a married man, who worked in the paid labor force, and his wife, who spent most of her time in their home caring for their biological children. Americans were strongly encouraged to conform to that norm. Other groupings of adults and children – even if they were considered families by some people – were generally disfavored by the predominant social values (and by the public programs) of the time (2008, p. 232).

To idealize a particular family form that was championed in a single era and to assume that it is an ideal family form that is historically sanctioned is at least misleading or more likely downright inaccurate. Family historian Stephanie Coontz captured the central fallacy of our assumption about the historical longevity of the "ideal" family form in the title of her book *The Way We Never Were: American Families and the Nostalgia Trap* (1992). In this myth-busting volume Coontz, by a careful historical tour of family forms over the last several centuries, documents not only that the "ideal" nuclear family form existed only briefly in the 1950s and 1960s but also that a wide variety of forms were common in our past. Moreover, Coontz underscores that the cultural endorsement of the 1950s family form is itself fraught with misconceptions. Yes, men worked, women stayed at home and looked after children and divorce rates were low, but all was not tranquil and peaceful in these supposedly ideal families. There was marital conflict, spousal and child abuse, maternal depression and despair, albeit masked by public displays of contentment and conformity that allowed the myth of this form of family to be perpetuated. Even the Nelson family who played the idealized nuclear family in the popular TV show *The Adventures of Ozzie and Harriet* in the 1950s and 1960s were later revealed to be fraught with father–son conflict and resentment in real life (Weinraub, 1998).

Nor is it just legal scholars and historians who have warned against acceptance of this very parochial and historically misleading view of the ideal family. Family therapist Froma Walsh has eloquently noted that our conception of family is too narrow:

> It is unfortunate when public discourse frames as 'profamily' those who adhere to the 1950's nuclear family as the sole standard for healthy families while denouncing as 'anti-family' those who hold a pluralistic view. Abundant research shows that children can be raised well in a variety of family arrangements. We need to be mindful that families in the distant past and in cultures worldwide have had multiple, varied structures and that effective family processes and the quality of relationships matter most for the well-being of children (Walsh, 2006, pp. 31–32).

If our conception of family is too restricted and too exclusive, what should it be?

## From Past to Present

In recent decades, new family forms have become more common and are challenging this definition of an "ideal" family. Many demographic and technological trends have contributed, among them the increase in divorce and remarriage, changes in maternal employment patterns, increased prevalence of same-sex parents, new routes to parenthood permitted by alternative methods of reproduction, new family models provided by Asian and Hispanic immigrants, and increased contact with family variations in other cultures around the globe. As we will see in this book, families with porous boundaries that allow a wide range of extended family and members of the community to contribute to caregiving and other responsibilities of family life were the historical norm and provide models for contemporary families as well. This book provides both an overview of some of these changing family forms and a critical examination of how they affect children's social, emotional, and cognitive development.

## Meet the Families

Let us introduce some families. Some meet the common definition of the "ideal" – nuclear – family, but many do not. Instead families come in many forms.

## The Evans: The "Ideal" Nuclear Family

Ellen and Tom Evans are married and live in a suburban home in a safe neighborhood. They both have good jobs. Ellen is a nurse and Tom is a high school teacher. They have raised two biological children who are now teenagers. When the children, Mike and Lisa, were in elementary school, Ellen stayed home to look after them, and she returned to her nursing career when the children were in their teens. They viewed it as important to manage child-rearing by themselves without the use of child care or nannies. They enjoy material comforts beyond Tom and Ellen's own European American, middle-class origins. Mike and Lisa, are good kids, doing reasonably well in school, who aspire to go to college and become successful professionals. The Evans represent the "ideal" American family, a standard against which other family forms are judged. As the Evans family illustrates, the assumption is that the ideal family form for successfully raising children should consist of two parents who are heterosexual, married, and residing in the same household. They are the biological parents of their teenage children and Tom is the major breadwinner especially when the children were young, while Ellen was the stay-at-home caregiver during the children's formative years.

## The Millers: The Dual Career, Outsourcing Family

Another family, the Millers, represents another version of the typical contemporary American family but one that nonetheless departs from the ideal family form. Even though Loretta Miller wanted to be a stay-at-home mom, she and her husband, Steve, decided that they need two paychecks to manage financially. Loretta is a teller at the local credit union while Steve, a certified plumber, works for a national plumbing company. They reluctantly enrolled their children, two-year-old Stacey in child care and five-year-old Rick in an after-school program to make it possible for both parents to work, an adaptation to the economic demands of modern family life. Just as the wealthy as well as many poor families of the past have done, the Millers "outsourced" child-rearing assistance in the form of child care and after-school care.

## Baker–Ashe: The Cohabitating Family

One of the fastest rising family forms is the cohabitating couple who chose not to marry but share a residence and raise children together. Elaine Baker and John Ashe are a typical contemporary cohabitating couple. They have lived together for five years and have two-year-old and four-year-old sons. Perhaps they will marry but for now they are content with their arrangement, except that their tax bill is higher due to their single tax filing status. They both work full time. Elaine is a dental technician and John is a real estate agent. As in the case of many families with small children, they rely on professional child care to attend to their children during the day since their extended family is too far away to offer aid with the caregiving duties. Elaine envies her African American coworker who relies on her extended kin to help out with child care.

## The Winstons: The Single-Mother-by-Choice Family

Mary Winston and her seven-year-old son Sam represent another form of family increasingly found in many North American neighborhoods. Mary, a college educated 39-year-old account executive at an advertising firm is a single mother by choice. When she was 30, she decided to start a family but had no husband in her sights so decided to go ahead and start a family with the "help" of a friend. She enjoys being a parent but has no immediate plans to get married. Instead she relies on her parents and other relatives including her sisters and an older brother as well as friends and neighbors for child care advice and assistance with child rearing and child care. Her sister Janice is a regular member of the household and often moves in and takes over when Mary has an out-of-town business trip. Mary enrolled her son Sam in a community Little League team as well. Mary is a member of the national organization of like-minded women, "Single Mothers by Choice," which offers support and opportunities to share with other older single mothers. Although Sam has only one mom, he has lots of other people who play an active "parenting" role in his life, especially his aunt Janice.

## The Fuller Family: The Adolescent Mother Family

Not all single mothers arrive in this position by choice. Sometimes pregnancies are unplanned, especially among young women like Jackie Fuller, who dropped out of high school after her daughter Elle was born. Elle's father, a high school senior, was unable to provide much financial support and left the day-to-day caregiving to Jackie. Fortunately, Jackie eventually completed high school and now works part time to support herself and her daughter. Like many single mothers, she relied on government support to help her out financially and enrolled Elle in the local Head Start program. She expects to enroll in community college to improve her computer skills so she can be independent. Her extended family, especially her aunt and her mother often share in caring for Elle.

## The Tremblay–Bailey Family: The Stepparent Family

For some, single motherhood follows divorce. Bethany Tremblay was a divorced single parent of six-year-old Eric for several years after her marriage collapsed. Then she met Oscar Bailey who was also divorced with joint custody of two children – nine-year-old Melissa and seven-year-old Frank. After a year of dating, they decided to marry and form a new combined stepfamily with their three children. Life is complicated for the new family but they are managing to coordinate their children's visits and stayovers with Eric's father and with Oscar's ex-wife who has custody of Melissa and Frank about half the time. These children have many parental figures in their lives as well as multiple sets of grandparents. Their arrangement is far from what is considered the "ideal" family form, but as we will see this type of family, including the children, can thrive in spite of the challenges and bumps that they encounter along the way.

## Standish–McCLoud: The Lesbian Parent Family

Down the block from the Evans and the Millers, the Standish–McCloud family resides. This family also has two children, Michele and Eric, but instead of a mom and dad, they have two mothers, Janice and Darlene. Janice is a sales representative for a pharmaceutical firm and Darlene is a librarian at an elementary school. They live in Vermont and have been married since 2009 and have been partners in a civil union since 2000. This couple achieved parenthood by adopting their children. Michele who is now 12 years old, was adopted from China when she was 2 years old, and 10-year-old Eric, her younger brother, was adopted from Russia when he was just six months old. Janice and Darlene have told their children about their origins and have bought books and videos to help them understand their cultural heritages. They have pictures of their birth parents in their house and plan to take a trip to see their birth place and meet their biological parents when their children are a little older. Janice's brother lives close by and he often comes to visit to play with the children and babysit to allow Janice and Darlene some time away from the children.

## The Lewin Family: The Reverse Role Family

Meet the Lewin family who are unusual in a different way. Both Mary Helen and Todd are computer software engineers but after the birth of their daughter, Pamela, Todd became a full-time stay-at-home dad. Mary Helen continued to work full time. They are pleased with the arrangement even though Todd initially got some strange looks from the mothers of the other toddlers at the playground and sometimes his former coworkers gently kid him about his choice to be a stay-at-home caregiver. However, that situation was short lived and now Todd is part of a neighborhood parent–toddler play group where parents exchange child-care advice and babysit for each others' children. Todd is also an active member of an on-line stay-at-home dads network, which has been a source of emotional support as well as practical parenting advice. Pamela has a close relationship with both of her parents. Todd enjoys his role as the primary caregiver, and Mary Helen is pleased to be moving up in her software company. The Lewins think that their unorthodox family arrangement is good for all of them, especially with the help of their neighborhood and virtual social networks.

## The Darcys: The Assisted Reproductive Technology Family

Get acquainted with another family, the Darcys. After being married for nearly a decade but without any success in starting a family, Joan and Harry Darcy discovered that they could not have biological children due to some medical issues. Harry discovered that he had a low sperm count and Joan had a scarred uterus due to an earlier infection. So they decided to have children the new fashioned way with aid of the Assisted Reproductive Technologies (ART). They contracted with a trusted family friend, Chad, who agreed to be a sperm donor and a fertility clinic to provide a surrogate mother, Marion who received an egg from Joan. They now have three children using the same surrogate, Marion, and their sperm donor friend Chad. Both Marion and Chad are regular participants in the Darcy family; they often babysat when the children were growing up, continue to join family celebrations, and are regularly consulted on child rearing dilemmas and even some medical and school decisions. Their involvement clearly extends well beyond their biological roles in helping to start a family; they are integral partners in the life of the Darcy family. Both the Darcys and Marion and Chad are satisfied with the arrangement. It has made the parenting tasks less demanding for Joan and Harry and the children enjoy close relationships with all of these adults and love having lots of people to help them with their school work and teach them new things. Neither Chad nor Marion have children of their own but gain lots of pleasure in being part of the Darcy family.

## The Dorados: The Extended Family

Maria and Jose Dorado are first-generation Mexican immigrants who live in Los Angeles, California. Maria works part time and Jose holds down two jobs – a daytime construction job and part-time evening work as a security guard – in order to support their four children, who range in age from 8 to 16. They live in a modest home on an urban street with lots of traffic and not much green space for recreation; they worry about the crime rate, homeless vagrants, and the gangs in their part of the city. In spite of their economic struggle, the Dorado family enjoys a high level of support from their extended family and community. Their home is located close to their jobs, and they are part of a tightly knit Mexican American community.

Many members of their extended family – grandparents, siblings, nieces, nephews, and cousins as well as nonkin compadres – live in the same neighborhood, and they frequently visit one another. They help a lot with money when things get tight, and, of course, look out for the children. They do most things together as a family such as taking walks, going to movies, socializing, and attending church. The older Dorado children sometimes serve as language brokers for their parents and experience a sense of pride and an increased sense of self efficacy as a consequence of helping their less language-proficient parents deal with tax officials or the educational and medical systems.

## The Benningtons and the Winfields:
## The Intergenerational Families

As a rule in Western cultures, individuals of different generations often live separate lives. Unlike the Dorado family, many grandparents often reside in different parts of the country from their children and grandchildren. Many older people choose to live in "seniors only" residential settings where children – their own grandchildren or anyone else's children – are not part of their daily lives. But older and younger generations need not live apart. Take Hope Meadows, for example, an innovative residential community in Illinois where multiple generations live in the same community and which explicitly encourages cooperation and contact across generations. Both Jennifer and Joe Bennington, a retired couple in their 70s with grown children who live in distant parts of the country, and Trish and Timothy Winfield, a couple in their mid 30s who are raising two adopted foster children are residents of Hope Meadows. This unusual residential program is a three-generation living arrangement in which children, parents, and seniors form a community that benefits all of the participants. In this community, seniors like the Benningtons are present and actively involved as playground supervisors, tutors, or crossing guards for the children of the community. Some are around just to listen to children and offer support and advice. Parents such as the Winfields benefit, too, by gaining support and wisdom from older and more experienced individuals in the same community. And the seniors feel useful, needed, and appreciated. This multigenerational community model is an example of how individuals at different life stages even though they are unrelated can form bonds and function as a child-centered cooperative community.

So far, we have met a diverse set of families and, with the exception of the Evans family, these families are departures from conventional views of the "ideal" family as two heterosexual parents who conceive and raise their biological children largely by themselves. A common characteristic that unites these other types of families is not only their clear violation of the traditional view of the nature of a family but the commitment to open or porous boundaries between parents and other individuals including extended family members, nonbiologically related community partners such as older children, friends, or mentors. This community-based cooperative model of caregiving can assume a variety of forms, but the argument is that it is a central aspect of alternative forms of family. So do the Evans, the "ideal" family, enjoy a better quality of life, tighter family bonds, and better adjusted children than the other families that we have met? The answer is not as simple as you might think.

A closer look at the Evans suggests that the traditional model of family is not necessarily the best one. When we examine the Evans family more closely, we find that Ellen and Tom are struggling to balance work and family obligations as they try to maintain their comfortable lifestyle. As in many "ideal" families, there are conflicts over the distribution of household labor. While Tom does some household chores, Ellen often feels that he does not do enough. She sometimes thinks that she is doing two shifts as Arlie Hochschild documented in *The Second Shift*, in which she argued that many contemporary mothers work a shift outside at a job as well as a second shift at home. Their closest relatives live in another state, and while they do get away for the occasional dinner or concert, without grandparents to step in, this means babysitters and more expense. They have acquaintances but few close friends in their suburban commuter community to whom they can turn for advice or help with their children. "It makes me sad that our kids don't see their grandparents regularly," says Ellen. "It's like they hardly know them." Although not divorced, Tom confesses that, "we have talked about it on and off but so far we are holding things together." Ellen and Tom value family activities, but most of the time they do things separately from their children. "We each like to do our own thing, even though Mom and Dad want us to do stuff together, I'd rather spend time with my friends," says 14-year-old Mike. The Evans, like many modern families are struggling to do it all by themselves and recognize that some extra help from grandparents or even neighbors might make family life more manageable. The Evans meet the definition of the "ideal" family but perhaps this form is not all that it is supposed to be.

Although there are lots of traditional and supposedly "ideal" families who are doing fine, many like the Evans are struggling. The example of the struggles experienced by this family argues for a reevaluation of alternative family forms to see what the Evans of our country can learn from these other models of family. As family historian, Stephanie Coontz (2010) has argued,

> It would be a terrible mistake to delude people into believing that if we could only restore the family values and forms of the past we would not have to confront the sweeping changes America is experiencing in gender and age relations, racial and ethnic patterns, the distribution of jobs and income, and even our experience of time and space. There are many historical precedents of families and communities reorganizing themselves in response to social change. But these examples should inspire us to construct new family values and social support institutions rather than trying to recreate some (largely mythical) "traditional" family of the past (2010, pp. 46–47).

So the aim is to move beyond the Evans and see how other family forms can work to the benefit of parents and children alike. In this book, I will document that children who grow up in the other versions of family that I described are not necessarily suffering negative consequences but, in fact, may even be as well off as children in "ideal" families. The empirical evidence shows that children in these alternative families can thrive socially, emotionally, and intellectually. Part of the reason that children succeed in a variety of family forms is that families do not exist in a social vacuum nor do families function as isolated self-sufficient units. Instead, we need to closely examine, learn from, and endorse alternative family forms and recognize that caregiving and the responsibility for the socialization of children is a community-based cooperative enterprise. Parents are less physically and emotionally taxed by having others available to share child-care responsibilities and to offer advice and guidance in the face of child-rearing challenges. And adults who form this network of caregivers and socializers benefit too. Adult caregivers who are active participants in cooperative family forms experience a heightened sense of self-worth and increased morale and receive affection and caring from their young charges. Even younger caregivers such as siblings benefit from their caregiving experiences. In light of the potential benefits of alternative family forms for children and adults, it is worth looking more closely at these family forms. In reality, as a society we have already moved beyond the ideal of the isolated, self-sufficient nuclear family, and all the forms of families introduced earlier rely on others to assist in the care and socialization of their children.

## How Did We Get Here? The Changing Historical Context of Families

To understand how the myriad of family variations we have just encountered evolved, let's look at the demographic changes that have occurred in family life over the recent past. Central to the theme of this book is the view of the family as an institution that is not static but always changing and evolving. In recent years, there have been a variety of social changes in American society that have had a profound impact on families. According to Urie Bronfenbrenner's ecological theory (Bronfenbrenner & Morris, 2006), children and families are embedded in a "chronosystem," meaning that they are affected by changes that occur over time. American families today differ from American families in earlier times – even a decade or two ago – in a variety of ways.

One change is that more mothers are working outside the home. In 1968, only 20% of mothers with a child under five years of age were in the labor force; in 2002, this number was close to 60% and by 2011 nearly 64%. For mothers with children of all ages over 70% are now in the labor force (Current Population Survey, 2002; U.S. Bureau of Labor, 2009, 2012). This shift is especially profound among White women. Historically, African American women, often due to economic necessity have participated more fully in the work force (Lee & Mather, 2008). The sharp rise in the number of working mothers is, in part, influenced by the changing economic landscape that requires two paychecks to make ends meet. Even in the Evans household, our example of the "ideal" family, once the children reached adolescence, Ellen joined her husband Tom in the paid work force. At the same time, fathers are playing a more active role as caregivers for their infants and children in part as a response to the increase in maternal involvement in the work place. Recall the Lewin family, in which Todd is the main caregiver while Mary Helen is the family wage earner.

Another change is that couples are waiting until they are older before they get married and have their first child. Many couples such as the Baker–Ashe family are simply living together and raising children without taking the formal step of marriage.

Opportunities to become parents have also expanded. A century ago, the new routes to parenthood were not available to infertile couples, nor were the opportunities for same-sex couples to openly raise children. Infertile couples such as the Darcys or same-gender couples can now become parents through a variety of ART. Similarly, changing attitudes and laws permit single gay and lesbian individuals as well as same-sex couples to adopt children. This was the pathway taken by Janice Stadish and Darlene McCloud, a lesbian couple who adopted children from other countries. The number of single-parent families has increased because more women are choosing to have babies without waiting until they marry. In 1960, there were 22 births per 1000 unmarried females; in 2002, the figure was 44 births (Children's Defense Fund, 2004). Today, births to unmarried women account for 41% of babies born in the United States (Child Trends, 2012a). As in the case of Mary Winston, an increasing number of unmarried women in their 30s are single mothers by choice, while others such as Jackie Fuller became a single mother in her late teens, an unplanned transition to motherhood.

Another reason that there are more single-parent households today is that the divorce rate has risen. Between 1960 and 1980, the divorce rate doubled. Although it has not risen since, demographers estimate that 40–50% of marriages today will end in divorce and 60% of these divorces will involve children (Amato, 2010). One third of children in the United Sates will also experience the remarriage of one or both of their parents, and 62% of remarriages end in divorce. As in the case of the Tremblay–Bailey stepfamily, more parents and children are undergoing multiple marital transitions and rearrangements in family relationships.

The Dorado family who migrated to the United States from Mexico represent the changing cultural diversity of the United States due to the waves of immigration that have resulted in new cultural perspectives concerning the form and functioning of families. Finally, due to advances in both cross-cultural work as well as our increased awareness of other cultures through travel, documentaries, and the increase in cross-country contact through the new media such as the Internet, we are reminded of the variety of ways in which families are organized around the globe.

In each chapter, as we discuss different family forms, we will examine the demographic changes in these forms so we can trace their fluctuating prevalence across different historical eras and explore how these changes in the family have affected parenting and child development. This will underscore that the assumption of an "ideal" family form is, in fact, a historical and cultural invention.

## Beyond the Nuclear Family: The Interdependent Model of Contemporary Parenting

In spite of the endorsement of the nuclear family and its anointment as the model of the "ideal" family form, which operates as an independent socialization unit, the modern family is increasingly an interdependent family which relies on the cooperation of others to care for and raise their children. In light of the trends that we have just discussed such as the increase in mothers employed outside the home, the rise of nonstandard work schedules and the proliferation of single-parent families, it is increasingly difficult to "go it alone" and raise children without the cooperation of other individuals and institutions outside the family. As psychologist Jean Rhodes in her book *Stand by Me* (2002) notes, " middle-class parents have purchased adult contact and protection for their children through investment in after school programs, sitters, athletic clubs, music lessons, summer camps and even psychotherapy" (p. 13). Similarly, sociologist Arlie Hochschild in her recent book *The Outsourced Self*

(2012), documents how many aspects of contemporary family life – from renting a womb to employing a nanny to hiring a professional children's party planner – have been turned over to nonfamily members. By restricting our focus only to the parent–child relationship, we fail to recognize other ways that parents actively manage their children's social and intellectual opportunities outside the family and that other socialization agents influence children's development. Parents actively facilitate children's access to physical and social resources outside the family such as schools, religious institutions, social clubs, and sports activities (Furstenberg, Cook, Eccles, Elder, & Sameroff, 1999; Parke et al., 2003). They serve as regulators of opportunities for social contact with extrafamilial social and academic partners such as teachers, coaches, and play partners. They partner with outside agents and organizations and enlist their aid in the socialization of their children. Some parents such as the Evans purchase assistance in the form of babysitters and music lessons. Others, including the Millers, outsource child care to a local child-care center, while Jackie Fuller enrolled her child in the local Head Start program. The Dorado family relies on extended family members to help care for their children; the Winfields rely on older unrelated residents in their community to provide after-school supervision and homework assistance. In all forms of families, multiple players and social organizations are involved in children's lives, even though the nature of the outsourcing varies across families. The key to understanding how different family forms succeed in raising well-adjusted children lies in a fuller appreciation of the roles played by these outside agents. For example, the success of the Millers, a family with two working parents, is highly dependent on their access to affordable and adequate quality child care and after-school care for their two-year-old and five-year-old children, while the Standish–McCloud's brother who helps with child care makes life easier for these parents and their children. Or consider Mary Winston, a single mom, who is not athletically inclined. To ensure her son's physical and social development she, enrolled Sam in Little League baseball so that coaches and peers could play a part in her son's socialization into the world of sports. Although contacts with nonfamily sources such as peers, teams, and schools increases as children develop, parents remain important and continue to play an important regulatory role as gatekeepers and monitors of children's informal and institutional social contacts, even in adolescence (Mounts, 2002) (Figure 1.1).

## Many Forms of Shared Child Responsibility

In response to the decrease in parents', especially mothers', time available to care for children's needs, a wide variety of institutions have emerged to share in the care and socialization of children. The proliferation of child-care centers, after-school programs, boys and girls clubs, and mentoring organizations is, in part, a response to the growing demand for assistance with the care, education, and protection of children. At the same time this represents the continuation of a long history of outsourcing family responsibilities to other institutions, such as schools for education and religious organizations for spiritual guidance and social support. Even the feeding role of the mother has been outsourced before: wet nurses were common among the wealthy in Europe in the seventeenth and eighteenth centuries. In France, for example, Louis XIV had a wet nurse as an infant as did many wealthy families in Great Britain. In the

"Just wait untill your nanny gets here."

**Figure 1.1** Outsourcing of parental responsibilities is increasingly common.
*Source:* Barbara Smaller, New Yorker.

United States, the outsourcing of nursing was widely practiced, especially in the southern states during the nineteenth and early twentieth centuries. Even today, when breastfeeding has soared in popularity among new mothers in the United States, there has been a minor resurgence of wet nursing as well as cross-nursing, in which mothers breast feed one another's babies. Even some men who adopt newborns may turn to wet nurses so that their infants can reap the benefits of being breastfed. In response to this need, there are companies such as Certified Household Staffing in California that offer a variety of household help ranging from butlers and valets to nannies and even wet nurses. However, at $1000 a week, professional wet nurses are probably out of range for all but the wealthy. For the less affluent, there are informal breast feeding sharing arrangements. According to one 29-year-old mother who has cross nursed with her California neighbor, "Breast milk is a communal commodity around here." In addition, she notes that cross-nursing brought her closer to her neighbor. "It takes female friendship to another level. You're trusting another person to nurture your child." And she adds that since she and her husband don't live near family, "It's also a way of building that village or community that a lot of us crave" (Lee-St. John,

2007). Another benefit is the fact that the infant may develop a close relationship with a "second mother," much the way that godparents play a parental role in children's lives. Nor is this the only form of biological outsourcing: The Darcys formed a family the new fashioned way; they accepted donated sperm and rented a surrogate mother's womb as a way to overcome their fertility issues and become parents.

Although wet nurses and borrowed wombs are still relatively uncommon forms of outsourcing, there are many forms that parents engage in on a regular basis to meet the needs of their own schedules and obligations and to assist in the tasks of rearing and educating their children. As the case of the Darcys, the ubiquity of out-sourcing is a reminder of how much contemporary families rely on others and how much these other institutions are part of the social and academic lives of children. The institutions and individuals who are part of the outsourcing network should not be viewed as competitive with families but rather as allies on behalf of children. As we will see, these outsourcing arrangements do not undermine family relation-ships and in some cases may even compensate for poor ties between parents and their children. Parents should be viewed as active partners with these other sociali-zation agents who cooperatively provide the experiences that children need to develop and flourish.

Schools are a long-standing source of extrafamilial responsibility. For several centuries, families have increasingly relied upon schools for the education of their children. And the centrality of schools in children's lives has increased. Children today spend more time in school than ever before – more hours each day and more days each year. Children in the United States now go to school an average of five hours a day, 180 days a year. In 1880, they attended school only about 80 days a year. Not only are children spending more hours and days in school, but they are beginning school at younger ages and staying until they are older.

In response to family needs, other forms of nonfamilial support have also become more prevalent. Because many parents often work full time, children may need some-where to go after school, although approximately 26% of school-age children in the United States (over 15 million) are on their own after school (After School Alliance, 2009). After-school programs provide an alternative to self-care. Although the rise of after-school programs is dramatic, only 8.4 million children (15%) are in after-school programs. Another 18.5 million children would be enrolled in some form of after-school care if quality programs were available in their communities (After School Alliance, 2009).

To illustrate how far we have come along the outsourcing road, consider the number of three- to five-year-olds who spend part of their time in nonfamily settings. In 1970, only about 25% of American children under age six were cared for by someone other than their mother for significant portions of each week. In contrast, by 2011 a majority were. In fact, more than 11 million children under age five in the United States are in some type of child care arrangement every week (U.S. Census Bureau, 2010b). On average, the children of working mothers spend 35 hours a week in child care. About one-third of these children are in multiple child care arrangements so that parents can meet the need for child care during traditional and nontraditional working hours. Today only one fifth of American parents can count on extended family to provide child care, which has led to an increase in various forms of nonparental or in many cases nonrelative child care.

Both formal and informal mentoring partnerships between adults and children or youth are becoming more prevalent in response to the need for nonfamily adult guidance. Mentoring can be an informal arrangement with an older individual in one's social network. Or in some cases, mentoring is a formal arrangement whereby an organization such as Big Brothers/Big sisters arranges the contact between the mentor and mentee (Rhodes & DuBois, 2006). Just as we saw in the case of other forms of nonfamily support such as child care and after-school programs, mentoring programs have increased in recent years. An estimated three million youth are in formal mentoring relationships (Mentor, 2006). Even larger numbers of youth report experiencing informal mentoring relationships with teachers, coaches, neighbors, or extended family members (Rhodes & DuBois, 2006). In fact, about 23% of youth have nonfamily informal mentors (coaches, employers, coworkers, neighbors, or friends' parents), and 35% have "professional" mentors (teachers or guidance counselors, ministers, priests, rabbis, doctors, therapists, or social workers) (DuBois & Silverthorn, 2005; Erickson, McDonald, & Elder, 2009). Researchers have documented a range of benefits from such having such informal mentors, including improved educational outcomes and decreased drug use and violence (Black, Grenard, Sussman, & Rohrbach, 2010; DuBois & Silverthorn, 2005). Similarly, formal mentoring programs improve social, emotional, behavioral, and academic development (DuBois, Portillo, Rhodes, Silverthorn, & Valentine, 2011).

As we will see in later chapters, many cultures share responsibility for their children with both extended kin and nonrelated members of the community. So instead of parents and mentors being in competition, it is best to view parents and mentors as partners on behalf of children and youth. Moreover, the positive effects of natural mentors are evident even after controlling for parental influence (Greenberger, Chen, & Beam, 1998), peer influence (Beam, Chen, & Greenberger, 2002), and even romantic partners (Haddad, Chen, & Greenberger, 2011). In sum, there is added value in having a mentor. As families continue to consist of single and divorced parents, who often live apart from natural support systems such as extended family or are simply overwhelmed, these types of nonkin mentors have a legitimate and needed place in the socialization mix.

Parental facilitation of children's involvement in religious institutions is another form of parental outsourcing. It is important to distinguish between religious institutions as sources of social support and personal and family religious beliefs and practices, because these two aspects of religion may have partially independent effects on family functioning and child outcomes (Mahoney, Pargament, Tarakeshwar, & Swank, 2001). First, religious institutions are social as well as spiritual entities and in their social capital role, they provide social support and social ties for their members. This form of social capital has been termed "congregational support" (Pargament, 1997). The support takes several forms including the social and emotional support provided by the social relationships among church members. For parents, this can often take the form of both child-rearing advice and direct child-care assistance. For example, religious mothers and fathers in North America exhibit greater supervision of their offspring and higher warmth toward their children and enjoy more positive relationships with their children than less religious parents. At the same time, some religious fundamentalist groups advocate harsh discipline, which may lead to less than optimal child development (Holden, 2010). In addition, marital satisfaction, commitment, and communication are higher, and conflict and divorce rates are lower among religious couples (Mahoney et al., 2001). Together these links between religious participation and family harmony and stability have a positive effect on child and adolescent outcomes.

As Glen Elder and Rand Conger (2000) found in their study of rural Iowa farm families, when both parents attended church on a regular basis, children were more likely to be involved in religious organizations. Involvement in church activities was associated with higher involvement in school, better grades, less deviant activity and – especially for boys – more participation in community activities. Although, the relative importance of beliefs and involvement in organized religious activities in accounting for these outcomes is unclear, it is clear that religious institutions are an important part of the outsourcing family model.

## Families Do Not Exist in a Social Vacuum: Parents, Extra Familial Partners, and the Development of Social Capital

As our exploration of the role of parents as managers of social opportunities suggests, families are embedded in a variety of other social systems, including extended networks of relatives and informal community ties such as friends and neighbors, work sites, and social, educational, and medical institutions. An important product that results from this embeddedness of families is the possibility of acquiring social capital – a concept introduced by sociologist James Coleman. As described by Coleman (1988), social capital considers the relations among people, institutions, and organizations of the community outside the immediate family structure; it involves both the flow of information and the sharing of norms and values that serve to facilitate or constrain the actions of people who interact in the community's social structures (e.g., schools, places of worship, or business enterprises). Later commentators, such as political scientist Robert Putman, who generated considerable debate with his book *Bowling Alone: The Collapse and Revival of American Community* (2000), in which he argues that there has been a decline in participation in community groups over the last four decades in American society, makes an important distinction between two kinds of social capital: bonding capital and bridging capital. Bonding occurs when you are socializing with people who are like you: same age, same race, same religion, or some other personal characteristic or social interest. Mary Winston's participation in a Single Mothers by Choice group is an example of this form of social capital. This is commonly seen in homogenous societies. But in a diverse multiethnic country, there is the need for a second kind of social capital: bridging. Bridging is what you do when you engage others who have a different perspective from your own. Bridging capital is the product of learning new ways of viewing the world as a result of this engagement with dissimilar others. Most scholarly work has focused on bonding capital; for example children benefit when bonding capital is high as reflected in the presence of norm and value consensus among members of their family and the wider community (Coleman, 1988). Monitoring of children is facilitated, as is their socialization, through multiple efforts of network members who hold shared family community norms and values (Elder & Conger, 2000). Moreover, if a child's own family is negligent in fulfilling the socialization role, other adults are available to assume the responsibility. However, my argument is that both forms of social capital are important for understanding contemporary families. Specifically, bridging capital, which flows from engaging others who have formed families that differ from one's own, can yield valuable lessons about the advantages of alternative family forms. The Evans family can learn about the value of kin networks from the Dorado family. As our society becomes increasingly diverse in the ways that families form and function, children and parents can benefit from exposure to different perspectives on family. Moreover, lessons from other cultures are another form of bridging capital that we will explore. The embeddedness of families and their reliance on both bonding and bridging forms of social capital for their smooth functioning and for promoting change in families is a central theme of this book.

In sum, the social capital in local communities or in the case of some immigrant families in cross-border communities can aid parents' socialization of their children through several pathways. First, when parents and children have community ties, more social support is available. Second, parental connections with community services and their participation in shaping the institutions of the community promote the maintenance of values and norms that influence their children. Third, parental participation in collaboration with parental surrogates in the community with their children enables closer supervision of children and reduces the likelihood of negative peer influence. Fourth, by exposure to dissimilar families, parents, and children can gain new perspectives on how families can be organized and operate and gain new respect and acceptance of diverse family forms. The concept of social capital embodies the notion not only that parenting is a community enterprise (Elder & Conger, 2000) but also that children and adults are active players in the distribution of social capital. As we will see in a later chapter, children in immigrant families can also play important roles as cultural brokers on behalf of their parents in dealing with physicians, lawyers, and government offices. We will explore the myriad ways in which the effectiveness of alternative family functioning is dependent on utilizing resources offered by extrafamilial agents.

## Some Further Guiding Assumptions

In our effort to understand various family forms, several assumptions guide the journey through this book.

First, family processes that govern family functioning in all family forms need to be recognized as important ways of understanding the successes and failures of different family forms. Second, we need to appreciate that there are universal socialization goals that are shared across most cultures and form the foundation for family functioning. Third, at the same time we need to be aware and informed of the ways that culture shapes our family values and strategies and appreciate the diversity of family forms that are evident historically and globally. Closely related is the fourth assumption that it is important to recognize the diverse ways in which different ethnic and racial groups within our own country organize their family lives. Fifth, it requires the collective perspectives of multiple disciplines to understand the forms, functions, and processes that define contemporary families. Finally, understanding families can benefit from a developmental life course perspective in which changes in individual family members, dyads, and the family unit itself all change across time. We examine each of these assumptions in more detail next.

## Process and Form Need to Be Considered for Understanding Families

An assumption that is central to the argument of this book is that there are multiple ways that families can be organized and internal processes of family life are just as important for the successful development of children as the form, status, or organization of the family. The quality of the relationships among family members, whether parent and child or between spouses and parents' methods of child rearing and their goals and expectations for their children are independent of family form. Just as the "ideal" family can be fraught with conflict, harshness, and lack of caring, other family forms can share these characteristics as well. At the same time, families of all forms – not just the "ideal" family form – can provide supportive, loving, and healthy environments in which to raise children. In short, family relationships of both good and bad quality exist in all family forms. However, some family forms have a tougher time than others. Single-parent families may experience special challenges related to inadequate economic resources and accompanying stress. Same-gender parents may confront discrimination and prejudice and their children may encounter negative reactions from peers and classmates. By focusing on both form and process, we can better understand the circumstances under which various family forms can function effectively. We can recognize the challenges faced by different family forms and open up an inquiry into how these challenges can be overcome.

## The Goals of Family Socialization

To appreciate how different families can raise children successfully, we need to investigate their common goals of socialization. Although it is important to recognize differences, there are some aspects of family socialization that are probably shared by parents in most cultures. As anthropologist Robert LeVine (2003) has argued, in any family arrangement the universal goals of physical survival, promotion and maintenance of physical health, and preparation for economic independence through education and instruction are evident as well as culture-specific goals of particular forms of intellectual achievement, culturally informed versions of social and emotional competence, and knowledge of culturally unique rules and norms. Moreover, LeVine suggests that these goals are hierarchically organized such that under conditions of high threats to infant and child mortality, the physical survival and health of offspring is likely to be a paramount aim. Next in LeVine's hierarchy of parental child-rearing goals is ensuring that the child will be prepared for economic independence in adulthood. Once these basic needs are satisfied, parents can and presumably do devote more resources to other specific cultural values. The form and content of these culturally specific goals vary across cultures and reflect the values and beliefs of the particular culture in which the child and family are situated. In each chapter, I will examine the processes by which these goals are met and how well these parenting goals and related child outcomes are achieved in different family arrangements.

## Different Cultures, Different Families

In order to understand families, we need to take off the blinkers that often blind us to the ways in which other cultures approach the topic of family. For the last several decades, social scientists have begun to critically examine the assumption that generalizations from a single culture (e.g., American) are appropriate (Rogoff, 2003) and a major shift has been to question the universality of our theories about families. Cultures vary enormously in how they organize their families, how they allocate family roles to different individuals, what outcomes they value in their children, and even what child-rearing tactics they choose to achieve their socialization goals. Although there are many similarities across and within cultural groups around the globe, we need to recognize variations and how we as contemporary Western societies can benefit from them.

To illustrate, consider the Aka, a group of hunter-gatherer pygmies who live in the Central African Republic and the northern Congo. They have been described as models for the Women's Movement, as they have very egalitarian male and female family roles. Throughout the day, couples share hunting, food preparation, and social and leisure activities. Aka fathers have even been called the best dads in the world for their devotion to their children. But the parents are not left to themselves to rear their children. In this culture, caretaking of infants and children is not only a maternal or even a paternal responsibility, but a community responsibility. Among the Aka not only relatives but other women in the community participate in the care and even the nursing of newborns and young infants. The active sharing of caregiving increases a sense of belongingness and ensures that infants are cared for even when parents are working or unavailable. We can learn from how other cultures organize family life and responsibilities.

## Different Ethnicities, Different Families

As the Dorado family illustrates, ethnicity leaves a clear imprint on how families are organized and function. Especially in the current era of increasing diversity within our society due to immigration, we need not only to recognize the variations represented by different ethnic groups within our society but to ask how we can learn from these differences as well. It is important not only to examine the diversity of familial organization, goals, and strategies across ethnic groups but it is equally critical to explore variations within different ethnic groups (Garcia Coll & Magnuson, 1999; Parke, 2004). Not all Hispanic origin families are alike; families from Spain, Mexico, Cuba, Venezuala, and Puerto Rico may share a common Spanish heritage but they may also have their own unique ways of expressing this shared heritage in their family values, customs, and organization. Nor do all immigrants follow a similar path. Some come as family units, whereas in other cases family members migrate separately and reunite or not later. Recognizing the ethnic diversity within our own culture is a necessity both for understanding and for guiding social policy.

## Many Disciplines Are Necessary to Understand the Variety of Family Forms

There is an increasing appreciation of the need for perspectives from a variety of disciplines to understand the family socialization process. No longer restricted to developmental psychology, the field of family socialization is increasingly multidisciplinary. History, biology, anthropology, sociology, demography, pediatrics, psychiatry, economics, and even architecture and urban planning are all fields that are playing a role in the study of families (Parke, 2004). Historians (Coontz, 2010) have provided a glimpse at families in earlier times, while demographers (Hernandez, Denton, & Macartney, 2008) are helping us track changes over time and aid in our policy planning for the future. In turn, families' links with the legal and medical establishments have enticed legal and medical scholars to join the effort to understand families (Maccoby & Mnookin, 1992; Pruett, 2000). Families are embedded in and influenced by biological systems, which has led to the assessment of hormonal changes in men and women across the transition to parenthood (Storey & Walsh, 2012). Sociologists remind us that families are embedded in a wider set of extrafamilal contexts such as neighborhoods, work, school, and religious institutions and underscore the importance of social class. Economists emphasize the centrality of monetary resources for family functioning and highlight the impact of poverty on families (Duncan, 2012). And not all families function adequately; some family members are depressed, others are violent; some are uninvolved. This has led psychiatrists, social workers, clinical psychologists, and educators to become involved in this inquiry as well (Bender et al., 2007; Cowan and Cowan, 2000). Anthropologists have alerted us to patterns of cultural variation around the globe in how families are organized while highlighting the ethnic diversity among families in our own society (Hrdy, 2009; Small, 2001). Psychologists help us understand the processes by which families affect children's development (Parke & Buriel, 2006). Finally, architects and urban planners can help us envision how the built environment affects families and how new housing and community designs can better support families (McCamant & Durrett, 2011). Clearly, families are too important and too diverse to be left in the hands of a single discipline; multiple disciplines are essential to advance our understanding of how families function and how they affect children's social and cognitive development.

## A Developmental Perspective on Families Is Useful

Another guiding assumption is that family relationships can be usefully considered from a developmental perspective. Although developmental changes in infant and child capacities continue to represent the most commonly investigated aspect of development, other aspects of development are viewed as important too. Under the influence of life-course and life-span perspectives (Elder, 1998; Parke, 1988), examination of developmental changes in adults is gaining recognition because parents continue to change and develop during adult years. For example, age at the onset of parenthood has implications for how women and men manage their parental roles. This involves an exploration of the tasks faced by adults such as self-identity, education, and career, and an examination of the relation between these tasks and parenting. For example, Mary Winston decided to become a single mother by choice because of her age and her ticking biological clock, a decision that is usefully conceptualized from a life-course perspective. Similarly, Jackie Fuller's unplanned entry into motherhood in her late teens had a subsequent effect on her education and occupational trajectories and can be understood through a life-course lens.

Developmental analysis need not be restricted to the individual level for either child or parent. Relationships (e.g., the marital, mother-child, or father-child relationship) may follow separate and partially independent developmental courses over childhood (Parke, 1988). In turn, the mutual impact of different sets of relationships on each other will vary as a function of the nature of the developmental trajectory. Families change their structure (e.g., through the addition of a new child or the loss of a member through death or divorce), norms, rules, and strategies over time. Tracking the family unit itself over development is an important and neglected task but one that can help us understand the challenges faced by Bethany Tremblay and Oscar Bailey, who divorced and then remarried and formed a new stepfamily.

To understand the nature of relationships in families, a multilevel and dynamic approach is required. Multiple levels of analysis are necessary to capture the individual, dyadic, and family unit aspects of operation in the family itself, and to reflect the embeddedness of families in a variety of extrafamilial social systems. The dynamic quality reflects the multiple developmental trajectories that warrant consideration in understanding the nature of families.

## A Brief Orientation to the Goals of the Book

The first goal of this book is to explore how the social, medical, and policy shifts are challenging our culturally constructed notion of the "ideal" family form. The argument is that we need to revise or expand our definition of the "ideal" family to accommodate current and new family forms and critically examine these forms as alternatives or complements to our view of the ideal nuclear family.

The second goal is to review and evaluate the empirical evidence concerning the effects of these variations in family forms for children's social, emotional, and intellectual development. In order to provide a coherent framework for evaluation of the effects of various family arrangements on children's developmental outcomes, we need to recognize a set of child rearing goals that are viewed as universally relevant.

As our review of the research shows, some aspects of development are affected by cooperative family forms in positive ways such as empathy, responsibility taking, perspective taking, and altruism (Hrdy, 2009); other aspects of social development such as gender roles are relatively unaffected. Still other aspects such as cognitive development may be detrimentally affected if stimulation is restricted to peers and siblings with minimal adult input (Weisner, 1987). At the same time, children learn valuable social skills as a result of either being a sibling caregiver or being part of a sibling or multiage social group; they learn how to manage conflict, take responsibility, and how to function effectively in a social group. My strategy is to present a balanced view of the advantages and disadvantages of different family forms for children's development.

The third goal is to go beyond describing children's developmental progress under various family forms by identifying gaps in our knowledge of how different family forms affect children's social, cognitive, and emotional development and to provide a framework for future research on these issues. By setting and defining an agenda for the next generation of scholars, the book will serve as a catalyst for a new interdisciplinary and multicultural approach to understanding how changing family forms affect children's development.

A fourth goal is to examine current social policies that are designed to support the optimal functioning of families but often fail because of their focus on one particular so-called ideal family form. Ways in which these policies can be modified to better achieve the goal of supporting the array of contemporary family forms will be explored.

To achieve these goals, I draw upon the following lines of scholarly research:

First, evidence shows that parental roles are to some extent interchangeable; fathers as well as mothers are competent caregivers and both can provide the critical ingredients for children's optimal development, such as nurturance and stimulation. Not surprisingly, children develop into competent social and intellectual individuals in families in which parental roles are reversed.

Second, the idea that two parents of opposite genders are necessary for the adequate development of children has come into question since research shows that same-sex couples can support children's normal development as well as heterosexual couples. Children's social, emotional and cognitive development is unaffected by being raised in a same gender parent families. Even children's gender roles and sexual preferences remain relatively similar in same- and opposite-gender parent families. Indeed, neither mothers nor fathers are necessary for healthy child development.

Third, relatives in extended families and nonrelatives in the community can provide children with socialization and stimulation beyond what is provided by their parents. Evidence suggests that these additional socialization agents have unique and beneficial effects on children's social-emotional development above and beyond the effects of the nuclear family. This suggests that we need to expand our view of the family as a two-parent unit and recognize the porousness of boundaries between nuclear families and extended families and communities.

Fourth, new routes to family formation made possible by modern reproductive technologies have separated the biological and social aspects of parenthood. A variety of individuals such as egg and sperm donors and surrogate mothers contribute to the child's biological family but are not necessarily part of the child's social family. While there is considerable evidence that children conceived through the use of the ART fare well in their social, emotional, and cognitive development, less is known about the role of nonkin contributors in children's lives. To what extent should they be involved in the child's life? What are the psychological and legal issues involved? I argue that these individuals ought to be able to be active participants in the life of the family because such involvement will be potentially beneficial for children, parents, and these nonkin players as well. In appreciation of the complexity of this issue not only the positive but also the potential negative effects of expanding the range of "nonkin players" for children's development and for family cohesion will be explored.

Fifth, cross-cultural and intracultural variations in family forms expand our view of the ideal family beyond the nuclear, two-parent form as Aka families and Latino families such as the Dorado family illustrate. A cooperative, community-based model of parenting, I argue is the universal norm not the exception and this model is a clearly viable alternative to our notion of the "ideal" family form. Both cross-cultural evidence and recent empirical studies of ethnic groups within our own Western culture will be reviewed to highlight some of the beneficial lessons that can be gleaned by expanding our cultural lens.

Sixth, to address concerns that multiple caregivers will be harmful to children, I show that infants are capable of forming multiple meaningful relationships beyond the parent–child relationship and that these extrafamilial ties are beneficial for children. Empirical work on infant attachment to multiple social figures in other cultures as well as studies of multiple attachments in our own culture are critically examined. The extensive literature on child care, especially children's attachment relationships with nonfamily caregivers reveals the potential protective functions of multiple attachments for young children.

Seventh, caregiving of both one's own children and others' children is beneficial for adults as well. The recent empirical evidence of the beneficial neurological effects of caregiving is highlighted as well as the long-term satisfaction for adults derived from caregiving activities. The role of a supportive social network in realizing the positive potential benefits of parenthood is examined as well as the costs and downsides of caregiving responsibilities for parents and nonparents alike. The positive aspects of intergenerational-caregiving is explored to illustrate that such cross-generational contact can be beneficial for children and adult care providers. The burdens and stresses associated with intergenerational caregiving are also examined as well as ways to maximize the positive potential of this cross-generational involvement for grandchildren, adults, and the grandparent generation.

In a final chapter, I explore the changes or policies that could help overcome barriers to a broader cultural view of the "ideal" family and lead to greater acceptance of and support for multiple family forms. Ways to support family diversity will be considered across legal, social policy, economic, architectural, and media domains. The potential positive effects of these policy-driven changes for children's social, emotional, and cognitive development are emphasized.

# 2

# Changing Parental Roles

## *The Sharing and Redistribution of Family Responsibility in Contemporary Families*

*The ideal that paid work was only for men and the ideal that only women belonged in the home is a myth rather than an everyday reality for most families* (Scott Coltrane & Michele Adams, 2008)

The Evans family represents the culturally endorsed "ideal" family form, with mother and father playing separate and distinct roles both inside and outside the home. Tom Evans is the main breadwinner while Ellen was a stay-at-home mother when their children were in elementary school. After that Ellen worked part time. For the most part, Ellen was the main caregiver in the household while Tom was the family breadwinner. However, the strict division of labor between mothers and fathers in traditional families has declined over the last several decades and been replaced by a view that roles are fluid and mothers and fathers are more interchangeable than in earlier generations. In recent decades as more women entered the workplace, men gradually assumed more responsibility for the care of their children (Coltrane & Adams, 2008; Ferree, 2010).

In some groundbreaking families, such as that of Todd and Mary Helen Lewin, Todd became the at-home caregiver while Mary Helen was the breadwinner. What does this interchangeability mean for both parents and their children? And if mothers and fathers are interchangeable, what does this mean for the criticality of either mothers or fathers for the adequate development of children? The answers to these questions tell us a great deal about the possible forms that families can assume and at a minimum presents a major challenge to the traditional views of the "ideal" family form.

Another major consequence of women's increased participation in the marketplace is the shift away from an isolated and self-sufficient nuclear family where mothers and perhaps fathers do child care by themselves. Loretta and Rick Miller, a dual-earner family is typical of many contemporary families; they found and purchased care for their two-year-old at a local child-care center and paid for after-school care for their five-year-old. They realized that child care is a cooperative venture and by outsourcing

*Future Families: Diverse Forms, Rich Possibilities*, First Edition. Ross D. Parke.

some of the child-care responsibilities, they could both work and at the same time be assured that their children were safe and being cared for. By exploring the ways that families have adapted to the changing demands of life as dual earner families we can better appreciate the shift away from the ideal family form to a more cooperative, community-centered view of child care, albeit one that involves in many cases the purchase of services on behalf of their children. To anticipate our general conclusion: Many family forms exist, children thrive in many family forms, and there is much variation within different family forms. The plethora of family forms, rather than a single culturally anointed "ideal" family form is not only a realistic reflection of contemporary family life, but a healthy alternative to a nostalgic but outdated view of how families ought to be.

## Setting the Stage for the New Roles in Contemporary Families

Several shifts in how social scientists think about families have set the stage for the changes in the roles played by men and women in modern families. Theories that were historically aligned with the traditional view of the family have been challenged and replaced by more flexible contemporary views of the roles played by mothers and fathers in families. Moreover, social change is often driven not only by our theories of how families work but by secular changes such as the women's movement, the men's movement, the rise of the dual earner family, and the outsourcing of child care. Putting these shifts into perspective, it is important to remember that social change is usually slow, gradual and evolutionary, seldom fast, abrupt, and revolutionary, and always multiply determined.

As a brief glance at either New Yorker cartoons or the syllabus of any first year social science course will reveal, one of the most influential shapers of our twentieth century cultural views of the family was and remains the psychoanalyst, Sigmund Freud. According to Freud, the feeding situation was the critical context for the adequate development of the infant's social and emotional development. Because mothers were the primary feeding agents and biologically better prepared for parenthood than fathers, he argued that mothers played the major role in shaping early infant development. However, there were challenges to the primacy of Freudian theory and its support of the superiority of women as caregivers. First, the British psychiatrist, John Bowlby (1969) suggested that the early development of social relationships and, in particular, the development of an attachment bond between infants and their caregivers was based not on the feeding situation but was a result of instinctive responses that are important for the protection and survival of the species. Infant behaviors such as crying, smiling, clinging, and following all elicit necessary parental care and protection for the infant and, in turn, promote contact and eventually an attachment bond between the caregiver and the infant. Bowlby stressed that the mother was the first and most important object of infant attachment while fathers played a secondary and supportive role. However, even though fathers are less involved in feeding, even bottle feeding, than mothers, the kinds of stimulatory interactions that Bowlby identified such as vocalizing, rocking, and touching that are part of routine parent–child interaction could be just as likely provided by fathers as by mothers. So it was ironic that while Bowlby championed the primacy of the mother's role in early development, his theoretical views on the importance of stimulation gave credence to the father's role as well. Although this was probably not the intended outcome of Bowlby's theory, it was a welcome one nonetheless.

A second blow to the primacy of the feeding context and therefore to the primacy of mothers in children's early development came from the classic studies by American psychologist Harry Harlow (1958) who showed that rhesus monkeys spent more time clinging to a terry cloth covered surrogate mother who provided warmth and "contact comfort" than to a wire-mesh surrogate who offered only food. This experiment suggested that attachment, at least in monkeys, was based more on the "contact comfort" provided by the terry-cloth covering than on the chance to feed. At about the same time, Scottish psychologists Rudolph Schaffer and Peggy Emerson (1964) found that human infants' attachment to their caregivers, including fathers and grandparents, was independent of the degree of their involvement in feeding. This set of empirical and theoretical advances led to a reevaluation of the potential role that socialization agents beyond mothers such as fathers and other kin and nonkin could play in infant and child development. This early work paved the way to greater acceptance of child care by nonfamily members as well as an awareness that infants and children can develop and maintain social ties with several individuals beyond their immediate family members, including their child-care providers (Howes, Rodning, Galluzzo, & Myers, 1988).

Another theoretical shift occurred in the 1970s that gave new impetus to the rethinking of men's and women's roles in the family came from gender role theorists. Although gender theorists have long viewed males and females in dichotomous terms in which there is little overlap in the typical traits possessed by males and females, psychologist Sandra Bem (Bem, 1973) questioned this rigid view of male-female differences and instead suggested that there is considerable overlap between men's and women's traits. Instead of viewing males as aggressive, strong, and independent but emotionally unexpressive, and females as weak, dependent, and deferential but emotionally open, kind, and nurturant, according to Bem both genders shared many of these traits, which were usually ascribed solely to one or the other gender. According to this androgynous view of gender, which rejects gender polarization, men could be nurturant, kind, and emotional, while women could be strong, assertive, and independent. This revised view of gender opened up the options available to both men and women and reduced the dichotomization of "the social world into the masculine domain of paid employment and the feminine domain of home and childcare" (Bem, 1993, p. 194). One of the major advances of the last several decades is the recognition that women can succeed in extrafamilial competitive work environments and men can be competent caregivers for their offspring at home. Documenting this shift toward the sharing of the care and nurturance of children regardless of caregiver gender is one of the primary aims of this chapter.

Evidence based on a lifespan view of development also changed our views of parents' roles by suggesting that certain behaviors and attitudes emerged in response to life course events such as the transition to parenthood. Men who became fathers were more sensitive to infant signals as indexed by their better ability to distinguish among different types of infant cries compared with men who had not yet become parents (Weisenfeld, Zander-Malatesta, & DeLoach, 1981). Parental behavior, in short, can be elicited under different circumstances rather than being viewed as a fixed set of traits. Another theoretical idea that influenced parental roles was the increased recognition of a family systems perspective (Minuchin, 1985) in which the interdependence of mothers and fathers is recognized. When mother or father shift roles, complementary reactions on the part of the other parent follow.

There were other cultural changes outside the musings of social scientists that were reshaping the possible ways in which family roles are divided and executed. In the 1970s, the Women's Liberation Movement, motivated primarily by the interests of white, middle-class women, challenged the prevailing notion that child care was women's work. According to a 1970 press release by the National Organization for Women (NOW), "The care and welfare of children is incumbent on society and parents. We reject the idea that mothers have a special child-care role that is not shared equally by fathers" (Hole & Levine, 1971). And later in that same year, NOW passed a resolution declaring that "marriage should be an equal partnership with shared economic and household responsibility and shared care of children" (Griswold, 1993). And in 1971, Ms.Magazine cofounder and feminist activist, Gloria Steinem proclaimed "It's clear that most American children suffer too much mother and too little father" (Steinem, 1971, p. 37).

In spite of subsequent conflicting opinions within the women's movement concerning the appropriate role of men in the lives of either women or children (Parke & Brott, 1999), there is little doubt that this early clarion call to action was an important catalyst for a renewed dialogue about the role of both fathers and mothers in family life.

Even the various strands of the men's movement helped focus attention on men's possible roles not only at work but in the family as well. Some branches of the men's movement such as the Men's Liberation Movement with its focus on divorce and custody laws, work-family issues, and equal opportunity in the workplace for men and women share some common goals with the Women's Liberation Movement (Farrell, 1993). The focus on men's capacity to express emotions and be nurturant are positive reminders that men are able to be active and competent parents. However, the conflicting views and lack of a clear and coherent message has lessened the impact on this movement on men's roles. For example, the Mythopoetic Men's Movement, with its focus on the centrality of masculinity, soul searching, and self discovery is not very helpful in aiding men reimagine more equitable family roles. And some strands such as The Promise Keepers are more champions of the traditional status quo with men off at work while subservient women are at home taking care of the kids than guides to more flexible and egalitarian mother/father family roles (Parke & Brott, 1999). Nonetheless, the focus on new possible roles for men contributed to an awareness that men need not be restricted by the past ideologies associated with traditional family forms.

As noted earlier the other major shift was the rise in mother's entry into the paid workforce. In 1960, only 20% of mothers with preschool children were in the labor force; in 2011, this number was close to 64% (U.S. Department of Labor, 2012). For mothers with school age children (6–17), only 40% were in the work force in 1960 but the rate nearly doubled to 76% by 2011 (U.S. Department of Labor). In 2011, most employed mothers worked full time (35 hours per week or more) with 71% of mothers with preschoolers and 76% of mothers with school age children working full time (U.S. Department of Labor). In turn, this shift in work patterns led to two other shifts, namely an increase in father participation in child care and an increase in the outsourcing of child care to nonkin child-care specialists.

In spite of the conflicting views and the inevitable tensions between those who pine for the past and those who wish for new social and economic opportunities for men and women, there have been and continue to be real shifts in how families are organized especially in terms of the roles played by mothers and fathers. Next we turn to a closer examination of the effects of these shifts in family functioning which were set in motion by these cultural and theoretical changes on children's development. How has the rise in maternal employment, the increased involvement of fathers as caregivers, and the greater outsourcing of child care to nonkin altered children's social, emotional, and cognitive development?

## To Work or Not to Work: The Implications of the Rise of Maternal Employment

One of the major and most sustained shifts in family role arrangements that has taken place over the last 50 years is the increase in the percentage of women who have entered the work force on either a part time or full time basis. As we noted, since the 1960s there has been more than a three fold increase in the percentage of women with three- to five-year-olds who are employed outside the home. As this dramatic shift indicates the assumption that the traditional allocation of the breadwinner role to men and the child caretaker and housekeeper roles to women is rapidly becoming obsolete. The Millers are typical of contemporary American families. Both Loretta and Rick Miller have full-time jobs, in part, in response to the economic necessity of making ends meet by the provision of two pay checks. And they each contribute to the household and child-care tasks at home too.

However, there has been plenty of anguish about women's more active role in the workplace and especially the presumed negative impact on children. Many assumed that children would be harmed by this realignment of roles which takes women away from their traditional roles as homemakers and caregivers. They assumed it because it was a departure from the "ideal" family form. An "underlying skepticism" lingers even today and implies that "maternal employment, even if the norm, is still not optimal" (Gottfried, Gottfried, & Bathurst, 2002, p. 209). Recent surveys of public opinion confirm that many are ambivalent about the trend toward mothers of young children working outside the home. Only 21% agreed that this trend was a good thing for society while 37% say this has been a bad thing, and 38% say it hasn't made much difference (Parker, 2009, 2012). Part of the reason for this failure to fully embrace maternal employment is due to the fact that for many families, especially nonaffluent families, working is not a choice but an economic necessity. However, public concern about the effects of maternal employment is decreasing and becoming more closely aligned with the empirical evidence on this issue (U.S. Department of Labor, 2009). Nevertheless, women themselves report feeling stressed about balancing work and family. A surprising number (40%) of working moms reported always feeling rushed in comparison to only 24% of the general public and 26% of stay-at-home moms. In contrast, only 25% of working dads said they always feel rushed. And most working mothers (62%) would prefer to work part time (Parker, 2009, 2012). In spite of these attitudes, as Kathleen Gerson reported in her recent book *The Unfinished Revolution* (2010), almost 80% of young adults from working mother homes did not believe that they would be better off if their mothers had stayed home. Many appreciated being the beneficiaries of their mother's outside labor.

Others were skeptical that fathers would be willing to pick up the slack and become more involved on the home front. As Arlie Hochschild (1989) famously argued in her book *The Second Shift*, mothers ended up with more overall work; they put in their time as outside paid workers and then were faced with a second set of responsibilities as unpaid caregivers and housekeepers at home. Even if men became more involved with child care some have questioned the capability of men to assume these responsibilities (Blankenhorn, 1995). As I will show, children are not harmed by maternal employment, women themselves often benefit, and men, in fact, have become more involved with their children. Moreover, the concerns that fathers are incapable of being competent and involved parents are not true either. The Millers need not be worried that their children will suffer because of this family arrangement in which both parents work outside the home.

In spite of the fact that both working mothers and their children complain that they have too little time to spend together (Booth, Clarke-Stewart, Vandell, McCartney, & Owen, 2002; Perry-Jenkins, Repetti, & Crouter, 2000), there is actually little difference in the amount of time working mothers spend with their children or the types of activities they engage in compared to nonworking mothers (Gottfried et al., 2002). "In the past several decades, mothers have actually increased the amount of time spent with their kids, a feat all the more remarkable considering that paid work has meant they're spending more and more hours outside the home" (Konigsberg, 2011, p. 48). What mothers have done as a result of taking on employment is reallocated their time and priorities, delegated some household work to others, increased the enrollment of their children in preschool, and redefined their parenting role. In turn, fathers have also become more involved in families in which mothers are employed (Pleck, 2010).

In addition, how they spend that time with their kids has become more labor-intensive as parenting styles have shifted toward what Annette Lareau, author of *Unequal Childhoods* (2011), calls "the concerted cultivation of children." This approach is

> an attempt to draw out children's talents with organized activities and groom them for success, which requires a lot of waiting around while they do Taekwondo (or other organized after-school activities). This phenomenon – largely an upper-middle-class one – is known as intensive parenting, although given the gender breakdown still in play, it would probably be more accurate to call it intensive mothering and involved fathering (Konigsberg, 2011, p. 48).

> Nor is this necessarily for the better. As one young adult with a stay at home mother reflected about her childhood, "She would become way too into her children's lives and spend way too much time paying attention to what we're doing and it becomes really oppressive. If I made the mistake of telling her anything, it would be all over town, as if I just won some blue ribbon or something (Gerson, 2010, p. 20).

So what have these changes in maternal work patterns meant for children's development?

*Maternal Employment and Children's Development:*   Does the increase in maternal employment negatively affect children's development? While there are still some who suggest that maternal employment is potentially harmful to children' social and intellectual development, most of the evidence suggests that there are few negative effects and a number of positive ones. Part of the reason that there are not the expected negative effects is that the perception that children with mothers employed outside the home are being deprived of maternal (or paternal) attention is simply wrong. For example, researchers have found no negative effects on children's attachment security (Huston & Rosencrantz Aronson, 2005), behavior problems or self-esteem (Harvey, 1999). In a longitudinal study from infancy to age 12, researchers found no association between maternal employment and children's socioemotional development (Gottfried et al., 2002; Gottfried, Gottfried, & Guerin, 2006). Some researchers have even found that, for children in low-income families, maternal employment is related to fewer behavior problems (Dunifon, Kalil, & Danziger, 2003). Similarly, according to a recent meta-analysis of nearly 70 studies, children's achievement outcomes (formal tests of achievement and intellectual functioning, grades, and teacher ratings of cognitive competence) were not negatively affected by maternal employment (Goldberg, Prause, Lucas-Thompson, & Himsel, 2008).

In some cases, maternal employment is associated with positive effects. Researchers have found that the role model provided by a working mother has a positive effect on children's perceptions of men and women. Children of working mothers have more egalitarian views of gender roles, and, in middle-class families, higher educational and occupational goals (Hoffman, 2000). These differences in goals are likely due to the fact that, in addition to modeling achievement or occupational goals, working mothers encourage their children to be self-sufficient and independent at earlier ages than full-time homemaker mothers do (Hoffman). Compared with homemaker mothers' daughters, daughters of working mothers are more likely to see women's roles as involving freedom of choice, satisfaction, and competence, are more career-oriented, independent, and assertive, and have higher self-esteem (Hoffman). Sons of working mothers not only perceive women to be more competent but view men as warmer and more expressive, perhaps due to the greater father involvement in routine care in families where both parents work outside the home.

The age of the child may complicate the picture. Some researchers have found negative associations between maternal employment when children are very young and children's later social-emotional well-being (Han, Waldfogel, & Brooks-Gunn, 2001) but others have failed to find such effects (Burchinal & Clarke-Stewart, 2007). One of the problems associated with maternal employment when children are young is the possible disruption of breast feeding opportunities if the workplace is not breast feeding friendly. Children may be at greater risk when they reach adolescence. Mothers who work encourage their children's and adolescent's autonomy (Zaslow, Jekielek, & Gallagher, 2005). If thoughtfully coordinated with the children's abilities, this may facilitate independence at a developmentally appropriate time. If not, working mothers' encouragement of autonomy and lack of supervision and monitoring may press independence on adolescents too soon and create problems. Boys especially are likely to respond negatively to premature pressure for autonomy. In terms of achievement, Goldberg, Prause and colleagues (2008) found that there was little evidence of age-related effects of maternal employment.

In general, it appears that individual differences among children and mothers are more significant for children's development than simply the mother's status as employee or homemaker. Next, we examine the effects of employment on women themselves.

*Maternal Employment and Women's Life Satisfaction:*   In spite of the challenges of balancing work and family, most but not all women benefit from outside employment. In fact, the "ideal" family form with mother at home and dad at work is not so ideal after all. Numerous studies suggest that work, especially challenging and rewarding work, is linked with better physical health, higher self esteem, and better mental health for women (Hyde, 2007). However, these benefits are likely to occur when mothers want to work. If women prefer to stay home, they are less likely to benefit from employment (Gerson, 2010). As is often the case, it is an issue of a match between a woman's expectations and preferences and her actual situation as well as her sense of fairness about the distribution of home and work responsibilities between herself and her coparent (Coltrane, 2009; Cowan & Cowan, 2000). Both mothers who derive a sense of satisfaction and self-efficacy from their homemaking role and working mothers who enjoy their employment report that they have more positive relations with children than unhappy homemakers who would like to be employed (Hoffman, 2000). Mothers who wanted to work outside the home, but did not were more depressed than mothers who worked outside and wanted to be employed (Hock, 1978). Even children recognize the need for a match between mother's feelings about work and her everyday reality. As one young adult looking back said, "As a kid, you don't realize your parent's unhappy. I thought she just wanted to be a mom and carpool, and it turns out, she didn't want to do that at all" (Gerson, 2010, p. 20). When attitudes and roles are congruent, satisfaction is higher. As we will see, having a satisfying job and adequate child care, contribute to better mental health outcomes among employed women (Barnett & Hyde, 2001). Tasha Howe (2012) nicely summed up the advantages to women of a dual career:

> Multiple roles allow people to move in numerous contexts where they can receive social support, encouragement, and a sense of appreciation for their talents and strengths. They gain a more complex and nuanced sense of who they are as people and travel in multiple circles where they meet diverse individuals who expand their world view (p. 344).

Neither mothers nor children are negatively affected by this departure from conventional family roles and, in fact, there are positive aspects accompanying this shift. At the same time we need to acknowledge that women often work out of necessity, not by choice and not necessarily in careers but just in jobs that help pay the bills. Next, we take a closer look not just at work but at the type of job, the rate of pay, the level of stress, and the scheduling flexibility, since these factors modify the effects of work on families too.

*Beyond Maternal Employment – Type and Quality of Work Matter:*   In recent years, many workers – men and women – have experienced an increase in work hours, a decrease in job stability, a rise in temporary jobs, limited scheduling flexibility and, especially among low wage workers, a decrease in income (Williams, 2010). These factors all play into the work–family equation and make it more likely parents and children will suffer. As a result of these changes, the theoretical questions have shifted.

   More recently, there is recognition that a focus only on whether mothers work or not misses part of the picture. Researchers have begun to address the issue of the impact of the quality and nature of work on the parenting of both mothers and fathers (Perry-Jenkins et al., 2000; Williams, 2010) and the effects of home obligations on work (Coltrane,

2009). How much, how stressful, and when parents work, all matter for children. When work is stressful it takes a toll on children, parents, and marriages.

Repetti (1994), who studied the impact of working in a high-stress job (air-traffic controller) on subsequent family interaction patterns, found that the male air-traffic controllers were more withdrawn in marital interactions after high-stress shifts and tended to be behaviorally and emotionally withdrawn during family interactions. In addition, distressing social experiences at work were associated with more expressions of anger and greater use of discipline during interaction with the child later in the day. After a particularly stressful or heavy work day, mothers, too, are likely to withdraw from their children (Repetti & Wood, 1997), and if they have negative experiences at work, they are angrier and more withdrawn from their husbands (Schulz, Cowan, Cowan, & Brennan, 2004; Story & Repetti, 2006). Similarly, Crouter, Bumpus, Maguire, and McHale (1999) found that parents who reported high work pressure and role overload had more conflicts with their adolescents. Repetti views this as a "spillover effect" in which there is transfer of negative feeling across settings.

Moreover, when household responsibilities mount and conflict with work roles, women are more likely to step up than are men, providing another source of inequality and stress between men and women. As Coltrane (2009) noted,

> In contrast to men, women's family obligations have traditionally been allowed to penetrate into their workplace. It is usually mothers who take time off from work when a child becomes ill, though we are seeing a small increase in the number of fathers doing this. The typical pattern has been for women, more than men, to move in and out of the labor force, regulating the number of hours they are employed in response to child care demands and other family needs (p. 398).

Women often view this asymmetry as unfair since it may undermine their career advancement.

Parental work schedules can be stressful and are associated with negative outcomes for children and adults (Williams, 2010). In our 24-hour economy, 40% of employed individuals in the United States work part of their time outside normal working hours or what Europeans call "unsocial hours." In 51% of two-job families with children, at least one parent works nonstandard hours, with the evening shift being the most common (Deutsch, 1999; Gornick & Meyers, 2003; Williams, 2010). As legal scholar Joan Williams observed in her book, *Reshaping the Work-Family Debate* (2010), this trend toward nonstandard schedules takes its toll on family relationships. People working "unsocial hours," not surprisingly, tend to have strained relationships. These schedules are associated with higher family-work conflict, lower marital quality, and reduced time with children. They are also associated with a lower likelihood of eating meals together, providing homework supervision, and sharing leisure (Williams). As one father who worked weekends and shift work noted, "I would always say to the kids: 'Daddy worked the night shift.' Then they would take it into account...because you are irritated much faster. I think it is about the biorhythms and the switches" (Taht & Mills, 2008, p. 15). Clearly, nonstandard schedules take a toll. In a Canadian study, children had more behavioral problems when parents worked nonstandard hours (Strazdins, Korda, Lim, Broom, & D'Souza, 2004). In another study, researchers found that children's language development was impaired if their mothers worked nonstandard schedules, including night shifts or rotating shifts (Han, 2005). Nor are marriages immune from the effects of work schedules; nonoverlapping work hours for husbands and wives had negative effects on marital relationships (Perry-Jenkins et al., 2000) and may increase the chances of divorce (Presser, 2003). And mother's household workload goes up more than dad's with nonstandard job schedules (Craig & Powell, 2011). Although such work schedules are often undertaken out of economic necessity, they are still a hardship for parents and children. Finally, job loss and underemployment have serious effects on family life, including marital relationships, parent-child relationships, and child adjustment (Conger et al., 2002; Parke et al., 2004).

In contrast, positive work experiences can enhance the quality of parents' behavior. Parents whose jobs were more satisfying and offered them independence, complexity, and problem-solving opportunities were warmer, less strict, and more supportive of their children's autonomy (Greenberger, O'Neill, & Nagel, 1994; Grimm-Thomas & Perry-Jenkins, 1994; Grossman, Pollack, & Golding, 1988), and their children had fewer behavior problems (Cooksey, Menaghan, & Jekielek, 1997). Work-based experiences can help, not just hurt, child and family outcomes, a reminder that work and family contexts are inextricably linked.

Together these studies underscore the importance of quantity, schedule, and quality of work as a further set of situational factors that may alter the parental involvement as well as the quality of their interactions with other family members. However, these variations suggest that the difficulties associated with maternal (or paternal) work are not due to the shift away from the "ideal" family form but the quality of the work experience and how it affects family life. Work-related processes and related family interactional processes are more important than simply who works. Finally, the effects of shifts in maternal work cannot be fully understood apart from two other interrelated changes: modifications of father's roles and responsibilities in response to this increase in maternal employment and the quality and quantity of the substitute care and supervision provided for children accompanying decreased availability of working mothers.

## The Emergence of Fathers as More Equal and Competent Caregivers

As we have just seen, the "ideal" family form in which men are breadwinners and women are child caregivers and housekeepers is becoming an endangered species. The Millers are a typical example of a contemporary American family. Both Loretta and Rick Miller have full-time jobs, in part, in response to the economic necessity of making ends meet by the provision of two paychecks. And they each contribute to the household and child-care tasks at home, too. A recent report (U.S. Bureau of Labor Statistics, 2011) found that

> husbands and wives have never before had such similar workloads. Men and women in 2010 who were married, childless and working full time (more than 35 hours a week) had combined daily totals of paid and unpaid work – which is to say, work at the office and all the drudgery you have to do at home – that were almost exactly the same: 8 hours 11 minutes for men, 8 hours 3 minutes for women. For those who had children under the age of 18, women employed full time did just 20 minutes more of combined paid and unpaid work than men did, the smallest difference ever reported. No, men were not

doing the same amount of housework as women, but neither were women pulling the same number of hours at the office as men (Konigsberg, 2011, p. 46).

However, we are clearly not at 50/50 yet. Working women decrease their time devoted to housework but they still spend lots of time on child care especially in the case of children under six (Bianchi, 2009). Women who do not work outside the home continue to do a significantly larger share of the child care than their husbands (Coltrane & Adams, 2008), but the compulsory aspect of it may contribute to the feeling of being more "time-poor." Picking your child up from day care, for example, or getting a nutritious dinner onto the table cannot be put off until the morning. In contrast, men do some of these tasks but often do household tasks such as fixing a leaky faucet or taking out the garbage, which are not as time-urgent as getting dinner on the table. Although women still do more paid and unpaid work than fathers, it is still a remarkable shift from only a few decades ago. Men are doing more child care – an average of 53 minutes a day in 2010 for children under 18, which is almost three times as much as they did in 1965. Working women are doing an average of 1 hour 10 minutes a day, which is only 17 more minutes (Konigsberg, 2011; U.S. Bureau of Labor Statistics, 2011). A glance at other countries reveals a similar pattern. From 1965 to 2000, fathers in Canada, Australia, the Netherlands, France, and the United Kingdom, showed a similar increase over time in the amount of "child care time" (Bianchi, 2006). However, with the exception of France, "child care time" for US fathers is lower than fathers in many industrial countries with British fathers being highest (Bianchi).

Nor are fathers always mere helpers; in over 20% of married employed- mother families, fathers served as the primary care provider during the hours that the mother was working (U.S. Census Bureau, 2008). However, mothers still do more of the child caregiving such as feeding and diapering in infancy and in providing meals, school lunches, and clothing as the child develops than fathers (Gray & Anderson, 2010; Pleck, 2010). And mothers continue to assume more managerial responsibility than fathers such as arranging social contacts, organizing schedules, taking the child for medical checkups, and monitoring homework and school-related tasks. However, these patterns change as a function of the time of the week and the age of the child. For example, fathers are more involved in household activities (shopping) and social activities on weekends than weekdays and fathers focus less on play interactions as the child gets older (Yeung, Sandberg, Davis-Kean, & Hofferth, 2001). Part of the explanation for the greater caregiving and managerial involvement of mothers is due to the fact that the maternal parenting role is more mandatory and more clearly scripted by our culture, whereas paternal parenting is still more discretionary and less clearly scripted by the culture. Nevertheless, this pattern of change even if modest underscores the plasticity and modifiability of maternal and paternal roles.

## Who Benefits from Increased Father Involvement?
## Mothers, Fathers, and Children Too

When fathers step up and share more of the child care and to some extent the household tasks, women benefit: they are less tired and experience less stress due to work overload at home (Coltrane & Adams, 2008). Increased involvement is good for fathers too. The father-child relationship is a two-way process and children have a positive influence on their fathers just as fathers can support their children's development. For example, becoming an involved father can promote self-understanding and self-identity (Cowan & Cowan, 2000). Moreover, involved fathers may be more generative as well. According to Erikson (1975), generativity refers to a caring activity that contributes to the development of future generations. Involved fathers contribute not only to their own children but engage in activities (coaching, teaching, mentoring) that nurture nonfamily members of the younger generation (Snarey, 1993). Even the quality of the marital relationship is positively linked with father involvement especially when there is a match between partners expectations about the level of father involvement (Pleck, 2010).

However, the major concern surrounding trends toward greater father involvement in the routine care of infants and children is whether it is beneficial or harmful for children themselves. We turn to this issue next.

## No Reason to Worry: Fathers, Not Just Mothers, are Biologically Prepared for Parenting

Some may fret and worry that this increasing involvement of men in caregiving is misguided, misplaced, and even perhaps "not natural" (Blankenhorn, 1995; Popenoe, 1996). However, parenting behavior is clearly a natural process and as recent evidence suggests both mothers and fathers are biologically prepared to parent their offspring.

*Hormones and Mothers:* The biological case for mothers is well established. Evolutionary theorists argue that women's greater investment in caregiving activities is due, in part, to the fact that relative to men their reproductive cycle is shorter and they therefore can have fewer children. In turn, women are more likely to ensure the survival of their offspring by a high expenditure of caregiving effort (Bjorklund & Pellegrini, 2000). Second, women invest nine months carrying their fetus, an investment that is enormous in comparison to men's burden. Moreover, women undergo a variety of hormonal changes during pregnancy, childbirth, and subsequent nursing experiences that "prime" maternal behavior. Considerable evidence suggests that these changing hormonal patterns are related to maternal responsiveness to their infants. For example, nursing mothers showed an increase in oxytocin, often called the "love" hormone, in response to infant crying and displayed more positive behavior toward their infant than bottle feeding mothers (Carter & Altemus, 1997). Mothers with high levels of oxytocin during pregnancy bond better with their babies (Feldman, Weller, Zagoory-Sharon, & Levine, 2007). Similarly, mothers with higher cortisol levels displayed more affectionate and stimulating behavior toward their infants, were superior at recognizing the odor signature of their infants, and responded more sympathetically to infant cries than mothers with lower cortisol levels (Fleming, Steiner, & Corter, 1997; Stallings, Fleming, Corter, Worthman, & Steiner, 2001). Clearly, mothers are biologically as well as culturally prepared for parenthood and this biological priming may be one reason for higher levels of maternal involvement with infants and children.

*Dads and Hormones:* But what about fathers? Until recently, the recognition of biological factors in shaping fathering behavior has been neglected. However, new evidence has challenged the assumption that hormonal levels are unimportant determinants of paternal behavior in both animals and humans (Fleming & Li, 2002; Rosenblatt, 2002; Storey, Walsh, Quinton, & Wynne-Edwards, 2000). In fact, males experience hormonal changes, prior to the onset of parental behavior and during infant contact. For example, Storey et al. found that human fathers experienced significant pre-, peri-, and postnatal changes in each of three hormones – prolactin, cortisol, and testosterone – a pattern of results that was similar to the women in their study. Specifically, prolactin levels were higher for both men and women in the late prenatal period than in the early postnatal period, and cortisol levels increased just before childbirth and decreased in the postnatal period, which corresponds to the first opportunity for interaction with their infants. As Storey et al. argue, the "cortisol increases in late pregnancy and during labor may help new fathers focus on and become attached to their newborns" (p. 91). Hormonal levels and changes were linked with a variety of social stimuli as well. Men with lower testosterone held test baby dolls longer and were more responsive to infant cues (crying) than were men with higher testosterone. Men who reported a greater drop in testosterone also reported more pregnancy or couvade symptoms. Men's changes in hormonal levels are linked not only with baby cries and the time in pregnancy cycle but also to the hormonal levels of their partners. Women's hormonal levels were closely linked with the time remaining before delivery, but men's levels were linked with their partner's hormone levels, not with time to birth. This suggests that contact with the pregnant partner may play a role in paternal responsiveness, just as the quality of the marital relationship is linked with paternal involvement in later infancy. Clearly, social variables need to be considered in understanding the operation of biological effects. Perhaps intimate ties between partners during pregnancy stimulate hormonal changes, which, in turn, are associated with more nurturance toward babies. Other evidence is consistent with a psychobiological view of paternal behavior. Fleming and colleagues (2002) found that fathers with lower baseline levels of testosterone are more sympathetic and show a greater need to respond when hearing infant cries than men with higher baseline testosterone levels. Moreover, fathers with higher baseline prolactin levels are more positive and alert in response to infant cries. Just as in the case of mothers, contact with the baby is linked to the level of the hormone oxytocin for new fathers too; paternal oxytocin correlated with the degree of stimulatory parenting behaviors, including proprioceptive contact, tactile stimulation, and object presentation (Feldman, Gordon, Schneiderman, Weisman, & Zagoory-Sharon, 2010; Gordon, Zagoory-Sharon, Leckman, & Feldman, 2010). Interestingly, this stimulatory play style is the typical and unique way that many western fathers interact with their infants (Parke, 2002a).

But all of these studies were cross-sectional snapshots, and alternative interpretations are possible. Perhaps men who show lower testosterone are more likely to partner and reproduce, whereas higher testosterone men stay single and do not become parents. Recent longitudinal work suggests that becoming a father does indeed lead to a drop in testosterone. Anthropologist Lee Gettler and his colleagues (2011) followed a group of over 600 men in the Philippines over a five-year period, from the time that they were single to the time some became fathers. Men with higher levels of testosterone were more likely to become partnered fathers over the course of the study than men with lower levels of the hormone, possibly because men with higher testosterone were more assertive in competing for women or appeared healthier and more attractive. However, the men who became partnered fathers showed nearly twice as large as the decline in testosterone as shown by the single nonfathers. These findings illustrate that relations between testosterone and men's reproductive strategies are bidirectional. High testosterone is helpful in the mating process but declines rapidly once men become fathers and begin the process of parenting where lower levels of testosterone are better for maintaining a family. As evolutionary anthropologist Peter Gray noted, "a dad with lower testosterone is maybe a little more sensitive to cues from his child, and maybe he's a little less sensitive to cues from a woman he meets at a restaurant" (Gray, 2011; quoted by Simon, 2011). Men need not worry since the drop in testosterone is unrelated to whether men have more children. Lower levels of testosterone do not make men wimps, just more sensitive parents.

Moreover, child-care experience also plays a role. At two days after the birth of a baby, fathers show lower levels of testosterone than non-fathers. Moreover, fathers who have more experience with babies have lower testosterone and higher prolactin levels than first-time fathers (Corter & Fleming, 2002), even after controlling for paternal age. In the Gettler et al. (2011) study, fathers with extensive involvement in child care (three hours a day or more playing, feeding, bathing, toileting, reading, or dressing them) showed larger decreases in testosterone than fathers who were less involved with the routine care of their children. Similar links between testosterone and involvement in child care have been found in Tanzania (Muller, Marlowe, Bugumba, & Ellison, 2009). In two neighboring cultural groups, fathers in the group in which paternal care is the cultural norm had lower testosterone than among fathers in the group in which paternal care is absent. In a study of a polygymous Senegalese society, fathers who were highly invested in their children, as reported by the children's mothers, had lower testosterone compared with fathers who were less invested (Alvergne, Faurie, & Raymond, 2009).

This perspective recognizes the dynamic or transactional nature of the links between hormones and behavior in which behavior changes can lead to hormonal shifts and vice versa. In contrast to the myth of the biologically unfit father, this work suggests that men may be more prepared – even biologically – for parenting than previously thought. Men just like women are biologically evolved to be parents and cooperation between parents is an adaptive strategy. In a recent interview, Gettler wisely noted,

> Humans give birth to incredibly dependent infants. Historically, the idea that men were out clubbing large animals and women were staying behind with babies has been largely discredited. The only way mothers could have highly needy offspring every couple of years is if they were getting help (Lende, 2011, p. 1).

More work is needed to explore the implications of these hormonal changes for the long-term relationship between fathers and their offspring. For example, are the ties between children and fathers who experience less hormone-related changes at birth weaker, or can experience compensate for lower levels of hormonal shifts? Do childless men or women show hormonal changes as a result of opportunities to engage infants and children as well? In spite of unanswered questions, it is clear that hormonal, in combination with social factors, are important influences on paternal parenting since the shifts in paternal hormones may decrease differences in maternal versus paternal parenting behavior. However, it is not just hormones that reflect fathers' biological preparedness for parenting.

*Insights from the Brain:* Perhaps some of the most striking evidence that humans – mothers and fathers – are biologically prepared for caregiving comes from recent studies of how our brains react when we are exposed to babies. From the earliest days of life, fathers as well as mothers are neurologically primed to respond to infants. Using brain imaging techniques such as fMRI, they show more neural activation when shown pictures of babies than pictures of animate objects (Swain, Lorberbaum, Kose, & Strathearn, 2007). Other brain imaging studies found that men respond neurologically more to the cries of their own infants than to the distress signals of unrelated infants (Swain et al.). Brain imaging reveals that mothers and fathers compared to nonparents exhibited more pronounced neural responses in the right amygdala (an area involved in emotional processing) in response to infant crying than to infant laughter (Seifritz et al., 2003). This suggests that parents may experience the cry as an emotionally important signal which requires their attention and demonstrates that the emotion areas of the brain may be involved in fathers and mothers listening/responding to their infant's distress signals (Seifritz et al., 2003). Moreover, fathers and mothers show higher levels of activity in emotional processing areas of the brain when exposed to infant cries than nonparents (Swain & Lorberbaum, 2008). This suggests that parents may experience the cry as an emotionally important signal which requires their attention and demonstrates that the emotion areas of the brain may be involved in fathers and mothers listening/responding to their infant's distress signals (Lorberbaum et al., 1999; Seifritz et al., 2003). In sum, our brains as well as our hormones prepare not just mothers but fathers too for the challenges of caregiving.

## Another Reason Not to Worry about Paternal Caregiving: Fathers Are Competent Caregivers

One reason for the increase in father's contribution to child care is not only that more hands are needed as mothers work more outside the home but that both mothers as well as fathers themselves have recognized that dads can be competent caregivers. And research evidence confirms this revision of our traditional views of fathers as incompetent and bumbling by clearly showing that fathers not just mothers are competent caregivers (Parke, 2002a). Both parents are capable of providing the basic caregiving that infants and children need for survival and to ensure appropriate development such as nurturance/affection, feeding, and stimulation as well as the teaching /guidance needed to become competent participants in their cultural milieu. These basic similarities are evolutionarily adaptive and ensure that infants and children will flourish if one parent of either gender is unable to provide adequate caregiving. As an example, consider the overlap in maternal and paternal styles of interaction with infants. When Sandra O'Leary and I (Parke & O'Leary, 1976) watched fathers and mothers interacting with their newborns, we found that mothers and fathers were equally "nurturant": they touched, looked, vocalized, rocked, and kissed their newborns the same amount. It is clear that mothers and fathers are capable of providing similar levels of nurturing behavior. Only in smiling did mothers surpass fathers – an often observed gender difference in which females routinely are higher than males across a variety of settings and social partners. Similarly, in observations of 30-month-old children at home, Clarke-Stewart (1980) found that fathers and mothers were similar in their stimulation, affection, and teaching. Even more important from an evolutionary perspective was the fact in our study of newborns the amount of formula consumed by the infants was comparable, regardless of whether it was the father or the mother who was holding the bottle (Parke & O'Leary). Fathers and mothers are not only similar in their parental nurturance but are equally competent in feeding the infant based on the amount of milk consumed by the infant.

And parents quickly learn to recognize their own offspring. For example, dads as well as mothers can recognize their babies by their smell. When presented with a shirt worn by their baby or another infant, they knew their baby by its signature smell (Weisfeld, Czilli, Phillips, Gall, & Lichtman, 2003). Fathers can even identify their infant by touch alone without looking at their infant just a few days after the baby is born (Kaitz, Shiri, Danzinger, Hershko, & Eidelman, 1994). And fathers and mothers can distinguish between the cries of their own infants from the cries of an unfamiliar baby.

However, competent parenting involves more than providing nurturance and stimulation or being able to recognize their baby by sight, sound, and smell. A competent parent needs to be able to recognize, interpret, and appropriately respond to their infant's signals such as smiles, cries, and movements. In fact, parents, including fathers, are better than nonparents in diagnosing why an infant is crying (Holden, 1988; Swain et al., 2007). Although mothers, probably due to their greater experience with infants are better than fathers in distinguishing among different types of cries (hunger vs. pain cries) both fathers and mothers show similar biological reactions (a rise in blood pressure) to a crying baby (Frodi, Lamb, Leavitt, & Donovan, 1978). As we saw earlier, even the maternal and paternal brains register similar reactions to infant signals. As this work illustrates, fathers as well as mothers are able to recognize to their infant's earliest communicative signals.

There is more to a successful interchange than merely recognizing an infant's signals. It is important for caregivers to respond contingently, sensitively, and appropriately to these social signals (Tamis-LeMonda, Bornstein, & Baumwell, 2001). Competent parenting is dependent on the parent's ability to correctly read or interpret the infant's behavior so that they can regulate their own behavior in order to achieve some interactional goal such as feeding or calming. To illustrate, in the feeding context the parent's goal is to facilitate their infant's food intake. The infant, in turn, by signals such as sucking, drooling, spitting, coughing, or moving provides the parent with feedback concerning the effectiveness and/or ineffectiveness of the caregiver's efforts to maintain the smooth flow of food intake. In this context, parental competence can be assessed by examining how well the parent tracks and appropriately responds to infant cues in this feeding situation; fathers were as competent as mothers in their ability to sensitively respond to changes in the newborn's vocalizations, mouth movements, or distress levels during feeding (Parke & Sawin, 1980). For example, both parents responded to infant vocal sounds by vocalizing more, touching more, and looking more closely at their infant. In short, both mothers and fathers reacted to newborn infant cues in a contingent and functional manner. Other evidence tells a similar story: mothers and fathers showed similar levels of sensitivity to their two-year-old children's behavior during a play interaction (Tamis-LeMonda, Shannon, & Cabrera, 2004), responded to the smiles and cries of their toddlers (Berman, 1980), and were responsive to their one-year-olds when engaged in a task (Notaro & Volling, 1999). Another sign of parental competence is how they adjust their speech when they address infants. In contrast to adult-directed speech, when talking to infants and young children, parents talk slower, use more repetitions, use shorter phrases, and speak at a higher pitch. This is useful because this speaking style increases and maintains the infant's attention. Fathers as well as mothers adjust their speech patterns when talking to babies (Golinkoff & Ames, 1979; Parke, 1981). Although this pattern  of speech has been called "motherese", perhaps "parentese" would be a more accurate label. In sum, Dads as well as mothers adjust their language to better suit their infants and can read and respond to their infants' social messages, key ingredients of competent caregiving.

Nor is it simply similarities in parenting but there is ample evidence that infants develop similar critical social relationships with both mothers and fathers. For example, infants form attachments not only to their mothers but to their fathers too. Many decades ago, Schaffer and Emerson (1964) showed that infants formed emotional attachments to fathers as well as mothers (see Lamb & Lewis, 2010 for a review). However, as Lamb (1976) showed, the mothers were preferred as a source of comfort in times of stress while fathers were sought out as a source of stimulation and play. Similarly, studies of social referencing indicate that fathers as well as mothers are used as objects of emotional reassurance in ambiguous situations such as an approaching unfamiliar figure (Dickstein & Parke, 1988).

This similarity in maternal and paternal caregiving competence provides a safety net for the child in case either parent is incapacitated or unavailable. Mothers and fathers are to a large degree interchangeable as caregivers. But do mothers and fathers provide redundant input for their children or do they provide unique experiences outside the caregiving realm? We turn next to mothers and fathers interactive styles as play partners to address this question.

## A Matter of Play: Do Mothers and Fathers Provide Unique Experiences for Their Children?

So far, we have shown that both fathers and mothers are capable caregivers and the increased involvement of fathers in their children's lives or the entry of women into the paid workforce is not a cause for concern. In spite of this overlap in mother and father roles in child care, there are clear gender differences in both the overall levels of involvement of mothers and fathers in the parenting of children beyond basic child care, in the parenting tasks for which parents of each gender are typically responsible and the style of interaction that parents adopt as they carry out their parenting responsibilities.

Both mothers and fathers play with their children but fathers spend a greater percentage of the time available for interaction with their children in play activities than mothers do, although in absolute terms mothers spent more time in play with their children than fathers (Yeung et al., 2001). The quality of play across mothers and fathers differs too. With infants and toddlers, fathers hallmark style of interaction is physical play, which is characterized by arousal, excitement, and unpredictability in terms of the pace of the interaction. In contrast, mothers' playful interactive style is characterized by a more modulated and less arousing tempo. Moreover, mothers play more conventional motor games or toy-mediated activities, and are more verbal and didactic (Clarke-Stewart, 1980; Parke, 1996, 2002a). And they engage in more pretend play and role play (Crawley & Sherrod, 1984) as well as more teaching activities than fathers by labeling colors and shapes as they engage their infant in play (Power & Parke, 1982).

Nor are these effects evident only in infancy and toddlerhood. In the preschool and elementary school years, father–child physical play decreases but fathers remain more physical in their play than mothers (MacDonald & Parke, 1986) while mothers were more actively involved in school work, reading, playing with toys, and helping with arts and crafts (Russell & Russell, 1987). In adolescence, the quality of maternal and paternal involvement continues to differ. By adolescence physical play on the part of fathers declines and is replaced by verbal playfulness in the form of sarcasm, humor, and word play even though this often increases emotional distance but perhaps encourages independence as well (Shulman & Klein, 1993). Mothers, on the other hand, are more emotionally available to their adolescents and mother–adolescent dyads spend more time together than father–adolescent dyads (Larson & Richards, 1994). Mothers continue to be more involved in arts, crafts, and reading than fathers, and they maintain more open communication and emotional closeness with their off-spring during adolescence. Just as in earlier developmental periods, mothers and fathers may complement each other and provide models that reflect the tasks of ado-lescence – connectedness and separateness. Mothers maintain social and emotional connectedness while fathers spur independence and autonomy.

There is clear evidence that mothers and fathers make independent contributions to their children's social, emotional, and cognitive development. Father's interactive physical play style is linked with less aggression, better peer relationships, and less risk taking (Le Camus, 1995), the capacity to manage unfamiliar situations (Grossmann et al., 2002) and the skill to manage competition (Bourçois, 1997). The effects of fathers on children's social outcomes are evident even after controlling for the contri-bution of mothers (Leidy et al., 2011). This is often referred to as statistical independence. Probably it is the ability to regulate emotional arousal that is learned in the context of father–child play that accounts for these advantages (Parke, 2013). At the same time, there is a long history of documentation that maternal involvement is related to child outcomes independently of paternal effects (Parke & Buriel, 2006). More interesting is fact that that mothers through their distinctive verbal style of inter-action may contribute to different aspects of children's development such as enhanced intellectual development including memory, problem-solving, and language advance-ment (Cabrera, Shannon, & Tamis-LaMonda, 2007). Perhaps children's knowledge of internal emotional states is a consequence of maternal labeling of emotions and feeling states during social interactions (Denham, 1998). Although there is overlap between the effects of mothers and fathers on their children's academic, emotional, and social development, evidence suggests that fathers and mothers make unique contributions to their children's development (Parke, 2002a).

## How Mutable Are These Stylistic Differences?

The common wisdom concerning these parent gender differences has been ques-tioned over the last decade. Instead, a profile of overlap of play styles between mothers and fathers as well as adoption of a range of play styles by both mothers and fathers has emerged. This revision does not diminish the contribution of either parent to children's development but opens up new questions about the processes through which parents contribute. Moreover, we may need to reevaluate the distinctiveness of maternal and paternal contributions to developmental outcomes but still recognize that both parents can play important roles.

*The Size of the Parent Gender Differences:* Despite this evidence about the unique styles of mothers and fathers, questions remain. The gender-of-parent differences, on average, are relatively small and there is a good deal of overlap between mothers and fathers in both the style of play as well as in the absolute amount of time devoted to playful interactions (Pleck, 2010; Yeung et al., 2001). And fathers do not own the physical play franchise; mothers have a mixed play repertoire too and can and do bounce and tickle as well as read and converse with their children. In the same vein, fathers, like mothers, play with toys, read books and engage in pretend play in addition to their supposedly signature style of rambunctious, arousing, and stimulating physical play. And parents may do a variety of types of play not only in a single play session but across different days, weeks, or even the time of day depending on their mood, their energy level, and the child's momentary interest and their child's daily schedule. Both mothers and fathers contribute to their children's development in a myriad of playful ways.

*Changing Times, Changing Styles:* The differences in play between fathers and mothers became enshrined in our cultural views of normative maternal and paternal play styles based on work conducted 20–30 years ago. In these earlier times, "traditional conceptions of fathers' role predominated, maternal employment was still relatively uncommon and was viewed negatively, and fathers were much less involved in the day-to-day care of their infants" (Lamb & Lewis, 2010, p. 116). As men in contemporary society have increased their type of involvement to include more caregiving and managerial parenting activities, the predominance of play as the distinctive feature of the father role has diminished in importance. Play has become merely one of a variety of ways that fathers (and mothers) are involved with their children. Even some leading father scholars, such as Michael Lamb and Charlie Lewis have revised their earlier views of the uniqueness of father play: "There is less and less justification for viewing the identification of fatherhood with play and companionship as something with unique psychological significance as was once thought" (Lamb & Lewis, p. 117).

*Other Cultures, Other Interactive Styles:* Another challenge to the uniqueness of these play distinctions comes from scrutiny of other cultures, where father physical play is less common. This evidence has challenged the assumption of the universality of paternal physical play as well as the widely shared view that physical play is the hallmark of fathers' interactive style (Parke, 2002a). In some cultures that are similar to mainstream US culture, such as England and Australia, there remain comparable differences between mothers' and fathers' play styles. However, in several other cultures physical play is not a central feature of the father–infant relationship. Neither in Sweden nor among Israeli Kibbutz families were fathers more likely than mothers to play with their children or to engage in different types of physical play (Hwang, 1987). Similarly, among Chinese Malaysian, Indian and Aka pygmy (Central Africa) parents, neither mothers nor fathers rarely engage in physical play with their children (Roopnarine, 2004). Instead, both parents display affection and engage in plenty of close physical contact. Perhaps societies who value sharing and cooperation will be less likely to encourage a physical playful interactive style, whereas industrialized societies which are characterized by a high degree of competition and value independence and assertiveness would commonly support this interactive style (Paquette, 2004). In fact, Western technologically advanced and highly individually-oriented societies are likely to have the highest levels of competition in their children's play (Hughes, 1999). However, there is less competitive play among North American children raised in cooperation-oriented communes (Plattner & Minturn, 1975) and perhaps less prevalence of physical play between fathers and children, although this has not been established.

*Other Cultures, other Nonparental Play Partners:* The most serious challenge to the traditional view of mothers and fathers as play partners comes from cross-cultural observations that parents are not always active play partners. Instead in some cultures the play duties are assumed by other members of the community. In Italy, neither mothers nor fathers but other women in the extended family or within the community are more likely to play physically with infants (New & Benigini, 1987), while in Mexico this physical play role often falls to siblings (Zukow-Goldring, 2002). These findings suggest that the physical play role of the father is not universal and that the play role may be assumed by other social agents in some cultures. Moreover, these cross national differences suggest that cultural context is one of the factors that may reduce the differences – in this case in terms of play style – between mother and father interaction patterns. These observations argue for a reevaluation of the pathways through which fathers influence their children and suggest that we reconsider the father's physical play role as a major contributor to children's emotional regulation – at least in some cultures.

The findings from other cultures suggest that our focus on the gender of the parent may be too narrow a conceptualization of the issue of the necessary adult input for adequate child development. Instead, it may be helpful to recast the issue by asking whether exposure to male and female parents is the key, or whether it is exposure to the interactive style typically associated with either mothers or fathers that matters. In an experimental examination of this issue, Ross and Taylor (1989) found that boys prefer the physical play style, whether it is mothers or fathers who engage in it. Their work suggests that boys may not necessarily prefer their fathers but rather their physical style of play. Together these studies suggest that gender of the agent of delivery of playful input may be less important than the type of stimulation itself. Further evidence is consistent with this interchangeability argument which suggests that mothers and fathers can substitute for each other as we saw in the case of care-giving. To illustrate gender of parent substitutability, consider a classic study of the effects of having a secure or insecure attachment relationship with mother or father on an infant's sociability with a stranger, a friendly clown (Main & Weston, 1981). One-year-olds who had secure attachment ties to both mother and father were most responsive to the friendly stranger, whereas those with insecure attachment relationships with both parents were the most wary and least responsive. Infants who had a secure attachment with either their mother or their father and an insecure attachment to the other parent exhibited a mid level of social responsiveness. However, whether an infant was securely attached to mother or father did not make a difference; the parents were substitutable for one another. A recent study of the effects of having a supportive or unsupportive parents on 36-month-old toddlers' cognitive development came to a similar conclusion (Ryan, Martin, & Brooks-Gunn, 2006). When both mothers and fathers were supportive, the children's cognitive development scores were highest and when both parents were unsupportive, the toddlers scored lowest. The cognitive development scores were between the high and low extremes when one parent was supportive and the other parent was unsupportive. However, the scores were similar regardless of which parent was supportive or unsupportive. Clearly, it is better to have two supportive parents but if the toddler has only one supportive parent, mother and father are equivalent. When the children were reassessed at age five, the same pattern emerged and supported the substitutability argument (Martin, Ryan, & Brooks-Gunn, 2007). As the authors concluded, "Among children with one supportive parent, the sex of the parent was inconsequential" (2007, p. 423).

Together, this evidence indicates that the style of parenting and the gender of the parent who delivers it can be viewed as at least partially independent. These data help us address the uniqueness of fathers' and mothers' roles in the family. Moreover, they help provide clarity on the important issue of how essential fathers (Silverstein & Auerbach, 1999) and mothers (Parke, 2002b) are for the successful socialization of their children. We directly address this issue in a later chapter devoted to same-sex parent families. Finally, the focus on parents themselves as the sole agents in the socialization matrix is too narrow a framing as well. As we saw in the cross-national examples, siblings in Mexico are the agents who provide playful stimulation, while in Italy extended family members such as aunts play this role. These findings remind us that a variety of socialization agents beyond mothers and fathers such as siblings, extended family members, and nonkin figures in the community play important roles in children's lives.

In terms of the family form debate and the impact of variations in family form on children's development, it is clear that fathers as well as mothers in dual career families have important and largely beneficial effects on children. This contemporary dual earner family form, although a departure from the "ideal" family form by redefining parental roles and responsibilities inside and outside the home and increasing involvement of fathers in children's lives, is to be embraced not feared. Next, we turn to another test of the parental substitutability issue by exploring the reverse role family form.

## A Further Challenge to the "Ideal" Family Form: The Reverse Role Family

In some cases, such as the Lewin family, role reversals occur, in which Mary Helen works outside the home and her husband Todd is the primary caregiver. This form is a clear departure from the "ideal" family form by fundamentally altering the conventional nurturing role of mothers and stripping dads of their breadwinning responsibilities. The media have, of course, chronicled the challenges of being a stay-at-home father (or SAHF) and have helped increase awareness of this family arrangement. Unfortunately, portrayals of stay-at-home dads in such movies as Michael Keaton's *Mr. Mom* (1983) or Eddie Murphy's *Daddy Day Care* (2003) were often geared more toward producing laughs and box office receipts than accurately depicting the reality of being a full-time dad. For example, when Michael Keaton's character in *Mr. Mom* lost his job, his wife went to work while he stayed home. Hijinks and mayhem ensued; he was so clueless he even offered his kids beer for breakfast. It has fallen to authors such as Jeremy Adam Smith in *Daddy Shift* (2009) to provide a realistic portrait of

reverse role dads from different economic classes and different races. And documentary film makers such as Mike Denning, creator of *Stay at Home Dads: The Dad
Revolution*, which chronicles the director's own experience as well as the trials and
triumphs of other stay-at-home dads have helped dispel the myths about SAHFs. TV
entries such as *Househusbands of Hollywood*, a documentary focusing on the lives of
five stay-at-home dads, and TV series such as *Parenthood* and *Brothers and Sisters*,
which include SAHFs, have offered authentic pictures of this family form as well.

As in the case of other deviations from the "ideal" family form, many remain as skeptical of the acceptability of this arrangement as they did over 40 years ago. In 1976,
James Levine (1976) a long time observer of trends in fathering wrote "There is still the
widespread belief that a man does not belong at home taking care of children" (p. 153).
A similar sentiment is echoed in a recent survey in Canada: two-thirds of Canadians "still
believe that it's more socially acceptable for a woman, rather than a man, to stay home
and take care of the family" (Leger Marketing Survey for the BMO Financial Group,
June, 2011). How prevalent is this family form and are these concerns warranted?

Although this arrangement is a relatively recent phenomenon and still far from
common, it is on the rise. In 2007, SAHFs in the United States made up approximately
2.7% of the nation's stay-at-home parents, triple the percentage from 1997 and has been
consistently higher each year since 2005 (Shaver, 2007; U.S. Census Bureau, 2009).
According to a recent census report, in 2010, there are 154,000 stay at home dads in
the United States up from 140,000 in 2008. These fathers cared for 287,000 children
(U.S. Census, 2010c). The news from Canada is even more dramatic. The number of
men self-identifying as stay-at-home dads has increased threefold over the past 30 years
(Statistics Canada, 2010). The same study showed that the number of stay-at-home
dads has been gradually rising, reaching 60,000 in 2011, up from 20,000 in 1976.
Canadian men now account for 12% of stay-at-home parents, compared with only 4% in
1986. To put these figures into perspective: one in every 100 stay-at-home parents were
fathers in the 1970s and in 2011, it is one in every eight. In spite of these shifts, as we
saw earlier many remain skeptical of the acceptability of this arrangement (Figure 2.1).

There are a variety of reasons for the increase in this family arrangement but also
challenges that may account for why only a small number of families choose this
alternative and persist in it. For many families it is simply economic; dad may be laid
off or mom makes more money so it makes more financial sense for dad to stay home
and mother to assume the financial provider role. In fact, between 2009 and 2010,
during the recent recession in the United States, the earnings of men with college
degrees dropped while women's earnings increased. In some cases, the wife's job provides a better set of health benefits than her spouse. As unemployment rises, the
number of men who are thrust into primary care roles rises, in part, because the
unemployment rates for men tend to be higher than for women (U.S. Bureau of
Labor Statistics, 2010). Or in some cases, women enjoy their job and prefer to work
outside the home and men may dread their work and prefer to become the primary
caregiver. As one stay-at-home dad in England noted:

> As my wife got more out of her job, had the better career and therefore, higher earnings
> than me it was clear that I should be the one to give up work and stay at home with the
> baby. It was something that we had thought about before so I was kind of accustomed

**Figure 2.1** More dads are staying home to take care of their children as more mothers work outside the home even though many in society remain skeptical of this arrangement. *Source:* © Leigh Schindler/iStockphoto.

to the idea beforehand and looking forward to the time when it would happen. My wife was much happier with the thought of going back to work knowing that our child was going to be at home with me than she would be if she had to leave them in a nursery (child care) full-time (Paul Smith, 2011).

In other families, parents reported that they simply believed that they should share the care of their children. Interestingly, the reasons for choosing this arrangement and the reasons for continuing it may be different. One father in Australia described the process:

We started out doing it because of the money...we wanted to buy a house. When we got the house, Sally wanted to stop working...she wanted me to go back to a 9 to 5 job. I didn't want to because that would have meant that I wouldn't have seen the kids as much. I felt I had as much right to see the kids as she did. We thought that we should both take care of them about equal time. I want it to stay that way (Russell, 1983, p. 129).

What are the pros and cons of this family arrangement for parents? Sharing or in this case switching roles has distinct benefits for both mothers and fathers. Mothers report increased self esteem and greater independence as a result of the opportunity to return to work (Russell, 1983). One mother commented: "After going back to work I started to value myself more...I have also become more pleasant." And fathers benefit too. In an Australian study, 70% of fathers who served as primary caregivers report that their relationships with their children improved: "I think that it has improved the amount of pleasure I get from them." "Being with them all of the time has helped cement my relationship with them." "I became a lot more involved, understood my daughter better and I got on a lot better with her." (Russell, pp. 126–131). Full time dads in the United States spoke with great enthusiasm about the satisfaction of being a caregiver as well. One father stated: "The best thing I can say is just how rewarding it is when my 8-month-old laughs, giggles, whatever, she just smiles at you from across the room 'Hey dad, so good to see you!' That's all she can give me right now, that's great" (Rochlen, Suizzo et al., 2008, p. 198). Canadian dads express similar sentiments. After four months at home with baby Callum, full time dad Rohan says, "I can't quite imagine doing anything else at the moment." Previously in an office job, Rohan loved being able to get out a lot. And he's cherished the chance to get to know Callum and earn his trust (Ryan, May 26, 2010).

Besides understanding their children better, these stay-at-home caregiving fathers showed greater awareness of the mother-housewife roles and an appreciation of the pressures and demands that are involved in the set of roles traditionally assumed by women. And some fathers felt the relief from career pressures. One reflected "I enjoy the freedom from the routine, pressures and hassles of work" (Russell, 1983, p. 128).

As is the case of with any social change that challenges our long-held views about the definition of the "ideal" family form, there is a down side too. Sixty percent of mothers who were working and sharing caregiving responsibilities with their partners experienced difficulties associated with the physical and time demands of a dual role. Even when dads take more responsibility, working mothers still feel the strain of doing a *Second Shift* (1989) as sociologist Arlie Hochschild described it in her book with this title. Twenty years later, journalist Catherine Rampell (2009) continues to caution us not to be overly optimistic about the implications for women's overall household responsibilities of the dramatic increases in stay at home dads:

> Bona fide primary caregiving fathers are still rare, and a man doesn't automatically become a primary caregiver of the children simply because he's unemployed or underemployed. The horrid worldwide economy has simply created a larger number of unemployed/ underemployed men who aren't picking up the slack at home. When women are unemployed and looking for a job, the time they spend daily taking care of children nearly doubles. Unemployed men's child care duties, by contrast, are virtually identical to those of their working counterparts, and they instead spend more time sleeping, watching TV and looking for a job, along with other domestic activities. So despite media fantasies, men getting laid off means that many moms are now acting as both the primary caregiver *and* primary wage earner (February 5, 2009).

Nor is the experience all positive for fathers either. While some dads adapted easily to the change in life style such as the dad who said "It just comes naturally to me," nearly half of the Australian fathers found the demands – the constancy, the physical work, and the boredom – associated with child care and housework to be difficult to manage. Over a two year period, in fact, tension and conflict in the father–child relationship increased – part of the realities of assuming an increased caregiving role. As one father reflected "When I first stayed home I found it hard. All the diaper changing and just the constancy of it." Still other fathers missed their jobs and the loss of status associated with the shift away from full time employment: "I had a lot of difficulty adjusting to the idea of not having a job. I didn't realize how important that was to me" (Russell, 1983, p. 127).

Others argue that we still view breadwinning and masculinity as linked and some men feel that their sense of manhood is undermined by not being employed in an outside job and instead taking on a traditional female role of caregiver (Doucet, 2004, 2006). To combat this feeling of threatened loss of masculinity after giving up participation in the full time labor force for a caregiving role,

> many fathers replace employment with 'self-provisioning' work that allows them to contribute economically to the household economy as well as to display masculine practices, both to themselves and their wider community. For example, fathers play a role in children's extracurricular activities such as sporting as well as in community work which emphasizes leadership, sports, construction, and building while also easing community scrutiny of their decision to give up work. Moreover, fathers' involvement in children's lives in a manner that builds on traditional male interests also provides for the possibility of building their own community networks on the basis of traditional areas of male connection such as sports (Doucet, 2004, p. 278, 279, 292).

In short, men who assume these primary caregiver roles adopt strategies to overcome some of the still remaining prejudice associated with this new family form and the prevailing narrow definition of masculinity.

Being a stay-at-home dad may put a marriage at risk as well. According to a recent study of 3600 couples who participated in the National Survey of Families and Households, sociologist Liana Sayer and her colleagues (Sayer, England, Allison, & Kangas, 2011) found that the rates of divorce to be higher in role reversal families.

> "It's emblematic of an asymmetrical revolution," says Sayer. "The role of women has changed a lot, but we have seen far less movement in the roles of men. That men be breadwinners still seems to be very salient for couples. If a man is not bringing in some money, it seems to be unacceptable. It's still unacceptable for men to stay home and take care of the kids. For men, not having a job increases the risk he will initiate leaving the relationship, and it also increases the risk women will leave the relationship. Men are still held to an older standard than women and penalized by employers and stigmatized if they are doing what's perceived as women's work" (Sayer interview with Rochman, 2011).

And it can be a lonely and isolating experience for many men who assume this role after losing the built-in social network provided by a company and colleagues. And stay-at-home mothers are sometimes skeptical or even wary of primary caregiver dads. Men expressed perceiving women as being suspicious of them, sometimes to the point of feeling regarded as perverted and even criminal. For example, one man stated: "They instinctively get together and they form playgroups and you will get this stink-eye from the moms, this sort of 'Who the hell are you and what are you doing here?' look" (Rochlen, Suizzo et al., 2008, p. 200). In light of these comments and despite the positive aspects of these reverse role arrangements, it is difficult to maintain this pattern.

To counter this sense of isolation, having a supportive significant other, a positive family, and a network of supportive friends helps. In a recent study of 213 stay-at-home dads, supportive friends was strong predictor of psychological well being while a supportive family and partner was related to higher levels of life satisfaction (Rochlen, McKelley et al., 2008). And more stay-at-home dads are turning to organizations devoted to this new family form for support and guidance. The attendance at the annual "At Home Dad" convention, for example, has increased dramatically in the past few years and numerous web sites and blogs devoted to this group of dads have become more numerous and more popular (Little, 2010).

How do fathers' styles of interaction shift when mothers and fathers reverse their customary roles as caregiver and outside the home worker? Evidence from the United States, Australia, and Israel suggests that when dads stay home, their style of interaction becomes more like that of primary-caregiving mothers. In the American study, psychologist Tiffany Field (1978) found that primary caregiver fathers smiled more and imitated their babies' facial expressions and high-pitched vocalizations more than secondary caregiver fathers. In these ways, the primary caregiver fathers acted very much like mothers who are primary caregivers. Being a primary caregiver and therefore spending more time with their infants seems to affect the fathers' style of play significantly – a reminder that fathers' style of play can be modified and is not entirely biologically determined. However, these stay at home fathers still played as physically – bouncing, tickling – as traditional fathers which suggests that some aspects of paternal style may be more resistant to change. The news from Australia is similar. Father expert, Graeme Russell (1983) found that role-sharing fathers engaged in a less stereotypically masculine style of parenting and instead exhibited a more maternal interactive style (e.g., more indoor recreational activities such as talking, singing and drawing, and less exclusive focus on roughhousing and outdoor games such as football). Finally, Israeli primary-caregiving fathers were more nurturant as reported by both themselves and their children relative to conventional fathers (Sagi, 1982).

But how do the children reared in reverse role families fare? The majority of mothers and fathers in Russell's Australian study did not believe that their children suffered as a result of this unorthodox family arrangement. According to one father, "There doesn't seem to be any bad side of it from Luke's (their child) point of view. He has adjusted well" (Russell, 1983, p. 130). Researchers who have examined how children are affected by having their father as primary caregiver agree with the father in Russell's study. There are no apparent major negative effects but there are some positive effects for children. In an early study of American families in which the father was the primary caregiver, psychiatrist Kyle Pruett (1987) found positive effects for the children. Toddlers who were followed across a two-year period from infancy scored above average on standardized tests of development including problem-solving skills as well as personal and social skills. Follow-up measures two and four years later revealed no negative impact on gender identity and clear evidence of a heightened appetite for novel experiences and stimuli. In another American study, Norma Radin (1982) found that not only toddlers benefited from this family arrangement but older children as well. In her study of three- to five-year-old children, she found that both boys and girls who were reared primarily by their fathers had higher verbal ability than children raised in traditional families. Child rearing fathers set higher educational and career expectations for their sons as well as their daughters than traditional fathers. An 11 year follow up when the children were adolescents showed that these arrangements had long term effects on children (Williams, Radin, & Allegro, 1992). They found that a greater amount of paternal involvement during the preschool years was associated with teens' support for nontraditional employment arrangements. They were more positive about both parents working full time and sharing child care and less positive about fathers working full time and mothers not working and caring for the children on a full time basis. Similarly, Pruett (2000) found that adolescents of primary caregiver fathers showed greater emotional balance, stronger curiosity, and a stronger sense of self-assurance than adolescents reared in homes with less involved fathers. Even more evidence that role reversal can have clear benefits for the children comes from an Israeli study of primary caregiver fathers. Six-year-old children of fathers of intermediate or high involvement exhibited more internal locus of control (a belief that you, rather than some external source, are responsible for your outcomes) than children of fathers with low involvement (Sagi, Koren, & Weinberg, 1987). Children of these highly involved fathers were higher in empathy as well. The fact that it was the children whose primary caregiver fathers were relatively highly involved were the ones who benefited most from this arrangement underscores the importance of peeking behind the "family form curtain" to examine the processes that are ongoing within the family organization. In addition, there was evidence of more androgynous gender – orientation on the part of girls, perhaps as a result of being reared by more nurturant, involved fathers who were not gender stereotyped themselves and who did not respond to girls in a gender stereotyped fashion. These data are consistent with Bem's (1993) argument in favor of gender depolarization by which men and women both act in nongender-stereotypic ways.

Although this role-reversal arrangement clearly violates the notion of an "ideal" family form, it is clear that men as primary caregivers not only do an adequate job of rearing children but their increased involvement may boost their children's development as well. At the same time, we still have a ways to go in terms of our cultural acceptance of men as primary caregivers. Finally, evidence suggesting that children from these families fare better must be treated cautiously rather than conclusively. Such parents may be different in other ways from parents who maintain more traditional roles. For example, they might have treated their children differently than traditional parents, no matter which parent stayed home with the children. At the same time, it is likely that parents who reverse roles are significantly affected by their choice, and that therefore the nontraditional environment in which children develop is at least partially responsible for the differences between children reared in role reversal and traditional families. This evidence provides further support for our earlier argument that that the style of parenting and the gender of the parent who delivers or enacts this style can be viewed as at least partially independent. These data contribute to the debate about how essential fathers (Silverstein & Auerbach, 1999) or mothers (Parke, 2002b) are for the successful socialization of children. Next, we address another issue that often accompanies an increase in maternal employment, namely the outsourcing of childcare to nonkin.

## And the Children Are Fine Too When Mom Goes to Work and Children Go to Child Care

Not only do fathers become more involved in child care when mothers work outside the home but in most dual earner families parents often turn to others to assist with child care. What parents have done as a result of both partners taking jobs is to reallocate their time and priorities, and rely on an outsourcing model whereby some of the parenting responsibilities are shared with others outside the family. Families have divided household work and child care more equally between mothers and fathers, increased their reliance on paid cleaning help (if they can afford it), purchased more prepared or frozen meals, and increased the enrollment of their children in child-care and after-school programs. In fact, one of the major consequences of maternal employment is the expansion of the range of players beyond the nuclear family who contribute to the child's daily care and socialization. As we saw in the opening chapter outsourcing of child-care and after-school supervision is increasingly common. This move toward a more cooperative and outsourcing model of care is an adaptive response to the time bind associated with both parents working outside the home and managing both household and child responsibilities. In addition, it moves American socialization models in closer alignment with both historical and cross culturally prevalent cooperative, community-based approaches to child care and away from the notion of the isolated self-sufficient nuclear (i.e., "ideal") family model.

However, the issue of child care remains controversial since there is still a cultural belief that the care and nurturance of young children should be the primary responsibility of parents, especially mothers. On average, the children of working mothers spend 35 hours a week in child care. About one-third of these children are in multiple child-care arrangements so that parents can meet the need for child care during traditional and nontraditional working hours. Today, only one fifth of American parents can count on extended family to provide child care which has led to an increase in various forms of nonrelative child care. A further reason for the increase in outsourced child care is that views about what children need for proper social and cognitive development have changed. Regardless of whether or not mothers work, most parents believe that children benefit from spending time in an organized setting where they can learn their colors, their letters, and their numbers to gain a cognitive "leg up" in preparation for formal school and learn how to interact successfully with their peers. As studies of child care have shown, the quality of and, to some extent, the amount of time in care are linked to children's cognitive and social development (Clarke-Stewart & Allhusen, 2005). One of the early fears, that child care would undermine the attachment bond between mothers and their children has proved to be unfounded: children in child care develop close attachments with their parents (Clarke-Stewart & Allhusen). This conclusion about whether child care interfered with infants' attachment development is based on the US government funded National Institute of Child Health and Human Development (NICHD) Study of Early Child Care and Youth Development, a large study in ten sites around the country. More than 1300 infants were randomly selected from hospitals at birth and tracked through adolescence. Their psychological and physical development was assessed repeatedly. The results showed that when factors such as parents' education, income, and attitudes were statistically controlled, infants in child care were no more likely to be insecurely attached to their mothers at age three than infants not in care. However, when they were placed in poor-quality care in which the caregivers were not very sensitive and responsive to their needs and their mothers were not very sensitive to their needs at home, infants were less likely to develop secure attachments than if they were in good-quality care and their mothers were sensitive and responsive (NICHD Early Child Care Research Network, 2005).

Good-quality child care can even compensate for poor care at home by giving children an opportunity to form secure attachments outside the family. Children with an insecure attachment to their mother but a secure attachment to a child-care provider are more socially competent than insecurely attached children who have not formed a positive relationship outside the family (Howes & Spieker, 2008; van IJzendoorn & Sagi-Schwartz, 2008). Having a stable child-care provider who stays in their role over a period of time is particularly important. Children more frequently seek caregivers who have been on the child-care staff longer, and these caregivers are able to soothe the children more effectively than caregivers with unstable employment records (Barnas & Cummings, 1994). Although, minimizing staff turnover in child care can help children's attachment development, low wages often means that staff turnover in many centers is high.

High quality care carries other benefits too. Children in higher-quality care are more sociable, considerate, compliant, controlled, and prosocial; they are better adjusted, less angry and defiant, and have higher self-esteem (Clarke-Stewart & Allhusen, 2005). They also have better relationships with their caregivers in child care. In the NICHD Study of Early Child Care and Youth Development, children in higher-quality care exhibited more positive interactions with other children and were reported by their caregivers to have fewer behavior problems and to be more socially skilled (NICHD Early Child Care Research Network, 2005). Child-care quality has a modest long-term effect on children's cognitive and socioemotional development through kindergarten and first grade (Peisner-Feinberg et al., 2001), and, in the NICHD Study, through age 15 (Vandell et al., 2010). Social behavior, despite the opportunity to have increased peer contact, is not consistently linked with day-care quality: Some evidence suggests that children who are in day care for more than 40 hours per week may show some increases in aggression (NICHD Early Childcare Research Network). Clearly, not all forms of child care are equal and the variations in the forms of child care that are available to families of different social classes and ethnic backgrounds have real consequences for the academic and occupational success of children from these different groups. In view of the fact that many poor families are less able to afford or access high-quality care for their children, their children are likely to be at a disadvantage in terms of academic preparedness for school.

After-school programs for their elementary school age children are an increasingly popular outsourcing choice for working parents. Children enrolled in such programs benefit in many ways, including improvements in school attendance, in social and emotional adjustment, and in course work and test scores (Mahoney, Parente, & Lord, 2007; Vandell, Pierce, & Dadisman, 2005). Parents whose children are in high-quality after-school programs feel better, too: "Justin's after-school program relieves me of the fear of him being caught on the streets unattended. He's playing with a selected group of kids. He's not strapped to the TV. I feel so comfortable with the program and teachers" (Belle, 1999, p. 88). Moreover, parents could avoid an average loss of five days of work if after-school care was more available and save American business about $300 billion each year due to lost productivity (Catalyst and Brandeis University, 2006). Poorly supervised and disorganized after-school programs, however, can be detrimental to children's development (Mahoney, Vandell, Simpkins, & Zarrett, 2009). While parents need to be aware of the importance of quality when choosing after-school care, communities need to ensure that quality after-school programs are available and affordable as well.

Contemporary families have moved away from the nuclear "ideal" family model and adopted a family form that involves regular outsourcing of some child care to extended family, other nonrelated families, childcare centers and after-school programs. This albeit sometimes reluctant acceptance of the involvement of both kin and nonkin in child-care responsibility is a major move toward a community based model of parenting in which it becomes normative and not suspect to enlist others in the socialization process. As we will see when we tour other cultures in a later chapter, this simply aligns our Western child-care arrangements with longstanding practices of earlier times and in other parts of the world.

## Reflections

As we have seen in this chapter, challenges to the dominance of the "ideal" family as the cultural ideal come in many forms. The roles that men and women play in the two parent family are evolving and changing in ways that an earlier generation of parents could not have envisioned. Women are participating in the workforce in increasingly large numbers, while men are taking more responsibility not only for household chores but for child care as well. While the economic reality of our contemporary society has played a major role in the rise of two earner families, emerging evidence that fathers can be competent caregivers has to a large extent eroded resistance to increased father involvement as a caregiver in the lives of children. And it is a welcome shift. Women value their increased opportunities for the self fulfillment, status, and financial independence that come with paid work. Men, in turn, are valuing their new roles as more equal partners in child care and the opportunity to display their reawakened nurturant side. Children benefit too by having two involved parents who are both competent caregivers and interactive partners. In turn, this provides a welcome safety net for children in case of the loss or unavailability of one parent. At the same time, this shift toward a wider range of family forms is still very much a work in progress and in spite of the changes toward greater sharing of household and caregiving roles by mothers and fathers, there remain many barriers to these shifts and much more to be done. In the closing chapter, we address some of these barriers and how we can overcome them. Our goal is to identify the social conditions under which a variety of family forms can be successful. In the case of both dual earner and reverse role families, with social, emotional, and material support from extended family and the wider community, children can thrive developmentally. The rise in outsourcing of child care to others outside the family further questions the narrow definition of family and even the meaning of family responsibilities. In its place a view of child care as not merely a family but a community based responsibility in which parents as well as others share in the care and socialization of children has emerged. Finally, the fact that children in role reversal families in which fathers assume the primary caregiver role develop well, raises a further challenge to the criticality of the gender of the parent for successful child developmental outcomes. Instead it suggests that internal family processes are of greater importance than either the form of the family or the gender of the parent. Our review mounts a major assault on the "ideal" family form and suggests that many family forms can support the successful socialization of children.

# 3

# Further Assaults on the "Ideal" Family Form

## *Divorce, Remarriage, Single Parenthood, and Cohabitation*

*We have witnessed over the past half century the unprecedented decline of marriage as the only acceptable arrangement for raising children* (Andrew Cherlin, 2009)

In the past century, one of the major challenges to the "ideal family" form has been the rise in divorce and the increase in both single-parent and stepparent families. Bethany Tremblay who divorced and found herself as a single parent raising her six-year-old son is an example of this recent trend. Oscar Bailey is another example of a parent in a contemporary family torn apart by divorce but in this case he has joint custody of his two children, nine-year-old Mellissa and seven-year-old Frank. Oscar is a single father – albeit only part of the time. For Bethany and Oscar, being single was temporary and they followed a well-trodden path by remarrying and forming a new stepfamily together. Not all follow the same route to single parenthood. For some women, such as Jackie Fuller, becoming a single mother as a teenager was unplanned. Others such as Mary Winston are part of a growing group of women who are single mothers by choice. The Baker–Ashe family represents another major shift in family forms – unmarried, cohabitating couples with children. Examining these new family forms and their effects on children is the aim of this chapter.

## The Changing Face of Divorce

One hundred years ago, the divorce rate in the United States was only about one divorce for every thousand people. By 1980, the rate had climbed to just over five divorces for every thousand people. This increase was associated with a reduction in the legal and moral restrictions against divorce and a shift in the focus of family life from economic dependence to emotional fulfillment. Since 1980, the tide has turned, and divorces have declined. Today, the rate is just under four divorces per thousand people – the lowest it has been in over 30 years. However, despite this decline, the divorce rate in the United States remains higher than that of any other

*Future Families: Diverse Forms, Rich Possibilities*, First Edition. Ross D. Parke.
© 2013 John Wiley & Sons, Inc. Published 2013 by John Wiley & Sons, Inc.

country in the Western world. As divorce has become more normative, attitudes toward divorce have changed from disdain and disapproval to grudging acceptance. According to a recent report on attitudes toward modern families "People aren't embracing these changes, but they are accepting them. The days when people were made to wear a scarlet letter or were shunned after a divorce are ancient history" (Morin, February 17, 2011).

A further shift in our attitudes toward divorce is the change that has occurred in the nature of custody arrangements following divorce. Although historically fathers were unequivocally favored in custody decisions, for nearly a century courts have viewed mothers as the "natural" parent in part due to the assumption of biological predisposition and in part due to the tender years doctrine which held that infants and young children should be raised by their mothers (Clarke-Stewart & Brentano, 2006). Since the 1980s there has been a shift away from the presumption that mothers are automatically the best parent and an increase in the proportion of children in joint custody arrangements in recognition of the fact that children need a continuing relationship with both their mothers and fathers. However, the vast majority of custodial parents are still mothers and more mothers than fathers have physical custody in joint custody arrangements. In a study of a nationally representative sample of 13,017 individuals age 19 and over, representing 9643 American families and households, Kelly, Redenbach, and Rinaman (2005) found that in 80% of the cases, the mother received sole physical custody of the minor child or children. The remaining 20% of the cases were evenly divided between the father having sole physical custody and joint custody. Of those cases designated as joint custody cases, about half of the cases involved situations where the children were spending approximately 50% of the time with each parent and the remaining were sharing physical custody but to a lesser degree (e.g., school year with the mother and summer with the father). However, the number of fathers with sole custody has increased over the last several decades as a result of the growing national fatherhood movement, the growing recognition of fathers as significant parental figures and perhaps father-friendlier courts (Clarke-Stewart & Brentano). These general demographic trends in custody are evident not only in the United States but internationally as well. Nonetheless, mothers continue to have more opportunities for involvement in their children's lives after divorce than do fathers. This is further evidence of the cultural assumption, albeit a questionable one, that mothers are a more central socialization agent for children than fathers.

## What Causes Divorce?

Divorce has no single cause, but the probability of divorce rises when husbands and wives come from different ethnic backgrounds, lack the religious conviction that divorce is wrong, abuse alcohol or other substances, have poor communication skills or mental health problems. Couples are especially likely to divorce if they experience high levels of stress – stress from having limited education, facing economic hardships, getting married too young, and being overwhelmed with the responsibility of having children, especially children with problems or children born before marriage (Clarke-Stewart & Brentano, 2006).

Divorce is not a single event. It involves a complex series of steps that start long before the couple separates, continue through the pain of separation, and the difficulty of setting up two separate households, and reverberate through often lengthy legal proceedings. Although a divorce may eventually prove to be a positive solution to a destructive family situation, for most family members the period following the separation is very stressful. During the first year after the divorce, parents' feelings of distress and unhappiness increase, relationships between parents and children become more troubled, and children's social and emotional well-being usually worsens (Hetherington & Stanley-Hagen, 2002). In the second year, when families are adapting to their new status, many parents experience an improvement in their sense of personal well-being, interpersonal functioning, and family relations. In the long run, children in stable, well-functioning single-parent households are better off than children in conflict-ridden intact two-parent families, another reminder that simply being in an intact two parent family, the "ideal" family form, is not necessarily beneficial. When "staying together for the sake of the children" means staying together in a conflictful household, it may not be the best option; children in high-conflict-intact families show more adjustment problems than children who escaped a conflict ridden family through divorce (Amato, Loomis, & Booth, 1995; Hanson, 1999; Morrison & Coiro, 1999). However, when the couple is not in overt conflict and keeps it from their children, staying together is better for the children (Booth, 1999; Hetherington, 1999). Process again trumps form. However, this does not mean that the path is easy or that divorce does not have consequences for many children.

## The Consequences of Divorce

How are children affected by divorce? Overall, researchers have found that children from divorced families have more behavioral and emotional problems than children from two-parent families. They are more aggressive, noncompliant, and antisocial, less prosocial, have lower self-esteem, and experience more problems in their peer relationships (Amato, 2001; Clarke-Stewart & Brentano, 2006; Hetherington & Kelly, 2002). Cognitive aspects of development such as school progress and grades may suffer too (Kim, 2011; Sun & Li, 2002). In addition, children in divorced families have less positive relationships with their fathers, especially when divorce occurs in early childhood and especially when the child is a girl (Amato, 2006). After divorce, fathers are less likely to maintain contact with their daughters than their sons (Hetherington & Kelly, 2002).

The differences between children in divorced and intact families are not particularly large. A meta-analysis of studies comparing children in divorced and intact families showed that for psychological adjustment (depression and anxiety), the effect size was 0.31, and for conduct problems (aggression and misbehavior) it was 0.33 (Amato, 2001). This means that, on average, children with divorced parents scored about one-third of a standard deviation lower than children with continuously married parents on assessments of psychological well-being and good behavior. Researchers have also found that compared with children from intact families children from divorced families are about twice as likely to skip school or get suspended, to get into trouble with the police, to get pregnant as teenagers, to be unemployed in their late teens and early twenties, and to experience clinical levels of distress and depression (Clarke-Stewart & Brentano, 2006; Hanson, 1999). About one-third of the children in divorced families have behavior problems or unwanted teen pregnancies and about one-fourth have adjustment problems or poor social relationships; in contrast, only one-tenth to one-seventh of children from intact families have these problems (Hetherington & Kelly, 2002; Wolchik et al., 2002). Divorce has a stronger effect on children's problem behavior and psychological stress than does race, illness, birth order, death or illness of a family member, or parents' low education. In fact, the link is larger than the association between smoking and cancer. The effects can be long-lasting, too: A long-term study showed that adults who experienced their parents' divorce when they were children died sooner than adults whose parents stayed married (Friedman & Martin, 2012). In spite of these possible negative outcomes, we will see that a variety of factors can either buffer or exacerbate the effects of divorce on children's adaptation.

## Who Is Affected Most?

Not everyone is affected equally by parents' divorce. The age of the child when the parents separate makes a difference. It is often assumed that if parents separate when their children are either very young or all grown up, the effect of the divorce will be minor. Effects may indeed be less severe for these two age groups, but researchers have found that divorce can affect children at all ages. Infants from divorced families are more likely than those in intact families to be insecure and disorganized in their attachments to their mothers and fathers (Solomon & George, 1999) and less positive and engaged in play with their parents (Clarke-Stewart, Vandell, McCartney, Owen, & Booth, 2000). Children who are a few years older when their parent's divorce are likely to be confused, fearful, and anxious and may regress to more immature forms of behavior (Clarke-Stewart & Brentano, 2006). As one college student recalls (Clarke-Stewart & Brentano, 2005):

> I was four years old when my parents divorced, and I felt confused and bewildered. I started sucking my thumb and withdrew from activities with other children. I was very fearful about being abandoned by my mother, and I did not understand why I was being forced to see my father. I felt I did not know him and was angry at him without understanding the reason. I remember only feeling really "safe" in my mother's presence. She was the only person I could trust (p. 111).

School-age children understand the concepts of "divorce" and "separation" better than younger children, but they, too, are usually shocked, worried, and sad when they find out that their parents are separating. Six- to eight-year-olds are particularly upset about the loss of their father and they experience anxiety and depression. At 8–10, children are more likely to get angry – about the divorce, about moving away from their friends, about their parents' suffering, and about custody problems, such as living in two homes. Many children of this age ruminate about the divorce: One study found that 40% of these children spent time thinking about the divorce at least once a day – even a year afterward (Weyer & Sandler, 1998). Many children at this age suffer psychosomatic stress symptoms – headaches, vomiting, dizziness, sleep problems, and inability to concentrate. As one young adult who was in fifth grade when her parents split up recalled (Clarke-Stewart & Brentano, 2005) "My parents' separation was the most devastating event in my life. I remember getting sick after I was informed of my parents' plans. I was sick for a week; all I did was sleep and vomit" (p.115).With adolescence comes increased awareness and understanding of the parents' problems, but adolescents still tend to see things from their own perspective: "How could you do this *to me*?" They are more likely than their peers in intact families to engage in risky behaviors involving sex, drugs, and alcohol, and, in turn, to get into trouble at school or with the law. They may feel abandoned, anxious, and depressed. These adolescents may contemplate suicide – especially boys (Hetherington & Kelly, 2002).

A number of studies have suggested that divorce is worse for boys than for girls. In Hetherington's study (Hetherington & Kelly, 2002), for example, preschool boys from divorced families were more likely than preschool girls to behave aggressively and immaturely. Boys might have more problems than girls for a number of reasons: boys are physiologically more vulnerable to stress than girls; parents and teachers are stricter with boys' outbursts; boys in divorced families usually lose their male role model because they live with their mother, not their father; and boys get less emotional support from their overstressed parents, who find that their noisy, physical, and oppositional behavior makes them more exhausting and difficult to parent. Gender differences are not always observed, however. Meta-analyses reveal that boys are not more adversely affected in terms of psychological adjustment (Amato, 2001). However, boys from divorced families have significantly poorer social adjustment compared with girls from divorced families: They have more problems with popularity, loneliness, cooperativeness, and parent–child relations.

It has been suggested that boys and girls are both affected by divorce but they express it in different ways: Boys are more likely to externalize their distress and girls to internalize it. There is some support for this idea. In letters written to their parents by children in divorce-adjustment groups, boys' themes were more angry; girls' were more anxious (Bonkowski, Boomhower, & Bequette, 1985). Boys also are more likely than girls to have fights with their divorced mothers and in adulthood, young women from divorced families have more long-term anxiety, depression, and relationship difficulties (Hetherington & Kelly, 2002). Another suggestion is that the reaction to parental divorce is stronger for boys at younger ages and for girls in adolescence. Supporting this suggestion, researchers have found that adolescent daughters of divorced parents show increases in antisocial behavior, emotional disturbances, and conflicts with their mothers; they may be sexually active, get pregnant, and get married (Hetherington, 2006). In later years, they are more likely than women whose parents did not divorce to have relationship problems and to find themselves, like their parents before them, in divorce court (Amato, 2006; Hetherington, 2006). Boys do not show these effects in adolescence and adulthood.

Perhaps more important than gender, however, are individual qualities that help children adjust to their parents' divorce. Children who are psychologically healthy, happy, and confident adapt to the new challenges and stressful experiences brought on by the divorce more easily than children with psychological problems before the divorce. In fact, they may even gain from the experience and become better at social problem solving. High intelligence and having an easy temperament help buffer children from the negative effects of divorce (Hetherington, 2006). Children adjust better to divorce if they have a more optimistic, constructive, and realistic outlook. These children have fewer psychological problems in childhood and, as young adults, are more secure in their romantic relationships (Clarke-Stewart & Brentano, 2006).

## Divorce and the Single-Parent Household

How do we account for these effects of divorce on children? Of the many explanations, one of the most important is that children of divorce are growing up in single-parent households, which are at increased risk for multiple stresses that make child rearing difficult. In fact, a period of diminished parenting often follows divorce (Hetherington & Stanley-Hagan, 2002). Mothers themselves are suffering from the divorce and therefore are likely to be self-involved, erratic, and inconsistent in dealing with their children. They often fail to control and monitor their children's behavior adequately. Children reciprocate in the immediate aftermath of divorce by becoming more demanding, noncompliant, and aggressive or by whining and being overly dependent. Divorced mothers and sons are particularly likely to engage in escalating, mutually coercive exchanges.

Children also suffer because they have lost the home and lifestyle to which they were accustomed. They often have to move neighborhoods, find new friends, even attend new schools. Their family income has dropped, and their mothers often have trouble making ends meet. Some children are forced to take on more household responsibilities after the divorce, which leads to resentment and rebellion. Not surprisingly, children find the adjustment to divorce easier if they experience fewer stressors, such as burdensome household chores, responsibility for younger siblings, moving to a new town, and repeated trips to court (Clarke-Stewart & Brentano, 2006).

Although parenting improves markedly in the second year after divorce, problematic parenting is more likely to be sustained with sons – especially temperamentally difficult sons. Divorced mothers and daughters are likely eventually to form close relationships, although mothers may have to weather their daughters' acting out in adolescence (Hetherington & Kelly, 2002). When divorced mothers manage to be warm and consistent in their discipline, their children – of both genders – have fewer adjustment problems (Wolchik et al., 2000). Authoritative parenting is associated with more positive adjustment of children in divorced families, just as it is in intact families. If divorce reduces stress and conflict and leads to better functioning of parents, children tend to benefit in the long run.

Other keys to the well-being of children in divorced families are the children's relationship with their nonresidential parent, most often their father and the relationship between their parents. Frequent visits with the nonresidential parent are linked to more positive adjustment in children (Dunn, Cheng, O'Connor, & Bridges, 2004; Fabricius, Braver, Diaz, & Velez, 2010). These visits are particularly helpful for sons. They are especially important if they allow the nonresidential parent to maintain a parental role by supervising homework, making meals, celebrating holidays, and so on rather than just becoming a casual adult pal. When conflict between parents continues, however, especially causing the child to feel caught in the middle, frequent contact with the nonresidential parent is associated with problematic behavior by the child (Buchanan & Heiges, 2001; Buchanan, Maccoby, & Dornbusch, 1991).

This underscores the importance of the other key factor – the quality of the relationship between the custodial parent and the nonresidential former partner. In fact, some argue that

> the benefits of nonresidential father involvement may depend on the father's ability to effectively work together with mothers in rearing their common child; father's involvement is associated with significantly lower behavioral problems when mothers and fathers have a high quality coparenting relationship (Carlson & McLanahan, 2010, p. 260).

Clearly, what counts is having positive contact with the nonresidential parent but under conditions whereby the child is not being exposed to inter-parent conflict and stress. In this case, children may be better off after divorce than in a two parent but conflict ridden home.

## Does Custody Matter?

Does it matter whether children are in sole custody with their mother or their father or in joint custody with both parents? Most children today are placed in sole custody with their mother. Mothers obtain primary physical custody in close to 80% of cases and fathers in about 10%; joint physical custody is awarded in only about 4% of divorces (Argys, Cook, Garasky, Nepomnyaschy, & Sorensen, 2006; Logan, Walker, Horvath, & Leukefeld, 2003). But is mother custody always the best arrangement? Researchers have found that father custody is advantageous for children's self-esteem, anxiety, depression, and behavior problems (Clarke-Stewart & Hayward, 1996). Custodial fathers have higher incomes than custodial mothers and are more likely to have emotional support from family and friends. Moreover, when children are in father custody, mothers are more likely to stay involved than fathers are when children are in mother custody; thus, children in father custody have the advantage of continued close ties with both parents. In addition, non custodial mothers "are less likely to act as a 'tour guide' parent. They advise, set rules, encourage mature, self controlled-behavior, and discipline their children more than non-custodial fathers do" (Hetherington & Kelly, 2002, p. 121). In a national study of 1400 adolescents ages 12–16 years, only one-third in mother custody maintained a positive relationship with their father, whereas more than half of those in father custody maintained a close relationship with their mother (Peterson & Zill, 1986). This does not mean that courts should automatically place all children with their fathers; however, fathers who *seek* custody are more emotionally invested in their children and more effective parents than fathers who do not seek custody. Moreover, in one study, even though children in father custody were found to do better than children in mother custody *on average*, they were not better adjusted than children in mother custody who also had high levels of contact with their fathers (Clarke-Stewart & Hayward).

If contact with both parents is important for children's adjustment after divorce, is the solution, then, joint custody? In a joint legal custody arrangement, both mother and father share the responsibility for decisions concerning their children's lives, but the children may reside with only one of the parents. In a joint physical custody arrangement, the children live with each parent for close to half the time and have physical access to both mother and father on a regular basis. This arrangement may give children a sense of security and lessen their sense of abandonment by one parent (Fabricius et al., 2010). According to a meta-analysis of 33 studies, children in joint physical or legal custody were better adjusted than children in sole custody; they showed fewer behavior problems and emotional difficulties and had higher self-esteem and better family relationships than children in sole custody arrangements (Bauserman, 2002). However, many factors can undermine the success of joint custody. If parents have dramatically different lifestyles, contradictory values, or poor communication skills, if they cannot set aside their conflicts, or if they want to move to different areas, joint custody is challenging and tends to be unstable. If children are very young, if parents use them as pawns in their battles, or if joint custody is court ordered against the parents' will, the results for children are likely to be negative (Clarke-Stewart & Brentano, 2006). Joint custody works best when the conflict between parents is minimal and children don't feel caught in the middle. Even with cooperating parents, children can feel torn by joint custody. Nor has this issue gone unnoticed by the publishing industry. There are even self-help books that promise to smooth relationships between spouses to make joint custody a more viable option (e.g., *Joint Custody with a Jerk: Raising a Child with an Uncooperative Ex* by Ross & Corcoran (1996)) and even books for children in joint custody(e.g., *We're Having a Tuesday* by Simoneau (2006)). Joint custody is clearly not a panacea for divorced families, and there are many ways to make it unworkable. In the long run, its advantage may be its symbolic value to parents and children (Emery, 2011). It offers a sign to fathers that they retain their rights and obligations as parents and conveys to children the message that both their parents love them and their fathers are still important.

## Not All Divorced Families Are Alike: Why Some Families Work Better Than Others

However, not all divorced families are alike and our question is "what conditions make the postdivorce family work most effectively to buffer children from possible negative outcomes." Several factors mitigate the negative effects of divorce.

As we noted earlier authoritative parenting in the post divorce period helps children cope better with the transition. Variations in effective parenting in the post divorce period are dependent not only on personal characteristics of the parents themselves but on the kinds of support that a custodial parent receives. Social support for parenting (emergency and nonemergency child care, practical support, financial support) from family and friends is related to better psychological adjustment and health among divorced parents, especially if the network is stable (Amato, 2000; Burell, 2002; Hetherington & Kelly, 2002). Members of support networks can relieve stress and anxiety by offering companionship, listening and of course assistance with the daily tasks of parenting. "Friends are good for child care and chauffering, companionship and comforting" (Clarke-Stewart & Brentano, 2006, p. 81). In turn, when mothers are in a supportive network and under less stress, their child rearing is more positive and their relationships with their children are better (Hetherington & Kelly). Nonresidential fathers can benefit from social support too. The parenting of dads who have social support is less affected by role overload and coparenting conflict while those without social support are less buffered from these postdivorce challenges (DeGarmo, Patras, & Eap, 2008). By outsourcing some of their child-care responsibilities to others, divorced parents can manage their parenting interactions more effectively.

Assistance from professionals can help too. Several parent intervention programs for divorced mothers have successfully improved parenting skills and, in turn, benefited children's adaptation as well (Sandler, Miles, Cookston, & Braver, 2008; Wolchik et al., 2002). Moreover, these improvements in children's behavior have been stable over a six year period (Wolchick et al.). Interventions aimed at divorced nonresidential fathers such as the Dads for Life program have focused on commitment to the parenting role, motivation and skills for managing conflict with the former spouse, and skills for parenting. Children of fathers in this program had fewer internalizing and externalizing problems than children of fathers in the control condition (Braver, Griffin, & Cookston, 2005). Following divorce, both parents and, in turn, their children can benefit from intervention efforts by community-based professionals.

Social support is important not just for parents but for children as well. Support from kin and nonkin helps children adjust to divorce. "A supportive social network can provide comfort and stability and let children know they are cared for and important; a supportive network can offer children advice, emotional support, positive feedback, and even opportunities for recreation" (Clarke-Stewart & Brentano, 2006, p. 168). Children with more social support are less anxious and worried and better adjusted than those with fewer social supports (Cowen, Pedro-Carroll, & Alpert-Gillis, 1990; Rodgers & Rose, 2002). And support comes from a variety of sources including siblings, neighbors, friends, adult mentors and, of course, extended family members such as grandparents (Hetherington & Kelly, 2002; Lengua, Wolchick, & Braver, 1995; Lussier, Deater-Deckard, Dunn, & Davies, 2002). For example, feelings of closeness to maternal grandparents after divorce was linked with lower levels of both externalizing and internalizing problems for school age children, which suggests that grandparents can serve as buffers during the transition following separation and divorce (Dunn, Fergusson, & Maughan, 2006). Moreover, the effects of grandmothers and grandfathers on children's adjustment were evident even after accounting for the variation due to nuclear family effects (e.g., quality of parent–child relationships, parental mental health). Here is a personal story recounted by a college student that illustrates the importance of support from others after a divorce:

> Fortunately, I had friends, my teachers, my grandparents and my brother to help me through the whole crazy-making time after my parents' divorce. The most important people were my brother and a teacher I had in sixth and seventh grades. My brother was important because he was the only constant in my life; we shared every experience. My teacher was important because she took an interest in me and showed me compassion. My grandparents also offered consistent support. They gave my mother money for rent and food and paid for private schools for my brother and me; they were like second parents to us. (Clarke-Stewart & Brentano, 2006, p. 169).

The message is clear: families, whether divorced or intact function more effectively when there is support for both parents and children from relatives, friends, and community. Parenting is a cooperative enterprise and by embracing this view of families as embedded in a matrix of supportive relationships, both adults and children have many sources of consistent care and function more effectively.

## Remarriage: Harmful or Helpful?

Is remarriage harmful or helpful? Bethany Tremblay and Oscar Bailey thought that it would be helpful not harmful to combine their separate families into a new stepfamily and for the most part it has proven true. As we will see, there are challenges to making the transition from single-parent family to a stepfamily but as the Tremblay–Bailey stepfamily illustrates with effort and patience it can work and be fine for adults and children too. However, remarriage is not a guarantee of happiness or a fix for children's problems.

High divorce rates create a large pool of experienced candidates for remarriage. So it is no surprise that about three quarters of divorced people remarry (Kreider , 2005). For divorced women, remarriage is the surest route out of poverty and in one study, about one third of women who remarried did it for economic reasons (Hetherington & Kelly, 2002). As one mother bluntly stated "I don't need Prince Charming. I'll settle for a guy who just brings home a paycheck and helps me with the dishes" (Hetherington & Kelly, p. 164). A new partner can, of course, provide more than a paycheck; they can provide affection, emotional support, and help in child rearing. However, creating a stepfamily, especially when children are involved is not easy since there are no clear guidelines for the roles and responsibilities of each parent. It is most often the case that a man father joins a mother and her children to create a "simple" stepfamily.

> As one stepdad lamented "I have no idea how I am supposed to behave, or what the rules are. Can I kiss my wife in front of my stepchildren? Do I tell my stepson to do his homework or is that exceeding my authority? It's hard living in a family where there are no clear rules or lines of authority" (Hetherington & Kelly, 2002, p. 181).

And when stepdads do try to take charge, especially if it is too early in the transition process of forming a new family, mothers may get upset and the stepchildren may rebel and disobey. Remarks such as "you're not my real father" are not uncommon. In fact, finances and disputes over children are the top issues of conflict in stepfamilies. In light of these challenges, it is not surprising that children in stepfamilies have more emotional problems than children in intact families or even divorced families (Cherlin & Furstenberg, 1994; Clarke-Stewart & Brentano, 2006; Hetherington, Bridges, & Insabella, 1998; Pryor, 2008). More antagonistic relations among siblings, especially brothers, are also found in stepfamilies compared with intact families (Conger & Conger, 1996; Dunn & Davies, 2001; Hetherington et al., 1998). Things are even more difficult for both the couple and the children if not just one parent but both parents bring their biological children into the new family to create a "complex" stepfamily.

> Stepfamilies, like machines are subject to the complexity principle: the more working parts, the greater the risk of breakdown. And in a complex stepfamily, breakdown

often occurs in family cohesion. Alliances, scapegoating, and divisive loyalties appear. The children in the family clash; each parent sides with his biological child and; the unit divides into hostile, sometimes warring camps (Hetherington & Kelly, 2002, pp. 196–197).

Not unexpectedly, dissolution rates are higher in complex than simple stepfamilies (Amato, 2005). Of course, many stepfamilies work out workable lines of authority and household routines that can benefit not only the couple but the children as well. And many of the problems exhibited by children in stepfamilies are not permanent (Amato, 2005). Although the majority of stepchildren exhibit problems during the transition period immediately following remarriage, most show considerable resilience, and three quarters have no long-term problems (Hetherington & Jodl, 1994). Younger children adjust more easily. Teen children have a difficult time accepting their parent's remarriage and are at greater risk for externalizing problems, including alcohol use, delinquency, and premature sexual intercourse. They also report more conflict with their stepparents than adolescents in intact families have with their parents (Hetherington & Stanley-Hagan, 2002). This is not surprising because stepparents are less nurturing and affectionate with their stepchildren than biological parents are with theirs (Clarke-Stewart & Brentano, 2006; Pryor, 2008). Adolescents, especially girls, are often resentful of stepfathers who displace them as the object of their mother's attention.

As one young woman recalled:

I was just jealous, I guess. I missed the times Mom and I spent together sitting on her bed eating Chinese dinner and watching TV. I resented Nick (her stepdad) being there at the dinner table when I wanted to get her advice about something-a romantic problem, an unreasonable teacher or a fight with a friend. I couldn't stand it when they hugged or kissed. I thought it was disgusting. There wasn't much they could do. I just felt shut out (Hetherington & Kelly, 2002, p. 191).

However, the differences between stepchildren and children in intact families – like the differences between children from divorced and intact families – are small. Most stepchildren do well in school and do not suffer from emotional or behavioral problems. The small differences suggest that there is a great deal of overlap between children in stepfamilies and those in intact nuclear families; in fact the overlap is greater than the difference. This suggests that children's adjustment is largely determined by the *quality* of the relationships in the stepfamily, just as it does in intact families, another indication that family process is more critical than form. Although remarriage is no simple panacea for the challenges after divorce and is no guarantee that it will improve happiness and affluence or solve children's social and academic problems, there is great deal of variability among stepfamilies and as a form it can work. However, how well the parents manage their new roles and how well they take into account the challenges children face in adjusting to a new parent and their own new roles and demands will determine how well stepfamily life will work for both adults and children. The success of Tremblay–Bailey stepfamily was due to the fact that both stepparents moved into their new roles slowly, cautiously, and with plenty of consultation with each other and with the children who were part of their new combined family unit (Figure 3.1).

**Figure 3.1** Capturing the diversity of families.
*Source:* Edward Koren New Yorker.

## Not All Single-Parent Families Are a Result of Divorce: The Rise of Other Types of Single-Parent Families

One of the realities that many modern parents face is parenting alone. It is widely recognized that this is a challenging family form in which a single adult, whether mother of father assumes responsibility for the care and rearing of a child or children. A glance at the demographic trends over the last few decades tells the story. In 2010, approximately 26% of children under age 18 lived with a single parent (U.S. Census Bureau, 2010a) which is nearly three times as high as it was in the 1960s (DeVita, 1996). In the current era, among single-parent families, most are mother headed families (87%) while only 13% lived in father headed families (U.S. Census Bureau). These rates vary by race of the family. In Asian families, the rates of single-parent households is low with 10.2% of children living with only their mother and 4.0% living only with their father. In contrast, among Black households the rates are markedly higher: 49.7% of children live in mother only homes and another 3.6% in father only homes. For White children, 15.5% live in mother only families, while 3.8% are in father only households. Finally, 26% of Hispanic children live with only their mothers and 2.7% live with only their fathers (U.S. Census Bureau).

In spite of the increase in single-parent families there is still a public perception that this family form is inferior to the "ideal" family form. It has been decades since then Vice President Dan Quayle famously lambasted the fictional TV character, and single mother, Murphy Brown, but public sentiment may not have changed significantly. In early 2011, former Arkansas governor Mike Huckabee called out pregnant Oscar winner Natalie Portman as glamorizing "the, idea of out-of-wedlock children" (Carroll, 2011). A recent national survey of 2691 Americans (Pew Charitable Trust, 2011) found that only 7 out of 10 respondents believed that a child raised by a single mother represented a true family (they did not ask about living with single dads). The survey further found that a mere four percent believed that single motherhood has a positive impact on society, while 70% believed those households are "bad for society."

Although parenting alone is a departure from the "ideal" family form, families arrive there by many different routes. As we have just explored, the largest group become single parents as a result of divorce or separation. Others are young single mothers or fathers who often reach parenthood well before they planned to become a parent or simply did not want to wait until they were financially secure enough to marry. Others are single parents by choice who purposefully set out to become a parent even though they lack a partner with whom to share the responsibilities of parenthood, part of the larger trend in which child bearing and marriage are no longer as closely linked as in the past (Cherlin, 2009). Still others become single parents as a result of the death of a spouse or partner. While all these individuals are going solo as parents, their economic and emotional challenges are different and their success as parents varies. And perhaps not surprisingly, the effects on children are different too. There are many faces of single parenthood and each has its own set of dynamics. Moreover, there is a great deal of variability within each of these types of single-parent families and our goal is to not simply explore the differences and similarities across the different forms of single parenting but to examine the internal variations within each of these distinctive forms of solo parenting. By doing so, we can discover what works and what doesn't work so that we can better assist all forms of single-parent families function more effectively. Finally, we ask a seldom posed question: are there advantages to being a single parent?

## Two Profiles of Single-Mother Families

Although nearly half of women in the United States become single mothers after a divorce, this route to single parenthood is decreasing. In its place, there has been a steady increase in the percentage of single mothers who have never been married. Among white single mothers, two-thirds (66%) have been previously married, compared with nearly half (48%) of Latino single mothers and a third (34%) of African American single mothers (Mather, 2010). The figures can be misleading since some single mothers cohabitate with a partner so the rates may be overestimated. We explore the issue of cohabitation later in this chapter. Forty percent of single mother families are poor which is five times higher than married couple families (U.S. Census Bureau, 2011). This impoverished group of single mothers has been of major concern to policy makers and child advocates since poverty is linked with a variety of negative outcomes for parents as well as children. Another group, single mothers by choice, is better off economically and usually older; women in this group deliberately decided to become a single parent even without a partner. Let's take a closer look at these two groups of single mothers.

## Poor Single Mothers

The public image of single mothers is not flattering. The public perception of single mothers as poor, impulsive, irresponsible, and unfit for parenthood is widespread. Many assume that they are an economic drain on the state and collect welfare to survive. However, is it a fair characterization and are the single mother and her offspring destined for a downward spiral? The answer is more complex than the stereotype of single mothers would suggest.

Although the societal focus has been on adolescent single mothers, young teen mothers represent an increasingly smaller portion of the single mother population. In fact, the US teen birth rate fell by more than one-third from 1991 through 2009, a long-term downward trend that has continued (Centers for Disease Control and Prevention, April, 2011b). In spite of this trend, teenage pregnancy remains a societal concern and grabs our attention every time a celebrity adolescent like Jamie Lynn Spears or former Alaska governor Sarah Palin's daughter Bristol reveals she is expecting. Most single mothers are in their 20s and 30s and not teens. Most (75%) single mothers are employed, a rate that is even higher than for women in married families (Mather, 2010). However, their unemployment rate is higher and they often hold poorly paying jobs in the service sector with limited benefits. Finally, their highest education attainment is typically a high school graduation certificate which limits their career prospects.

Why do poor women have babies out of wedlock? The immediate causes include the facts that young people among all major cultural groups in the United States are initiating sexual behavior earlier and that people generally are marrying later. In addition, the cultural acceptance of single motherhood has increased dramatically over the last several decades. According to a recent survey of poor women, 79% agreed with the statement that "A women should have children if she wants to even if she is not married" (Cherlin, Cross-Barnet, Burton, & Garrett-Peters, 2008). Moreover, for some young women, especially poor women, entry into motherhood is a valued and attainable goal. As a recent close examination of over 160 poor mothers has shown, motherhood for many young women is a higher priority than marriage and for many a fulfillment of a central life goal (Edin & Kefalas, 2005). In contrast to middle class women who privilege career above children, many poor women take the opposite view. They simply see children as more central to their lives than middle class women. Poor women believe their lives would be empty without children (McLanahan, 2004). While middle class women strive to establish a career and marriage before child bearing, many young poor women choose to have children first and address issues of career and marriage later especially in view of their often bleak prospects for economic success or finding a viable partner (Edin & Kefalas). As Edin and Kefalas observe "unlike their wealthier sisters, who have the chance to go to college and embark on careers – attractive possibilities that provide strong motivation to put off having children – poor young women grab eagerly at the surest source of accomplishment within their reach: becoming a mother" (2005, p. 46). It is not that they do not value marriage as well as motherhood. In fact, they hold marriage as a high value but do not think that they have reached the level of financial or relationship quality where marriage is a viable alternative. This may, in part, explain why more than half the women who get pregnant decide to keep their babies and become single mothers and only a quarter of teenage mothers are married, and another third have fairly stable relationships with the fathers of their babies. This latter group of "single" mothers underscores that at least some of these mothers are, in fact, not parenting alone but have a male figure in their life who may contribute to helping raise the child by providing informal financial or instrumental assistance (Carlson & McLanahan, 2010). Variability among single mothers needs to be recognized as does the lack of clarity in the meaning of the term "single" parent.

What are the prospects for poor single mothers? Most women who are single mothers face personal, economic, and social problems that make it very difficult for them to support and care for their children (Moore & Brooks-Gunn, 2002). Stress, financial hardship, and lack of social support all contribute to poorer child outcomes in single-mother families, just as they do in two-parent families (Golombok, 2000; Lipman, Boyle, Dooley, & Offord, 2002). As one British single mother reflected:

> "You have to be all things to all people. You can never be ill, you can never be tired and you can never run out of resources even when you are on your knees. If I was confronted with the same choices I would do it again, but I wouldn't choose it as a way of life" (Golombok, p. 4)."

Many scholars have argued that it is the poverty-related challenges that account for many of the difficulties that young mothers face rather than the lack of a second parent (McLanahan & Sandefur, 1994). However, the stereotype of single mothers as welfare queens who do not work is a myth. In spite of the economic challenges associated with being a single mom, and contrary to popular beliefs, among children with single mothers 41% get food stamps and 59% do not. Moreover, only 5–10% of all single mothers receive other forms of government assistance (eg Temporary Assistance for Needy Families program (TANF) (Daly & Kwok, 2009). This does not mean they do not struggle. If they have already left school, they are unlikely to return; if they have not yet dropped out of school, they are likely to do so and are unlikely to catch up educationally after the baby is born. Without education, they are limited in the kinds of jobs they can secure, and their earning power is low. They can rarely afford child care and, unless relatives or others can care for the child, they may give up their jobs and go on welfare at least temporarily. Without money or education, they find themselves in a recurring cycle of low educational attainment, few skills, economic dependence, and poverty. Being poor and a single mother is not easy and providing support for this group of mothers is a continuing concern for communities and policy makers.

## The Fate of Children in Single-Parent Families?

Children who grow up in poor single mother families are at risk for serious social, emotional and academic problems (McLanahan & Sandefur, 1994). In fact, it has been suggested that the negative impact of the conditions under which poor single mothers and their children live is greater for the children than for the mothers. This may be because the children have always lived under these conditions, whereas some of the mothers grew up in better times. The children of young single mothers are more likely to develop behavior problems and to do poorly in school than children whose parents are older (Furstenberg, Brooks-Gunn, & Chase-Lansdale, 1989; Moffitt, 2002). Preschool children of single mothers display higher levels of aggression and less ability to control impulsive behavior. By adolescence, they have higher rates of grade failure and more delinquency. They also become sexually active at younger ages and are more likely to become pregnant before age twenty (Kiernan, 2001; Kiernan & Smith, 2003). The negative effects on children are to some degree due to the less effective caregiving provided by single mothers; they are less warm and provide less verbal and cognitive stimulation than married mothers. Not all single mothers behave this way, nor are all children who grow up in poor single mother homes adversely affected. Being in a single mother family may elevate the risk of negative outcomes but it does not imply that negative outcomes are inevitable.

Some fare well under these family conditions, others not so well. Next, we examine potential factors that can reduce the negative effects associated with growing up in a poor single mother home.

## Not All Poor Single Moms Are Alike; Not All Children Have Problems

There is considerable variability among young single mothers and it is unfair and inaccurate to assume that all poor single mothers are troubled and all their children are suffering developmental problems. When the effects of poverty and stress are taken into account the effects of single parenthood are lessened which suggests that poverty-related stress rather than single mother status alone may be the culprit which causes the poor outcomes for children. For example, during preadolescence, children in single mother families with high levels of stress were described as having the most behavior problems. However, when stress was low, children from single-parent and two-parent families were similar (Gringlas & Weinraub, 1995). Social support of either children or single parents themselves is related to improved functioning for parents as well as children. Nonresidential fathers, grandparents, other extended family members, nonkin, as well as community organizations can all provide support. Just as we saw in our exploration of children's postdivorce adjustment, nonresidential fathers provide a variety of forms of support to single mothers including help with child care, child supervision, or by financial assistance; these assistance efforts are related to better child outcomes (Amato & Dorius, 2010). Moreover, children do better if they have a strong attachment to their nonresidential father (Whitman, Borkowski, Keogh, & Weed, 2001). Nonresidential father's parenting style is important as well. Positive involvement and authoritative parenting by nonresident fathers are linked with more adequate development (Carlson, 2006; Fabricius & Luecken, 2007). For children living in single mother households, father provision of cognitive stimulation was positively related to children's cognitive development at 9 and 24 months; the link was even stronger for children in single mother families than for children in two parent households (Fagan & Lee, 2012). Single mothers do better if their own mothers are supportive and provide guidance to help daughters improve their parenting skills

(Oberlander, Black, & Starr, 2007). Social support reduces the stress associated with being a single parent and lessens the negative effects of being in a single parent home for the children (Weinraub, Horvath, & Gringlas, 2002). In one study (Deleire & Kalil, 2002), teenagers living with their single mothers and with at least one grandparent in multigenerational households have developmental outcomes that are at least as good and often better than the outcomes of adolescents in married families. Similarly, increased availability of instrumental support, as perceived by single mothers of adolescents predicted fewer depressive symptoms in those mothers, less punishment of adolescents, and less negativity about the maternal role. In turn, the adolescents were better adjusted (McLoyd, Jayaratne, Ceballo, & Borquez, 1994).When children in single-parent homes receive support from extended family members or are involved in extracurricular activities or active in religious institutions, they do better academically and socially (Benson & Roehlkepartain, 1993; Riley & Cochran, 1987).

Race matters too. The more time that white children spend in single-parent families, the poorer their math outcomes and the greater their delinquency. In contrast, for black children, time in a single-parent family was unrelated to these outcomes (Dunifon & Kowaleski-Jones, 2002). Higher levels of social support in black communities combined with the greater acceptance of single-parent family structure may contribute to these race related patterns (Heard, 2007).

Long term prospects of young single mothers: Not all young single mothers are destined for problems in the long term. Happily, some young parents develop good lives for themselves and their children. In two studies, researchers have followed African American teen mothers into middle adulthood (Furstenberg, Brooks-Gunn, & Morgan, 1987; Horwitz, Klerman, Kuo, & Jekel, 1991). Not all ended up in a life of poverty and welfare dependence. In their early 30s, one-third had completed high school and nearly one-third had completed some post–high school education. About three quarters were working; only one quarter were on welfare. They were most likely to be doing well if they had attended a special school for pregnant teens, had high aspirations at the time the baby was born, and if their parents were well educated. Teenage parenthood does not necessarily doom either the teen parent or their offspring to a lifetime of negative outcomes; some do just fine or even better. Just think of King Henry VII of England, whose mother gave birth at age 13, or Barack Obama, whose mother was 18 when he was born. The key seems to be finding ways to reduce stress by garnering social support from family and community to aid the young single parent do their job as a parent by developing a quality relationship with her children and an authoritative approach to control and discipline. Parenting processes, not family form, continues to be a better approach to understanding the effects of single and two- parent families on children.

## A New Group of Single Mothers: Single Mothers by Choice

Another major change in families is that more women are deliberately choosing to go it alone and become a single mother. In contrast to young poor single mothers, there is a sizeable group of older women such as 39 year old Mary Winston, a single mother by choice who we introduced in the opening chapter. Mary and others like her are choosing to become single mothers without a husband or partner. There are a variety of reasons for this trend including the unlinking of marriage and motherhood, the decreasing stigma associated with single motherhood and the growing economic independence of women (Cherlin, 2009). Many of these single mothers by choice are older (age 35–40), well-educated, upper middle class socioeconomically and employed in well paying professional jobs (Bock, 2000; Hertz, 2006; Weinraub et al., 2002). They can afford to have a child on their own, have not found a marriageable partner, and are motivated by the "ticking of their biological clock" which may run out and limit their biological ability to conceive a child. Therefore, they achieve motherhood by the use of the assisted reproductive technologies or become pregnant with the assistance of a cooperative male partner who is not under any obligation to serve as a parent (Hertz). Others adopt a child either domestically or internationally as a means of achieving motherhood (Gailey, 2010). Still others, including women across the economic spectrum, may find themselves pregnant and choose to have the baby and rear the child on their own, in part, because the father may either be uninterested in marriage or unwilling to assume a parental role. Or the women themselves may view the partner as unworthy marriage material due to perceived unreliability, untrustworthiness, or lack of positive economic prospects (Edin & Kefalas, 2005). For these women, it is better not to marry at all than to marry badly. From their perspective there are some upsides to being a solo mother. No partner is better than an abusive one or one who cannot be relied upon to contribute either emotionally or financially.

Just as we saw in the case of poor single mothers, the level of support makes a difference in how well even economically viable single parents by choice fare. In a study of Israeli older single mothers (average age of 43), their success as single mothers was found to be due, in part, to the fact that they did not raise their children alone, but received support from others (Weissenberg, Landau, & Madgar, 2007).

> As the mothers shared with us, they indeed need much help, such as daily taking care of the children or regularly babysitting for them, or receiving financial help, and are aided particularly by their parents. Some of the mothers said that although they enjoy their motherhood very much, they did not think how demanding the role of a single mother will be (p. 2789).

To access social support needed to raise a child alone, some women moved back to their parent's home, moved close to their extended families, or even to an apartment in the same building with their parents, in order to get support from them. Some even outsourced some of the household responsibilities by employing full-time maids. And these single but well-supported mothers perceived their toddlers and young elementary children as well-adjusted. The children were reported to function well at kindergarten or school. Very few of them had difficulties with their teachers and the majority of them did not experience any problems with their peers. Further evidence of the importance of social support in helping single parents cope with the challenges of parenting comes from an American study of 65 single mothers by choice (Hertz, 2006). In her study, Hertz found that there are a variety of models that women develop to cope successfully with the challenges of raising a child on their own. While some women were consummate single mothers who parented alone and were technically responsible for the child 24/7, even they relied heavily on extensive social networks to cope. Others in the Hertz sample sought out another adult to serve as a coparent even though there were no romantic ties. Here is how Trish, who became a single mother at age 37, described her goal: "I wanted another parent whose relationship is about the kid and not about our romantic situation" (Hertz, p. 147). Just as we saw for some of the women in the Israeli study, some chose to reside with their parents and in effect to coparent with their mothers. Hertz interviewed one single mother who adopted an infant and agreed beforehand to both share a residence and be a coparent with her mother. Still others made coparenting legal arrangements with nonrelatives; in some cases they might share a residence and in other cases the child would go back and forth between the houses of the two coparents. For example, Trish coparented with two gay men, one of whom was the sperm donor, and they met as a group weekly and shared responsibility for their daughter who spent time with both her dads as well as her mom in their separate houses. The advantages of this kind of coparenting arrangement are nicely summed up by Trish:

> I really wanted another parent because I wanted to have built-in time when I wasn't going to be responsible for a child. I also felt like there are other parts of my life, separate from motherhood, that I really love and care about, and I didn't want to give it all up (Hertz, p. 151).

Adaptation to the social circumstances of being a single parent by seeking and using social support from others is a key to being a well-functioning single parent. However, there are many forms that social support can assume, and there are clearly many creative ways of managing single parenthood. These findings underscore our view of parenting as a cooperative responsibility and regardless of the family form, social support can aid in reducing the burdens of parenthood. Beyond the recognition that there are many types of single mothers, many single mother families are functioning well and their children are thriving in spite of the clear departure from the "ideal" family form.

## Are There Advantages of Being a Single Mother?

In spite of the challenges, there are, in fact, positive aspects associated with being a single mother. A peaceful single-parent household may be preferable to a conflict-ridden family for both mother and child (Cummings & Davies, 2010) just as we saw earlier in the comparisons of low-conflict divorced family units with intact but highly conflictful families. The hassles of joint-decision making are avoided and one's autonomy is preserved in a single mother family. Other advantages involve close and interdependent relationships with their children. As one 16-year-old girl who lived with her mother and younger brother noted:

> "I just feel a lot closer to her because it's only her." She went on to explain: "I think it's the fact that, like, she spent, like, all my life with me. I mean she had her other friends around. I don't know, she's had boyfriends or whatever. I presume she has, but it's mainly been only...it's just the fact that it's just me and her, that's kind of why our relationship would be so strong" (Nixon, Greene, & Hogan, 2012, p. 146).

And some children learn important prosocial lessons. For example, some children develop an ethic of care, whereby, they become aware of their mother's stress and respond by attending to her emotional needs and actively participating in the household duties. A 12-year-old boy explained:

> If she's stressed at work, if she has to meet a deadline or something, she can come back and I can help her out with stuff around the house and everything.... I'd bring her up a cup of tea or whatever and put my brother into bed (Nixon et al., 2012, p. 149).

Of course, the long term implications of these prosocial lessons are unclear, but other work suggests that responsibility-taking is associated with other forms of altruistic and prosocial behavior (Whiting & Edwards, 1988). At the same time, issues of parent–child boundaries and the hazards of assuming responsibility earlier than is maturationally appropriate are downsides that need to be recognized and better understood. Nonetheless, turning our attention to the possible healthy aspects of single mother families serves as a corrective to the decidedly negative view of single mother families that has pervaded both the scientific literature and the public consciousness.

Next, we turn to another violation of the "ideal" family form – single fathers.

## Single Fathers: A Growing Family Form

In spite of the early recognition of the challenges of single fatherhood when Dustin Hoffman became a single father in the 1979 movie, *Kramer vs Kramer*, our understanding of the role of single fathers in the lives of their children has lagged far behind our knowledge about single mothers. Although Hoffman depicted a single father after his wife, played by Meryl Streep, leaves him to care for his young son after a divorce, custody after divorce is not the only route to single fatherhood. As in the case of women, there are a variety of routes to becoming a single father. Some single men adopt a child, others become single fathers as a result of the death or desertion of their spouse, while still others like the Dustin Hoffman character receive custody of their child after divorce. Family courts, which used to be wary of granting custody to fathers after divorce, have become much more willing to do so as a result of the increased recognition that fathers as well as mothers can be competent caregivers (Clarke-Stewart & Brentano, 2006). In this age of Assisted Reproductive Technologies, single men can become fathers through the assistance of a surrogate and an egg donor, a topic that we explore in Chapter 5. Just as we saw in the case of single motherhood, variability is clearly evident and there is no single profile of single fathers, only multiple ones.

How prevalent are single fathers? In 2010, there were 1.8 million single fathers or about 15% of all single parents (U.S. Census Bureau, 2010b). About 46% were divorced, 30% were never married, 19% were separated and 6% were widowed. In other words, about one in six single parents is a man. In spite of their growing numbers, there are many more books and other resources available for single mothers than single dads. As one observer noted "If you could conjure any single mother's circumstances, any circumstances whatever, you could find a dozen books offering her advice and guidance. For single fathers, not so much" (McCloskey, 2010).

How do single dads fare as parents and how do the children they care for develop? One of the challenges faced by single fathers is the dichotomous cultural stereotypes as either superdads or needy and perhaps even incompetent fathers (Grief, 1985; Weinraub et al., 2002). Some view single fathers as special and perhaps extraordinary, in part, because they are so few in number compared to single mothers. As one observer noted about her nephew, a single dad of 6-year-old twins and a 15-year-old:

> The women in our family think he's the greatest, because he parents mostly alone and does a pretty good job. This same praise is never given to the single moms in my extended family who have done just as well (Ernestine Avila, personal communication, 2012).

On the one hand, their willingness to go it alone and their relative success as a parent is viewed as praiseworthy and admirable. On the other hand, many are viewed with skepticism and doubt that single men are up to the task of parenting alone. He is seen as needing help and advice on everything from diapers to dishes, and single fathers often receive more assistance than single mothers who are assumed to be able to cope. Neither view has much merit and serves only to perpetuate outdated myths about men's abilities to be competent parents. While our views are changing, there is still a lingering expectation that single men are going to be less competent parents than single women.

## Single Fathers: Myth versus Reality

Single fathers who have custody of their children experience the same stresses and challenges faced by single mothers including balancing work and family demands, financial woes, and finding adequate child care. Fathers, however, have more difficulty than mothers with monitoring their children's whereabouts, activities, and progress in school. In contrast, single mothers report more problems remaining firm and patient. These differences reflect pre-divorce roles, in which mothers tended to assume more managerial responsibilities and fathers often acted as disciplinarians. Moreover, as a group, they do differ not only from single mothers but from men who do not gain custody. Fathers who gain custody of their children after a divorce are often older, better educated, more affluent, and enjoy better overall psychological well-being (Amato, 2000). Moreover, custodial father who seek custody rather than merely agree to it have been found to be more emotionally invested in their children than men who do not actively seek custody (DeMaris & Grief, 1992).

In light of this selection bias, it is not surprising that many custodial fathers are quite competent homemakers and parents. Fathers with custody are not bumbling and ineffectual characters who can't change a diaper, fry an egg or vacuum a carpet. Divorced fathers can raise their children competently and effectively. In an early study of single fathers, Helen Mendes (1976) asked single dads how they coped with the daily chores of homemaking: Nearly 90% of the fathers regularly cooked, cleaned, shopped, and managed their homes. In light of the increased number of households where parents share responsibility for a variety of household tasks, it is likely that the current crop of divorced single dads is even better prepared for the responsibilities of single fatherhood (Deutsch, 1999).

How do the children develop when dad is the lone parent? Most of the evidence about this question is based on studies of children in father custody. As we noted earlier, in the United States, most children today are placed in mother custody. Mothers obtain primary physical custody in about 80 % of the time, while fathers are awarded primary custody about 8–14% of the time. Joint physical custody occurs in 2 to 6 % of the cases (Argys et al., 2007; Clarke-Stewart & Brentano, 2006; Logan et al., 2003). Early evidence suggested that children fared better when in the custody of the same gender parent: boys were better adjusted when with their dads and girls were better off when residing primarily with their mothers (Warshak & Santrock, 1983). Later studies have found that there is an advantage of father custody for children's self-esteem, anxiety, depression, and behavior problems, especially for boys (Clarke-Stewart & Hayward, 1996).While there continues to be a debate about whether children are better off with a same-sex parent, it is clear that father custody does offer children some advantages. As we noted earlier, custodial fathers tend to have higher incomes than custodial mothers and are more likely to have emotional support from family and friends. Moreover, when children are in father custody, mothers are more likely to stay involved than are fathers when children are in mother custody, so that children in father custody have the advantage of continued close ties with both parents. In a national study of 1400 12–16-year-olds, only one-third of the adolescents in mother custody maintained a positive relationship with their fathers, whereas over half of those in father custody maintained close relations with their mothers (Peterson & Zill, 1986). In the long run, the nature of the custody arrangement may matter less than whether there is continued contact with both parents. For example, in one study of custody, even though children in father custody were found to do better than children in mother custody *on average*, they were not better adjusted than children in mother custody who also had high levels of contact with their fathers (Clarke-Stewart & Hayward).

To understand how effective fathers are as single parents, it is critical to consider their social ties to people and institutions outside the family. As in the case of single mothers, single fathers are more effective parents when they are embedded in a network of social support so that the burden of caregiving is a shared responsibility. Single fathers recognize both the necessity and value of outsourcing some of the child-care responsibilities. They use additional caregivers such as their child's mother, babysitters, relatives, daycare centers, and friends more than single custodial mothers. Just as do single mothers, single fathers with children tend to have more involvement with their parents than married fathers (Marks & McLanahan, 1993). Children in father custody are enrolled in childcare for more hours a week (24 vs. 11 hours) than children in mother custody (Clarke-Stewart & Allhusen, 2005). Even if they fail to reach out for assistance, single dads are more often the recipients of unsolicited help, especially from females, than single mothers (Hetherington & Kelly, 2002). Nor is this social support used by single fathers inconsequential; the total amount of contact with additional adult caregivers is directly linked to the child's warmth, sociability, and social conformity (Hetherington & Kelly). Perhaps children in single father families benefit not only from more nonparental adult involvement, but by better relationships with their dads as well, whose resources are less depleted due to this extrafamilal support. The viability of single father families is a further challenge to the "ideal" family form not only as a one parent unit but as a single gender parent form as well. We return to this issue of men as parents without a mother in the household in the next chapter when we examine same gender parent families.

## The Cohabitating Family: An Increasingly Common Alternative to Marriage

The Baker–Ashe family who are cohabitating with their children represents one of the fastest growing family forms in the United States. Since 1990, the number of cohabitating parents has nearly doubled. And in 2010, over 7.5 million US households were headed by cohabitating couples who were rearing either their own children or their partner's children (U.S. Census Bureau, 2010a). In 2008, 5% of households were headed by a cohabitating couple, up from 3% in 1990. In some Scandinavian countries such as Sweden, the rates of cohabitation are closer to 25% (Gubernskaya, 2010). At the same time the percentage of married parents has declined; the share of married-couple households fell to 51% in 2008 from 57% in 1990. For many contemporary families cohabitation is an alternative to marriage or for some a step or trial period before they take the plunge into marriage. In fact, nearly 30% of couples cohabitate before getting married while only 18% of men and 23% of women skip the cohabitation step and go directly to marriage (U.S. Census Bureau). As demographer and family expert, Andrew Cherlin noted in his book *The Marriage-Go-Round* (2009):

> We have witnessed over the past half century the unprecedented decline of marriage as the only acceptable arrangement for having sexual relations and for raising children. Marriage is still important but it is now optional: people can start relationships or have children without it (p. 7).

According to some estimates, almost 40% of children will spend time in a cohabiting household by age 12 (Kennedy & Bumpuss, 2011). Approximately half of these cohabiting families include a biological father and half involve a stepfather (Kreider, 2008). Most of the increase in the percentage of children being born to unmarried women since 1990 is due to births to women who are living with an unmarried partner (Cherlin, 2009). A recent Census Bureau report estimated that of four million women who gave birth in 2008, 425,000 were living with an unmarried partner (Dye, 2010). As in the case of all family forms, not all cohabiting families are alike. First, couples attitudes toward this arrangement varies. In some cases, it is a prelude to marriage, in other cases it is an alternative to marriage, and in still others an arrangement without clear commitment (Smock, 2000). Second, the composition of cohabiting families varies too. Some consist of a couple with their biological children, while others involve a mother with biological children and a live-in stepfather. Still others are hybrid arrangements in which there are both biological and stepchildren in the household (Manning & Brown, 2012). In yet another type of unmarried-parent household, a mother and child maintain a "visiting" relationship with the child's father who is present periodically but not on a regular basis. In McLanahan's study of poor unmarried families, she found that between 16% (White) and 43% (Black) of fathers were visiting dads (Carlson & McLanahan, 2010). Moreover, cohabitation varies in duration from relatively brief periods to decades. Overall cohabitation arrangements tend to last for shorter periods of time than married relationships (McLanahan, 2011). A major barrier to understanding cohabitating families is the fact that there may be selection effects which determine who chooses to marry and who decides to cohabitate (Brown, 2010). Selection factors include socio-economic and educational resources, race, level of relationship commitment, and perhaps personal characteristics as well. Without taking these selection factors into account it is difficult to attribute differences in child outcomes between this family form and other forms such as married or single-parent households to family structure itself (McLanahan & Percheski, 2008).

This shift is part of a larger pattern that we have seen with divorce and remarriage, namely an increasingly high rate of change in family stability as parents and partners move in and out of various living arrangements. And this rate of social transitions is especially high in the United States compared to other western countries. By age 35, 10% of women in the United States have three or more husbands or live-in partners (married or cohabitating) while in Canada and France it is only 2%. Even in liberal Sweden only 4.5% of women have experienced three or more live-in partners by their mid 30s. (Timberlake & Heuvline, 2008, cited by Cherlin, 2009). Children born to cohabiting couples, for instance, are at least twice as likely to see their parents separate as are children whose parents are married at the time of their birth (Heuveline, Timberlake, & Furstenberg, 2003).

In spite of the increasing prevalence of cohabitation as a family form, the preference for the "ideal" family form is still alive and well. Public sentiment lags behind social reality with 43% saying that is "bad for society for a cohabitating couple to be raising children" while another 41% indicated that it made no difference (Pew Research Center, 2011).

## Challenges for Cohabitating Families

Just as we saw in the case of divorced- and single-parent families, cohabitating families face a variety of challenges. First, they tend to be less well off economically than two parent married families, even though cohabitating families have more resources than single-parent families (Manning & Brown, 2006). College educated cohabitating families are equivalent or higher in terms of income while cohabiting noncollege graduates are less well off than married families (Fry & Cohn, 2011). Second, they experience more transitions which can be stressful for both parents and children alike and harmful to children's development (Teachman, 2008). However, instability early (vs later) in the child's development is most likely to be detrimental (Cavanagh & Huston, 2008). Moreover, not all transitions are equal. Sometimes moving from a cohabitating stepfamily to a single mother family can be beneficial to children's school engagement while moving into a cohabiting stepfamily from a single-mother family decreased adolescent well-being (Brown, 2006). Third, they may receive less support from extended family than married families due to the still lingering cultural stigma associated with living together without a formal marriage contract.

## What Happens to the Children of Cohabiting Parents?

The jury is still out on this issue. Some early reports found that the marital status of the biological parents – whether married or cohabiting – made little difference in children's social adjustment or their school engagement or achievement (Clark & Nelson, 2000; Manning, 2002). Comparisons between children in married and cohabitating stepfamilies yield a similar story in terms of behavioral and emotional outcomes and levels of school engagement and achievement outcomes (Clark & Nelson). However, children in cohabitating-stepparent families exhibit more behavior problems at school than children in married stepfamilies (Acs & Nelson, 2002; Clark & Nelson, 2000) but again the effects are small and most children in either family type do not exhibit problems. Moreover, compared to single-parent families, children in cohabitating families are often similar and in some cases may be better off economically (Hao, 1996) and do better in school than children from single parent families (Dunifon & Kowaleski-Jones, 2002). In a study of over 10,000 kindergarten children, the investigators found no differences in child well-being for children living in cohabiting stepfamilies and cohabiting two-biological-parent families (Artis, 2007). Instead, any effects of cohabitation on child well-being were accounted for by economic resources, maternal mental health (i.e., depression) and parenting practices. Similarly, in another study, six to eleven year old children who lived in a two biological parent cohabiting or a stepparent cohabiting family did not differ from children in married parent families in either social and behavioral problems after taking into account economic resources (income and education) and parental resources (parental effectiveness and mental health) (Brown, 2004). These findings underscore that variations in family resources and parenting processes are critical for understanding the effects of different family forms on children's outcomes.

However, developmental level of the child matters too. Adolescents in cohabitating family forms had higher levels of emotional and behavioral problems even after taking into account economic and parental resources (Brown, 2004). Smoking and drinking among adolescents varies by family structure as well (Brown & Rinelli, 2010) with higher levels of both behaviors in cohabitating stepfamilies. However, family processes make a difference: maternal warmth and control and parental education are both negatively related to smoking: the more maternal warmth and the higher the parents' level of education, the less likely the adolescents are to smoke. Others report that children are more aggressive with their peers and, more likely to be expelled from school and steal (Manning & Lamb, 2003). Onset of sexual behavior and increased likelihood of teen pregnancy is higher among adolescent girls in cohabitating than married families (Bulanda & Manning, 2008). As we saw in our discussion of remarriage after divorce, adolescents often have more difficulty accepting a new parent and perhaps may be especially wary of a cohabitating parent than younger children (Hetherington & Kelly, 2002). The lack of acceptance may reduce the effectiveness of parental monitoring, which in turn, could account, in part for the increases behavioral problems. So what accounts for these differences in child outcomes between cohabitating and married families? We turn to this issue next.

## Is Family Form the Culprit? In Search of Explanations

Several explanations have been suggested for these profiles of children from different family forms. Perhaps differences in parenting process account for these findings. Or the quality of the couple relationship may underlie the differences. Others point to the instability of cohabitating arrangement while others offer selection effects as the explanation. Some suggest that increasing marriage rates is the answer.

*Parenting processes in cohabitating families:* While some expect that parenting processes would be poorer in cohabitating families, recent evidence suggests that this is not the case. Recent evidence suggests that there are few differences in parenting practices between cohabitating and married mothers (Gibson-Davis, 2008). Mothers were similar in their positive engagement (i.e., play together, read, tell stories to their child), parental aggravation (how hard it is to be a parent), and paternal instrumental support (i.e., father helps with child), regardless of marital status. Do cohabitating fathers and married fathers parent differently? Apparently not. In this same study, Gibson–Davis found that fathers like mothers were just as positively engaged and no more aggravated about their parenting role whether cohabitating or married. In a more detailed look at dads, similar findings emerged. Cohabitating fathers were just as involved as married dads in their children's lives (Manning & Brown, 2012). Dads in both types of families went on as many outings with their children and in the case of infants and preschoolers they did similar amounts of feeding, bathing, and playing. In the case of older children and adolescents (5–18), cohabiting and married fathers report similar levels of involvement in helping with homework, taking to activities, eating meals together, and participating in the PTA. And men in the two types of families did not differ in their self assessments of their competence as fathers (Manning, Brown, & Stykes, 2012) "Among men, marriage and involvement in fatherhood activities do not seem to be a package deal" (Manning & Brown, p. 292). Cohabitating fathers were slightly more involved with their stepchildren if their own biological children were also in residence. Perhaps more practice in the fathering role may carry over to all the children in the household. As one commentator noted "these results are contrary to a structural hypothesis, which posited that marriage itself is advantageous to parents, and that cohabiting parents have lower levels of investment because of cohabitation's ambiguous social norms and legal uncertainty" (Gibson-Davis, p. 463).

*Selection effects:* As noted earlier, the lack of differences in parenting processes between cohabitating and married family forms suggest that selection effects may play a larger role than previously thought and that those who marry may be different individuals than those who do not. For example, those who marry rather than cohabitate are better educated and more economically advantaged, which suggests that the poor child outcomes that are sometimes found in cohabitating families may be due less to family form than educational and economic factors.

*Couple relationships:* As decades of research has shown, the quality of the couple's relationship is a major determinant of parenting quality not only in married families

(Cowan & Cowan, 2000) but in cohabiting couples as well. Among cohabitating couples, Carlson and McLanahan (2006) found that the better the quality of the biological parents' relationship at birth, the better the parenting skills they demonstrate one year after the birth. In turn, this would bode well for the developmental outcomes for the child. In addition, programs aimed at bolstering couple relationships and reducing break ups would enhance children's well-being by shielding children from dissolution related transitions.

*Social support:* Even if separations do occur, social support from extended family members can mitigate some of the ill effects for children. The leave taking of cohabitating partners has a less negative effect on African American than white children, in part, due to the prevalence of a community oriented cooperative model of parenting in which African American female kin such as aunts and grandmothers play an enhanced and more sustained parent-like role in children's lives (Fomby & Cherlin, 2007).

*Cultural context:* Similarly, cultural context which dictates the normativeness of this family form modifies the effects of cohabitation on children. Children born in cohabitating parent families in Puerto Rico or the Dominican Republic suffered fewer externalizing problems than children born to parents of either group residing in the United States (Fomby & Estacion, 2011). The presence of extended kin provides stability and a safety net to cushion the loss of a parent. In addition, the lessened stigma associated with cohabitation in their country of origin may contribute to the lessened effect of cohabitation on children's development. We return to this issue in a later chapter.

*Too many transitions?:* Another explanation for the differences between married and cohabitating forms is that there is more instability in cohabitating unions. This is due, in part, to the often short duration of cohabitating relationships, the lack of any binding contracts and lower levels of commitment to the relationship. In view of the fact that children who undergo multiple transitions are more likely to develop academic, social, and emotional problems, it is not surprising that children in cohabitating relationships are less well off than children in either stable married or even stable single-parent families. Transitions are stressful and challenging for children and they often suffer under the strain. In the NICHD study of over 1300 children followed from infancy, those children who experienced more transitions were more disruptive and disobedient in first grade (Cavanagh & Huston, 2006). However, recent studies have not confirmed that transitions alone account for these child effects. For example, in one recent report, transitions associated with a dissolution in a cohabitating relationships had no negative effect while divorce-related transitions were negatively linked with child outcomes (Wu, Hou, & Schimmele, 2008). In another study (Fomby & Cherlin, 2007), the number of transitions were related to white children's cognitive development but was largely due to selection effects (i.e., maternal characteristics). For Black children, there were no effects of the number of transitions on children's cognitive or behavioral developmental outcomes. Sometimes transitions can even be helpful. As Brown (2006) found, the transition from a cohabitating family to a single-parent family was associated with an increase in school achievement. As this discussion shows, the effects of cohabitation on children is probably less due to the family form itself than a myriad of other factors associated with this arrangement, especially selection effects.

# Is Marriage the Solution for Improving Children's Development?

Since the mid 1990s, a central concern of many political leaders in the United States has been the promotion of marriage as a solution to poverty, as a way of stabilizing couple relationships and as a way of improving child outcomes. However, "the message hasn't been particularly effective: the United States has just experienced the most sustained period of promarriage rhetoric in a century, and yet little increase in marriage has occurred" (Cherlin, 2009, p. 193). In cohabiting families, some parents marry after a child is born; most remain as cohabiting partners. In fact, only about 15% of cohabiting parents marry after the birth of their child (Carlson, McLanahan, & England, 2004). However, both among the general population as well as among poor families, the decision to marry does not result in improved child outcomes (Brown, 2006; Heiland & Liu, 2006). So simply promoting more marriage is not the solution especially if the relationships are fragile and likely to end in dissolution or simply increase stress and poor parenting (Cherlin, 2009; Osborne & McLanahan, 2007). While it was thought that cohabitation before marriage would contribute to lower later marital stability, recent evidence suggests that the stability of marital relationships is very similar for those who cohabited before marriage and those who did not (Manning & Cohen, 2012). This is likely due to the normalization of the cohabitation to marriage sequence among recent generations.

# What Is the Future of This Family Form?

Our review suggests that selection factors and family processes such as either economic resources or parental socialization processes are likely more critical than family form itself in accounting for differences in child outcomes between cohabiting families and married couple families. Moreover, as this form becomes increasingly common accompanied by a drop in marriage rates, it is likely that attitudes toward this form will shift toward greater acceptance and toward increasing recognition as a legitimate family form. As the stigma associated with cohabitation decreases some of the benefits that are now the province of married families may flow to cohabiting families as well. For example, as this becomes a more normative family form, family and community support of the couple and their children will increase. The gap between the support of extended family for married and cohabiting families can be expected to narrow. Just as in the case of divorce, where children of divorce suffered less rejection from peers and teachers as divorce became more normative, it is likely that children in cohabiting families will experience less stigma as this becomes a more normative family form. Perhaps, this shift toward a more positive view of this form will lead to better outcomes for children as well. Since cohabiting couples are generally poorer and less well educated, shifts in the economy will make a difference to the outlook for these families. As the economic situation improves, the economic disparities between married and cohabiting families which account, in part, for the elevated rate of problems for children in cohabiting families may decrease. In turn, with more economic resources the developmental outcomes for children may improve.

Finally, lessons can be learned from other countries such as Sweden and Norway where there are high rates of cohabitation but fewer problems for either children or adults in these family forms than in the United States (Cherlin, 2009). In these countries, this family form is already viewed as normative and the government programs that benefit married couple families are available to cohabiting families as well. As we examine in the closing chapter, government policies can help support new family forms and better ensure the well-being of children and parents in all family forms not just "ideal" family forms.

## Reflections

As we have seen in the last two chapters, challenges to the dominance of the "ideal" family form as the cultural ideal come in many guises. The rise of single-parent families either through the increased prevalence of divorce or through active plans to be a solo parent has challenged another plank in the "ideal" family platform, namely the necessity of two parents for adequate child adjustment. While single parenthood, especially following divorce presents difficulties in the short term, a majority of adults and children adapt to the changed life circumstances and in the long term adjust well. Our goal is to identify the social conditions under which a variety of family forms can be successful. In the case of both intact and single-parent families, with social, emotional, and material support from extended family and the wider community both parents and children can do well. As we noted in the opening chapter, our western model of the isolated nuclear family unit bearing sole responsibility for the care and rearing of children is less common in many other societies. Instead a more communal approach to the socialization and care of children is found in many other cultures. And in contemporary families in our own culture, outsourcing care to others is becoming a common and increasingly accepted strategy in response to changing roles of men and women. Single parents have led the way in rediscovering the value of this communal approach to child care; moreover, they appear to function more effectively when they embrace this model. Being a single parent does not mean that you need to be the only responsible adult in a child's life; in fact, involving others in your child's life is a common and effective strategy for addressing the challenges of being on your own as a parent. Since children in single-mother or single-father families can manage well in terms of developmental outcomes, it raises a further challenge to the cultural notion that only children reared in the "ideal" family form of two opposite gender parents will develop successfully. Moreover, the work on single-parent families brings into question the importance of gender in our dialogue about parenting. Instead it suggests that the quality of internal family processes is of greater importance than either the form of the family or the gender of the parent. Finally, examination of the emerging family form of cohabitation suggests another assault on the "ideal" family form, namely the necessity of marriage as a family form in which to raise healthy children. As we have noted, the prevalence of this form is rapidly increasing and as it becomes more normative, the negative effects on children which are evident in some studies may decrease in frequency and magnitude. Our review mounts a major assault on the "ideal" family form and suggests instead that many family forms can support the successful socialization of children.

# 4

# Same-Gender Families

## *Are Two Mothers or Fathers Good Enough?*

*A child will benefit from a healthy, loving home, whether the parents are gay or not.* (US President Barack Obama, 2008)

Another change that has challenged one of the central assumptions of the ideal family form is the increase in lesbian and gay families. Janice Standish and Darlene McCloud, the lesbian family that we introduced in the opening chapter is one of these new families. Not only does the Standish–McCloud family challenge our notions of the "ideal" family it also "challenges and exposes the meaning and limits of gender – and inextricably, standard or traditional conceptualizations of family" (Goldberg, 2010, p. 11). The goals of this chapter are to examine the implications of growing up in a family of two same-gender parents on children's development and to explore the family processes in this new family form to better understand these developmental outcomes. As I will show, in spite of some challenges, children are not harmed by being raised by two same-gender parents but instead seem to be quite normal in their social, emotional, and cognitive development. Another goal is to continue our exploration of the critical issue of whether it is the gender of the parent or the types of family processes irrespective of the family form or the parents' gender that is most important for the successful socialization of children. This is a hotly contested issue in American culture, with many skeptics and many supporters. My goal is to present the science behind the headlines so cooler heads can prevail as we try to sort out the scholarly research aimed at achieving a better understanding of the issues surrounding same-gender families.

## The Controversy about the Wisdom of Same-Gender Parent Families Is Alive and Well

Early as well as contemporary critics of nonheterosexual parent families were and are concerned that the lack of a male figure or in the case of gay parents a female parental figure would disrupt gender role development, expose children to peer ostracism, and

*Future Families: Diverse Forms, Rich Possibilities*, First Edition. Ross D. Parke.

**Table 4.1**  The Changing Attitudes Toward Gay Parenting

| More gay and lesbian couples raising children | *Views of Gay Parenting Less Negative* | | | |
|---|---|---|---|---|
| | Feb 2007 (%) | Jan 2010 (%) | Oct 2010 (%) | Mar 2011 (%) |
| Good thing for society | 11 | 13 | 12 | 14 |
| Bad thing for society | 50 | 42 | 43 | 35 |
| Does not make much difference | 34 | 40 | 41 | 48 |
| Don't know | 5 | 4 | 4 | 3 |
| | *100* | *100* | *100* | *100* |

Pew Research Center (2011) Political Typology 2007–2010 trend from Pew Social and Demographic Trends.
*Note:* Figures may not add to 100% because of rounding.

cause emotional and relational problems (Blankenhorn, 1995; Dobson, 2004; Wardle, 1997). In the words of David Popenoe, author of *Life Without Father* "Children need a committed male and female couple – a mother and father in a joint partnership – to provide them with dependable and enduring love and attention" (1996, p. 197). In addition he notes, "we should disavow the popular notion that 'mommies can make good daddies' just as we should disavow the popular notion of feminists that 'daddies can make good mommies'" (1996, p. 197). To put aside any doubts that these new family pioneers are not always accepted by the wider culture, consider these results of a recent national survey. In response to the statement "we should do everything we can to encourage that children are reared by their biological parents," 81% agreed with this sentiment (Cultural Cognition Project, 2009). At the same time, acceptance of gay and lesbian parent families has increased from earlier eras, when there was not only less acceptance of gay and lesbian parents but also fewer opportunities for gay or lesbian couples to become parents (Pew Research Center, 2011; see Table 4.1). The laws restricted the ability of gay/lesbian couples to adopt, and only in the last few decades did the advances in assisted reproductive technologies(ART) such as sperm- or egg-donor based artificial insemination and the use of surrogacy open up new ways for gay and lesbian couples to achieve parenthood. Even the popular media are catching up now, and in the process increasing acceptance of gay and lesbian families. We see gay families in more and more TV shows such as *Modern Family* and *The New Normal* and in movies such as *The Kids Are All Right*. At the same time, we need to examine the prevalence of these types of families and see how they work as families. Only then can we properly assess whether the concerns behind the controversy are real or imagined.

## How Prevalent Are Same-Gender Parent Families?

The exact number of children in America currently being raised by gay, lesbian, and bisexual parents is unknown. Resistance to lesbian and gay rights continues to force many lesbian and gay people to remain silent about their sexual orientation and relationships. But several studies indicate the numbers of children with same-sex parents in America are significant. Beginning with the 2000 US Census, two same-gender adults who were living together could identify themselves as an unmarried couple.

This allowed an estimate of the number of gay and lesbian couples as well as the number of children under age 18 who were living in their homes. According to the 2010 Census, there are approximately 650,000 same-sex couples in the United States (Gates & Cooke, 2011) and 20% of these couples identified as spouses. Furthermore, 19% of all same-sex couples are raising children. Of these child-rearing couples 31% identified as spouses and 14% as unmarried partners. Therefore, parents of the same sex are raising at least 200,000 children – possibly more – in America (these numbers do not include single lesbian or single gay parents). In contrast, 43% of heterosexual couples have children in their homes. Race and ethnic variations are evident. About a quarter of individuals in same-sex couples are nonwhite, and they are generally as racially and ethnically diverse as those in different-sex couples, though individuals in same-sex couples are less likely to be Asian, Native Hawaiian, or Pacific Islander (Gates, 2013). Fully a third of same-sex Hispanic couples and a quarter of African American same-sex couples are raising children, compared to 17% of white same-sex couples (Gates, 2012).

There are limitations in the Census report that suggest that the numbers are an under-estimate and the real numbers are probably higher (Gates & Cooke 2011). Some same-sex couples may have failed to disclose their couple status to census interviewers. Single gay and lesbian parents were not counted nor were children over 18 of same-sex parents. "These data were nevertheless valuable because they demonstrated that, even when undercounted, substantial numbers of gay and lesbian parents live in all parts of the United States" (Patterson & Riskind, 2010, p. 328).

The social stigma surrounding gay and lesbian identity, the legal barriers concerning same-sex marriage as well as the higher hurdles associated with adoption all contribute to this lower rate of parenthood among nonheterosexual adults (Patterson & Riskind, 2010). Even though most women (90%) have or intend to have children it is significantly less likely that lesbians will fulfill this dream (Chandra, Martinez, Mosher, Abma, & Jones, 2005). The evidence we have, however, suggests that substantial percentages of gay and lesbian adults want to become parents although the rates are lower than for heterosexual adults. In one national study (the 2002 NSFG project), although 52% of childless gay men and 41% of childless lesbians expressed a desire to have children, these rates are lower than the level of desire to become a parent among heterosexual males or females (Riskind & Patterson, 2010). In the 2002 NSFG survey, 53% of childless heterosexual women and 67% of childless heterosexual men expressed a desire for children (Gates, Badgett, Chambers, & Macomber, 2007). Thus, reduced desire for children may be responsible, in part, for lower parenthood rates among gay and lesbian adults. Whether this lower desire to become parents among gay men and lesbians is due to a truly diminished desire or due to the societal barriers imposed on gay men and lesbians who wish to have children is unclear. Perhaps if the obstacles are removed and gay- and lesbian-parent families become socially acceptable, the discrepancy between the desire to become a parent and the actual rates of parenting for heterosexuals and gay men and lesbians will diminish.

A final caveat is in order. We know more about both prevalence and process among white, middle class and relatively well educated same-sex couples, and significantly less about same-gender couples from other ethnic and racial groups in our society. There are exceptions such as Mignon Moore's recent book *Invisible Families* (2011), a study of

Black lesbian women and mothers. We highlight some of this recent work later in this chapter. The fact that the proportion of minority gay/lesbian couples who are raising children is higher than white same-sex-couple families (Gates, 2012) underscores the need for more information about minority same-sex parents and their children.

## Routes to Parenthood among Gay/Lesbian Couples

In contemporary Western societies, there are a variety of ways in which gay and lesbian couples can achieve parenthood. Many of the same-sex parents studied 20 or 30 years ago in the initial period of investigation of this issue were, in fact, previously married individuals in heterosexual relationships who later self identified as gay or lesbian after a divorce (Barret & Robinson, 1990; Bigner, 1999). In some cases, a lesbian or gay man would continue as a single parent and in other cases, he or she would partner with another person of the same gender and coparent as a same-sex family. It was difficult to sort out whether the effects of growing up in these families on children was due to divorce, single parenthood, or same-gender parents (Biblarz & Stacey, 2010). However, more recent studies have included gay and lesbian individuals or couples who have followed a diverse set of pathways to parenthood (Goldberg, 2010; Golombok & Tasker, 2010). Instead of becoming a parent in a heterosexual relationship, common routes today are artificial insemination and adoption. Janice and Darlene Standish-McCloud, the lesbian couple we introduced earlier chose the international adoption route but other lesbian couples choose the artificial insemination path to parenthood. As we will see in the next chapter, the access to ART may be limited by income and possibly race (Moore, 2011). One US survey of lesbians found that only 2.8% of Black lesbian mothers had their children this way compared to 5.6% of white lesbian mothers (Morris, Balsam, & Rothblum, 2002). Other lesbians pursue the old fashioned route – engaging in heterosexual sex in order to become parents, which some may view as more natural or a way to increase the chances of conception (Lev, 2004). Some lesbians and gay men pursue surrogacy, whereby a contracted female carries a baby to be raised by the couple. Some are even more unorthodox and devise unusual parenting arrangements (e.g., a lesbian couple coparenting with a gay couple; a single lesbian coparenting with a lesbian or gay friend or friends). Family forms seem to be limited only by our imagination.

Some have suggested that there has been a generational shift in the routes to parenthood (Patterson & Riskind, 2010). One large scale survey of over 2000 lesbian women, found that 96% of lesbian and bisexual mothers at least 60 years of age reported that they had become parents in the context of a heterosexual relationship, before coming out (Morris et al., 2002). In contrast, only 59% of those 30–40 years of age reached parenthood in this way. There has been a similar generation shift in the paths to parenthood for gay men as well. An online survey of nearly 900 gay men found that older men (over 50 years of age) were more likely than younger respondents to have become parents in the context of a heterosexual relationship (Tornello & Patterson, 2010). A few older men achieved parenthood through adoption and foster care but rarely through the more recently available new reproductive technology routes of surrogacy, donor insemination, or sperm donation. For younger gay men, parenthood was rarely achieved through a prior heterosexual relationship but more likely through adoption and surrogacy (Goldberg, 2012). New Internet sites which provide information about parenting possibilities for gays and lesbians and specific resources such as "Maybe Baby" groups for lesbian and gay prospective parents and more same-gender couple-friendly adoption agencies and fertility clinics are all contributing to the changing landscape for same-sex couples (Lev, 2004). New surveys may provide even stronger support for the generational shift hypothesis as more lesbian women as well as gay men are taking advantage of the new pathways to parenthood afforded by both adoption and ART.

Regardless of the route to parenthood that is chosen, all involve a violation of the "ideal" family form. Artificial insemination is a solution to fertility problems for heterosexual couples but when used as a route to parenthood for lesbian couples or single lesbians, it is viewed as a violation of the "ideal" family form. The use of the new reproductive technologies by nonheterosexual couples is viewed by some as a distortion of the purpose for which these medical advances were intended (assisted reproductive technology as a route to parenthood is discussed in the next chapter). Even adoption is sometimes viewed as subverting American kinship ideology since it involves the separation of biological from social kin (Gailey, 2004). In the case of gay or lesbian adoptive singles or couples, there is even greater concern about the departure from the cultural "ideal" family form. In fact, in some states, such as Utah and Louisiana, only married couples can adopt, while in other states single gay/lesbian individuals can adopt but not gay/lesbian couples. This requires that the second or nonadopting parent petition to be legally recognized as a parent. About two-third of all states allow second-parent adoptions by the unmarried partner of an existing legal parent either by legal statute or by generally being permitted by the courts. In a handful of states, courts have ruled these adoptions not permissible under state laws (Fenton & Fenton, 2011).

Enlisting a male partner only to be able to conceive, is a departure from the ideal that two heterosexual individuals should not only conceive but also serve as parents of the child; in this case the biological father is not involved and the child may either be raised by a single lesbian mother or in a lesbian couple family. As Goldberg (2010) notes, there are other risks as well.

> When a coupled lesbian engages in heterosexual sex to become pregnant, this threatens both the legal and symbolic parental role of her partner, in that the biological father is often awarded greater symbolic and legal recognition than the non-biological lesbian partner (Goldberg, p. 55).

The use of surrogacy is also a departure from the "ideal" family form since a third party is involved in achieving parenthood rather than the child rearing couple. Furthermore, in the case of gay and lesbian couples, their parenthood violates the cultural norm of two heterosexual parents who conceived their child. Complex coparenting in which multiple figures play roles as parents, although a creative social form in which to rear a child is again a violation of the "ideal" family form which includes the mother and father as the primary caregivers. (As we explore in Chapter 6, more cooperative forms of parenting are, in fact, common in other cultures). In sum, regardless of the route to parenthood chosen, gay/lesbian parents face societal discrimination, in part, due to their departure from the cultural notion of the "ideal" family form. The question is whether this discrimination and prejudice directed toward same-gender parents adversely affects their adequacy as parents. As we noted earlier, critics have been concerned that children who are raised in these families will suffer cognitively, socially, and emotionally, in part, due to the suspected inadequacy of same-gender couples as parents. To assess the validity of these claims, we examine both the parenting of same-gender couples and single gay or lesbian parents and the development of children reared in these families.

## The Challenges of Same-Gender Parenting

When partners become parents, both heterosexual as well as gay and lesbian couples face many challenges. These include decisions about the division of labor inside and outside the household, the roles and responsibilities of each partner and decisions about child-rearing practices. As we will see, there are many similarities across heterosexual and gay/lesbian parents in terms of how they deal with these challenges but also some unique and specialized ways in which gay/lesbian parents approach these decisions about their parenting roles and responsibilities.

## Division of Household Responsibilities in Same-Gender Families

Research comparing gay and lesbian parent families with heterosexual families finds that gay and lesbian parents tend to share household duties more equally than do heterosexual couples (Farr & Patterson, 2009; Goldberg, Downing, & Sauck, 2008). Heterosexual couples specialize more than same-sex couples: in heterosexual families, mothers do more unpaid child care while fathers work outside the home more. In contrast, gay/lesbian couples are more equitable in their parenting tasks and roles and more satisfied with their division of responsibilities than heterosexual couples (Farr, Forssell, & Patterson., 2010a; Farr & Patterson, 2013b). Similarly, lesbian and gay couples report that they divided child care (feeding, bathing, dressing) more evenly than did heterosexual couples and perhaps even preferred this equitable division of caregiving (Farr et al., 2010a; Farr & Patterson, 2013b; Patterson, Sutfin, & Fulcher, 2004). Observations confirmed this pattern: – lesbian and gay parents participated more equally than heterosexual parents during family interaction (Farr & Patterson). Not surprisingly, lesbian couples generally coparented more compatibly than heterosexual parents and were more satisfied with their division of parenting responsibilities (Bos, Van Balen, & Van den Boom, 2004, 2007). Heterosexual couples were more undermining as coparents compared to lesbian and gay couples (Farr & Patterson).

Nevertheless, in some lesbian families, the biological mother tends to be more involved in child care and the nonbiological mother spends longer hours in paid employment (Goldberg et al., 2008; Johnson & O'Connor, 2002). This pattern is particularly evident among Black lesbian couples where the biological mother does more housework, child care, and management of the household schedule than her partner (Moore, 2011). Similarly, in Black stepparent families, the biomother is highly involved while the stepmother may be more detached and removed from child decision making. As Moore argues, Black lesbian women may be less committed to the "ethic of equality" endorsed by white lesbian mothers and instead view the investment in household tasks as a sign of being a good mother. However, this pattern of greater involvement of the biomother may occur more in the early years of a child's life when feeding responsibilities (especially if breast feeding) are a central focus than when the child is older (Patterson & Farr, 2011). Without biological factors as a constraint as in the case of lesbian adoptive couples, the division of labor was more equally divided than in either lesbian couples who achieved parenthood through artificial insemination or in heterosexual adoptive couples (Ciano-Boyce & Shelley-Sireci, 2002).

As in the case of heterosexual couples, there is much variability among gay and lesbian couples in how they organize the tasks of child care and paid work. As Goldberg (2010) notes

> some lesbian and gay parents may enact labor arrangements that appear similar to traditional heterosexual parenting arrangements (one woman does more paid work, one woman does more unpaid work), others may execute labor arrangements that look very different (e.g., both women contribute equally to paid and unpaid work) and some may enact arrangements that we likely have yet to imagine, conceptualize, or understand (p. 102).

Some lesbian couples, even those who used donor insemination do manage to share child care tasks relatively equally between the biological and nonbiological coparent. In fact, they shared more equally than heterosexual couples and in this study the lesbian nonbiological mothers were more involved in child care than heterosexual fathers (Chan, Brooks, Raboy, & Patterson, 1998). Similarly, in some lesbian parent families the amount of outside paid work undertaken by biological and nonbiological parents is relatively similar (Gartrell, Rodas, Deck, Peyser, & Banks, 2006; Patterson, Sutfin, & Fulcher, 2004). This is sometimes at the expense of career advancement which may reflect women's socialization into the motherhood role as mandatory rather than discretionary. As in heterosexual families, when both partners share in the child-care tasks, they are more satisfied and their children are better adjusted in terms of social–emotional development (Patterson, 1995). However, a rigid commitment to the equality principle may not always be best especially if equality of care is associated with resentment or dissatisfaction due to the thwarting of personal preferences for different time allocations. As earlier studies (Hock & DeMeis, 1990) of maternal employment among heterosexual families found, satisfaction was greatest when there was a match between a woman's preferences for the balance of paid/unpaid work and the actual work arrangement regardless of the specifics of the work plan. Others found a similar pattern for gay/lesbian couples: the subjective evaluations of parents – gay, lesbian, and heterosexual – predicted child adjustment; those who were dissatisfied with their division of labor due to a discrepancy between their real and preferred arrangements had children with more behavior problems regardless of the actual division of labor (Farr et al., 2010b; Farr & Patterson, 2013b). Forming new family forms is to some degree a creative process, and finding a workable solution that satisfies the couple involved is more important to the partner's satisfaction than the final division of labor that ensues.

To sum up, the take home message is threefold. First, the pathway to parenthood for lesbian/gay parents makes a difference in who does what in the household. Second, satisfaction with the division of responsibilities is more important than a strict accounting of who does what and third, there are individual differences within the lesbian and gay communities that make overall generalizations difficult. The story sounds a lot like the tale of heterosexual couples as chronicled by so many others (e.g., Cowan & Cowan, 2000).

# Parenting Practices in Same-Gender Families

Do child rearing practices and parenting skills differ between same-sex and heterosexual families? This is one of the hot button issues that has kept a cloud over same-sex parents for decades since social critics and perhaps more importantly the judicial system have questioned whether gay or lesbian individuals could be competent parents. As we have noted, concerns include the lack of an opposite-gender parent in the home, the negative impact of discrimination on children in these families, and even doubts about the mental health and psychological stability of nonheterosexual adults (Goldberg, 2010). To illustrate the extent to which these attitudes affect legal decisions, consider the historic case of Sharon Bottoms, a lesbian mother in Virginia who lost custody of her son to her own mother who felt that a lesbian was unfit for motherhood. Sadly the court agreed with the grandmother's claim that her grandson's well-being was undermined by living in a lesbian mother household. The evidence based on numerous research studies suggests that both the judge and the grandmother were wrong (Patterson, 2006).

*Adjustment and Parenting Knowledge of Lesbian Couples:*   In several studies, comparisons between donor insemination lesbian couples and donor insemination heterosexual families revealed no differences in parental adjustment, parental self-esteem, or relationship satisfaction (Chan, Raboy, & Patterson, 1998; Flaks, Ficher, Masterpasqua, & Joseph, 1995). Others find a similar pattern: lesbian women's well-being and psychological health is similar to females in general (Rand, Graham, & Rawlings, 1982). Nor are there differences in parental knowledge of the skills necessary for effective parenting or in the self-reported parenting skills between lesbian and heterosexual parents (Bos et al., 2007). Parenting stress levels were similar across adoptive gay, lesbian, and heterosexual couples (Farr & Patterson, 2009). It would be surprising if gay or lesbian parents were not just as capable as heterosexual parents of fulfilling the basic set of universal parenting tasks that we reviewed in Chapter 1.

*Parenting Quality of Lesbian Couples:*   Does parenting quality vary across same-gender and heterosexual coparent family forms? The short answer based on numerous studies in both the United States and Europe is *No*; parenting is not very different in these types of families. Several studies in the United States found few differences between the parenting practices of lesbian couples and heterosexual couples (Patterson, 2006). In Belgium, Brewaeys (1996) found no differences between donor insemination lesbian and heterosexual families and naturally conceiving families in the quality of parenting or the quality of the couple's relationship. In Great Britain, Golombok, Cook, Bish, and Murray (1997) compared lesbian donor insemination families, heterosexual donor insemination single mother, and two-parent families; they found no differences in parental warmth and mother–child interaction patterns. Other work by this British team found that lesbian and heterosexual mothers were similar in warmth and sensitive responsiveness in interacting with children, adolescents, and young adults (Golombok & Badger, 2010; Golombok et al., 2003; Golombok, Spencer, & Rutter, 1983). When differences in parenting style are found, there is no indication that these stylistic differences are cause for concern; some would argue that the differences in style may, in fact, be better for children. For example, lesbian coparents tend to play with their children more than heterosexual parents (Golombok et al.) and are less likely than heterosexual mothers to physically discipline (spank) their children (Bos, Van Balen, & Van den Boom, 2007; Johnson & O'Connor, 2002; MacCallum & Golombok, 2004). Although the moral justification and the effectiveness of physical punishment is debatable, many experts agree that such child rearing tactics can lead to a variety of negative outcomes such as an increase in aggression (Gershoff, 2002). Other studies (Bos et al., 2007) report higher rates of structuring and limit setting for lesbian biological mothers compared to lesbian nonbiological mothers. Since in many cases the biological lesbian mother takes more caregiving responsibility and spends more time with the child than her coparent partner, this pattern is not surprising. Parenting by lesbian coparenting couples has been aptly described as "a double dose of a middle class 'feminine' approach to parenting" (Biblarz & Stacey, 2010, p. 11). More importantly these child-rearing characteristics are part of the style that Diana Baumrind (1991) has described as authoritative, a style that is widely recognized as an optimal approach to child rearing. So rather than concern, there may even be some positive advantages to the parenting styles of lesbian mothers (Figure 4.1).

**Figure 4.1** Parenting styles of lesbian couple families are more similar than different from heterosexual parent families (Marcie and Chantelle Fisher-Borne, North Carolina mothers). *Source:* © Tiburon Studios/iStockphoto.

*Parenting Quality of Gay Fathers:* What about gay fathers? Women are culturally prepared from an early age to be nurturant and sensitive, characteristics that are critical for successful parenting. Most play with dolls, many babysit and take care of younger siblings. For lots of girls, childhood is an extended apprenticeship in parenting. Boys have a very different set of childhood experiences. They are more likely to play with trucks than baby dolls and fewer neighbors provide them with opportunities to babysit. For boys, childhood is an apprenticeship in sports and mechanics – wonderful training for the working world, but not particularly helpful to future fathers (Parke & Brott, 1999).

In spite of the lack of cultural support for parenting during childhood, we saw in the last chapter that men can be competent and effective caregivers. Is the same true for gay men? Gay parents face unique challenges. They encounter more discrimination and experience more stress than heterosexual fathers because gay dads are a stigmatized group (Golombok & Tasker, 2010). Moreover, gay fathers may be less accepted than lesbian mothers since women are culturally expected to be mothers while men's roles as parents are less culturally scripted. The fact that some gay fathers assume a primary caregiver role is a further departure from the cultural norms of fatherhood. In the context of two men as parents there are other challenges. "Both men must cooperatively negotiate the actuality of engaging in both mothering and fathering and they must navigate the realities of (co)constructing and sharing the parenting role without the societal support and guidance that heterosexual couples receive" (Goldberg, 2010, p. 106). At the same time, gay men who decide to become parents are a self-selected group just as in the case of heterosexual men who seek or gain custody after divorce (Biblarz & Stacey, 2010; Clarke-Stewart & Brentano, 2006). They are committed to the responsibilities of parenting, are generally better educated, and earn more than those who do not choose parenthood. Although there has been much less attention given to gay men as fathers compared to lesbian mothers, current evidence suggests that gay men are competent parents in spite of the challenges faced by these parenting pioneers. Early studies comparing divorced gay fathers and divorced heterosexual fathers found no differences in their self reported levels of involvement or intimacy with their children; gay fathers were even more sensitive and responsive to their children's needs than their heterosexual counterparts (Bigner & Jacobsen, 1989). However, gay fathers were more strict and set more limits on their children but also used more reasoning (i.e., provided more explanations for their decisions) and involved their children more in family decisions. As we saw in the case of lesbian couples, gay couples use less corporal punishment than heterosexual coparents and even somewhat less than lesbian coparents (Johnson & O'Connor, 2002). It is clear that when two gay men parent together they do not "provide a double dose of masculine parenting" (Biblarz & Stacey, p. 12). Instead, their parenting approach more closely resembles lesbian than heterosexual coparents (Mallon, 2004; Stacey, 2006) or mothers rather than heterosexual fathers. These observations suggest that it is overly simplistic to assume that gay and lesbian parenting is always based on a heterosexual-couple model which provides clear guidelines for role divisions between males and females based on both biological differences and cultural expectations. Same-gender families are exempt to some degree from these constraints, although as we saw in our discussion of the division of labor, the biological mother in a lesbian couple family sometimes assumes a traditional role of caregiver, while the nonbiological mother takes on more paid work. Unlike the roles prescribed by gender in heterosexual couples, gay men, in some ways, are least hindered by biological constraints and often develop what has been termed "degendered parenting" (Schacher Auerbach & Silverstein, 2005). In this case, each father enacts and blends aspects of both mother and father roles into a creative, flexible, nonconventional but workable parenting role. "The gay fathers (in the Schacher study) described themselves as having a hybrid parenting role, where both they and their partner divided child-care duties by preference, aptitude, or equality, rather than splitting into 'mother or father' roles" (Golombok & Tasker, 2010, p. 327). For gay men the concepts of father and mother may be obsolete. As one gay man questioned, "Am I a mother or a father? So what does that make me when I nurture him? What's a father and what's a mother? I don't really know" (Silverstein Auerbach, and Levant, 2002, p. 366). And another gay man observed, "It's not about gender…males and females can be equally mothers and fathers" (Schacher et al., 2005). Another gay dad expressed a similar sentiment,

> As a gay dad, I'm not a mom, but sometimes I think I have more in common with moms than I do with straight dads. I mean, these straight dads that I know are essentially weekend dads; they don't parent with the same intensity that I do or that their wives do. In many ways, despite being a man, I am a dad, but I am like a mom too (Mallon, 2004, p. 138).

Often gay male coparents both share child caretaking as well as organize their lives to permit both of them to participate in the workforce (Goldberg, 2012; Schacher et al., 2005). This balance between home and work responsibilities is especially important to gay male coparents who tend to be more committed to maintaining a full time career than lesbian coparents but less so than heterosexual fathers (Sears Gates & Rubenstein, 2005). While some gay fathers challenge the traditional concepts of masculinity by taking on more caregiving responsibility, "They cannot fully escape hegemonic masculine roles, such as those that assign greater value to breadwinning than to caregiving" (Goldberg, 2012, p. 107). As we explore next, dichotomous labeling of parents based on biological gender may prevent couples from fully exercising their preferences and utilizing their unique talents and predispositions. Some fathers may eschew the breadwinner role in favor of more home time with the children but still coach his children's soccer team while his coparent may both work outside but still be a nurturant and involved dad.

This emerging evidence of the plasticity of roles among gay fathers in which they combine elements of "maternal" and "paternal" into a hybrid role is a further reminder of the fluidity of gender roles and is consistent with a more general story of gender role flexibility, regardless of gender identity. For example, other work illustrates that heterosexual men and women are more flexible in their family roles than cultural stereotypes would suggest. Recall the Lewin family who we introduced in the opening chapter in which Todd was a full-time dad while his wife Mary Helen worked full time. The success of these reverse role arrangements in which men become primary caregivers and women become the chief breadwinners illustrates this flexibility and fluidity of gender roles (Radin, 1994; Russell, 1983). Clearly, caregiving can be effectively provided not only by mothers by a variety of partners, including both gay and

**Figure 4.2** These gay parents share a happy moment with their 5 year old son.
*Source:* © kali9/iStockphoto.

heterosexual fathers (Figure 4.2). Both adults and children can benefit from more flexibility in how we define parent roles and who assumes these roles.

## Is Gender of Parent or Family Process More Important?

The quality of the parenting in both same-sex and heterosexual-parent families, is more important than the gender of the parents for children's development (Patterson, 2006). British family expert, Susan Golombok agrees: "Family structure, in itself, makes little difference to children's psychological development. Instead what really matters is the quality of family life" (2000, p. 99). A parenting pattern of warmth and sensitivity and responsiveness in conjunction with appropriate limit setting and control (Baumrind's classic authoritative pattern) is associated with better outcomes in both same-gender parent families and in heterosexual-parent families. Support for this claim comes from Charlotte Patterson and her colleagues (Chan, Raboy et al., 1998; Wainright, Russell & Patterson, 2004; Wainright & Patterson, 2006) who found that the quality of parent child relationships (i.e., adolescents perception of parental warmth, parents perception of the quality of the parent–child relationship) were associated with less trouble at school and greater school connectedness, especially in same-gender parent families. Substance use and delinquent behavior were also related to the quality of the parent–adolescent relationship. A good quality parent–adolescent relationship is related to lower use of tobacco, alcohol, and marijuana as well as less delinquent behavior across all types of families. Moreover, the quality of coparenting in heterosexual, lesbian and gay adoptive families was related to lower levels of externalizing in young children (Farr & Patterson, 2013b). Finally, both quality of the parent–child relationship and care from other adults and peers were linked with more positive peer relationships (Wainright & Patterson, 2006). Another factor that is associated with child adjustment across heterosexual, lesbian and gay parent adoptive families is parental stress. When parents agreed with such items as "I feel trapped by my responsibilities as a parent;" "I expected to have closer and warmer feelings for my child than I do and this bothers me;" and, "My child seems to cry or fuss more than most other children," their three-year-olds were rated as higher in both externalizing and internalizing outcomes (Farr et al., 2010b). Process emerges once again as trumping family form or parent gender.

## Factors that Alter Parenting Processes in Same-Gender Families

Several factors influence the success of gay and lesbian parents in rearing well-adjusted children. Consistent with a family systems view, it is not only parenting processes and, in turn, parent–child relationships that are important but partner–partner relationships are critical family processes as well (Cowan & Cowan, 2000; Cummings & Davies, 2010). Sharing the tasks of parenting with a cohabitating partner is linked with more positive parenting among gay parents. Compared to single gay fathers, gay couples rated themselves as better able to meet the financial emotional and practical challenges of parenting (Barrett & Tasker, 2001). This parallels findings with heterosexual single mothers: in general single mothers have more stress and challenges in meeting their parenting responsibilities than two-parent families (McLanahan & Sandefur, 1994). It is not simply sharing that matters, it is the degree of satisfaction with the partner relationship that is important. When couples who were satisfied with their relationship, their children had fewer behavioral problems (Chan, Brooks et al., 1998; Farr et al., 2010). In a Belgian study, Bos and colleagues (2007) found that school-age children were rated by their parents as having fewer externalizing and internalizing problems when parents – lesbian or heterosexual – were satisfied with their partner as a coparent. One of the determinants of relationship satisfaction is how satisfied the couple is with the division of labor in the household. When lesbian, gay, or heterosexual parenting couples were satisfied with the division of labor, relationship satisfaction was higher and, in turn, child adjustment was better (Chan, Brooks et al., 1998; Farr et al., 2010). The effect of feelings about the division of labor was linked to couple relationship satisfaction which suggests that couple contentment mediated the links between division of labor and child adjustment. Interpartner harmony is a positive influence on children in both heterosexual and same-gender parent families. Again, the centrality of process for understanding families is evident.

On the other hand, interpartner conflict clearly has a negative impact on children's adjustment. There is a plethora of evidence that intercouple hostility and conflict is linked with poorer social and emotional functioning among children and adolescents in heterosexual families (Cummings & Davies, 2010). Similar findings are evident in investigations of both donor insemination lesbian-parent families and heterosexual-parent families. Regardless of family form, when parent–parent conflict was high, there were higher levels of behavioral problems in the children (Chan, Raboy et al., 1998). Finally, family systems theory suggests that marital discord not only adversely affects parent–child and coparent–child relationships but also impairs quality of the triadic parent–parent–child relationships by reducing the effectiveness of how well partners work together as coparents with their children. Although there has been some progress on this issue in heterosexual families (McHale & Lindahl, 2011), more work on gay and lesbian coparenting is needed (Patterson & Farr, 2011).

Another factor that is linked with parenting and family satisfaction is the openness of the gay parent about their sexual orientation. Those who are more positive about their sexual identity experienced less parenting stress than those who were less positive (i.e., I often wonder whether others judge me for my sexual orientation; Tornello, Farr, & Patterson, 2011). Among gay divorced fathers who had come out to their children, many reported greater honesty and openness in their parent–child relationships and felt that their children were similarly more open and honest with them (Benson, Silverstein, & Auerbach, 2005).

Families do better when there is social support from friends, relatives, and community; as in the case of heterosexual couples, gay and lesbian parents benefit from the acceptance, assistance, and advice of a social network (Golombok & Tasker, 2010; Tornello, Farr, & Patterson, 2011). Friends may be even more important than family as a source of social support for gay parents (Tornello et al.) and lesbian parents (Goldberg & Smith, 2008) since families of origin are not always reliable sources of support due to lack of acceptance and understanding of their relative's sexual orientation. Interestingly, the members of the network who provide assistance in child care and rearing among gay father families are not as restricted to close kin as in heterosexual families. Rather than the closed nuclear family unit which is typical for the "ideal" family paradigm, some gay fathers incorporate several adults into their childcare system including not only people who are biologically related such as the "birth mother" and members of the "birth family" but others who are neither biologically related nor even in the same residence (Schacher, Auerbach, & Silverstein, 2005). As is the case for African American and Latino families, gay couples base their definition of family on sentiments such as love and loyalty rather than biology. In this conceptualization of family, "bonding transcends biology" (Schacher et al.). Another departure from the traditional "ideal" family model among gay couples is the interracial and interethnic nature of their families. Most gay men who adopted were unconcerned about the racial identity of the child. As one gay adopting father commented, "We don't see in Black and White" (Schacher et al.). This pattern of interracial adoption is especially evident among younger gay men. According to a survey of gay men (Tornello & Patterson, 2010), about half of gay fathers under 40 adopted a child of a different race while only a quarter of older gay men (over 60) had formed an interracial family through adoption. The barriers gay men face in the adoption arena may, in part, make them more accepting of a range of possible adoptive children than culturally conforming adopting families who face fewer obstacles. In Judith Stacey's (2006) discussion of gay adoption, she describes the gay men of Los Angeles as having to search through the state's "overstocked warehouse of 'hard to place children,' the majority of whom have been removed from families judged negligent, abusive, or incompetent. Most of the state's stockpiled children are children of color, and disproportionately boys with 'special needs'" (p. 39). However, it may not simply be availability; younger generations may be more open to a wider variety of nonconforming family forms including interracial families.

## Growing Up in a Same-Gender Parent Family: Harmful or Helpful for Children's Development?

Contrary to the concerns and fears of many cultural critics that children reared in same-gender families will be poorly adjusted (Blankenhorn, 1995; Popenoe, 1996), the vast body of evidence suggests that these fears are not borne out by the research evidence. Instead, children of lesbian and gay parents are well-adjusted (Goldberg, 2010; Patterson, 2006). While a wide range of outcomes have been examined, the central issue has been gender identity, gendered role behavior, and sexual orientation. Let us look at the evidence.

*Gender Development:*    Studies in both Europe and North America have tried to answer this question: "Is children's gender identity – their self identification as male or female – affected by being reared in a same-gender parent household?" While some commentators have expressed concern that boys in lesbian parent families who lack a male model would identify as female (Wardle, 1997), there is little support for this concern. Over 30 years ago in a study of American 5–12-year-olds raised in either a lesbian mother family or a heterosexual-mother family, Kirkpatrick, Smith, and Roy (1981) found no differences in children's gender identity. In Britain similar results were found, namely that gender identity was unaffected by the nature of the sexual orientation of the parent (Golombok, Spencer, & Rutter, 1983). In short, there is no evidence that gay or lesbian parents produce children with a poorly defined sense of their gender. Boys know they are male and girls identify as female, regardless of the gender of their parents.

Another aspect of the gender development issue that has been examined is the extent to which children's gender role behavior is affected by the type of family in which they are raised. Do children raised in same-sex parent families exhibit more androgynous sex role behavior patterns whereby they exhibit aspects of both male and female gender appropriate behavior than children raised in heterosexual parent families? As Goldberg (2010) argues,

> to the extent that lesbians and gay men hold less rigid gender stereotypes, may be more tolerant of cross-gender interests and behaviors, and may model less rigid conformity to gendered roles in their dress, behaviors and overall comportment, they may also facilitate similar nonconformity in their children (p. 130).

Some American studies have found no differences between children from lesbian single mother and heterosexual-single mother families in their preferences for gender typed toys (Hoeffer, 1981) while others found no differences in knowledge of gender stereotypes nor any differences in gender toy or activity preferences (Fulcher, Sutfin, & Patterson, 2008). Boys preferred trucks and girls liked dolls regardless of their parent's sexual orientation. However, children with lesbian parents were more tolerant of gender transgressions (e.g., boys wearing nail polish or girls playing football) than children of heterosexual parents. A closer look at the gender attitudes of lesbian and heterosexual parents helps us better understand these findings. Lesbian mothers endorse less traditional gender attitudes than heterosexual parents (e.g., lesbian parents approve of active play for girls as well as boys more than do heterosexual parents). In turn, the children of the lesbian parents were less traditional in their attitudes than children from heterosexual (i.e., more traditional) families (Sutfin, Fulcher, Bowles, & Patterson, 2008). In a British study, MacCallum and Golombok (2004) found that children in lesbian parent households show less gender-typed behavior; but their work suggested that parent gender rather than sexual orientation may be more important. Comparisons of gender typed behavior of 12-year-old children from either lesbian–mother families, single heterosexual-mother families, or two-parent heterosexual families revealed that boys in both types of father absent families were higher on a femininity scale than boys from two-parent heterosexual families. Boys from the three family types were similar in terms of masculinity scores. Girls were similar in both masculinity and femininity, regardless of family type. According to the authors, single mothers may encourage their sons to act in caring and sensitive ways, which would account for the higher femininity scores. However, these scores were not outside the normal range and present a profile of androgyny or gender balance which may have some advantages in later life. After all what is wrong with a dose of androgyny? Adult men who are more androgynous are more involved fathers (Russell, 1983), score higher on emotional intelligence (Guastello & Guastello, 2003), and may be better adjusted (Shimonaka, Nakazato, Kawaai, & Sato, 1997). Less is known about gender role development among gay father families. However, in a recent comprehensive study of parenting and child development, Farr and Patterson (2009) compared gay couples, lesbian couples, and heterosexual couples who had an adopted child between one and five years of age. The gender role development of the children from the three types of families as assessed by their toy and activity preferences did not differ.

The biggest worry expressed by critics of same-gender parenting is that children who are reared in these homes will grow up to adopt a nonheterosexual orientation. In spite of these fears, the alarmists are misguided as there is no evidence that children of gay or lesbian parents are any more likely to adopt a gay or lesbian sexual orientation than children from heterosexual families. Several American studies of lesbian and heterosexual mothers found that the rates of adolescents who identified as nonheterosexual did not differ (Huggins, 1989). British studies tell a slightly more complex story but the conclusion is similar. In a comparison of young adults from single-mother lesbian and heterosexual-mother families, Tasker and Golombok (1997) found no differences in rates of same-sex sexual attraction. However, young adult females but not young adult males reared by lesbian mothers were more likely to have entertained a possible same-sex relationship and to have experienced a relationship with a person of their own gender than their peers raised in a heterosexual-couple family. In a more recent Dutch study of preadolescents raised by lesbian and heterosexual couples, Bos and colleagues (2007) found similar patterns: boys who were raised in either lesbian couple or heterosexual-couple families were not different in their heterosexual identity score but girls from lesbian couple families scored lower on the heterosexual orientation index than girls from heterosexual-couple families. Perhaps the presence of only female parents may lead to lower expectations that they will form heterosexual relationships (Biblarz & Stacey, 2010). Or a family climate of tolerance and acceptance of same-sex relationships could, in part, be responsible for the lower heterosexual orientation among females from lesbian mother homes just as we saw in the case of greater acceptance of nontraditional gender attitudes by children reared in lesbian mother homes. Biblarz and Stacey offer an interesting interpretation of this gender difference:

> The fact that lesbian parenting did not diminish heterosexual desires in sons supports research finding greater fixity in male and fluidity in female sexual desires over the life course (Butler, 2005; Diamond, 2008). The lower heterosexual identity scores of these girls (but not their brothers) might reflect this gender difference (p. 15).

More longitudinal work is needed to determine whether these gender differences in heterosexual orientation are stable across adulthood or whether they are transient and part of adolescent experimentation.

What are the effects of being raised by gay coparents on sexual identity? To address this issue, Tasker and Barrett (2004) studied 72 British young adults, half of whom were raised by gay fathers and half by heterosexual fathers. All of the young adults from heterosexual father families identified as heterosexual, as well as the majority of those from gay father families. However, in the gay father families two sons identified as gay, one daughter as lesbian, and two sons and one daughter identified as bisexual. Moreover, children of gay fathers were more likely to have been attracted to or have had a sexual relationship with someone of the same gender than children of heterosexual dads. As in the case of the lesbian reared preadolescents and young adults, perhaps the more positive response by gay fathers to their children's partners may, in part, account for the increased attraction to and experimentation with same-gender partners. Perhaps genetic factors play a role but in all likelihood in combination with environmental factors as is the case of other aspects of development (Rutter, 2006). The take-home message is clear: most children of both gay and lesbian parents identify as heterosexual, and the sexual orientation of parents is a minor influence on their offspring's sexual orientation (Golombok & Tasker, 2010). To put this work into perspective, Goldberg (2010) suggests that

> treatment of sexual orientation as a relevant indicator of children's well-being per se is inappropriate given that homosexuality is no longer considered a mental illness....While inclusion of sexual orientation as a child outcome is arguably justified, it should be clearly distinguished from other true mental health and well-being outcomes and accurately identified as one aspect of sexual identity development (p. 134).

Finally, it is important to note that most gay/lesbian individuals were raised by heterosexual parents.

*Social Adjustment Outcomes:*  There are many other important aspects of social development beyond gender-related issues that merit close scrutiny. How well do children of gay or lesbian parents get along with their peers? Are they more depressed or anxious than their peers from heterosexual parents? Are there differences in other aspects of mental health?

*Peer Relationships:*  One of the central challenges of childhood is developing satisfying and amiable relationships with your peers. And peers can be tough and are renowned for their low tolerance for kids who are different (Rubin, Bukowski, & Parker, 2006).The possibility that children with two lesbian mothers or two gay fathers may be rejected by their age mates is a concern. In fact, it is a serious enough fear that some judges have used this concern as a basis for denying custody to gay or lesbian parents (Stacey & Biblarz, 2001). Is this concern warranted? Scholars in both the United States and Europe have addressed this issue with early and middle school age children and found no differences in parent ratings of peer sociability, acceptance, or social competence between children of lesbian and heterosexual mothers (Gartrell, Deck, Rodas, Peyser, & Banks, 2005; Golombok et al., 1983, 2003). Nor do the children of lesbian or heterosexual mothers themselves perceive their peer relationships differently (Golombok et al.). A similar story is found among adolescents. In a large national sample of male and female adolescents, self and peer reports of the quality of peer relationships were similar regardless of family type (Wainright & Patterson, 2008). Peer relations remain satisfactory in young adulthood as well. Eighteen year olds reared from infancy by single heterosexual mothers, single-lesbian mothers or two heterosexual parents did not differ in the quality of their peer relationships (Golombok & Badger, 2010). There is no evidence of impaired social ties with peers as a result of the gender orientation of one's parents.

Another related concern is that children from lesbian mother families will be teased more. Again, the fears are generally not warranted. A Belgian study, found no differences in the rates of teasing among school age children in lesbian mother and heterosexual-parent families. Instead some children, regardless of their family type were teased, laughed at, excluded, and called names (Vanfraussen, Ponjaert-Kristoffersen, & Brewaeys, 2002). As is common among children, different clothing, odd behavior, unusual appearance (being overweight; disabled), or even being too smart are all reasons for teasing. Nor do adolescents from lesbian mother and heterosexual families differ in their rates of being teased, victimized, or bullied (MacCallum & Golombok, 2004; Rivers, Poteat, & Noret, 2008). Even when young adults who were raised in either a lesbian-divorced mother household or in a divorced heterosexual mother family reflected on their childhood experiences, they recalled similar levels of bullying in childhood (Tasker & Golombok, 1997).

While there is the good news about rates of teasing, there is some bad news for children of same-gender parents regarding the reasons for being teased. When children from lesbian mother families were teased it was often about family-related issues. Typically, they were teased about their parent's sexuality or about their own presumed sexual orientation (Vanfraussen et al., 2002). In a European study, nearly a quarter of the children in lesbian mother families experienced teasing that was directly linked to their family type. An Australian study of gay or lesbian families reported that just under half of third to sixth grade children and approximately one-third of secondary school children, had experienced teasing, bullying, and homophobic language (Ray & Gregory, 2001). Such comments as "Your mother is a lesbian," "How come you have two mommies?" "Where is your dad?" or "Are you gay too?" were typical comments directed toward these children. Similarly, in the study of young adults in Britain (Tasker & Golombok, 1997), boys from lesbian mother families recalled being teased about their own sexuality more than males from heterosexual mother families. Others report a similar pattern of family specific harassment for children from nonheterosexual-parent families. Such verbal insults as "fag," "lesbo," "devil's daughter" were directed at the school-age children from nontraditional families (Kosciw & Diaz,

2008). Although the rates of teasing may be similar, it is likely that these more personal and family focused comments hurt more than generic insults that are commonly used in classrooms and school playgrounds.

Here is one British girls's experience of being picked on and rejected because her mother was lesbian:

> When I was about 13, my friend found out about my mum. I wasn't allowed to go to her house anymore. Her mum and dad forbade me to go anywhere near. And that hurt me because she had been my best friend for a long, long time. I lost that friend. And then, of course, there was a chain reaction. Everyone found out. They said 'Don't go near her, she'll just turn out like her mum, so don't go near her.' And I lost a lot of friends through that. But there was one friend who really did stick by me and she is still around today (Golombok, 2000, pp. 55–56).

Does the teasing and social challenges encountered by some children raised in same-gender families lead to problems in psychological adjustment? American and British studies of the mental health of young children (ages three to nine) raised in lesbian or heterosexual households found few differences in psychiatric disorders (Golombok et al., 2003) or in psychological adjustment (Flaks et al., 1995). Nor were there any differences in children reared in gay adoptive-parent and heterosexual adoptive-parent families in emotional or behavioral adjustment as rated by their teachers (Farr & Patterson, 2009). Among older children and young teens; rates of anxiety, depression, and other socio-emotional problems did not differ across family groups (Gartrell et al., 2005; MacCallum & Golombok, 2004; Rivers et al., 2008). Finally, in one particularly impressive study using a large national sample, Wainright and colleagues (Wainright & Patterson, 2006; Wainright, Russell, & Patterson, 2004) found that adolescents in female same-sex and heterosexual families were similar in positive aspects of development such as self esteem just as they were similar in negative ones such as depression, anxiety, delinquency, and substance abuse. Clearly, children and adolescents are developing just fine in same-gender parent families in spite of the concerns of critics and commentators who worry that damage will result from being raised in these new family forms.

Several factors make a difference in the degree of acceptance of family differences or in how well children cope with teasing. The community, the neighborhood, and even the part of the country in which you live matters. In some communities with liberal leaning views, the degree of acceptance of same-gender families is likely to be greater. Growing up in the San Francisco Bay area, for example, a child in a lesbian or gay parent family is less likely to be harassed than a child in such a family growing up in a small town in Mississippi where homophobic attitudes are more prevalent. Living in a favorable social environment (e.g., a high proportion and large number of same-sex couples) for sexual minorities was related to better well being for adult offspring of lesbian/gay parents, regardless of their own sexual orientation (Lick, Tornello, Riskind, Schmidt, & Patterson, 2012). The type of school influences teasing and harassment rates too. Children in progressive private schools may experience less harassment than children in poorer public schools which suggests that parental income and education matter. More affluent parents have more choices about where to live and which school their child will attend than those further down the socioeconomic ladder. Having supportive parents can help too. Adolescents from lesbian mother families who enjoyed closer relationships with their parents had more friends and higher quality peer relationships (Wainright & Patterson,

2008). And having a best friend, even one, can buffer a child from the loneliness and sadness of being rejected or ostracized by the larger peer group (Rubin et al., 2006). A final factor is age. Children in late elementary and middle school are most likely to be victims of homophobic-related teasing but children in the early grades and in the later years of high school are spared some of the wrath of their peers (Gartrell et al., 2005; Ray & Gregory, 2001). This is more than just a list of mitigating factors but a reminder that there is a great deal of variability in children's experiences in same-gender parent families. Even though these families are structurally similar, not all same-gender families are alike and not all children in these families experience the same joys or difficulties.

In sum, there are some heightened risks of being teased about the nontraditional nature of one's family for children in same-gender parent households but the overall rates of teasing across children from same-gender and heterosexual families are similar. It is likely that as homophobic attitudes decline and same-gender parent families become more common, more children will understand and accept that families come in a wide variety of forms and not just in the "ideal" family variety.

*Achievement and School Success:* Perhaps children from same-gender families suffer academically as a result of their prejudicial treatment by peers and perhaps some teachers. Just as we have concluded in the case of social and emotional outcomes, children from these nontraditional families are not behind academically. In a study of nearly 90 teens, half living with female same-sex couples and the others with heterosexual couples, both groups fared similarly in school (Wainright et al., 2004). Teen boys in same-sex households had a grade point average (GPA) of about 2.9, compared with 2.6 for their counterparts in heterosexual homes. Teen girls showed similar results, with a 2.8 GPA for same-sex households and 2.9 for girls in heterosexual families. Recently, Rosenfeld (2010) used the 2000 census data to examine school progress among children in different family structures (2000 children with lesbian mothers and 1500 children with gay fathers). After controlling for socioeconomic status, there were no differences in school retention between children from gay/lesbian and heterosexual families. Comparisons between children in same-gender parent families and cohabitating heterosexual families yield a similar picture. In all cases, retention was between 7 and 10%. However, families, regardless of their form, do give children a clear academic advantage since children in group homes, awaiting adoption or foster parents, had a grade retention rate of 34%, while incarcerated children had a grade retention rate of 78%.

> The similarity in school performance between children of same sex couples and children of heterosexual couples fails to support the gender essentialist theories of parenting, which argue that child development depends on having parental role models from both gender groups (Rosenfeld, p. 773).

## Beyond Neutral: Advantages for Parents and Children of Same-Gender Families

While it is important to address critics and concerns about new family forms that violate the "ideal" family model, it is equally and in the long run more important to carefully evaluate the potential advantages of living in alternative family forms such as a same-gender family. Lessons can be learned from alternative family forms that could be valuable for not only our understanding of parenting more generally but for identifying ways that parenting among heterosexual families can be improved. Parenting is a generative activity and most adults benefit from parenting (Snarey, 1993). However, parent pioneers such as gays and lesbians benefit from the unique satisfaction of achieving parenthood in the face of societal barriers. Among the gay parents interviewed by Schacher et al., "most spoke of a strong sense of satisfaction in helping make social change and paving the way for others. Many felt that they had beat the system simply by successfully navigating all the obstacles to having a family" (p. 45). Many experienced personal growth and fulfillment by becoming fathers as well as closer ties to their partner and to their family of origin (Schacher et al., 2005).

Sharing the experience of parenthood can even change attitudes toward and relationships with heterosexuals; most gay/lesbian parents felt a new sense of commonality with heterosexuals. According to one new gay father, "it's not a straight versus gay world anymore" (Schacher et al., 2005, p. 47). Perhaps increased acceptance and tolerance for nonconforming families is a by-product of successful models of gay and lesbian parenting. For children and adults who grew up in gay or lesbian families, there are valuable benefits too. The experience of growing up in a marginalized family form may provide appreciation of other marginalized and minority groups. According to an interview study of over 400 lesbian and gay parents, 89% of lesbian mothers and 82% of gay fathers believed that their children benefited from growing up in a gay or lesbian family (Johnson & O'Connor, 2002). The most common theme was the feeling that children would show a greater tolerance and acceptance of differences and diversity. Here are the thoughts of one adult who grew up in a lesbian couple family: "I think knowing from a very early age what it is to be different or not, to be like the mainstream or not accepted…that gives me an understanding that people just come from so many different walks of life and that respect and an open mind and encountering the world with love and flexibility is definitely how I live my life" (Goldberg, 2007, p. 555). In addition, in a study of lesbian stepmother families, Lynch and Murray (2000) found that parents modeled openness and communication within the family which, in turn, led to more openness and disclosure by their children. Another common theme is the example of sharing and equality in gay/lesbian households that helps children understand alternatives to more traditional and often unbalanced role allocations and responsibility in "ideal" family forms. The focus on less gender stereotyping in these families allows children to explore more flexible roles for men and women both domestically and in the workplace. In fact, daughters of lesbian mothers had higher career aspirations and were more likely to choose traditionally male occupations such as lawyers or doctors than daughters of heterosexual mothers. The development of more androgynous gender attitudes with an emphasis on both caring and instrumentality especially for males (Bigner, 1999; MacCallum & Golombok, 2004) and perhaps girls as well (Sutfin et al., 2008) may flow from life in a gay or lesbian family. In turn, this higher androgyny may be linked to positive adjustment and a higher emotional IQ (Guastello & Guastello, 2003; Shimonaka et al., 1997). The experience of growing up in a nontraditional family can have advantages and offers opportunities to learn valuable life lessons.

## Challenges to the "Ideal" Family Form

Evidence of the adequacy of same-gender parent families poses serious challenges to our traditional views of the "ideal" family form with its focus on two opposite-gender parents with children with biological ties to both parents. Are either mothers or fathers necessary for the healthy psychological development of children? The traditional focus on the gender of the parent is too narrow a conceptualization of the issue of adequate parenting. Instead, the issue needs to be recast by asking whether exposure to a male or female parent is critical for adequate development or whether it is the provision of the universal and fundamental ingredients of parenting – nurturance, protection, nourishment, and stimulation – regardless of the gender of the person who provides these ingredients that is critical (Parke, 2002b). Nor is the argument restricted to these core components of parenting. Parental play, a common form of interaction and an important contributor to children's social and emotional development just as in the case of caregiving can be provided by a parent of either gender. The ingredients of parenting from caregiving to play are more critical for adequate child development than the gender of the parent who provides these experiences.

As our discussion of parenting processes suggests parent gender is clearly less important than the processes themselves. As we saw in the chapter 2 in our discussion of reverse role families, fathers and mothers are equally effective as caregivers. Our review of same-gender parent families tells a similar story: two mothers can successfully socialize children who are well adjusted and psychologically healthy. This raises the fundamental question of whether a male presence as part of the parenting mix is necessary for the successful development of children. In an influential but controversial article "Deconstructing the essential father," Silverstein and Auerbach (1999) concluded that "the empirical research does not support the idea that fathers make a unique and essential contribution to child development" (p. 403). Fathers may, in fact, be unnecessary for children's development but this does not mean that they are unimportant in children's lives. Just as Silverstein and Auerbach have questioned the essential father, the data on the ability of gay couples to successfully rear children without a female parent raises a similar question about the essential mother. Just as fathers may be unnecessary but still important for a child's development, mothers remain important even though not necessary.

However, the fact that same-gender couples can successfully raise children does not negate the extensive data that suggests that mothers and fathers are similar in many ways but may also provide some unique experiences to their children as well. Two key issues need to be addressed. More needs to be understood about the extent to which role division in lesbian or gay families approximates role division in heterosexual families, and more needs to be understood about the degree to which same-gender couples expose their children to opposite-sex role models. If mothers and fathers make different contributions to their children's development, do same-gender parent families adjust their roles to mirror more traditional maternal/paternal roles with each partner enacting the behaviors and actions associated with the paternal and maternal roles? Some support for this possibility comes from the evidence that the biological mother in a lesbian couple family may assume more caregiving duties while the nonbiological coparent may spend more time in outside employment, a pattern that mirrors, in part, traditional male/female role divisions. Whether nonbiological mothers enact other aspects of more traditional male roles, such as a physical play style, remains to be established. To date, the evidence is mixed (Patterson, 2009). Moreover, we know little about the ways in which gay men enact their family roles and whether one partner is likely to enact a more traditional maternal role. In short, children may be afforded opportunities to experience both maternal and paternal interactive styles in same-gender households, but more systematic research is needed to evaluate this possibility. Moreover, the critical issue is whether differentiation of roles between coparents in same-gender parent families is associated with the apparent advantages that this bestows in heterosexual families (Ricaud, 1998). Again this allows us to address the issue raised earlier, namely the relative importance of parental style versus gender of parent who is the delivery agent of this style.

Or does each partner engage in some aspects of both maternal and paternal roles as suggested by the "degendered" parenting notion described by Schacher et al. (2005) for the gay male couples in their study. Presumably, lesbian couples could decide to engage in this same kind of "degendered" parenting as well. In both cases, the parenting components are not only independent of the gender of the parent but the components themselves are itemized and used in novel combinations across partners rather than paternal behaviors being provided by one partner and maternal components by the other partner. The same set of experiences are available to the child but may come from either parent or perhaps both, depending on how the couple divides the components. Parenting can be viewed as a "cafeteria model" in which parents select different ingredients but as long as the selection produces a balanced meal of parenting ingredients the child will be fine. It matters less which parent chooses which ingredient than that a balance from all the critical "food groups" is achieved.

There are other strategies for providing a child with exposure to a range of stylistic experiences in both same-gender parent and traditional opposite-gendered parent households. Not only can two male or two female parents provide the range of experiences that children need for healthy development but others outside the family can play roles as well. This suggests that not only is the gender of the socializing parent not critical for children's development but that parents themselves are not solely responsible for their children's socialization. As noted earlier, it is increasingly common practice for families, regardless of whether they are heterosexual or same-gender families, to follow a communal model of socialization in which some parental responsibilities are outsourced to others. They hire babysitters, enroll their toddlers in child care or preschool, and sign up their school age children for soccer teams or girl scouts.

The question is whether the family form – heterosexual or same-gender – dictates the nature of these choices of supplementary assistance. In the case of nonheterosexual families, does the lack of an opposite-gender parent shape their choice of individuals to whom their child is exposed? Some evidence suggests that lesbian and gay parents have concerns about the lack of either a father or mother figure and some may actively engage others to compensate for the absence of an opposite-gender parent. As Goldberg (2010) has argued,

> lesbians and gay men experience anxiety about how the absence of a female or male parent might affect their children's development...these anxieties are related to ideological

assumptions about the functional and moral superiority of the heterosexual nuclear family. Families that lack a father or mother are assumed to be deficient, and the children in these families are presumed to be at risk (p. 94).

Although the evidence that we have presented suggests that these perceptions and concerns are not well founded, nonnormative families may be motivated to more closely conform to the cultural ideal by engaging outside surrogates to compensate for their departure from the cultural expectation about the gender mix of families. In short, they violate the norm of the "ideal" family form and these efforts are a way to address this concern.

Do these same-sex parent families engage either female or male figures from outside the family to respond to these concerns? When lesbian mothers were interviewed after the birth of their child and again at three months, two-thirds were highly aware of the lack of a father figure and expressed some concern about the absence of a male model (Goldberg & Allen, 2007). They were actively planful in their efforts to secure role male models by talking with brothers, fathers, male friends, and neighbors about possible involvement even before the baby was born. This was especially true in the case of male infants, while there was less focus on male involvement in the case of baby daughters. Lesbian and gay parents feel less accountable to the wider society for their daughter's gender development while they are more concerned about their son's gender development (Kane, 2006).

Lesbian parents give a range of reasons for planning for male involvement (Goldberg & Allen, 2007). Some women, especially with sons were sensitized to the societal view of the importance of male involvement and sought out males as a way to reduce their anxiety about the cultural expectation of male involvement. Others did it out of fairness to their offspring; for example, they wanted to provide the same kind of father–child experience that they enjoyed as a child. Others did this because they wanted to expose their children to a diverse range of people – males, females, gay, straight, white, nonwhite – as part of their commitment to teaching acceptance of many types of individuals. As they develop children often maintain contact with these "father" figures. In one study, 58% of children of lesbian mothers had regular contact with their biological mother's father, 24% with their nonbiological mother's father and 62% with unrelated male adults (Patterson, Hurt, & Mason, 1998). Men who served as donors for lesbian couples also play roles in the lives of their children. Among known donors 29% had regular contact and 71% saw their five-year-old children occasionally (Gartrell et al., 2000).

Involvement of a male from outside the nuclear family circle does not necessarily mean that the figure acts as a father. This is, of course, consistent with the view that children can grow up well without their biological fathers, but instead benefit from the activities and stimulation that fathers typically provide but can be delivered by either one of their lesbian mothers or another outside figure. In fact, while many lesbian mothers value male involvement, they do not necessarily prefer this involvement to be as a father figure. Instead the relationships that donors and male friends and relatives have with children in lesbian-mother families are often described as "uncle-like" (Goldberg et al., 2008). Not all lesbian mothers feel this way; some choose a male donor specifically to provide a father-figure for their child (Almack, 2006; Touroni & Coyle, 2002). It is less clear what factors determine the type of male relationship different lesbian mothers prefer or what the advantages and disadvantages of "uncle-like" or "father-like" relationships are for either children or for the lesbian parental couple. It also remains unknown whether there are clear advantages of using opposite-gender others as supplementary socialization figures rather than providing a range of parenting experiences by the coparenting same-gender couple alone. Finally, some argue that the active recruitment of opposite gender figures by lesbian parents signals an acquiescence to societal expectations and reinforces the stereotype that men are necessary adjunct parent figures for lesbian parent families (Clarke & Kitziner, 2005).

Do gay men invite their mothers, sisters, aunts, female cousins, or friendly female neighbors over for child-care advice or for baby sitting duties? While we know less about gay men who are parents than about lesbian parents, it is likely that they pursue a similar set of strategies. For example, some gay adoptive fathers consider the birth mothers of their children to be part of the family, at least symbolically (Berkowitz & Marsiglio, 2007). Moreover, gay fathers often prefer open adoption arrangements in order to ensure a female figure in their child's life (McPheeters, Carmi, & Goldberg, 2008). Whether gay parents view females as mother figures or as aunt-like figures or just another set of nurturing hands is unclear.

*A Word of Caution:*   Little is known about the effects of the exposure to and involvement of opposite-gender "surrogate parent" figures on the development of children, especially their gender role development. Nor do we know about the duration and frequency of contact necessary to confer any potential developmental advantage if such exposure were found to be beneficial. Perhaps most fundamentally, we lack data on the kind of relationship needed if exposure is to prove beneficial for the child's development. And of course, the larger question is whether this exposure, after controlling for parent effects, makes a difference in child outcomes. However, work on adult mentors and other nonparental adults suggests that the positive effect of nonfamilial mentors on adolescents' social behavior is independent of the effect of parent–child relationships (Greenberger et al., 1998). Moreover, it remains to be determined whether or not any positive effects of involving opposite-gender socialization surrogates in the families of same-gender couple on children are due specifically to the gender-related role models or behaviors provided by these individuals. Or are the positive effects due to the increased social support provided by these family adjuncts, regardless of their gender or their gender-related activities.

Just as we have argued in the case of same-gender parents, the gender of the outside figures may be less important than the support resources that they bring to the family. Social support, regardless of the source, is an important predictor of parental well-being, effectiveness as a parent and, in turn, the health and adjustment of children – for both heterosexual (Mayes & Leckman, 2007) as well as lesbian parents (Vyncke & Julien, 2007). Although some studies report that lesbian and gay parents may receive less social support than heterosexual parents (Kindle & Erich, 2005), others report the opposite with gay/lesbian parents receiving more family support (Goldberg, 2006), while others report no differences in the amount of support (Patterson, 2009). Part of the inconsistency may be due to the fact that the support of lesbian and gay parents increases as children develop and grandparents increasingly desire and value contact with their grandchildren. Some support for this argument comes from the increasing number of grandparents who are open and forthcoming about their daughter's sexual orientation as their grandchild develops. While only 29% of grandparents with a two-year-old grandchild were open about their daughter's lesbian status, the percentage increased to 63% by their grandchild's fifth birthday and 73% when their grandchild was 10 (Gartell et al., 1999, 2000, 2006).

The level of family support varies depending on which lesbian parent is the biological mother: grandparents and other family relatives of the biological mother were more involved than the nonbiological mother's relatives with their grandchildren (Patterson et al., 1998). This is, of course, consistent with evolutionary theory that suggests that biologically based kin ties are a strong basis for social investment (Bjorklund & Pellegrini, 2000). However, it is not all based on biological ties; when the nonbiological lesbian mother gains second-parent adoption rights, this legal recognition led to increased involvement on the part of the grandparents as well. Being recognized as legal, even if not biological kin, apparently increases investment by grandparents in their grandchild (Hequembourg & Farrell, 1999). Social class matters too; more educated, middle class gay and lesbian families gain more family support and acceptance than their working class counterparts. This is a reflection of the well-established finding that there is more acceptance of gays and lesbians, in general, among more educated individuals (Carrington, 2002; Goldberg, 2010).

As I show in Chapter 6, in many other cultures, children have a range of parental figures beyond their biological parents. While evidence concerning the effects of variations in contact on children's development remains unclear, these contacts, at a minimum, can be viewed as significant and stable sources of social support for these developing children. Perhaps these adjunct male parent figures also provided assistance and advice for the parents as well. While the cultural push to include males in the mix of lesbian families may not necessarily be welcomed by all lesbian partner families (Clarke & Kitziner, 2005), the expanded network of parental support figures is likely beneficial for parents and children alike. Traditional heterosexual two-parent families ("ideal" families) could learn a lesson about the value and benefits of porous family boundaries. The burgeoning literature on the influence of nonfamily mentors on child and adolescent social, academic and even spiritual development supports the value of including both family and nonfamily agents in the socialization mix (Rhodes & DuBois, 2006).

## Reflections

The presence of not just two parents but parents of opposite genders remains a central-defining feature of the "ideal" family paradigm. In our continuing exploration of alternatives to the "ideal" family form, it is not surprising that the issue of the centrality of either a mother or a father for the adequate development of children continues to generate debate and controversy. The increasing prevalence of same-gender families in which either two lesbians or two gay men become parents provides a unique opportunity to critically address the issue. As our review suggests, the necessity of either a father or a mother for children's socialization is challenged by the success of children raised in same-gender parent families. Although we have an incomplete understanding of the internal interactional dynamics, the role distributions across partners and the extent to which other nonfamily socialization agents play a role in these families, it is clear that these alternative family forms are sufficient to produce well-adjusted children. However, most of our knowledge is based on a narrow set of samples – white, middle class, and educated – and whether or not similar findings will be evident for other racial or ethnic groups is unknown. Since the degree of acceptance of nonheterosexuality in general and same-gender parent families in particular may be lower among these groups (Herek, 2007), it is critical that samples be expanded so that the generalizability of the findings can be assessed. As we have seen in earlier discussions of other family forms such as single-mother families, stepfamilies or reverse role families, family processes that are common across a range of forms are better predictors of child outcomes than the form itself. The main impediment to the continued success of same-gender parent families is the fundamental misunderstanding that the underlying sexual preferences of same-gender individuals is independent of their ability to be loving and skilled parents. It is not inadequate parenting that contributes to children's experiences of prejudice and discrimination but the continued intolerance of these nonconforming families by many in our society. As our society progresses in understanding that diversity is not deficiency, greater acceptance and appreciation of these alternative family forms will follow. Finally, it is clear that these new family forms present a significant challenge to the "ideal" family form. Although same-gender parent families deviate from the tenets of the dominant family paradigm they work just as effectively as socialization contexts for our children.

# 5

# How Many "Parents" Are Too Many? Insights from the Assisted Reproductive Technologies Front

*Technology's gift to women (and men) during the latter half of the twentieth century was contraception, the first 50 years of the new millennium may well be considered the decade of conception* (Carl Djerassi, 1999)

Another assault on the "ideal" family form comes from the new routes to parenthood allowed by the Assisted Reproductive Technologies (ART) (Parke, Gailey, Coltrane, & DiMatteo, 2012). In this century, the routes to parenthood promise to be increasingly diverse. As we saw in the opening chapter, many families like the Darcys are following in the footsteps of Louise Brown, mother of the first test tube baby in 1978. Since that time, more than 50 million couples around the world have turned to ART to overcome infertility or the absence of a partner to achieve parenthood. Over five million children have been conceived as a result of these procedures (International Committee for Monitoring Assisted Reproductive Technologies, 2012a,b). In fact, more than 15% of births in the United States and in Europe involve these new reproductive technologies (Centers for Disease Control and Prevention, 2012; de Mouzon et al., 2010; Schieve, Rasmussen, & Reefhuis, 2005). The use of new reproductive technologies has significantly expanded the ways in which individuals become parents. This choice as a route to parenthood is especially welcome to individuals who have had medical challenges such as infertility, a condition that affects between 10 and 15% of adults (Spar, 2006). In other cases such as single females or males and same-sex couples who wish to become parents, the problem is the unavailability of a partner which can be solved by the use of these new medical advances. Recent changes in technology-assisted childbearing include *in vitro* fertilization (IVF) and its variations as well as intracytoplasmic sperm injection (ICSI), techniques involving genetic donation such as sperm or egg donations and the utilization of surrogate mothers.

The spread of reproductive technologies throughout the world has sparked debates among philosophers, social scientists, and physicians as well as policymakers about regulation of the use of these new techniques, the safety of these procedures, and the ethical and moral implications of their use. There are deep ethical issues surrounding

*Future Families: Diverse Forms, Rich Possibilities*, First Edition. Ross D. Parke.
© 2013 John Wiley & Sons, Inc. Published 2013 by John Wiley & Sons, Inc.

the search for perfectibility through new reproductive technologies. As I will argue, the newly discovered ability to manipulate, select, and, in the end, design offspring with desired traits and characteristics taps into a deep-seated cultural value, namely our preoccupation with the pursuit of perfection in many spheres of life. Like the inhabitants of Garrison Keilor's imaginary Lake Wobegon, where "all the women are strong, all the men are good looking, and all the children are above average," we are obsessed with striving for perfection. In the movie *Gattaca*, "parents routinely screen embryos for sex, height, immunity from disease, and even IQ" (Sandel, 2004). Is the present reality far removed from the imagined future depicted in *Gattaca*?

While the advances in ART allow parents to choose the sex of their child and beyond as part of the search for the perfection of offspring, paradoxically, these same advances raise the central question of this chapter – How do the families produced through these alternative routes to parenthood square with our cultural definition of the "ideal" family form? While these new pathways to parenthood allow more individuals to become parents, the resulting families do not conform to our cultural definition of the ideal family form. In fact, "ART represents one important tributary contributing to the torrent of social change that is already redefining the traditional procreating nuclear family as the normative ideal" (Leon, 2008, p. 21). And some social critics are clearly displeased by this threat to the cultural image of the "ideal" family and have lamented

> That children are conceived pursuant to contractual arrangements involving the exchange of money; that conception need not begin with sexual intercourse, and need not occur within the body of a woman; that the genetic makeup of a child (and its cloned twin or triplet) can be selected from a panoply of genetic options – these factors pose a profound threat to the ideology of family as it developed in the early years of the Industrial Revolution and was elaborated and glorified in the succeeding two centuries (Dolgin, 1997, p. 246).

Moreover, what are the implications of the deviations from our cultural definition of the "ideal" family form for the contracting families as well as for the other players who are partners in these new routes to parenthood? In this chapter, we also examine not only the increasing availability of these new routes to parenthood but also the vexing issue of inequalities associated with access to these new routes to parenthood as a function of social class, sexual orientation, and ethnicity. What are the developmental implications of these new advances for children produced through ART? Are they as socially and cognitively competent as naturally conceived offspring? Next, we provide a brief overview of the various techniques involved in the new reproductive technologies.

## What Are the Assisted Reproductive Technologies?

There is a good reason that the term "new reproductive technologies" is plural. There are a wide range of medical approaches that have been discovered since the first IVF baby in 1978. The original procedure, developed by British obstetrician Patrick Steptoe and embryologist Robert Edwards allowed a mother with blocked fallopian tubes to conceive by transferring her ova from her ovaries to a petri or glass dish (hence the term *in vitro* or in glass), where they were combined with the father's sperm. Drugs were used to stimulate the ovaries in order to produce 10–20 eggs rather than the usual one or two each month. In turn, the eggs were combined with 75,000–100,000 sperm. If successful fertilization occurred, then the embryos were transferred back to the women's womb or to the fallopian tubes if they were healthy. No part of this procedure is easy or without risk. Fertilization may be unsuccessful, the surgical removal of the ova can be painful, and the process interferes with daily routines since the mother needs to be monitored to harvest the eggs at the right time and for implanting the embryo later. Many cycles are sometimes needed and mother and partner experience anxiety and often disappointment if the procedure fails to produce a viable pregnancy. In fact, success is by no means guaranteed; the rate of a successful pregnancy is about 34% in the United States, 30% in Europe, and even lower (27%) worldwide (Nyboe Andersen et al., 2008). However, these rates are a dramatic improvement over the rates of 5–10% in the early 1980s (Mundy, 2007). Many factors affect the success rate, including the number of monthly attempts, the skill of the medical team, and the type of procedure used. Perhaps the best predictor of success or failure is the age of the mother, although recent evidence implicates father's age as well. Success declines as the mother ages: Twenty-six year olds have a 43% chance of pregnancy per cycle of ART, 38-year-olds, a 30% chance and 42-year-olds only a 16% chance (Centers for Disease Control and Prevention, 2003). For a would-be mother in her mid-40s the chances diminish to close to zero even after three cycles (Klipstein et al., 2005). Even with medical assistance, a women's ticking biological clock clearly limits her chances of becoming pregnant. As Marcel Cedars, a reproductive endocrinologist, correctly but wryly noted, "You know the old real estate adage: location, location, location. Well in IVF, it's age of the female partner, age of the female partner, age of the female partner" (cited by Mundy, p. 42).

However, the development of cryopreservation or freezing of extra embryos was a major advance and allows some older women to conceive using eggs harvested when they were younger. In this procedure, some of the eggs produced in response to drug assisted superovulation but not used in a current cycle can be frozen for use in later cycles. In the 1990s, as women were choosing to establish careers before having children, "young women began to consider egg freezing as a possible way to delay childbearing for an extended period – a way, at last, to beat the fertility decline hovering in the mid thirties" (Spar, 2006, p. 61). And the egg bank business became a major industry not only in the United States but worldwide as more women took advantage of this new way to beat the biological clock (Mundy, 2007; Spar, 2006).

Other procedures have been developed since the discovery of IVF. One, gamete intrafallopian transfer (GIFT) is a laproscopic procedure by which the unfertilized ova and sperm are procured and transferred to the fallopian tube, the natural site of fertilization. Under normal conditions the embryos live in the fallopian tube for five days after ovulation, so this procedure mimics nature to some extent. Unlike traditional IVF, fertilization takes place in the body and not in a dish, a procedure that some religious couples prefer as it is "closer to the way God intended conception to occur" (Paulson & Sachs, 1999, p. 98).

Zygote intrafallopian transfer (ZIFT) also entered the ART scene in the 1980s. In this procedure, the embryos developed *in vitro* in the lab were placed in the fallopian tubes after 24 hours. Another variation, tubal embryo transfer (TET) follows a similar protocol but transfer to the fallopian tubes is after 48 hours. These procedures expand the pool of women who can be helped. Both procedures are appropriate for women who have difficulty transferring embryos back through the cervix. However, these procedures involve surgery under anesthesia at more cost and more risk and are used only under unusual circumstances.

Another by-product of the advent of IVF is embryo donation (ED), another form of third party reproduction. In this approach one or more of the embryos formed during the IVF procedure of another party but not used in their pregnancy attempts is donated, usually without charge to another woman or couple in order to achieve a pregnancy. The issue of the disposition of unused "extra" embryos has become a controversial issue in the United States with some groups promoting embryo adoption programs to avoid the discarding of these embryos, while others argue that it is the parents' right to decide on the disposition of their embryos.

Of course, it is not always a female problem. "It's sometimes the case that a man has very few sperm, very slow sperm, badly formed sperm which can't make their way into an egg or no sperm at all" (Paulson & Sachs, 1999, p. 212). Up until the early 1990s, a couple would have to rely on a sperm donor but with the development of a technique called ICSI the treatment of male fertility was revolutionized. Using this approach, a single sperm is injected into a mature egg so that fertilization can take place in the laboratory.

Egg or sperm donors are sometimes necessary even though they complicate the family formation process. In this scenario, if your sperm is defective or absent, you can use someone else's sperm. Or if your eggs are not healthy, you can find someone who is willing to donate their eggs or more commonly sell you some of their healthy ones. Since 1983 when the first child conceived using a donated egg was born, it has been possible for women to become pregnant with a child to whom they are genetically unrelated. The most recent figures show that the number of assisted reproduction cycles involving egg donation in the United States increased from around 2000 in 1996 to nearly 18,000 in 2009 (Centers for Disease Control and Prevention, 2011), a number that is increasing exponentially each year.

Several decisions must be made that have important psychological, emotional, and social implications. Do you want to use a known donor such as a sister or a friend or an unknown source for your needed genetic material? For those who are concerned about avoiding genealogical confusion and wish their child to know their genetic history, choosing a known donor is often the preferred option. Other parents who prefer to avoid the social complications associated with having a known donor in their lives more likely use the more impersonal route of the unknown donor. Whatever the choice, the donor option clearly expands the chances of family formation for many childless individuals and couples.

Finally, some couples in which the female partner is unable to carry a fetus due to an earlier medical problem enlist the aid of a surrogate who carries the fetus throughout pregnancy. In traditional surrogacy, the surrogate provides the egg or genetic material and the womb and the sperm is provided by the male partner of the contracting couple. In this case, the baby has genetic ties to both the surrogate birth mother and the contracting father. The idea is hardly a new one as this quote from the bible indicates:

Now Sarai, Abram's wife, had borne him no children. And she had an Egyptian maidservant whose name was Hagar. So Sarai said to Abram, "See now, the Lord has restrained me from bearing children. Please, go in to my maid; perhaps I shall obtain children by her." And Abram heeded the voice of Sarai. So he went in to Hagar, and she conceived (Genesis 6:1–3).

In biblical times, of course, sperm donation was not possible so normal sexual relations between the male and the surrogate was the only possible route to conception. However, as the story of Sarai, Abram, and Hagar continues, this was a problematic solution; Sarai was jealous of Hagar while Hagar felt superior to her mistress as a result of her reproductive success. "And when she (Hagar) saw that she had conceived, her mistress became despised in her eyes." Then Sarai said to Abram, "My wrong be upon you! I gave my maid into your embrace; and when she saw that she had conceived, I became despised in her eyes" (Genesis, 16:4–6). Although modern sperm donor procedures avoid some of these negative social and emotional complications among the three partners, the wife can still be jealous or ambivalent about the surrogate. And because biological parenthood is held in "higher" esteem than ART achieved parenthood, there may be complications especially about the wife's feelings about the child.

With the advent of IVF, gestational surrogacy became possible. In this case, the contracting couple can use the male sperm with the intended mother's egg (or if necessary a donated egg) in which case the genetic ties to the surrogate are eliminated. Or if both contracting parents are unable to provide viable biological material, donor eggs and sperm can be used to create an embryo which is carried to term by a surrogate. In this case, there are neither genetic ties to either the surrogate or the contracting parents. In spite of concerns such as Warnock's (2002) warning that surrogacy is "an extremely risky enterprise and liable to end in tears," as we will see next, this approach is a viable and positive alternative route to parenthood for some families.

As this brief survey of the new paths to parenthood suggest, all of these methods of conceiving violate in various ways and to different degrees the concept of the "ideal" family form. We will explore the implications of these nontraditional alternatives for parent–parent relationships, for the offspring produced by these arrangements and for the social relationships with other parties involved in these new techniques.

## Is the Myth of the "Ideal" Family at Risk When Family Formation Is Achieved by Use of ART

Families such as the Darcys who became parents through ART violate the culturally scripted family portrait of the "ideal" family form as a two-parent nuclear family unit who are biologically able to produce a child. First, one or both partners may be infertile which in itself is stigmatizing and a violation of the expectation that reproductive capability is expected and normative. In spite of the fact that no one is to blame for infertility, infertile couples perceive higher levels of stigma and discrimination especially women than fertile couples which, in turn, may lead to lower rates of disclosure as a way of coping with this culturally induced distress (Slade, O'Neill, Simpson, & Lashen, 2007). Being infertile in and of itself is viewed as a cultural anomaly.

Second, by solving the infertility problem through the use of ART as an alternative route to parenthood uncouples biological and social aspects of family formation and parenthood by distinguishing between procreative aspects of parenting and later social or child rearing aspects of parenting. According to the "ideal" family form these two aspects of parenthood – biological and social – are linked as part of a unified process involving two partners who become parents without outside assistance. In a recent international survey of attitudes toward ART (Fundación BBVA, 2008), interviewees were asked to rate the best option for a couple who wished to become parents but had fertility problems: ART, adoption, accept the situation and stay childless. In all countries, a majority chose either adoption or the use of assisted reproduction techniques, with only a small percentage in favor of accepting the situation. Countries where the majority would opt for assisted reproduction were the Netherlands, Sweden, France, Denmark, Israel, and the Czech Republic. In Spain too, this option was supported by a relative majority. Countries where a relative majority preferred adoption were Germany, Austria, Italy, Poland, and the United States. In the United Kingdom and Ireland opinions were more evenly divided between the two alternatives. Depending on the type of new reproductive assistance, there are variations in the extent to which there are genetic ties between the contracting parents and the child. In the case of IVF, there are the genetic ties to both mother and father and only the unnaturalness of the test tube based assistance. However, in other cases such as those involving sperm or egg donors the genetic links may be to only one parent although the mother may carry the fetus through the pregnancy. In the case of gestational surrogacy, where donated sperm and egg are used, there are neither genetic ties to the contracting or social parents or involvement of the social mother as the womb provider. While all of these procedures represent a departure from naturalness and, in turn, the "ideal" family form, the degree of violation can best be viewed as a continuum of deviation from the "ideal" family form.

Third, in some cases, a single, unmarried man or women may be the contracting party, a further deviation from the cultural script that a married couple is the proper social unit for reproduction and child rearing. According to the international survey (Fundación BBVA, 2008) in nearly half of the countries (Czech Republic, Spain, Israel) involved, average acceptance was just above the midpoint and the rest (including the United States, Japan, Italy, and the United Kingdom) found this unacceptable. Similarly, an Australian survey found that only 38% of respondents approved of the use of donated sperm for single women while 54% disapproved (Kovacs, Morgan, Wood, Forbes, & Howlett, 2003). And same gender couples – either lesbian or gay – may be the contracting agents who are using these new reproductive technologies as a route to parenthood, another "violation" of the cultural norm concerning the "appropriate" gender composition of the parenting unit. When asked about their acceptance of the use of sperm banks by lesbian couples, most respondents in the international survey (Fundación BBVA) (with the exception of Denmark, the Netherlands, and Spain), rated it as unacceptable, especially Poland, Italy, Austria, and Japan. The Australian survey revealed that only 31% approved of the use of donated sperm by lesbians, while 59% disapproved of this practice (Kovacs et al.).

Fifth, the number of contributors that are potentially involved in order to complete the reproductive cycle goes beyond two "parents." The cast includes not just the contracting couple but potentially an egg donor or a sperm donor. In this case, there are three parties involved in the reproductive scenario namely the contracting couple and the sperm or egg donor. This trio of possible family members clearly violates the view of the family as a mother and father in a nuclear family arrangement. The complexity is increased if a surrogate who carries the fetus is involved in the process. In this scenario, there are four or five individuals involved who are potential family members – the contracting couple, a sperm or egg donor or both, and the surrogate (Parke, 2002b). In the Australian community survey, many (59%) were negative about the use of commercial surrogacy with only 44% approving of this approach to solving fertility challenges (Kovacs et al., 2003). More (59%) were accepting if the surrogate was deemed to be acting altruistically rather than merely for commercial gain. Not only the rights of parents need consideration but the rights of the children as well as the social and legal rights and obligations of the nonfamily contributors namely the egg and sperm donors and the surrogate mother. These issues raise new legal and ethical dilemmas concerning what rights are appropriate for each party. This expanded set of possible family "members" clearly violates our notion of the ideal family form. At the same time, these new techniques are increasingly part of our contemporary culture and allow many individuals and couples to fulfill their desire to become parents. Although this new reality presents challenges for children and parents, these challenges are clearly surmountable. As we will document, children and families can thrive even though their routes to family formation are unusual.

## Who Are the Consumers of ART? Another Case of Class, Race, and Age Discrimination

Although the primacy of the "ideal" family form is challenged by these new medical advances, access to these forms of reproductive assistance is not equal. Whether you are a consumer of these new advances in reproductive medicine and how much you will pay for these services depends on where you live, how old you are, and at least in some countries how wealthy and how educated you are.

Access to the new reproductive technologies in the United States is restricted by class, ethnicity, and education. The total cost incurred for successful delivery after successful IVF can be $41,000 in American dollars for the first cycle to $73,000 by the sixth cycle. Similar costs are found in Great Britain as well (Chambers, Sullivan, Ishihara, Chapman, & Adamson, 2009). Obstetrical and perinatal costs are considerably higher for twins and triplets than for singletons (Centers for Disease Control and Prevention, 2012). In other parts of the globe such as Scandinavia and Japan, the cost is much less at $24,500 (Chambers et al., 2009). Many insurers/public health systems in the United States do not cover or only partially cover these procedures, making IVF and related therapies available only to those with the ability to pay. Not only are costs prohibitive for most working class couples in the United States; but insurance coverage varies by state with little federal coverage or oversight. Although 15 states offer some coverage for infertility diagnosis and treatment, the level of coverage varies by state (National Council of State Legislators, 2012).

For example, IVF is fully covered in some states (Massachusetts), but not covered in other states (California, Louisiana, and New York). In contrast, some countries such as

Israel, Great Britain, and Denmark make ARTs available – regardless of income. However, in other countries such as Great Britain, there are usually restrictions such as providing National Health Service insurance coverage for a limited number of cycles. Others (Egypt, South Africa) provide no insurance coverage for IVF interventions (Spar, 2006; Twine, 2011). Still others ban the procedures such as Costa Rica who regard the approach as a "violation of life," while other countries such as China place restrictions on who is eligible to use these technologies. In China, Government agencies passed bans on the use of IVF in 2003 by unmarried women or by couples with certain infectious diseases.

Government and insurance related support depends largely on whether or not infertility is treated as a medical problem. If it is viewed as a medical issue it will be covered like any other medical problem such as a heart bypass or hip replacement. "If infertility is seen as fate, a decision, or bad luck, then states stay out of the market and prices flutter upward" (Spar, 2006, p. 213). For example, in the United States, the costs of IVF are high even when the procedure involves using a woman's own eggs and even higher for donor eggs. Advertisers are willing to pay $50,000 for an egg with the desired characteristics: Some Ivy League newspapers ran ads seeking "an egg from a women who was at least five feet ten inches tall and athletic, had no major family medical problems, and had a combined SAT scores of 1400 and above" (Sandel, 2004, p. 59). And one can cruise the internet not just for cheap books but for a vast array of eggs offered by fashion models or for sperm for sale by struggling medical interns eager to sell their reproductive wares for $10,000 and up! The commercial market in eggs and sperm is no longer restricted to east coast newspapers or exotic web sites. To illustrate, consider this advertisement from the Genetics and IVF Institute in *American Way*, a commercial airline magazine. The ad reads:

> We offer approximately 100 fully screened donors immediately available for matching and utilization by our patients. These donors include many Doctoral Donors in advanced degree programs and numerous other egg donors with special accomplishments, talents or ethnicity (American Way, 2006, p. 92).

As one newspaper writer observed, "egg donor technology has gone as mainstream as selling cereal" (Rubin, 2007). Clearly, the search for perfection in terms of "designer infants" is becoming pervasive if not commonplace and is a deviation from the original goal of these ART services as a way to help infertile would-be parents. Surrogacy represents a similar income based imbalance. In this case, poor women can rent their wombs to rich women for $20,000–$30,000 and for much more ($50,000 plus) if twins are involved and legal and medical costs are taken into account (Twine, 2011). Or increasingly, surrogacy is outsourced to poor women in other countries such as India where there is a thriving surrogacy industry. The attraction to European and North American women is clear: the cost of surrogacy services in India is considerably less expensive ($6500–$12,000) than in their home countries. This is a considerable and attractive payout for poor or even middle class women for a nine month period, especially among women in countries with limited economic opportunities (Figure 5.1). As Spar points out "surrogacy is fundamentally a market relationship, but one that almost always leaves poorer women serving their better-heeled sisters" (p. 93). In contrast to the United States, commercial surrogacy is illegal in most (if not all) European countries especially Western European countries.

**Figure 5.1**   Outsourcing of surrogacy to women in other countries such as India is increasingly common.
*Source:* India Today Group/Getty Images.

As noted earlier, in the United States, insurance will often cover only part of the cost of the procedures and sometimes it will not cover these costs at all (American Society for Reproductive Medicine, 2010) with the result that the rich have access while the poor do not. Clearly, these costs are likely to limit access to these techniques with the result that homogeneity in class and race is virtually guaranteed. This is merely another reflection of the differential access to health and medical support in the United States as a function of social class and ethnicity. In short, ART represents a middle class and generally white enterprise and by implication is limiting the reproductive rights of less wealthy and nonwhite individuals. The average user of IVF services in the United States is white, college educated with an average income well above national medians. As Paulson and Sachs (1999) argue, this situation is a reflection of our capitalist system.

> In a system that uses money as an evaluation of what things are worth it is hard not to wonder whether we are evolving into a culture that pays hard cash for everything good, and pities the poor individual who can't participate because she doesn't have the means. Whether the prize is a deluxe Caribbean Cruise, a heart transplant, a Porsche or a late-life baby, you have to put your money where your mouth is. And this clearly puts a restriction on such luxuries. If you don't come from wealth, achieve wealth or have wealth thrust upon you, you're out of the game (p. 252).

There is another form of discrimination that has received less attention than the economic barriers associated with race and class, namely the exploitation of the young (and often poor) in the service of providing for older (and often rich) recipients. Paulson and Sachs (1999) framed it as "Society's bargain: young, poor women help older rich women" (p. 251). Users of ART are often older women and/or couples who have turned to these procedures after encountering infertility problems. On the other hand, the providers – egg donors, sperm donors, or surrogate mothers – are often younger. In effect, we have another division based on age between the recipients and providers. It is not unwarranted to recall Margaret Atwood's *The Handmaid's Tale* in which one class of women service another – higher – class of women by providing eggs as well as a uterus. The contemporary surrogacy market "employs women to produce children, creating families as well as inequities in the process" (Spar, 2006, p. 94). Although we have not institutionalized the form of reproductive slavery that Atwood imagined, the unintended parallels are more than a little unnerving and raise serious questions about income-based access to health services in general and to reproductive assistance in particular.

## The Rights of Parents, Children, and Biological Contributors and the Protection of the "Ideal" Family Form

The right of parents (especially fathers) to define their family form and their family boundaries is long-standing and firmly established in our legal heritage. However, as new family forms have evolved, new legal guidelines have been developed to deal with new complications in cases, for example, of divorce and adoption (Gailey, 2004; Grotevant, 2007). Similarly, legal guidelines are gradually emerging to deal with the rights, responsibilities, and obligations of the various contributors to ART assisted births (Katz Rothman, 2002). In this section, we explore these issues as a way of understanding how the resolution of these challenges reflects on our efforts to align the realities of new-reproductive technology families with the lingering vision of the "ideal" family form.

*Restrictive versus Inclusive Definition of the Family Form:* Many of the current debates about the rights and responsibilities of each of the individual contributors to the infant production scenario flow from disagreements about the nature of the concept of family in general and of their acceptance or rejection of the culturally endorsed definition of a "ideal" family form. On one side of this debate, a restrictive definition of family and resulting family boundaries suggest that the contracting couple and their technologically reproduced child should be viewed as the rightful and responsible family unit; all other players could simply be viewed as paid contributors of either biological material – in the case of egg and sperm donors – or as providers of biological/physical services – in the case of surrogates. None of these players would have any claims in term of physical access to the child that was produced or any financial, emotional, or social obligations to the child. By endorsing this restrictive definition of "family," the ART family can, in part, achieve the "ideal" family form by the social presentation of a family arrangement (mother, father and child) to the outside world that is consistent with the cultural standard. By excluding the other players, the social untidiness and possible embarrassment associated with these other individuals who have no culturally scripted roles in this ART family can be avoided and the "ideal" family myth can be maintained. And the contracting families were aided in this myth maintaining scenario by the other players such as egg and sperm donors who were assured of their anonymity. Until the last decade donor anonymity was common and many donors provided eggs and sperm with the understanding that they would remain anonymous and would have no obligations to their offspring.

This contract between donors, donor brokers and agencies, and contracting families made the boundaries between contracting parents and egg and sperm donors relatively clear and unambiguous.

On the other end of the debate continuum is the definition of ART-produced families as "expanded family forms" with porous boundaries that not only permit, but encourage the development of social relationships among and between various contributors, but especially between the child and the nonchild rearing contributors (e.g., egg and sperm donors, surrogates). The feasibility of this new view of family boundaries and the expanded definition of possible family participants has been greatly facilitated by a shift away from donor anonymity toward a more open attitude toward donor identification. This set of family arrangements, of course, violates the "ideal" family form, but as we will argue, variations on this expanded family form need to be carefully considered and may, in fact, be a new "ideal" family form that may benefit not only the noncustodial players, but also may have potentially positive outcomes for the contracting couple and the child as well.

As we show next, the issues are not clear-cut in terms of either rights or responsibilities of various contributors to these new technologically assisted births or the rights and responsibilities of the contracting parents and children. In fact, it is probably more profitable to view possible variation in the amount and type of relationships between the contracting family and nonfamily members as a continuum rather than a simple dichotomy between family and nonfamily member categories.

*The View from the Contracting Parents:*  Although child rights have become increasingly recognized, parental rights generally supersede child-based considerations. This argument is rooted in a long-standing historical assumption that children are viewed as property and only as mature adults do they possess rights that equal parental prerogatives. As Murray (1996) argues, "the idea that a child is the property of its biological parents is out of favor, but not dead, either in our laws or our customs even though the concept of child as property is based on faulty evidence and truncated ethics" (p. 59). A more contemporary version of this perspective argues that parents – in their greater wisdom – will take children's best interests into account. Murray refers to this as the "parent as steward" model and argues that it is clearly more attractive than the property ownership model of parent–child relationships.

*Secrecy as a Tool for Maintenance of the Appearance of the "Ideal" Family Form:*  Based on this view, it is argued that parents have a right to manage the amount of information and the timing of disclosure of information to children about their origins (egg, sperm donor, surrogate). Although parental decisions to limit children's access to knowledge about their origins is justified on a number of grounds, according to the theme of this chapter, the underlying concept that unites the various arguments for withholding information about their origins and the cooperative nature of their production is the parental desire to preserve the public presentation of their family as culturally conforming both for themselves and for their child. Once a child understands the fact that multiple players are involved in their production, the child's conception of the "ideal" family form is undermined. In order to preserve the myth of the "ideal" family for their child, parents fail to disclose this information to their child. Parental secrecy may be motivated by a desire to protect the child from the stigmatization associated with their living in a nonconforming family. By maintaining a sense of "normality," parents are better able to protect their child and their family from negative social reactions. Secrecy is not restricted to the child. ART parents may hide their reproductive information from friends and relatives in the wider community for a variety of reasons, including their desire to maintain the appearance of an "ideal" family form. Public disclosure or awareness may undermine individual parental self worth or even perhaps the marital relationship by causing embarrassment or shame due to their public disclosure of their single or joint infertility. In turn, threats to individual mental health of one or both parents and/or marital strife could have negative effects on the child (Cummings & Davies, 2010). Moreover, the possibility of social contact between the "social" (contracting) parents and the donors or surrogates could further opportunities for public disclosure of their route to parenthood and further violate the restrictive and culturally defined "ideal" family form.

Although there is variability across different types of ART families in their disclosure patterns, disclosure is far from the norm. Withholding of information is highest in the case of sperm donor insemination (DI) families (Golombok, 2002). In one recent study, nearly 75% of DI children had not been told by their parents by age seven (Readings, Blake, Casey, Jadva, & Golombok, 2011). The level of secrecy is somewhat lower among parents who used donated eggs. Still nearly 50% of seven year old children in egg donation (ED) families had not been told by their mothers how they were conceived (Readings et al.). Part of the reason for the differences in rates of disclosure across ED and DI families is due to a desire to protect the infertile husband from the stigma of male infertility, which is thought to be more shameful than female infertility. Another reason is lack of information to give the child about the genetic father in cases of anonymous sperm donors (Golombok). For some couples the pain of the infertility was still felt and appeared to have some impact on the decision not to tell their child: "I'm not sure how [father] would feel about it, because he was really hurt at the time when he found out he couldn't conceive naturally, it was a real, you know, struggle (DI mother)" (Readings et al., p. 490). The least secretive were parents who used a surrogate. In one study all surrogate assisted parents either shared or planned to share this information with their 7 year-old children (Readings et al.) and by age 10, 90% of the surrogacy assisted children had actually been told (Jadva, Blake, Casey, & Golombok, 2012). As MacCallum, Lycett, Murray, Jadva, and Golombok (2003) noted

> Surrogacy families are like adoptive families in their readiness to disclose the child's origins to their family and friends. This may be due to the fact that, as for adoptive families, the absence of a pregnancy means that the commissioning couple cannot pretend that they have had the child through natural conception. Thus, the wish expressed by some families created through gamete donation to present themselves as a 'normal' family is not an option in the case of surrogacy. Parents did not seem to see surrogacy as something to keep secret, as shown by the large numbers who reported that there was no reason not to tell the child or others" (p. 1341).

Overall, lesbian donor insemination families and single mothers are more likely to disclose than heterosexual families (Golombok, 2002). Parents offer other reasons for secrecy. "Some parents were concerned that their child would not feel 'normal' if they were told and they wanted them to have a normal childhood" (Readings et al., 2011, p. 490).

Other parents worried about the child's lack of awareness about the possible negative social attitudes concerning the use of the new reproductive technologies. As one mother who used an egg donor to reach parenthood said

> I am concerned that my child is not old enough to understand the potential sensitivity of the subject and might tell other people, including peers, leaving themselves open to negative reactions or teasing: "I don't know how to approach that bit. I just don't want him to compromise himself, you know, without realizing" (Readings et al., p. 491).

Another common reason for secrecy about their child's origins is to avoid misunderstanding and confusion due to children's young age and their inability to comprehend issues surrounding their conception. Some parents struggle with the decision about the best time to disclose and how to tell the child's conception story. Others admitted to concerns about the negative effect that disclosure might have on the relationship between the child and their parents, in particular the nongenetic parent. The realization that one or both of their social or functional parents are not their biological parents may weaken the child's ties to their social parents. As one donor insemination mother worried: "Um, I think as well that she might feel that [father] wasn't her 'dad' dad" (Readings et al., p. 490). In turn, by undermining the quality of the parent–child relationship, the child's development may be impaired. Parents may be worried about their child's possible desire to search for, locate, and even form a relationship with their donor parent(s). The contracting parents may be concerned that contact with and potential social ties to biological parents may be a further threat to the quality of their own relationship with their child. Closely related is the concern that the introduction of others (donors, surrogate) within the social boundaries of the family may create ambiguity and confusion for the child and further undermine the stability of not only the parent child ties but the marital relationship as well. Moreover, the potential disruption of daily family rhythms and routines by the need to include or accommodate other "expanded" family members is a further argument for secrecy as well as for endorsing a restricted definition of family boundaries. Unfortunately, in their quest to protect the parent–child relationship by withholding information, parents may be inadvertently undermining the relationship. To illustrate, mothers in nondisclosing gamete-donation families showed less positive interactions with their seven year olds than mothers in natural-conception families which argues for greater openness about a child's genetic origins rather than secrecy (Golombok, Readings, Blake, Casey, Mellish et al., 2011).

*The Case Against Secrecy:*    Not all parents and experts agree that secrecy is either justified or even necessary. Many question whether the effort to protect the child from their conception history is in the child's best interests. Parents cite several reasons for a full disclosure policy. Some parents believe that the child has the right to know the truth about their origins, while other parents simply endorse a policy of being honest with their children.

> With respect to the desire to be honest, some parents felt their child ought to know about their own "story" and felt it was positive for their child to know. Some felt that knowing about the conception would show the child how 'wanted' they were: "I think it's very important for children to know where they came from and it would be just wrong, morally wrong, to withhold that information from him" (DI mother); "You

know it's not a shameful thing and there's nothing for her to be ashamed of being born in that way, it's something that she should be proud of really" (gestational surrogacy mother) (Readings et al., 2011, p. 489).

Another reason for disclosure is to avoid the child finding the truth in other circumstances or from other people: As one genetic surrogacy mother noted "I don't like lies.... And I didn't want it to be a sort of dirty secret." Similarly, a genetic surrogacy father cautioned "If you try not to tell them ever, if ever they find out, it destroys any trust they've got in you" (Readings et al., 2011, p. 490). Secrecy only complicates matters for the offspring as well as the parents. Another reason for disclosing their child's genetic/biological history is that this information can serve as a valuable guide in their child's future health decisions. As we increase our knowledge about the genetic bases of disease, children who are armed with an awareness of their genetic ties will clearly be advantaged. Some have argued (Bauman, 2001) that a child has a right to information about the donor, especially if evidence of a genetic illness is present. Another reason for disclosure is that knowledge of their genetic history can be helpful in their identity formation process. Although less concrete than the health issues, this identity formation issue may be just or more important for the developing child – in this case for their mental rather than their physical health. Knowing whether the biological parent is a musician, an accountant, or an antique dealer may be helpful in forming one's own sense of self. As one donor assisted young adult lamented "There's so much curiosity, I want to see how we're alike, how we're different. Is he in business? Is he not? Does he run marathons? All the stuff that is unique to me, you wonder how much of it comes from my mom or comes from the environment or comes from the donor." Another young man in his early 20s put it this way "There's this whole half of me that is completely missing," says Hunter, who has been looking for his biological father for two years. "To be asked why you want to look (for your parent) is like asking why you have to breathe. It's an essential component of human nature to want to know more about yourself and how you got to be here"(Ogilvie, 2009).The issue of identity is often reported by young children and adolescents as a major motivator of their desire to know their conception background (Readings et al., 2011). While the debate about disclosure continues, it is not surprising that ART children are curious to unveil their biological past.

## Who Is Right – the Nondisclosers or the Disclosers?

So who is right – the parents who keep the secret about their child's conception or the other parents who tell it like it happened and give their child an accurate account of their unique route to life? To try to answer this question, we will assess whether the fears are justified. As we will see, most of the evidence suggests that these parental concerns about revealing the facts about their child's origins are unwarranted.

*The Confused and Misunderstanding Child:* The evidence does not support parental concerns that the child will be confused or distressed by the news of their conception. In spite of the fact that nondisclosure is the rule in ART families, in one study of parents who did inform their children, the majority (57%) reported good feelings about the disclosure (Rumball & Adair, 1999). In surrogacy assisted families, parents reported that 90% of their 10 year old children had either a full or some understanding of the process (Jadva et al., 2012).As one 10 year old explained "Well my Mum's womb, I think well it was a bit broken, so [surrogate mother] carried me instead of my Mum" (Jadva et al., p. 4). Other reports confirm that these fears are unwarranted. In one study, four to eight year old donor insemination children reacted positively to parental disclosure of the truth about their origins (Lycett, Daniels, Curson, & Golombok, 2005) while seven year old children who were told that they were conceived with the help of either a sperm or egg donor reacted either neutrally or had no reaction at all (Blake, Casey, Readings, Jadva, & Golombok, 2010). No high drama was evident, in part, because parents delivered the news in a story like fashion and in language that children understood. For example, one mother described the egg donation process as follows: "I didn't have any eggs and some very kind person very kindly gave them to us, because we wanted you so much and that we've, you know, got you, which is the most wonderful thing" (Blake et al., p. 2530). Another mother who used donor sperm to conceive gave this explanation "Daddy's run out of tadpoles and that we had to go out and get some tadpoles from somebody else" (Blake et al., p. 2530).

As these parental explanations suggest, by tailoring the way in which the conception history is told to the developmental level of the child, much of the concern about upset and misunderstanding can be avoided or at least minimized. Moreover, we should not underestimate children's capacity to understand these issues. In fact, children begin to understand the causal nature of the reproductive process by ages 7 or 8 and gradually develop a relatively accurate comprehension of the process by ages 11 or 12 (Bernstein & Cowan, 1975). Moreover, there are books available for young children (two years and up) such as Schaffer's (1988) *How Babies and Families Are Made (There Is More Than One Way)* that explain the new reproductive technologies in a simple, but accessible way to children. Others such as *My Story* (Cooke, 1991) and *Mommy Was Your Tummy Big?* (Nadel, 2007) focus on donor conception families. In her book, *Kangaroo Pouch: A Story About Gestational Surrogacy for Young Children*, Sarah Phillips Pellet (2006) addresses the issue of surrogacy for two to eight year old children. Work that explores in more detail the development of children's understanding of various aspects of ART would be useful not only for better assessing the impact of disclosure but as a guide for parents who are the first responders in the disclosure process. Therefore, while parents need to be sensitive to the age related limitations of their children's comprehension, there are means of communicating the central "facts" about their child's origins that are age appropriate.

As ART procedures become more widely used and accepted, perhaps the curtain of secrecy will gradually fall just as it has in the case of adoptive families where openness is now relatively common (Grotevant, 2007). In fact, adoptees are encouraged to seek their birth parents and are aided by government and private registries in their search. By contrast, parents who use third party gametes need not tell children the truth about their conceptions. Nor is anyone who knows the identity of the genetic parent required to disclose this fact to the child, even when the child becomes an adult. However, based on related work on open versus closed adoptions, it is clear that disclosure rather than secrecy is better for children's emotional adjustment (Grotevant, 2007). The Standish -McCloud family who we met earlier not only followed an open adoption policy with their two adopted children but plan to include the biological parents in their children's lives as well.

# Is Three or More a Crowd? The Effects of Contact between Surrogates, Donors, or Donor Siblings

Another major concern of social parents is that parent–child ties and the stability of their family lives will be disrupted by the disclosure and possible involvement of other contributors such as egg or sperm donors or surrogates. However, the landscape of secrecy and anonymity of donors is rapidly shifting, which means that this is a reality that many parents are going to confront even if their initial goal is to be secretive. Although anonymity was common in the early years of egg and sperm donation, in recent years,

> The principle of donor anonymity has now been questioned and, in many instances, removed from regulatory frameworks that guide the provision of assisted conception. Various systems of open-identity donation now operate in the USA as well as in Sweden, Austria, Switzerland, the Australian State of Victoria, The Netherlands, New Zealand and, most recently, the UK (Freeman, Jadva, Kramer, & Golombok, 2009, p. 505).

Even in countries where anonymous sperm donation is available, such as the United States, some clinics offer "open-identity donors," where the identity of the donor can be given to the child once she/he reaches the age of 18. This reflects the changing understanding that *donor-conceived* children have always been" the missing voices" in the debate over how we handle infertility according to bioethicist Juliet Guichon (2010). And many offspring are eager to know their conception history. The proliferation of websites, search engines, and online registries devoted to help locate sperm or egg donors is making the task easier and more likely to lead to success. (See DonorOffspringRegistry.com, donor sibling registry; Inside parentcentral.ca; Searching for my donor father.org; DonorOffspringHealth.com.DonorOffspringMatches.com.) These are busy and active sites; for example, the Donor Sibling Registry (January, 2012), has helped to connect more than 9007 half siblings (and/or donors) with each other. The total number of registrants, including donors, parents and donor conceived people, is 35,100. And there has been a new documentary film released that presents the voices of offspring of sperm donors, entitled *Anonymous Fathers Day*. The film features male and female offsprings from 17 to 65 from three continents who share their views on being the product of a sperm donor.

*Contact between Surrogates and Contracting Families (Parents and Children):*   What happens to the family relationships when children learn the identity of their donors or their surrogate mother? Although there are horror stories of surrogates who do not want to relinquish the infant that they have carried in their womb or wish to play central and intrusive roles in the family, the vast majority of the empirical evidence suggests that these dire predictions of family mayhem or worse are unfounded. The Baby M case in which the surrogate mother, Mary Beth Whitehead refused to turn over the baby who was biologically related to the contracting father, William Stern even though she had agreed to relinquish the baby to the Sterns captured national attention in the mid 1980s but was an anomaly rather than a harbinger of future problems (Twine, 2011). Nearly all surrogacy arrangements proceed according to plan with the infant being placed with the contracting couple. And the post birth contacts between surrogates and the contracting parents generally proceed smoothly as well. Assessments of both surrogates and contracting couples suggest that there are few reports of conflict or difficulties with the post birth social contact arrangements. According to a British study (Jadva, Murray, Lycett, MacCallum, & Golombok, 2003), surrogate mothers do not generally experience major problems in their relationship with the commissioning couple, in handing over the baby, or from the reactions of those around them. Most surrogates maintained some contact with both the contracting parents and with the child; nearly 80% saw the parents between once a month and once a year, clearly enough to maintain social ties but far from intrusive in the lives of the contracting parents. The surrogates kept in touch with the child as well: 32% had contact with their "womb child" once a month and another 44% between once a month and once a year. Only 24% had no contact with the child. Follow up assessments after 10 years since the birth indicated that contact between surrogacy families and their surrogate mother decreased over time, particularly for families whose surrogate was a previously unknown genetic carrier (i.e., where they had met through a third party and the surrogate mother's egg was used to conceive the child). Contact decreased less when there was a previously established relationship between the family and the surrogate (Jadva et al., 2012). Even when contact was absent, 67% of surrogates were satisfied with this outcome since they had made a mutual decision with the intended parents not to maintain contact with the child (Jadva & Imrie, 2013).

Moreover, the quality of the surrogate–child relationship depends on whether the surrogate is known such as a sister, a friend, or a mother rather than unknown (a stranger). While 86% of the known surrogates reported that they felt a special relationship with the child, only 30% of the unknown surrogates felt this way. Finally, even the surrogates' own children were generally positive about the arrangement with 88% being positive; the rest were neutral or ambivalent (Jadva et al., 2003). Over half of the children (12–25 years old) of gestational surrogates were in contact with the surrogacy child in contrast to only 33% of genetic surrogates. Some of the children did not have contact with the target surrogacy child but had contact with some of their mother's other surrogacy children. In total, 81% of children of gestational surrogates had contact with a surrogacy child, compared to 50% of children of genetic surrogates (Jadva & Imrie, 2013).

The contracting couple report similar positive experiences regarding their relationships with the surrogate who carried their child (MacCallum et al., 2003). Over 90% of commissioning mothers and commissioning fathers had seen the surrogate mother at least once since the birth, while 76% of the surrogates had been in contact with their "womb child." Sixty-four percent of mothers and children and 60% of fathers, continued to see the surrogate mother every couple of months over the first year. Over 90% of the contracting mothers reported harmonious relationships with their surrogate following the birth of the child while nearly the same was true for fathers (89%). In cases where there had been contact between the child and the surrogate mother, 92% of mothers and 90% of fathers felt positive about the surrogate mother's involvement in the child's life. There is little evidence of problems between surrogates and contracting parents. Instead, these accounts of the integration of other individuals such as surrogates into the lives of ART families illustrate the ways in which multiple nonfamily players can contribute in meaningful ways to a child's life.

*Contact between Egg and Sperm Donors and Contracting Families (Parents and Children):* The issue of the relationships between egg and sperm donors and the children who are conceived through donor assistance and the impact of contact between donors and their offspring on social parent–offspring relationships has only recently been examined. In spite of the limited attention to this issue, a large numbers of adults who were conceived with sperm donor assistance are curious about their sperm donor father. To better understand the experiences of adolescents and adults who were searching for and contacting their sperm donor fathers, Jadva and her coworkers (2010) studied 165 offspring; she found that over three quarters of the offspring were searching for their donor. Although concerns have been raised that searching for their sperm donor would have negative effects on their social relationships with the parents who raised them, the investigators found that many had positive reactions from their mother (27%) and another 63% indicated that their mother's reaction was neutral/mixed; only 2% reported that the search caused a negative impact on their relationship with their mother. One might expect fathers would be threatened by their sons' and daughters' search for their genetic donor and lead to strained father–offspring relationship. However, the offspring's relationship with their fathers did not suffer either: most offspring (78%) reported a neutral/mixed reaction, 19% reported a positive response and only 3% indicted that the search had a negative effect on their relationship with their father. While only a small number of offspring (9%) found and contacted their donor, most (80%) of those who had contact reported that their experiences were positive, some were neutral (10%) and a small minority (10%) were negative. Moreover, they stayed in touch with their donor figure with half seeing him at least once a month and another 40% every 1–3 months.

Here is a sample of respondent reactions to contact with their donor father

> I am so glad that I met him, and would not trade the world for the experience I had. We communicate in some form or another at least every other day, and he is one of the most important people in my life to this day (13-year-old male, from heterosexual couple family).

> I used to think of the donor as sort of a super-human…perfect in a lot of ways (based on knowing he was chosen out of a catalogue). Now I know he's just a normal guy (19-year-old female, from lesbian couple family).

The one offspring who reported that contact with her donor had been a negative experience commented:

> I did not meet my biological father. I only exchanged a few letters with him. His responses were clear that although he's glad that I was born, he is not proud to have participated in donor conception.... It is a pretty bad feeling that my life has been such a source of shame and embarrassment, through no fault of my own, by the people who brought me into the world (40-year-old female, from heterosexual couple family) (Jadva et al., 2010, p. 530).

Nor was the contact limited to just their donor father. Donor offspring were also in contact with their donors' family, including the donor's children and parents who are effectively the offspring's half siblings and grandparents, respectively.

As one young woman wrote:

> In addition to the donor, I have met one of his children from his marriage, his mother, one of his brothers, sister in-law, niece, and 2 other half siblings and their respective mothers (15-year-old female, from single mother family) (Jadva et al., 2010, p. 530).

> Donor offspring viewed these individuals as members of their extended family. Thus the practice of donor conception is in some cases leading to new family relationships based on genetic connections and between individuals who had grown up apart (Jadva et al., 2010, p. 531).

Just as we saw in the case of contact between surrogates and their gestational off-spring, searching for and contacting a sperm-donor dad was overall not a disruptive or harmful experience.

Similarly, recent findings on intrafamily egg donation from a sister or sister-in law suggests that the children and the recipients and their partners have a positive relation-ship with the donor relative and the mothers reported to be satisfied with the donor's level of involvement with the child (Jadva, Casey, Readings, Blake, & Golombok, 2011). No problems of role ambiguity were found. Most egg donors maintained their social roles within the family and were treated as aunts while the recipient mother continued to be viewed as the mother. For example, one mother described the donor's role this way:

> She's very, um, I don't know what the word is really, not detached, but just very much, you know, stepped back... If she sends a card she always sends it 'to my nephew'. (Jadva et al., p. 3).

Other mothers reported that the donor played a special family role such as a god-mother. While many do not disclose the conception story, when they do, effort is made to stress the separate roles played by donor and birth mother. In spite of the intention of most mothers to tell their child, by age seven, only one mother had done so. This mother had explained to her child that the egg had been donated by her sister (the child's aunt) but stressed her own connection to the child:

> But we're always very clear that she grew in mummy's tummy and all of that so she knows that that connection is there.... I don't want her to think that (egg donor) is her mummy... and I don't think to be fair that (egg donor) wants that either (Jadva et al., p. 4).

*Contact between Half Siblings and the Contracting Family (Parents and Children):* The search for donors by children conceived with donor assistance is well known and increasingly common just as in the case of adopted children's search for their biological parents. But many donor assisted children are conducting another search – the search for half siblings who are the consequence of the use of a single sperm donor by several parents. In this case, a single sperm donor may be the genetic father of several donor children who are therefore donor siblings or their genetic half siblings, what one observer described as "an extended family of sorts for modern times."

Here is a typical scenario: Hunter, 24, and Martin, 23, were conceived with donated sperm by supposedly different donors. In the mid-1980s, their mothers sought help from the same small fertility clinic at the Health Sciences Centre in London, Ontario. After their husbands were deemed infertile, the two women chose to be impregnated with a stranger's sperm. Neither one wanted – or was encouraged – to meet the donor. However, when their offspring learned about their conception history, these two young men found each other – their long lost half siblings.

While meeting one or two half siblings is desirable and manageable, sometimes the number of half siblings can be over whelming. Since there is little regulation of how often the donated sperm of one individual can be used, this can lead to an extreme extended family size! In one case, a single sperm donor was the genetic parent for 150 offspring – an outcome that has led to demands for better regulation (Mroz, 2011).

> Now, there is growing concern among parents, donors and medical experts about potential negative consequences of having so many children fathered by the same donors, includ- ing the possibility that genes for rare diseases could be spread more widely through the population. Some experts are even calling attention to the increased odds of accidental incest between half sisters and half brothers, who often live close to one another (Mroz, p.1).

Although there are few guidelines to follow about contact between these half siblings, some recent studies have described the process of searching for siblings who share a genetic father. In one study (Freeman et al., 2009), nearly 800 parents from different family types (heterosexual couples, lone mothers and lesbian couples) discussed their reasons for searching for their child's half siblings. Family type matters as we saw in the search for donors. The minority (19%) of those searching for donor siblings were heterosexual-couple parents, compared with 43% who were lone mothers and 38% who were lesbian couple mothers (Freeman et al.). Eighty-five percent of the parents cited "curiosity (e.g., about similarities in appearance and personality)" as one of the reasons for their search for their child's donor siblings while over 60% men- tioned the desire for their child to have a better understanding of who he/she is or to help them have a secure sense of identity. Other reasons included: To have a better understanding of their child's genetic makeup and to gain a better understanding of their child's ancestral history and family background. Nearly a third of the parents wanted their child to have a sibling and develop a sense of kinship. In several studies, the investigators found that most parents who had contacted their child's donor siblings reported this to be a positive experience (Freeman et al.).

What about the experiences of the children themselves who are searching for and make contact with their genetic half siblings? In a related study, 78% of the children were searching for their donor siblings, nearly the same as the percentage of children who were searching for their donor parent (77%) (Jadva et al., 2010). The offspring them- selves gave similar reasons (curiosity, identity) as their parents for wanting to find their half siblings but their reasons vary with the age at which they discovered their conception history. Offspring who had found out about their conception after age 18 were more likely to be searching for medical reasons, whereas those who had found out before age 18 tended to be searching out of curiosity (Jadva et al.). As we saw in the case of relation- ships with donors, the majority of children who located and contacted their half sibs reported positive experiences and remained in regular contact with them. Here is the reaction of one respondent who had met six half siblings:

> It has become like a common occurrence and I don't expect any of the meetings to go badly, because it is like we have known each other all our lives even though we did not grow up together (16-year-old male, from heterosexual-couple family) (Jadva et al., p. 528).

Moreover, there was little evidence that the discovery of their half siblings interfered with or undermined their relationships with the siblings that they grew up with. In fact, some commented on how they did not see their donor siblings in the same way as their full siblings:

> I still think of my full-blood sister as more of a sister than my 2 donor siblings. But then again, I have had my full-blood sister in my life since the day I was born, so there's just a stronger feeling of connection and understanding in the relationship. My donor siblings are not quite in the 'family fold' (19-year-old female, from lesbian couple family) (Jadva et al., 2010, p. 529).

Many questions remain, especially the long-term relationships between ART children and their biological donors or surrogates. Do the relationships remain cordial and limited or does the child seek greater contact especially during adolescence, a time of identity formation and self exploration? Nor do we know the potential positive effects of having another caring person such as a surrogate or a donor in a child's life. Just as relatives and nonrelated adults can play supportive supplementary roles in children's lives, it is quite likely that surrogates or donors could potentially have positive effects on children as they develop. The child can enjoy an expanded set of "family" members who can offer stimulation and guidance. Perhaps the nonfamily players themselves can benefit by being part of "their" child's life, just as the parents can benefit from the support and assistance of these other figures. This expanded family form is common in other cultures (Hrdy, 2009; Rogoff, 2003 and as discussed in the next chapter) and perhaps such an alternative family model can benefit children and parents in our culture too. Finally, "these studies highlight the way in which donor conception is resulting in the creation of new family formations that are based purely on genetic relatedness" (Jadva et al., 2010, p. 524). Not only the forms that families assume but the ways that families are created are undergoing a transformation. Family forms in which multiple players beyond the contracting parents play a role in the child's life are clearly viable and increasingly common alternatives to the more restricted "ideal" family form. The "ideal" family form is clearly not the only feasible one and perhaps not the most desirable one.

*Children Cannot Handle Multiple Social Relationships:*  Another concern is that children will be confused and unable to manage multiple social relationships that may result from the involvement of other individuals such as sperm or egg donors or surrogates in their family world. Again the evidence suggests that these fears are largely unfounded. From early in life, children are socially, emotionally, and cognitively equipped not only to understand multiple relationships but form healthy, but separate social ties with multiple individuals including not only parents but with members of their extended families such as aunts, uncles and grandparents, and nonfamily members as well (Howes & Spieker, 2008; Thompson, 2006). Moreover, infants, children and adolescents form meaningful social relationships with a variety of nonfamily members including nannies, teachers, preachers, and coaches (Greenberger, Chen, & Beam, 1998; Thompson, 2006). In spite of the concerns on the part of the Millers, who we introduced in the opening chapter, about using child care for their children, we know that children are not only capable of forming close ties to nonfamily caregivers, but this does not undermine the quality of the child's attachment relationship with their primary caregivers (Clarke-Stewart & Allhusen, 2005; Rankin, 2005; see chapter 2).

As we will show in Chapter 7, evidence from intracultural inquiries in the United States of African American, Latino, and Asian American families suggest that these concerns about the involvement of extrafamilial social players in the lives of nuclear family members are misplaced and unjustified. For example, many African American and Latino families develop extensive networks of kin and fictive kin who play a role in family life and in the socialization of children (Baca-Zinn & Wells, 2000; Parke & Buriel, 2006). Similarly, an abundance of cross cultural evidence (see Chapter 6) suggests that shared responsibility for child rearing with members of the community are the rule rather than the exception. And the social–emotional and economic support provided by these nonfamily social networks are beneficial to both adults and children (Cochran & Niego, 2002; Coleman, 1988; Stack, 1974). In short, the imagined violation of the "ideal" family form often prevents families from embracing more fluid social boundaries that may, in fact, be valuable.

## The New Legal Landscape and the Rights of Donors and Surrogates

Together these lines of evidence are consistent with the view that the development of multiple relationships with nonfamily members are not harmful for children but normative in many cultures and potentially beneficial for the developing child. It is not only the child and the contracting parents who merit consideration but the rights and responsibilities of the other players – the egg and sperm donors and surrogates need to be recognized as well. A narrow and exclusionary view of family boundaries in the case of the ART-conceived family, comes at a price paid for by the other players whose rights to contact with either the child or the contracting couple are severely restricted or eliminated. However, not all donors or surrogates wish to either remain anonymous or be excluded from being part of "their" child's life and, in fact, can benefit by playing a role in the family. Some recent court decisions in North America recognize that in this era of new reproductive technologies, three may not be a crowd. A 2007 Pennsylvania case, *Jacob v. Shultz-Jacob*, involved two lesbians who were the legal coparents of two children conceived with sperm donated by a friend. The panel held that the sperm donor and both women were all liable for child support and both had visitation rights. In another case in Ontario, Canada, the courts ruled that a child can legally have three parents. Not only did the biological mother and father have parental rights but the biological mother's lesbian partner, who functions as the boy's second mother had such rights as well. The idea of assigning children three legal parents is not limited to North America (Marquardt, 2011). In 2005, expert commissions in Australia and New Zealand proposed that sperm or egg donors be allowed to "opt in" as a child's third parent. Entertainment of a new or at least a more expanded definition of the "ideal" family would be welcome and potentially helpful for both the social parents and their ART offspring as well as for the other partners in this cooperative reproductive process.

## Are ART Parents Adequate and Are Their Children Developing Normally?

Any discussion of alternative formulations of family forms needs to address the ultimate test: are the children reared in new family forms or in the case of the present chapter conceived in new ways developing adequately? And since quality of parenting is the process through which children's development is to a large degree affected, a related concern is whether alternative routes to parenthood leads to less than adequate parenting. This concern – whether well founded or not – flows from a cultural belief that naturalness and perfection are closely intertwined. In turn, as noted earlier, parents may feel less adequate and confident as parents due to their experience with infertility. In the case of individuals or couples who choose nonnatural strategies such as the use of a surrogate to achieve parenthood, the lack of biological preparation associated with pregnancy and birth such as the myriad of hormonal changes that occur for women and as we saw earlier for men as well are absent. In turn, without the hormonally linked biological preparedness, perhaps parenting will be less adequate. While there is clear evidence from animal studies, there is less evidence that hormonal priming is necessary for adequate parenting in humans (Lamb, 1975).The adoption literature (Brodzinsky & Pinderhughes, 2002; Grotevant & McRoy, 1998) provides rich and persuasive evidence that satisfactory parent–child relationships, including parent–child attachment can develop between adopted infants and their adopting parents in the absence of biological preparedness. Nonetheless, the parent may perceive and behave differently toward a nongestational child than toward a child that one has conceived and delivered naturally. Moreover, in the case of surrogacy, the separation of gestational parenthood from social parenthood is similar to adoption – in that the mother who gives birth relinquishes the child to other parents. It might be expected, therefore, that children born through surrogacy, like adopted children, will show more psychological problems.

Even in less extreme cases where no surrogate is involved, such as IVF or ICSI families, cultural attitudes concerning the inadequacy of couples or individuals who need to resort to these nonnatural means to achieve parenthood may undermine parental confidence or lead to overly high expectations for themselves as parents. For example, Louise Brown, the mother of the world's first IVF baby, reported that she felt pressure from others: "Having a miracle was a lot to live up to. I felt as if the whole world expected me to be the perfect mother" (1979, as cited in McMahon & Gibson, 2002). As a result of these lofty expectations IVF parents may be more anxious, as they strive to meet these standards of parenting (McMahon, Ungerer, Beaurepaire, Tennant, & Saunders, 1995). Or parents worry that IVF children may be seen as different within the family (Van Balen, 1998). Other concerns involve being overprotective of an IVF child as a result of the long and sometimes difficult period of failure to produce a child (Hahn & DiPietro, 2001). On the other hand, infertile parents who rely on egg or sperm donors may be less involved with their nongenetically related children just as stepparents are often more distant from their stepchildren than their genetically related offspring (Dunn, Davies, O'Connor, & Sturgess, 2000). In spite of the concerns, there is little evidence that ART parents are very different from parents who achieve parenthood the old fashioned natural way (Golombok, 2006). Several aspects of parenting have been examined: the quality of their relationships with their children, the psychological well-being of parents themselves, and their security and sense of confidence in the parental role.

*Parent–Child Relationships:*   To evaluate these concerns and in view of the fact that parent–child relationships are important predictors of subsequent child adjustment, several studies have examined this issue. The worries seem to be not as evident as the doomsayers might expect. Even during pregnancy, IVF mothers were bonded to their unborn children just as much as natural conception mothers (Hjelmstedt, WidstrÖm, & Collins, 2006). Observational studies of mothers interacting with their young infants found no differences in the security of infant–mother attachment between IVF and natural conception families (Colpin, Demyttenaere, & Vandemeulebroecke, 1995; McMahon & Gibson, 2002). With infant offspring IVF mothers are more positive and warmer than naturally conceiving mothers (Gibson, Ungerer, Tennant, & Saunders, 2000). With preschoolers and early school age children, IVF parents are more emotionally involved, showed greater warmth, interact more and report less parenting stress in comparison to natural conception parents. IVF dads are more involved and report less parenting stress as well. Since IVF parents tend to be older, this heightened involvement may reflect the general trend that older parents are more involved than younger parents (Bornstein & Putnick, 2007).

And the pattern persists into adolescence. In their multicountry, longitudinal European Study of Assisted Reproduction Families (United Kingdom, the Netherlands, Spain and Italy) Golombok and her colleagues found that IVF parents exhibited similar levels of affection and appropriate levels of discipline and control with their teens in early adolescence as natural parents (Golombok, MacCallum, & Goodman, 2001; Golombok et al., 2002). However, the more positive findings for the IVF families in comparison with the natural conception families were no longer apparent in later adolescence (Golombok et al., 2001, 2002). In a study of 15- to 16-year olds conceived by IVF, no differences in parenting style or parenting stress were found between IVF and natural conception mothers or fathers (Colpin & Bossaert, 2008). At age 18, IVF adolescents were continuing to get along as well with their mothers and fathers as children of natural parents; similar levels of closeness, warmth, and attachment were evident and there were no differences in parent adolescent conflict either (Golombok, Owen, Blake, Murray, & Jadva, 2009). Moreover, Owen and Golombok (2009) reported that donor insemination mothers were warmer with their late adolescents than either IVF or natural conceiving mothers. Since the natural conception mothers were not low in warmth, it suggests that the DI mothers were especially high in their expressed warmth. There were no differences in parent–adolescent conflict across the groups. Fathers from different groups were similar in their warmth and conflict scores even though one might have expected that father–adolescent relationships among sperm-donor families might be more distant or conflictful. Even without genetic ties the parent–adolescent relationships were not different than naturally conceived children and their fathers.

Another route to parenthood is through surrogacy. Comparisons between egg donation families in which the mother experienced the pregnancy and surrogacy families, where the mother did not experience the pregnancy revealed no differences in the quality of parent–child relationships when the child was three years of age

(Golombok, 2006). In follow up reports, Golombok and her colleagues (Golombok, Readings, Blake, Casey, Marks et al., 2011; Golombok, Readings, Blake, Casey, Mellish et al., 2011) examined the mother–child relationships in families of seven year olds created through surrogacy, egg donation, and natural conception. Again no differences were found for maternal negativity or positivity. However, the surrogacy and egg donation families showed less positive mother–child interaction than the natural conception families. These differences were largely accounted for by the gamete donation families who had not disclosed the donor conception to the child, which underscores the importance of open communication between parents and children about their origins. In spite of these small differences, it seems clear that the parent–child relationships in both surrogacy and egg donation families are not a cause for concern in the early school years. This suggests that the absence of a genetic or gestational link between the mother and the child does not appear to negatively alter parent–child relationships. The downside was small and mainly centered on more overprotectiveness by IVF parents (Hahn & DiPietro, 2001), a not surprising finding in view of the arduous steps and investment in time, money, and anxiety that is often associated with ART. The thinking seems to be: It was a tough road to get here and we are going to do our best to make sure our baby is going to be ok!!

One caveat: many of the studies of parent–child relationships involved single child births so that the route to parenthood was not confounded with the issue of multiple birth families. However, in light of the fact that a significant proportion of ART families result in multiple births, it will be important to revisit this issue of parent–child relationships to determine whether the conclusions apply not just to ART singletons but to families of twins and triplets as well.

*Parental Psychological Well-Being and Problems:*   In the case of both IVF and ICSI families, the rate of psychological maladies such as anxiety or depression among these parents in comparison with "natural" parents was similar (Golombok, 2006). In surrogacy families, one year after their child's birth, mothers and fathers were less stressed and reported better well-being compared to egg donor or natural conceiving families (Golombok, Murray, Jadva, MacCallum, & Lycett, 2004). Across several countries including not just the United States but Great Britain, Australia, the Netherlands, France, Greece, Sweden, Belgium and Denmark, ART mothers are well adjusted (Golombok). In the case of both naturally conceiving parents and ART parents, adjustment varies with the social support provided by others in the nuclear and extended family and friendship networks (Cowan & Cowan, 2000; Gameiro, Moura-Ramos, Canavarro, & Soares, 2011). In a recent Portuguese study, social support, especially from close family members such as siblings and extended family members is negatively related to postpartum stress in naturally conceiving parents and ART mothers (Gameiro, Moura-Ramos et al., 2011). For fathers, emotional and instrumental support from friends rather than family play a significant role in alleviating stress over the first few months after the transition to parenthood in both natural and ART families (Gameiro, Nazaré, Fonseca, Moura-Ramos, & Canavarro, 2011).

Similarly, marital satisfaction in most cases does not vary across parents who use different routes to parenthood (Moura-Ramos, Gameiro, Soares, Santos, & Canavarro, 2010). There are some exceptions: in Australia, Cohen and colleagues (2000) found that both ICSI mothers and fathers reported elevated levels of marital stress. Similarly, according to this same Australian study team, fathers of 12 month old IVF infants reported lower levels of marital satisfaction than spontaneously conceiving fathers (Gibson et al., 2000). Perhaps mothers are more protective of these IVF infants and act as gatekeepers to limit paternal involvement or devote large amounts of time to the baby and not enough to their partner to maintain high levels of marital satisfaction. Others have suggested that using a sperm donor may produce "confusion about paternity" (Snowden, 1988), negative feelings about not being able to act like a real father (David & Avidan, 1976) or feelings of inadequacy (Warnock, 1987). However, later studies of DI parents found that fathers reported that DI did not influence their relationship with their child and felt themselves to be "real" fathers (Brewaeys, 1996, 2001). This may reflect an increase in the acceptance of ART procedures and a greater understanding of these alternative routes to parenthood. However, it is clear that more work needs to be focused on differences in mother/father adjustment following the use of different ART procedures.

## Are Children Conceived through the Use of ART at Risk?

Although infertility treatment, including ART, is generally safe, adverse outcomes have been described both in women undergoing ART and in infants born from these procedures (Van Voorhis, 2006). Women are at elevated risk for pregnancy complications, especially if they are carrying multiple fetuses. Both birth related risk of physical–cognitive defects and later social, emotional, and cognitive developmental risks have been noted among some infants and children conceived with ART. The risk of birth defects in infants conceived through ICSI or IVF is about 30–40% higher than in spontaneously conceived infants (Hansen, Bower, Milne, de Klerk, & Kurinczuk, 2005).

*Multiple Births, Multiple Problems:* This higher incidence of problems is, in part, due to the fact that there is a higher rate of multiple births among infants conceived through ART approaches, which increases the risk to both mother and infant. While twins, triplets, and beyond occur in only 1% of natural births, the rate is dramatically higher – at least 25% – among IVF births (Nyboe Andersen, Gianaroli, & Nygren, 2004) due to the fact that multiple embryos are often transferred in the hope that a viable pregnancy will ensue. Although there is scant government regulation aimed at limiting multiple births associated with ART procedures in the United states, Europe has been more successful in reducing the rate of multiple births by mandating that only a single embryo be transferred into a women under thirty-six and only two in older women (Spar, 2006).

The chance of having twins skyrocketed between 1980 and 2009, when the rate of twin births in the United States doubled and the rate of triplet births increased over threefold (Centers for Disease Control and Prevention, 2011). In 2009, there were 33.2 twin births for every 1000 births, for a total of 137,217 sets of twins born and there were nearly 6000 triplet births, 355 quadruplet births and 80 quintuplets and other higher order births (Centers for Disease Control and Prevention). While some of this increase is due to ART, some is due to women conceiving naturally at older ages when ovulation produces more than a single egg and also to the increased use of fertility drugs (Mundy, 2007).

Multiple birth infants compared to singletons are more likely to be low-birth weight, be born prematurely, suffer restricted fetal growth, and even die at birth (Jackson, Gibson, Wu, & Croughan, 2004). This is especially evident in developing and newly industrialized countries such as Latin America where the rate of multiple births for assisted reproduction pregnancies was 50%; nearly 14% of these ART births yielded triplets or quadruplets (Zegers-Hochschild, 2002). Recently, public health experts recommend that

> For infertile women who have a good prognostic profile (i.e., a high expected probability of success with ART), perhaps the simplest and most effective strategy for reducing the risk of adverse ART outcomes is elective single embryo transfer (SET). The SET protocol carries a much lower risk of multiple delivery, with consequently lower risk of adverse maternal and child health outcomes (Macaluso et al., 2010, p. e6).

Moreover, it is not merely the prenatal and birth related problems associated with multiple births but the special challenges for parents of raising more than a single infant at a time (Segal, 2007). Parents of twins frequently report more emotional and financial stress, fatigue, and depression as a result of the increased demands placed on the family raising twins or triplets. Parents express regret at not being able to spend as much individual time as they wish with each child. They are even at elevated risk for separation and divorce (McKay, 2010). In one illustrative study of IVF mothers, 22% of those who gave birth to multiple infants reported severe parenting stress in comparison to 5% of mothers of IVF singletons and 9% of mothers of naturally conceived singletons (Glazebrook, Sheard, Cox, Oates, & Ndukwe, 2004). Later work (Vilska et al., 2009) indicated that having twins is equally stressful for both naturally and ART mothers and fathers compared to parents of singletons during the first year after birth. Twin parenthood, but not ART, has a negative impact on the mental health of mothers and fathers during the transition to parenthood. However, there are positive as well as negative aspects to rearing twins. As one Australian mother of twins observed,

> "It's quite expensive having two children at the same time. You can't rely on hand-me-downs and the extra expense will be ongoing. But on the other hand, it's so much fun to watch them develop. They have their own relationship and play all these little games together. They interact in a way that is completely independent of me. It's really nice to watch that" (Raising Children's Network, 2011).

Finally, social support from spouses, friends, and relatives matters; support may be particularly helpful for parents of twins and triplets (Feldman, Eidelman, & Rotenberg, 2004) by reducing depression among mothers of twins (Kendler, Myers, & Prescott, 2005), a reminder that parenting needs to be viewed as a community responsibility rather than as the sole responsibility of parents.

*Cognitive and Social Outcomes:* In spite of some rocky beginnings for some IVF conceived children most of these children develop emotionally, socially, and cognitively as well as naturally conceived children (Golombok, 2006). However, our understanding of these outcomes is uneven and varies across the type of ART and the domain of development under consideration.

Let's begin with cognitive development of children in IVF and ICSI families. In comparisons of IVF infants and naturally conceived infants, cognitive development is very similar (Ron-El et al., 1994). Among school age children, both intellectual development and educational attainment were similar across the two groups (Levy-Shiff et al., 1998). In the case of ICSI conceived infants, few cognitive delays are evident (Golombok, 2006) and when occasional delays in ICSI infants were found (Bowen, Gibson, Louise, & Saunders, 1998), they were no longer present by age five. Similarly, no differences in the cognitive development between surrogacy supported children and naturally conceived children have been found (Golombok). To date, the use of ART approaches to parenthood is not a cause for concern about the offspring's intellectual progress. Long term follow-up studies are needed to tell us whether this holds true across time.

Perhaps socioemotional development is adversely affected as a result of parental anxiety, overprotectiveness, or marital dissatisfaction. Again to the relief of parents who have selected these alternative pathways to parenthood, there is mostly good news. Maternal anxiety among IVF mothers may contribute to parental perceptions of their infants as more temperamentally difficult, but there were no differences across IVF and naturally conceived mother–infant pairs in their security of attachment, a strong predictor of later social adjustment (Gibson et al., 2000). And in toddlerhood no behavioral differences were observed during mother–infant interaction (Colpin et al., 1995) nor any differences in children's psychological problems (Montgomery et al., 1999) among children born through IVF. In the European Study of Assisted Reproduction Families, naturally conceived and IVF four to eight year children did not differ in terms of self rated self esteem, nor in ratings of social emotional functioning by teachers or parents (Golombok et al., 1996). As expected, similar results were found for ICSI children as well: at age five there were no more social or emotional problems for these children compared to their naturally conceived peers (Barnes et al., 2004). A study of early school age children in Great Britain found continuing evidence of similar secure patterns of child–mother attachment and no differences in psychological problems across the two groups (Golombok, Cook, Bish, & Murray, 1995). No delayed effects appeared either as the children in both groups were similarly well adjusted at age 12 (Golombok et al., 2001). At age 18, a similar profile of overall satisfactory social emotional adjustment was evident (Golombok et al., 2009). Test tube babies and naturally conceived children in late adolescence both had satisfactory peer relationships, even though the IVF adolescents had greater confidence in their relationships with peers than did the naturally conceived adolescents. Contrary to expectations regarding the potentially negative consequences of high levels of parental involvement and in some cases overprotectiveness in childhood, IVF adolescents and naturally conceived teens did not differ in their levels of depression or anxiety.

In the case of gamete donation families in which either a sperm or egg donor is involved, the 5–12-year-old offspring are well-adjusted socially as well (Golombok et al., 1995, 1999, 2002). In a recent study, Golombok, Readings, Blake, Casey, Mellish et al. (2011) examined the psychological adjustment of seven-year-olds in families created through surrogacy, egg donation, and natural conception. No differences among the groups were found in child adjustment as assessed by mothers, teachers, and clinical psychologists, nor were there any differences in psychiatric symptoms. Another British team (Shelton et al., 2009) compared the adjustment of nearly 800 five- to nine-year-old children conceived through IVF, sperm donation, egg donation, ED, and surrogacy. Again there were no consistent differences in children's

adjustment problems (as rated by mothers and fathers) between the assisted reproductive technology groups and in comparison with naturally conceived children.
ART-conceived children, regardless of whether or not they are genetically related to
their parents, do not differ in their psychological adjustment. Nor do they appear to
be at greater risk of adjustment problems in middle childhood compared to naturally
conceived children. This study is noteworthy because it included not only healthy singleton births born at term but a subsample of multiple births and compared them to
an age-matched twin sample. Therefore, their sample reflects the range of children
born following ART and gives more confidence in the generalizability of the earlier
studies of social adjustment of ART children. As these studies suggest there are few
reasons for concern about the mental health of ART-conceived children.

*Long-Term Outcomes:* Most studies of assisted reproduction have focused on
relatively short-term outcomes in childhood. Less is known about long-term outcomes. To date, it appears that donor assisted adolescents are well-adjusted and not
different from their peers (Golombok et al., 2002; Golombok, Readings, Blake, Casey,
Mellish et al., 2011). Although a recent Internet survey has raised concerns about
possible negative consequences, there are limitations in the study's sampling strategies, analytic approach, and reliance on self-reports (Marquardt, Norval, Glenn, &
Clark, 2010). Moreover, since the short-term follow-up studies which found few negative effects were methodologically sound and often used multiple raters and objective
observationally based assessment of adjustment rather than self-reports, there is little
basis for expecting long-term negative outcomes. While rigorously designed long-term
follow-up studies are needed, several ongoing longitudinal studies in both Europe and
the United States will help clarify these issues.

In spite of early concerns that children raised in families who differed from the
"ideal" family form as a result of their use of nonnatural routes to parenthood would
be socially and cognitively deficient, the evidence to date suggests that these fears are
largely unfounded. Instead these findings of both satisfactory parenting and normal
social and cognitive adjustment in the children and adolescents suggests – once again –
that intrafamilial processes are better predictors of child outcomes than family form,
regardless of the roles played by ART and other social and biological contributors.

## Reflections

The new reproductive technologies are transforming and expanding the routes to
parenthood. Many individuals for whom parenthood was out of reach just decades
ago can now achieve this goal through these advances in reproductive technologies.
Moreover, these advances present a serious challenge to the "ideal" family concept
and have compelled us to reexamine our assumptions about the definition of family,
the range of family forms, and even the range of the participants in family life. At the
same time this revolution in reproduction has led to a series of vexing ethical and
social questions. The ethical debate about unequal access to these technologies as a
function of race, education, and income and the related exploitation of the poor, the
less educated, and the racial minorities in the United States is far from settled. Lessons
learned from other countries where access is more equal can be usefully applied to our

own social policies. The insights from the families formed in these alternative ways raise serious questions about the value of restricting ourselves to a single model of family and instead leads to a recognition of the strengths of various family forms. In spite of dire predictions about the serious social, emotional, and health-related problems that parents and children would confront in the brave new world of ART, our review suggests that these predictions are largely unsupported. Not only are many new families being formed that might not have been possible in the past, but the children and their parents who form these new families are thriving and flourishing just as well as naturally conceived families. The findings that parenting processes are markedly similar across various family forms created through ART is simply another reminder that family process is a better predictor of both children's and parents' adjustment and well-being than family form. Moreover, there is a growing consensus that the rights of children and the rights of the new players in the ART scenario need to be more fully recognized. Children need to know their biological roots and adult contributors of sperm, eggs, or wombs need to be recognized openly for their contributions to the family formation process. New family forms are emerging in which there are more porous boundaries that permit all players not just the contracting individuals or couples to carve out roles in the life of the family and in the lives of "their" children. The rules, roles, regulations, and responsibilities that govern these new "extended" family relationships are only beginning to be discussed, but it is clear from the early returns from the field that an expanded network is workable and perhaps beneficial for all parties – the social parents, the reproductive partners, and the children themselves. It is clear that the "ideal" family form that has dominated our views of family is not the only viable form and in the final analysis may not be the most desirable. Only more time will allow us to offer a clear verdict but it is clear that the future will embrace many more forms than the restrictive "ideal" family model. In the next two chapters, we will glimpse into the future by examining other contemporary and past cultures as well as our own ethnically diverse culture that support the possible benefits of an expanded family form for children, parents, and other nonfamily players alike.

# 6

# Many Mothers, Many Fathers, Many Others

## *Insights from Other Cultures*

*Children do best in societies where childrearing is considered too important to be left entirely to parents* (Stephanie Coontz, 1992)

As Westerners learn more about other cultures, we come to realize that our Western "ideal" family form is the exception rather than the rule across the cultures of the world. In fact, extended family arrangements and various degrees of nonfamily member involvement in the care and rearing of children is both historically and cross-culturally the norm rather than the exception (Hrdy, 2009; Rogoff, 2003). While our Western culture endorses a narrow view of the ideal family form, other cultures embrace an expanded view of the family form that includes other players beyond a mother and father in a nuclear family. This type of distributed child care has been variously described as cooperative caregiving or alloparenting. In this chapter, we will explore variations in cultures across the globe and in the next chapter, we will continue this examination by taking a close look at the variations among families of different ethnic backgrounds in our own society.

In Chapter 1, we met the Aka, a group of hunter-gatherer pygmies living in the Central African Republic and the northern Congo who are models of both mother–father equality and community-based child care. Aka fathers have been described as the "best dads in the world" in view of their active role in caregiving. When the mother is not available, the father calms his baby by giving him a nipple to suck (figure 6.1). Among the Aka not only do relatives but other women in the community participate in the care and even the nursing of newborns and young infants. The Gusii of Kenya consider child rearing a shared enterprise involving both parents as well as child caretakers. As in the case of our own contemporary society and in past times, even when caregiving duties are shared, mothers or at least parents are still the central caregivers. Anthropologist Melvin Konner (2005) has termed this the "maternal primacy" hypothesis. The issue is whether there are advantages associated with this cooperative caregiving arrangement that can inform our current discussions about family forms. The purpose or adaptive function of this shared childcare arrangement in past times

*Future Families: Diverse Forms, Rich Possibilities*, First Edition. Ross D. Parke.
© 2013 John Wiley & Sons, Inc. Published 2013 by John Wiley & Sons, Inc.

was to allow women the opportunity and energy to reproduce by reducing their child-care load and to shorten the length of time between births. Another function of cooperative parenting was based on reciprocal altruism: you help me now and I will help you later. Finally, especially in the case of younger children and adolescents, the involvement in the care for another person's offspring provides an opportunity to learn how to be a competent caregiver, a set of skills that will be valuable when the young caretakers become parents themselves. In cases of caring for their younger siblings, older siblings would increase their parents' reproductive success as well as increasing their own inclusive fitness (Crognier, Villena, and Vargas, 2002). Of course, we need to be cautious about assuming that these examples from other cultures with their own unique ecology, customs, and traditions can easily be transferred to our own culture. Anthropologist Meredith Small (2001) has addressed this issue of the relevance of our ancestors to how we think about families today.

> We have come a long way away from the Pleistocene era of a million years ago. Surely our child rearing skills have evolved since then. Yes, but when we assume that the nuclear family is the "natural" way for parents and children…it is wrong. The natural human child care situation, the one through which our species evolved our hearts and minds, is a more communal, kin based extended family system (2001, p. 215).

This observation by Small suggests that the lessons learned from other cultures serve as reminders that other models of family organization and role allocation have been successful in our past and merit renewed consideration in the present.

**Figure 6.1**   Aka Pygmy Father.
*Source:* Barry Hewlett.

## Many Fathers, Many Mothers, or No Fathers: One of Each Is Not Always the Norm

To Western eyes with our laser focus on the "ideal" family form, it is a surprise to discover that the current increase of two father or two mother families in our own culture has precedents in other cultures. Although Janice and Darlene Standish–McCloud, the same gender parent family who we introduced in chapter one, view themselves as pioneers on the frontiers of new family forms, they are, in fact, continuing in a long-established tradition of multiple mother or multiple father families found in some other cultures. As anthropologist Stephen Beckerman and his colleagues (Beckerman and Valentine, 2002; Beckerman et al., 2002) discovered during their frequent visits with the Bari Indians of Venezuela, these people believe that a child can have several biological fathers. In contrast to our view of conception of one man and one women as the procreational unit, the Bari have an understanding of conception as a shared enterprise. According to the Bari version of conception, although the husband always begins the conception process "a fetus is built up over time with repeated washes of sperm – which means that, of course, more than one man can contribute to the endeavor" (Small, 2003, p. 54). These secondary fathers along with the husband or primary father are all expected to contribute to the child's well-being by contributing food and gifts. While not all of the Bari follow this multiple partner route to conception, the presence of secondary fathers has evolutionary implications: infants with secondary fathers in contrast with infants without additional fathers are more likely to survive to adulthood. Further probing found that the extra contributions of food by the secondary fathers during pregnancy was a major factor in protecting the viability of a fetus and in its long-term survival (Beckerman et al., 2002). Nor is this belief in shared biological paternity restricted to the Bari. According to a recent survey, 70% of Amazonian cultures share this belief in shared paternity (Walker, Flinn, and Hill, 2010). Other indigenous groups in New Guinea and India have similar beliefs about multiple paternity (Beckerman and Valentine, 2002).

> Partible paternity may have benefits for both sexes, especially in societies where essentially all offspring are said to have multiple fathers. Despite a decrease in paternity certainty, at least some men probably benefit (or mitigate costs) by increasing their number of extramarital partners, using sexual access to their wives to formalize male alliances, and/or sharing paternity with close kin (Walker, Flinn, and Hill, 2010, p. 19195).

Similarly, wives benefit not only by increasing the survival of their children but by having a paramour available as a possible future husband if their current husband dies or defaults. There are downsides too: male sexual jealousy and sexual conflict are not absent from even the most sexually liberal of partible paternity societies (Crocker and Crocker, 2004; Kensinger, 2002). In short, these beliefs and reproductive practices may have some benefits but may also be the source of social tension. In any case, the Bari customs clearly challenge our western beliefs about the "ideal" family form, especially regarding the ideal number of parents. According to the Bari, a husband and wife may not be enough and that for them two or more fathers and a mother is an improvement.

What happens if there are no fathers present? In some cultures such as the Na of Yunnan Province in the Himalayan region of Southern China, multiple mothers in the same household are found while neither fathers nor husbands are anywhere in the household. In his book *A Society Without Fathers and Husbands:The Na of China*, Chinese anthropologist Cai Hua (2002) describes a matrilinear and matrilocal society in which descent and resources are passed through the maternal line and siblings and their children lived in the household of their maternal relatives. Brothers, sisters, their mother, and in some cases grandmothers live together as a family and economic unit in the same household. "Biological fathers" of the children are recognized neither as husbands nor social fathers in this society and they have no responsibility for or power over either their offspring or the mother of their children. In fact, there is no word for father in the Na language (Hua, 2002). According to Cai Hua, "the identity of her children's genitors is never important" (2002, p. 296) but only in rare cases is the biological father not known to the mother, her sisters and brothers who reside together with the children. In this arrangement, the mother along with aunts and uncles raise the children, who are well adjusted and well adapted to life in their cultural group (Hua, 2002). Presumably the uncles (and possibly aunts) provide the kinds of experiences usually provided by fathers, a reminder that the identity of the socializing agent may be less important than the social/cognitive input that they provide. The fact that boys or girls develop normally when there is neither an intact married family unit nor a biological father present in the household clearly challenges our notion of the "ideal" family form as necessary for the socialization of children. A woman may have several male lovers but these men reside in their own maternal household and are treated as visitors but never as members of their offspring's family unit. These sexual arrangements are sometimes called "walking marriages" which for the Na means literally "going back and forth." (Shih, 2010). Even the houses are designed to reflect these social arrangements with rooms and spaces for the mother, her sisters and brothers, and the children, but no space for a father or husband. Just as we saw earlier that introduction of ART led to the uncoupling of sex, reproduction, and parenting, this unusual arrangement "separates sexuality, and romantic love from kinship, reproduction and parenting" (Stacey, 2011, p. 182). These customs have some benefits by allowing both women as well as men a high degree of independence and freedom. Moreover, this arrangement is relatively free of gender of child preference and unlike in other parts of China, girls and boys are equally valued. There have been vigorous efforts by Chinese government authorities to bring the Na in conformity with dominant Chinese norms of monogamous marriage, by offers of land to monogamous couples, outlawing conjugal visits and even withholding food rations from children who could not identify their father. In spite of these efforts, the Na have tried to maintain their patterns of matrilineal decent, living arrangements, and sexual practices, and, of course, their right to define the concept of family in their own unique way. The Na have captured the imagination of not just anthropologists but film makers as well. More than ten documentary accounts of the customs of the Na in Mosuo (the Na language), in Mandarin, and in English have been produced. Unfortunately, some have sensationalized and distorted their actual practices which has raised both visibility and curiosity about this group and their customs among Chinese and foreign tourists. As tourism to this region has increased, some worry that the Na may succumb to modern pressures to conform to a more stable, monogamous relationship model (Stacey, 2011).

Evidence of these practices and beliefs is not in and of itself support for the viability of multiple father or multiple mother households in our own society but a reminder that throughout our evolutionary history, there have been many alternatives to the "ideal" family form. Anthropologist Beckerman summed it up this way: "One of the things this research shows is that human beings are just as clever and creative in assembling their kin relations as they are putting together space shuttles and symphonies" (cited by Small, 2003, p. 61).

## Beyond Mothers and Fathers: Siblings as Caregivers

In some cultures, caregiving responsibilities are commonly distributed among a wide number of individuals beyond the biological parents including siblings, extended family members and nonkin (Weisner, 2008). Sibling caregivers, especially girls are common among some African communities such as the Nyansango of Kenya, the Mali of West Africa, and among the Kahuli in New Guinea (Weisner, 2008). In these cultures, five- to ten-year-old sibling caregivers often assume responsibility not only for their own younger siblings but for children from other nonbiologically related families in the community. In some cultures such as Polynesia, by the time they are able to walk infants are cared for by three to four year old siblings (Martini and Kirkpatrick, 1992). The older siblings supervise, transport, calm and play with the younger children, and serve as models for their younger charges.

> Children may carry a younger sibling or cousin around on their back or hip to be entertained by the sights and sounds of the community and the play of other children. If the young one becomes hungry, the child caregiver returns to the mother to allow the child to nurse. Adults are available to supervise child caregivers, but the entertainment of young children falls to other children (Rogoff, 2003, pp. 122–123) (Figure 6.2).

As this quote suggests it is not just typical maternal activities such as calming and carrying that are distributed among other members of the family such as siblings. Functions such as play, which, in our culture, is a central role of mothers and especially fathers are "outsourced" to others as well. In one culture, the island of Tonga in the South Pacific, adults rarely play with their children for a simple reason: they view parent–child play as a waste of time. Children play with their siblings and peers instead (Mavoa, Park, Pryce, 1997; Morton, 1996). In Mexico, older siblings from working class families assume not only the role of caregiver (Kramer, 2002) but the role of play partner for young children as well (Zukow-Goldring, 2002). Neither father nor mother serve as play partners but leave this activity to siblings. Nor is the quality of sibling play inferior: play between siblings is just as complex as mother–child play and siblings were just as nurturant and supportive as mothers as well. And sibling playmates are welcome. Polynesian mothers reported that toddlers preferred to play more with their siblings than adults, in part, because young children found the play of older siblings more interesting while parent activities are viewed as boring (Martini and Kirkpatrick, 1992).

Sibling caregiving has benefits too. At the most basic level, recent analyses suggest that the help provided by older siblings (at least three years older) is related to higher

**Figure 6.2** In southern Mali, West Africa, older siblings are often caregivers.
*Source:* Photographer: Line Richter (2011). This photo originally appeared in Profile Global Health #2, p.19, University of Copenhagen.

survival rates for the younger siblings (Sear and Mace, 2008). There are other, though less dramatic benefits. The presence of older children in the social world of younger children offers opportunities to learn more advanced skills from their older sibling and peer models. The younger siblings learn not only a variety of motor and physical skills such as running and jumping but other practical skills such as learning to dress themselves, toileting routines as well as a variety of social rules such as handling multiple relationships in a group and how to manage conflict and settle disputes (Weisner, 2008). In contrast to our North American age-segregated society, one of the central features of sibling caregiving in more traditional cultures is the mixture of children of a wide range of ages in the sibling and peer caregiving and play groups (Rogoff, 2003). Unlike studies of the links between birth order and intelligence in the United States, which suggest that intellectual achievement is lower for later born children who primarily interact with siblings rather than parents (Herrera et al., 2007), cross-cultural evidence suggests that when sibling caregiving is culturally normative, children do not show these intellectual deficits (Rogoff, 2003). In cultures where child and sibling caregiving is common, it is generally carried out in collaboration with adults present who ensure that the experience is competence building for both the child and the sibling caregiver (East, 2010). Moreover, this caregiving builds strong bonds between siblings which is seen later when adult siblings act as supplementary coparents for their nieces and nephews. As cross-cultural scholars (East and Weisner, 2009; Rogoff, 2003; Weisner, 2008) argue, the routes and processes of learning vary across cultures but the outcomes are similarly positive in producing culturally competent children and adults.

# Beyond the Nuclear Family: Grandparents as Caregivers

As we saw in the case of the Na of China, in some cultures, relatives such as aunts, uncles, or grandparents share caregiving responsibilities with members of the nuclear family. Are grandparents important? In many cultures, grandparents, especially grandmothers, play a significant caregiving role either as a supplementary figure who occasionally provides direct care or in cases where the mother is unavailable as the main custodial caregiver (Hayslip and Kaminski, 2008; Smith and Drew, 2002).

Even in our own society the number of custodial grandparents or at least coparenting mother–grandparent dyads has increased in recent years (Pew Research Center, 2010). The role of grandparents has been widely recognized by anthropologists and other cross-cultural scholars who have examined family relationships in traditional societies. We will explore these issues and then ask whether grandparents are still relevant in our own contemporary society.

In all cultures, grandparents influence children's development directly through the quality of their interactions with their grandchildren in their roles as occasional caregivers, playmates, advisors, and support figures or indirectly through emotional and financial support, guidance, and child-rearing advice that they provide their adult children in their parenting role (Smith and Drew, 2002; Tinsley and Parke, 1984). As we saw earlier in Chapter 2, grandparents can be attachment figures for their grandchildren and function as an additional source of emotional security for the developing infant and child. These close ties often emerge from the grandmother's part-time or custodial caregiving role. Observational studies reveal that grandmothers are competent caregivers and engaging playmates. For example, in a study of seven-month old American infants, Tinsley and Parke (1987) observed that grandmothers who engaged in more stimulating and engaging behavior with their grandchildren and infants who had more contact with their grandparents had higher cognitive development (Bayley Mental Development Index scores). Nor is it simply cognitive development that is related to grandmother availability and support. In his studies of hormonal reactions to stress among poor children on the Caribbean island of Dominica, anthropologist Mark Flinn found that access to kin networks enhance children's ability to regulate stress (as measured by cortisol, a biological stress marker), which, in turn enhanced social competence (Flinn et al., 2011). Children with a rich network of kin are able to escape stressful family situations (e.g., marital discord) by visiting a nearby relative such as a grandmother. Kin connections are even related to physical development. Among the poor children in Dominica, those with many kin relationships are taller and heavier than their peers with fewer kin ties (Flinn et al., 1996). Even more dramatic is the finding that grandparents, particularly maternal grandmothers, exert a positive effect on the survival rates of infants and children in traditional societies. In an analysis of 12 traditional societies, Rebecca Sear and Ruth Mace (2008) found that the presence of grandmothers was positively linked with higher child survival.

There are several circumstances under which grandmothers are important players on the cooperative parenting scene. Grandmothers matter more when the mother is inexperienced or has fewer older children with whom to share the caregiving responsibilities (Hawkes et al., 1998). They are particularly helpful at developmental transition points such as weaning (Biese, 2005; Sear and Mace, 2008).

Weaning is a dangerous time for children. It increases their exposure to pathogens in food and is often associated with the arrival of a younger sibling, when mothers divert their attention away from weaned children and to their new babies. Maternal grand-mothers may be stepping in to protect children from the dangers associated with this stage of childhood (Sear and Mace, 2008, p. 10).

And it is not just any grandmother. In our own culture, maternal grandmothers have more contact with their grandchildren than do paternal grandmothers (Cox, 2007; Pollet, Nelissen, and Nettle, 2009) and the grandchildren notice: they feel closer to their maternal than their paternal grandparents (Dubas, 2001; Sheehan and Petrovic, 2008). Anthropologists show us that this modern pattern has deep histor-ical roots in older cultures. Maternal grandmothers are more reliably associated with childhood survival than paternal grandmothers (Sear and Mace, 2008). Several factors may account for this discrepancy between paternal and maternal kin. Since females tend to reproduce at a younger age than males, paternal grandmothers are older than their maternal counterparts and therefore less able to assist. Maternal gatekeeping may play a role as well and mothers may simply be more comfortable and feel closer to their own mother than their mother-in-law. As a result the maternal grandmother is allowed more access to her grandchildren. Perhaps for some, it is their relative uncertainty about their level of genetic relatedness to their patrilineal descendants as a result of the lingering issue that their son may not be the biological father of their grandchild that decreases paternal grandmother involvement (Sear and Mace, 2008). Therefore, sticking with the offspring of daughters and sisters is the safest strategy of ensuring that one's genes are being protected and passed along. However, in some cultures such as rural Greece where paternal lineage is paramount, there is greater involvement of paternal than maternal grandparents (Pashos, 2000). Hence, cultural norms as well as evolutionary considerations may play a role in deter-mining contact patterns.

What about grandfathers? On average grandfathers are much less important to children's survival in traditional societies. According to Sear and Mace (2008), 83% of maternal grandfathers had no effect on child survival, though 17% had a positive effect. Paternal grandfathers had either no effect (50%) or a negative one (25%) while only 25% had a positive effect on child survival. Perhaps grandfathers help in material ways but clearly not in ways that are as effective as their wives. However, although their role may be limited in traditional societies, it is too soon to give up on grandfathers.

Are grandparents relevant in our own society? Coall and Hertwig (2011) recently offered this thoughtful reflection:

Because of substantial increases in human life expectancy in industrial societies, grand-parents and grandchildren have more shared lifespan than ever before (Murphy and Grundy, 2003). Consequently, grandparents have unprecedented opportunity to invest in their grandchildren. Simultaneously, however, low fertility rates and later ages at first childbirth mean that fewer people are becoming grandparents, and those who do become grandparents have fewer grandchildren. Paradoxically, although extended life span offers more opportunity for grandparents to invest, low childhood mortality rates and low fertility rates mean grandparents' altruistic acts may have less impact than ever before, when measured on these classic fitness indicators. However, this does not mean that grandparental investments in industrialized societies are wasted. With reduced mortality and fertility, the resources invested in children (e.g., education) have increased exponentially to ensure that they can fare well in employment and mating markets (Borgerhoff Mulder, 1998). Thus, the need for grandparents to invest their time, money, and affection in their grandchildren may actually be stronger than ever. Ironically, there may be a good fit between the high levels of investment required by grandchildren in industrialized societies and grandparents having fewer grandchildren in whom to invest their resources; benefits may materialize more than before on less tangible dimensions such as psychological adjustment and cognitive ability (p. 93).

The role of contemporary grandparents has been extensively examined and most accounts portray grandparents as actively involved in their grandchildren's lives. The majority of grandparents have contact with their grandchildren once or twice a month, according to surveys in the United States and Great Britain (Smith and Drew, 2002). In modern times, grandparents often play recreational, playful, advisory, or confidant roles rather than being critical contributors to the child's survival. Nonetheless, these contributions are viewed by both grandparents and grandchildren and their parents as significant and enriching experiences which serve to bind the generations together (Smith and Drew, 2002). There is considerable variability in the amount and type of contact between grandparents and their adult children and grandchildren due to geographical proximity, age, and health of grandparents, gender of grandparent and grandchild, and lineage (Tinsley and Parke, 1984). For many contemporary families, even in "ideal" families such as the Evans, geographical separation often limits children's contact with their grandparents.

Do grandparents play a unique role in children's development? In an examination of grandparents' impact on adolescents academic outcomes, economist Linda Loury (2008) found that grandparents' education made a difference in whether their grandchildren attended college even after controlling for the effects of the nuclear family. She found that when grandfathers had completed high school, their grandsons but not their granddaughters were 13% more likely to attend college. In contrast, the granddaughters of grandmothers who had a high school diploma were 10% more likely to attend college. While the differential gender effects of grandfathers having a greater impact on their grandsons and grandmothers on their granddaughters are interesting, the important message is that grandparents have a separate and added influence on their grandchildren after taking into account parental influences.

Just as we saw in traditional cultures, in our own culture, grandparents may be particularly influential in high-risk family environments such as poor or single-parent families or at times of family transitions such as divorce, parental incarceration, an adolescent pregnancy, or economic hardship. For example, Jackie Fuller, the adolescent mother who we met in the opening chapter benefits from her mother's help in caring for her daughter Elle. The depression or physical illness of a family member especially a custodial parent are other circumstances where grandparent aid is particularly important (Coall and Hertwig, 2010). For example, a study in Bulgaria (Botcheva and Feldman, 2004) found that perceived economic pressure during an economic downturn was linked with harsher parenting which, in turn, was associated with higher levels of depression among adolescents. However, the depression of these adolescents was reduced when there was a supportive grandparent in the household who played a buffering role. Similarly, among American children, the buffering role of grandparents on children in the presence of a depressed mother even extended into adulthood (Silverstein and Ruiz, 2006). Children who grew up with a depressed mother were less depressed as young adults if they were emotionally close to their grandparents, saw them frequently and viewed them as a source of social support. This work underscores that buffering is not inevitable but depends on the quality of the relationship between the grandparents and the grandchild. Finally, as we will explore in the next chapter, grandparents sometimes become custodial parents as well. And they are well prepared to take on this role since grandparents – grandmothers and grandfathers – are able to nurture and respond to children's needs in a competent manner which reminds us that even in our own era grandparents can function as custodial parents in time of need (Tinsley and Parke, 1987). Although the roles of grandparents may have changed across time, even in our own era, they are an important part of the socialization mix by providing direct and indirect support to parents and their grandchildren.

However, grandparents can be a negative influence on both grandchildren and their parents. The grandparent may undermine the parental role by overindulgence ("Oh, he is my grandson so I can spoil him"). Or grandparents can undermine a parent by acquiescing to a child's request which a parent has turned down ("When Mom says no, ask Grandma"). Listen to this tale of interference:

> "Oh, you're being too hard on Bobby. It's okay Bobby. Grandma says you don't need a nap." I look at my mother like she is from another planet. Are you kidding me? Is this the same person that raised me? "No, Bobby does need a nap," I say and lead my crying son into the bedroom. After a few minutes of kicking and throwing a fit, the exhausted child fell into a peaceful and well-needed sleep (Suttor, 2008).

And criticism of the parent's parenting style and behavior standards ("we were strict with you when you were this age but now you let her get away with everything") can undermine parental effectiveness and confidence.

Many of these issues can lead to serious conflict between grandparents and their adult children, especially when the grandparent is a coparent living in the same household with the parent or parents (Moore and Brooks-Gunn, 2002). However, a variety of factors including economic well-being, the age of the mother, and the health and age of the grandmother will increase or reduce the level of conflict. For example, conflict is less likely when the grandmother is a coparent with a relatively young and inexperienced mother rather than a more confident older mother (Chase-Lansdale, Brooks-Gunn, and Zamsky, 1994).

And some grandparent–grandchild relationships are unhealthy and characterized by lack of involvement, conflict, and nonsupportiveness. In a minority of cases especially grandfather–granddaughter interactions can lead to sexual abuse as well (Smith and Drew, 2002). As in all family relationships the quality of the processes that characterize the interactions is paramount. Just as families are better off if divorce reduces maltreatment on the part of a parent so it is in the case that reducing contact with troublesome grandparents is advisable as well. Not just any grandparent will do; a warm, sensitive, and responsive one who respects the parent's authority and household routines, treats their grandchildren appropriately, and provides support when needed is the type that is going to be a valuable member of the cooperative socialization network.

The influence of grandparents even reaches across generations. Grandparents teach their own children lessons about child rearing by how they raise them. Harsh parenting by the grandparent generation is sometimes repeated by the next generation and, in turn, the grandchildren may suffer the consequences. In one study, young parents who had been treated by their own parents in a hostile and angry fashion when they were adolescents were more likely to be hostile with their own children a decade later. In turn, the more they were treated in a hostile manner, the more toddler grandchildren were disobedient, aggressive, and withdrawn, especially children with emotionally reactive temperaments (Scaramella and Conger, 2003).

Grandparents across time and cultures have played important, even critical roles in the matrix of caregivers and support figures upon which families and children rely for survival and well-being. In recognition of this historical tenet, we need to elevate our appreciation of the significant role of grandparents can and do play in the lives of families. Parents and children can potentially benefit by giving grandparents along with other extended kin a clear and deserved place in our broadened view of families as cooperative ventures consisting of multiple players beyond the nuclear (i.e., "ideal") family form. Next, we turn to other extended but often neglected kin – aunts and uncles.

## Beyond the Nuclear Family: Aunts and Uncles

Are aunts and uncles helpful? In many cultures aunts and uncles play important and helpful roles in the socialization process. For example, Kipsigi children in Kenya do better if they have either paternal or maternal uncles (Borgerhoff Mulder, 2007). However, Chewa children in Malawi have lower survival in the presence of maternal aunts but only in households in which women own resources. In households in which men own resources, maternal aunts protect against child mortality (Sear and Mace, 2008). Nineteenth-century Mormon children benefited from maternal uncles and both maternal and paternal aunts (Heath, 2003). On the other hand, Venetian children apparently neither gain nor suffer from access to aunts or uncles (Derosas, 2002). In a study of child-care arrangements in Efe hunter-gatherers, Ivey (2000) found that children were frequently looked after by individuals other than their mothers, but these allocarers were rarely other women who had nursing infants of their own. Childless females may be more available and more willing to assist in care of their nieces and nephews since they are not responsible for children of their own. Just as we saw in the case of grandparents, maternal uncles and aunts were viewed more favorably by parents than paternal aunts and uncles (Gaulin, McBurney, and Brakeman-Wartell, 1997; McBurney et al. 2002). This is consistent with the paternity uncertainty hypothesis that evolutionary theorists have invoked in the case of grandparents as well. In general, individuals seem to invest more in kin associated with the maternal line.

Although it is clear that aunts and uncles are important figures in other cultures, are they relevant in our contemporary society? In North American culture, aunts and uncles have been viewed as "the forgotten kin" (Milardo, 2010), an observation which is supported by the fact that less than 1% of the research literature on family relationships is focused on collateral kin such as aunts, uncles, nieces, and nephews (Fingerman and Hay, 2002). This is surprising because people rate these collateral kin ties as relatively important and just behind spouses, children, parents, and siblings in importance (Fingerman and Hay, 2002). For example, parents, spouses, and children received a rating of 8 (on a 10 point scale), siblings a 7.5 and aunts and uncles a rating of 6. Most of us think that our collateral kin are more central in our lives than do family scholars.

Before we explore the various roles that aunts and uncles play in children's lives, let's address the question "do aunts and uncles make a unique contribution beyond the nuclear family"? Whether their impact is unique and distinct from parental influence seems likely in view of other work on nonfamily mentors (Rhodes, 2002). In fact, recent evidence suggests that there is added value contributed by aunts and uncles to adolescent educational involvement even after controlling for the effects of the nuclear family. Specifically, the level of schooling attained by aunts was a significant factor in whether their niece attended college (Loury, 2006). The number of aunts who were high-school dropouts significantly lowered the probability of their niece attending college while the number of aunts who were high-school graduates increased college attendance by their niece. Uncles' educational level was linked with how well their nephews performed in high school tests and their college attendance. The number of uncles who graduated from high school significantly raised age 14 test scores for nephews and increased their likelihood of attending college. Uncles had larger effects on nephews, while aunts had larger effects on nieces. Aunts and uncles do indeed make a unique contribution to children's development. Next we turn to the ways in which this influence is achieved by examining the myriad of roles that these kin play in the lives of their adult brothers and sisters and their children.

In his recent book, "The Forgotten Kin: Aunts and Uncles," Robert Milardo (2010) has documented, in an in-depth qualitative interview study, the family roles of over 100 aunts and uncles in New Zealand and the United States. He shows that these kin play a variety of roles in the lives of both their nieces and nephews as well as in the lives of their adult siblings. They both complement and supplement the roles of parents in children's lives, they serve as third parties with unique outsider perspectives and even act as surrogate parents or as second mothers or fathers. Here is a sample of the voices of aunts and uncles that illustrate the myriad roles that they play in family life.

Aunt Denise, who is single and childless and who provided additional care for her twin nieces, especially when they were infants noted that "The infants had irregular sleeping hours and somebody would have to get some sleep in that house. So I would go over for a few hours. It was a kind of changing of the guard" (Milardo, 2010, p. 72). Mary Winston, a single-mother-by-choice who we met at the start of the book is another example of a mother who relies on her sister, Aunt Janice, to help out with her son Sam when she is out of town.

They not only help parents in child care but provide alternate sources of information and act as confidants, especially around sensitive issues that may be "too hot" for parents to handle such as sex and drugs. For example, one uncle described counseling his nephew about experimenting with drugs by sharing his own experiences, good and bad, as a way of providing perspective on the issue but in a nonjudgmental way. It goes beyond touchy topics and includes educational or occupational advice as well. Another uncle, a university librarian, recounted helping his nephew with a term paper that was beyond the expertise of his parents. Rather than feeling jealous or violated by this assistance, many parents condone and even welcome the help. Aunt Harriett captured this appreciation of the importance of aunts and uncles for children in the following comment: "It is nice to know that her sons and daughters can have these other adult supportive relationships" (Milardo, 2010, p. 73).

Aunts and uncles are especially important during times of family conflict and when communication is strained between parents and children; these alternative adult figures can step in as confidants and buffers. As one niece said: "my aunt was more of a confidant than my mother ever could be" (Milardo, 2010, p. 74). Not surprisingly, aunts and uncles often play a larger role when their relative is single or undergoing a divorce or separation. According to Aunt Susan, "My sister struggled and had to work and work just to take care of Nika and her two brothers. Nika used to beg me to come and take them out and have fun. And that's what I did when they were little. We'd go camping and shopping" (Milardo, 2010, p. 75). In some cases, the aunt or uncle function as a second parent due to the absence of one or both parents or as a member of an extended multigenerational family household including an aunt or uncle, a mother and a grandparent. Or these relatives may provide temporary housing in times of parent–adolescent turmoil or parental unavailability due to illness or incarceration. In these cases, children often describe their aunts and uncles as second moms or dads. This type of family work is similar to the role played by grandparents, especially grandmothers who often provide supplementary child care for single mothers (Hayslip and Patrick, 2006; Milardo, 2010). At the same time this does not imply that the types of relationships between adult siblings and between parents and grandparents are similar. Age and generational differences characterize grandparent–parent relationships. In contrast, aunts and uncles have very different relationships with their siblings since they are close in age, share a distinct developmental history including their childhoods and major milestones such as graduations, marriages, parenthood, and the aging of their parents. In contrast to the grandparent–parent relationships, siblings are more peer-like in their relationships (Milardo, 2010).

The ways that aunts and uncles participate in the lives of their nieces and nephews shift as the children develop. While direct child-care assistance is welcome in the early years as the child develops, these relatives help with issues of identity development and conflict management during the adolescent years. And the parents themselves benefit from their siblings who can provide social, emotional, and material support as well as being confidants (Milardo, 2010).

Aunts and uncles focus on different issues with their nieces and nephews. While only 19% of uncles and nephews discussed relationship issues, 48% of aunts and nieces talk about romantic partners and sexuality issues. As one uncle put it: "That's not something I'd really want to get involved with. How somebody selects a person (romantic partner) is pretty much their own taste" (Milardo, 2010, p. 106). In contrast, aunts provide relationship advice and guidance more regularly and not only about boyfriends and sexuality but about marriage and breakups too. As one aunt told her niece about a boyfriend who was "being weird": "dump him and move on" (Milardo, 2010, p. 109). Of course, children continue to rely on their parents' counsel but often turn to aunts and uncles for a fresh and perhaps a more detached and objective perspective. Just as with parents, nieces and nephews sometimes accept and other times reject the advice of these extended family members. Much more needs to be learned about when aunts and uncles are influential and when they are rebuffed.

Sometimes aunts are more than just aunts and designated by their relatives as Godmothers, a practice that is common in but not restricted to Catholic communities. Instead of the more informal relationship that often characterizes aunt–niece relationships, the godmother role carries with it both more responsibility and more long term commitment (Falicov, 1998). As one godmother saw it: "I took it as a commitment that I would always look out for my niece," while another said "It is a promise that I will always protect my niece's well-being throughout her life" (Milardo, 2010, p. 111). Nor is it just women who play this role. In the next chapter, we will examine the role of male and female compadres and comadres who are coparents in Latino culture and serve as guides and mentors for children and youth.

Together, these observations illustrate the variety of roles that these "forgotten kin" play in the lives of nuclear families and dispel the myth that families are isolated and self-sufficient. Finally, these findings are even more striking since the Milardo sample was largely White non-Hispanic, not the African American or Hispanic families who we would expect to show porous boundaries between the nuclear and extended family.

## Beyond Family: Nonrelatives as Caregivers

Most challenging to our western ideal family form is the fact that in many cultures nonrelatives in the community either assume or share the tasks typically performed by parents in our culture. The caregiving unit is no longer just the family but the community. In West African Cameroon, unborn babies are viewed as the property of parents but after birth, children are no longer solely a parental responsibility but are the responsibility of their extended kin group (Nsamenang, 2004).

Here is one example from Polynesia where the community is the caregiver

> Children often grow up in an environment where many adults and children have responsibility for their upbringing in enduring social networks (Martini and Kirkpatrick, 1992). Children belong to the community and everyone is expected to comfort, instruct, and correct them. Within the extended family, a new baby belongs to the family, and adults all care for, teach, and discipline the child as it grows. Children have "many laps" to sit in and many models of adult behavior. Often children are adopted and raised by kin other than their biological parents in a system in which children are shared and help to strengthen ties among households (Rogoff, 2003, p. 129).

Nor is this an isolated example. Among the Efe pygmies who reside in the Ituri forest of Zaire, child care is shared between mothers and women in the community (Ivey, Morelli, and Tronick, 2005; Tronick, Morelli, and Ivey, 1992). As soon as the baby is born the infant is attended by a group of midwives who had assisted with the delivery. As the infant develops so does the network of caregivers. When the mother returns to work, child care is shared among members of her work group. As early as 3 weeks the infant spends 39% of their time in physical contact with community members other than their mothers and this increases to 60% of the time by 18 weeks. The average Efe infant is cared for by 14 different individuals and, in some cases, as many as 24 different community members (Tronick, Morelli, and Winn, 1987).

Among the Aka of the Central African Republic, we find another example of multiple or cooperative caregiving. As in the case of the Efe, members of the community share in the caregiving tasks, including other women in the community who even nurse others' newborns and young infants. For example, one to four month olds are held by other adults about 60% of the time and may interact with as many as seven different caregivers a day (Hewlett and Lamb, 2005). Fathers and mothers do the rest but it is clearly a cooperative, community wide venture. The active sharing of caregiving increases a sense of belongingness among members of the community as well as protects the infant by ensuring their care even when the mother is working or unavailable.

As anthropologist Meredith Small (1998) notes, this opportunity to interact with multiple caregivers in cultures such as the Efe and the Aka has advantages for children beyond merely being ensured of adequate care:

> Early on, Efe infants experience and presumably learn all about the interpersonal connections (of the Efe social system); they quickly learn social skills by navigating a series of coordinated and miscoordinated interactions while being held and cared for by several adults. Whereas a Western child experiences most of its interactions from one or two adults – thereby placing excessive demands for interaction on one or two people – the Efe child (who experiences multiple caregivers) will presumably be more socially adept at interactions with a multiple of others, and will probably be less demanding in general (p. 216).

Being reared in a cooperative community caregiving network is not only associated with more social and emotional advancement for children but decreases the chances of being physically abused as well. A network of supportive others not only lowers the stress of parenting by providing relief from the constant demands of parental responsibility but these individuals can provide child rearing advice and guidance that leads to better management of child-related conflict and, in turn, lowers the risk of abuse (Cicchetti and Toth, 2006). A network of supportive community members can intervene early and prevent disciplinary actions from escalating to abusive levels. Moreover, cooperative caregiving cultures may place higher value on children which may act as a further deterrent to abuse (Small, 2001). Finally, cross-cultural evidence suggests that children living in these child rearing contexts are more likely to survive and reach adulthood than children in less community based arrangements (Hrdy, 2009). In our own society, families such as the Millers who rely on child care and after-school programs to allow them both to work, of course, understand the value of "outsourcing" child care duties to others in the community. We are clearly rediscovering useful lessons from other times and places.

## Variability in the Distribution of Caregiving Responsibilities

Family organization and the degree to which different kin and nonkin beyond the parents play a role in caregiving is best viewed as dynamic and flexible; the distribution of care changes in response to a variety of ecological factors. As anthropologists (Konner, 2005; Valeggia, 2009) have claimed there is a continuum of care arrangements among both our foraging and hunter gatherer ancestors.

This spectrum takes us from no use of allomothers among the Aché of Eastern Paraguay, to intermediate use among the Hadza of Tanzania and the Hiwi of the Venezuelan llanos, to the Efe of the Ituri Forest, the most extreme example of allomothering in a foraging population. Among the Aché, childcare seems to take priority over all other maternal activities, including foraging. Aché mothers carry infants and toddlers all the time; they even sleep in a sitting position, cross-legged with the infant on their laps (Hill and Hurtado, 1996). In contrast, Efé infants as young as three weeks old spend almost 40% of their time in physical contact with individuals other than their mothers and by five months of age, babies spend more time with other caregivers than with their own mother (Ivey et al., 2005; Tronick et al., 1987). In between these two extremes we find a whole range of childcare practices (Valeggia, 2009, p. 101).

Several factors have been identified that alter the extent to which cooperative care-giving is prevalent such as number of adult women without children available, density of the setting, the danger level of the environment, fertility and mortality patterns, and sex and age distribution in the social group (Hewlett and Lamb, 2005). The degree of use of others as allomothers would be directly related to the availability of caretakers. As expected, the more women without children in the group, the higher their rate of fulfilling this alternative mother role. Residence arrangements matter too. Meehan (2005) found that among the Aka, other females provided more care when the couple resided with maternal kin while fathers provided more care when they resided with paternal kin. Finally, and no surprise to contemporary parents, flexibility in schedules and degree of leisure time in each society influenced the pattern of care. Multiple caregiving arrangements are more prevalent in the hunter-gatherer societies who have more leisure time, than in the more rigorously scheduled farmer/herder groups (Hewlett and Lamb, 2005). The local ecology affects the type of childcare pattern as well. Cooperative caregiving of infants and children is less common in more dangerous environments. Among the Aché who live in heavily forested areas of Eastern Paraguay, there are many threats to young children (snakes, poisonous insects, jaguars, poor visibility in the underbush, among others) and alloparenting, especially by young siblings is uncommon (Hill and Hurtado, 1996). The use of alternative caregivers such as siblings is more common in less dangerous settings occupied by such groups as the Efe (Ivey et al., 2005). The identity of alternative caregivers vary too. Female kin, particularly grandmothers and sisters, are more frequently engaged as caretakers than other sex and age categories (Valeggia, 2009). These cross-cultural examples support our earlier argument (Chapter 2) that the ingredients of care/stim-ulation can be delivered by a variety of different individuals independent not only of agent gender but age and/or kinship ties as well. Finally, alternative caregivers are more involved as the child develops, in part due to the decrease in breast feeding as children grow older. However, as we noted earlier, in some societies such as the Efe, even breastfeeding of infants is a task shared by women in the community.

To further illustrate that caregiving arrangements are adaptive, dynamic, and responsive to changing conditions, consider the impact of a shift from rural to a more urban environment on caregiving patterns among the Toba, a foraging group in Formosa, Northern Argentina. When some of their members moved from rural to more urban environments, there was a drop in the amount of cooperative caregiving arrangements. Compared to those who remained in their historic rural setting where infants were cared for by others about 60% of the time, cooperative infant care was present only 20% of the time for the market economy-based urban-dwelling Toba (Valeggia, 2009). Identification of conditions that would encourage, support, and sustain cooperative caregiving in contemporary contexts is a critical step if the lessons from the past are going to be successfully adopted.

## Cautionary Tales: The Israeli Kibbutz and American Communes as Extreme Forms of Cooperative Childcare

To provide a balanced discussion of this issue, some social experiments in cooperative child rearing that have not succeeded such as the American Commune movement and to some degree the Israeli Kibbutz merit review in order to better specify the circumstances under which cooperative social child-rearing efforts can be effective (Van IJzendoorn and Sagi-Schwartz, 2008). The importance of maintaining the central role of the family while at the same time providing a supportive social context for families and children is the lesson from this work. If child socialization as a cooperative venture involving a network of kin and nonkin rather than a strictly nuclear family affair has been successful and adaptive in other cultures, I argue that we need to give serious consideration to its utility and applicability for our own culture.

A well-known illustration of modern multiple caregiving comes from the Israeli Kibbutz in which children are reared in a "children's house" with professional caregivers. Parents have regular contact with their children on a daily basis but most of the children's activities take place in the children's house. In many traditional Kibbutzim, as early as a few months after birth, the children followed a communal sleeping arrangement which involved sleeping in bedrooms shared by three or four other children rather than in their parents residence. This is a highly unusual arrangement: a survey of 183 societies found that none had a sleeping arrangement in which children are away from their parents (Barry and Paxton, 1971). Sagi and his colleagues (1984, 2005) compared the infant–mother attachment patterns of infants reared in the kibbutz in which communal sleeping in children's houses was practiced with infants reared by their urban parents in nuclear family arrangements. They found that only 59% of the kibbutz children were securely attached to their mothers compared to 72% of the infants who were residing with their nuclear family. To determine if the communal sleeping arrangement may have contributed to this pattern, Sagi et al. (1994) compared two groups of cooperatively cared for children: kibbutz children who were reared in communal sleeping arrangements and other kibbutz children where family-based sleeping practices had been established. While only 48% of the children in the communal sleeping group were securely attached to their mother, 80% of the children with family-based sleeping arrangements had secure infant–mother attachments. This suggests that children who are in communal care are similar to those in more traditional parental care arrangements if there is the opportunity to sleep in the parental household (Sagi-Schwartz and Aviezer, 2005). Moreover, the involvement of multiple caregivers does not negatively affect the quality of the infant–mother relationship. As we noted earlier (chapter 2), a similar finding is evident in studies of children in child care (Clarke-Stewart and Allhusen, 2005). Further work by these Israeli investigators suggested that when children are in cooperative caregiving, the relationships that they form with their professional caregiver as well as with their parents are both contributors to the child's socioemotional adjustment. They compared the predictive power of the network of infant's attachment relationships (i.e., attachments to mothers, fathers and professional caregiver) with the infant–mother attachment alone. The extended network was the best predictor of children's social functioning in kindergarten (van IJzendoorn, Sagi, and Lambermon, 1992). At later ages, the network continued to contribute but to a lesser degree (Sagi-Schwartz and Aviezer, 2005) and instead the infant–mother relationship even among cooperatively reared children emerged as the most robust predictor of children's functioning (Van IJzendoorn and Sagi-Schwartz, 2008). This work is a further reminder that multiple caregiving is a workable alternative to a more restricted nuclear family form but that variations such as communal sleeping arrangements that interfere with or undermine the quality of the parent–child relationship may have unwanted negative effects on the child. Natural experiments such as these studies of variations in Kibbutzim child care arrangements give us insights into both the feasibility and the limitations of alternative child-care models.

Another natural experiment that is instructive is the commune movement in the United States in the 1960s and 1970s. In a 25-year study comparing 150 middle-class, two-parent married couples and 150 counterculture families, anthropologist Tom Weisner (1986) tracked their children's school achievement, peer relations, behavior problems, drug use, as well as values and social attitudes. The countercultural families had unconventional family configurations – single parents, cohabitating couples, and couples in communes or other group arrangements. Although the alternative family forms varied, a subset were committed to sharing of parental responsibility for child care. However, as often seen in western contexts as well as traditional societies, parents remained the primary caregivers. As Weisner observed "such parents made a real effort to extend the caretaking network and 'share out' the child to some extent with a circle of friends and like spirited kin and mates, yet retained American ideals of intense parental bonding" (1986, p. 203). How did children fare being reared in these more communal family forms? Weisner concluded that "contrary to some who had dire predictions regarding the children of the nonconventional or 'hippie' families, for the most part they seem to be doing as well or better than our comparison group" (1986, p. 205). In spite of their efforts and the generally positive outcomes for the children, these types of countercultural arrangements are often short-lived since they are out of step with the norms and demands of the mainstream culture. In contrast, in cultures where communal approaches to parenting are more normative, such as the Aka, the long-term stability of these caregiving strategies is more likely.

As both of these examples illustrate, the parent–child relationship is central and important for the healthy development of the child; parents are not easily replaced by a cooperative or communal child-rearing arrangement. However, supplementary caregivers can be beneficial for both parents and children and need not undermine the quality of the parent–child bond. The "ideal" family form is clearly not the only viable form for the care and socialization of children.

## Reflections

This brief tour of other cultures reminds Westerners that our focus on the "ideal" family form is not shared by many other cultures. Instead this tour indicates that cooperative child care is, in fact, not a deviant arrangement but a commonly practiced form by families in a myriad of other cultures. Moreover, as we argued earlier in Chapter 2, there is much more interchangeability among caregivers than our rather rigid views about the correct roles for mothers and fathers assume. In some cases, no fathers are actively involved but mother's male relatives are part of the caregiving network. Whether they provide similar or different roles than fathers in nuclear families is not fully understood but the children growing up under these social conditions develop normally. In other cases, there are multiple fathers who contribute to the support of the child instead of a single father; although a clear departure from our cultural view of the "ideal" family form, these children also thrive. And other family actors beyond mothers and fathers are involved in child care including siblings and extended family members. Their involvement benefits children by broadening their social–emotional experience and guaranteeing protection in case of parental incapacitation or loss. And nonrelatives commonly play active roles as caregivers in many cultures as part of a commitment to cooperative, community-based caregiving. Recognition of the value of a cooperative approach to care need not weaken or replace the parent–child relationship; instead, the parent–child unit and child care by others coexist and together can enhance the child's well-being. These cross-cultural examples present a major challenge to our narrow definition of the "ideal" family form and at the very least remind us that this minority view is neither universally endorsed nor necessarily in the best interests of Western children and parents. Much can be learned from these cross-cultural examples as we struggle to accommodate the changing roles of parents and families in our own society.

# 7

# All about Relatives and Fictive Relatives

## Insights from Diverse Ethnic Groups in Our Own Culture (Past and Present)

*Ask not what we can teach immigrants, but ask what immigrants can teach us*
(Anonymous)

It is not only other cultures but varied ethnic groups in our own society that can offer insights about alternative family forms. The family forms adopted by some subgroups within our own culture provide a further challenge to our cultural beliefs about the "ideal" family form. Some of these insights are based on historical and current accounts of North American Indigenous and African American families, while others are more recent insights based on related family forms practiced by Asian and Latino immigrants. Remember the Dorado family from the opening chapter. Maria and Jose Dorado are first-generation Mexican immigrants who are struggling economically but are managing, due in part to a high level of support from their extended family and community and to the strong sense of family responsibility shared by their children. We can learn important lessons from the Dorado family and families of other ethnic and racial backgrounds who share this focus on cooperative extended family forms. The retention of these traditional cooperative family forms by various native as well as recently arrived groups serve as protective factors for children and youth. On the other hand, paradoxically, becoming more acculturated and committed to "American" values may not necessarily be good for children's academic and social progress. By exploring these alternative family models offered by both long time natives as well as more recent arrivals, I present a further challenge to the contemporary "ideal" family form.

## Lessons from North American Indigenous Families

Although North American Indigenous Families (American Indian/Alaska Native/ First Nations) were known as the "Vanishing Americans," in the United States the American Indian population has increased at every census count since 1940. American Indians are a socioculturally diverse group consisting of over 560 federally recognized

*Future Families: Diverse Forms, Rich Possibilities*, First Edition. Ross D. Parke.
© 2013 John Wiley & Sons, Inc. Published 2013 by John Wiley & Sons, Inc.

tribal groups in the United States alone (U.S. Department of the Interior, 2007), who speak over 100 different languages (Trimble and Medicine, 1993). Although American Indian families are often in the news because of land disputes, poverty, and alcohol-related problems, these original North American families have much to teach us about alternative views of the family as they have a very different conception than the notion of the "ideal" family form that we have been discussing. Instead of the focus on the two parent nuclear family, these pioneering and historically very successful groups were organized into extended family forms which have served them well for centuries. In contrast to European American families which focus on the parent–child dyad as the unit of socialization, for Indigenous people the extended family is the central unit of interest (Whitbeck, Sittener Hartshorn, and Walls, 2013). The loss of their traditional tribal culture, with its extended family focus, occurred in part by the efforts by government authorities to assimilate North American Indigenous people into mainstream European American culture by shipping the children to Government schools. Unfortunately, this policy led to serious economic, social, and emotional problems for many "First Families."

As Sarche and Whitesell (2012) noted:

> Although Native children carry the rich legacy of their cultural traditions, they also bear the legacy of the massive traumas endured by their ancestors. Native children are born into communities shaped by a long history of government policies designed explicitly to disrupt tribal lands, cultural practices, language, and family relationships. After years of outright warfare on Native people ended in the late 19th century, attempts to deal with the 'Indian problem' shifted to numerous policies aimed at the forcible assimilation of Native people into the dominant culture and, ultimately, at the elimination of a culturally distinct Native population. The General Allotment (Dawes) Act of 1887 ushered in this era and targeted the very basis of tribal communities by dividing communal tribal lands into individual allotments. Furthermore, by forcing individual land ownership, Western views of the 'nuclear family' were also imposed. Ultimately, tribal land bases were drastically reduced as allotted lands were quickly lost to White settlement, and tribal sovereignty was significantly eroded (p. 43).

Despite their treatment by government officials, a number of features of American Indian family organization has helped them survive and adapt to their changing lives. In turn, there are important insights to be gained from their family forms and practices.

*The Focus on the Extended Family:* Among Indigenous North Americans, kinship ties define both one's identity as well as responsibilities and obligations to others in the kinship network (Allen, Mohatt, Markstrom et al., 2012). One of the important parts of the kinship community is the extended family which is centrally involved in child care and child rearing (Coleman, Unau, and Manyfingers, 2001; Stubben, 2001). These families may be characterized as a collective cooperative social network that extends from the mother and father union to the extended family, the community and the tribe (Burgess, 1980). Moreover, the structure of the American and Canadian Indian family networks is different from other extended family units in Western society (Light and Martin, 1996). For example, in most traditional European American families the extended family is limited to three generations either within a single household or across separate domains. In contrast, North American Indian extended family networks are more structurally open and can include several households representing significant relatives along both vertical and horizontal lines, thus assuming village-type characteristics. In such families, grandparents retain an official symbolic leadership role. Children seek daily contact with grandparents, who monitor children's behavior and have a voice in child rearing (Lum, 1986). Grandparents are a significant source of support, approval, and even discipline for children and youth (Whitbeck et al., 2013). Grandparents assume child-care responsibilities for their grandchildren and parents often seek advice from community elders, including their own parents (Whitbeck et al., 2013). In fact, in one study, nearly a quarter of adolescent boys and a fifth of adolescent girls lived away from their parent's home for a month or more during their teen years either at another parents' or a grandparent's home (Whitbeck et al., 2013), a further indication of the porousness of family boundaries among Indigenous peoples. As one Native American observer noted:

> Everything revolves around the extended family unit, and cousins are as close as brothers and sisters. For this reason, adoption is almost unheard of in Indian tribes. When a child is orphaned, someone in the extended family raises it as their own. Perhaps this stems from the fact that in aboriginal times, survival of the tribe as a group was all-important, and the family was the basic unit of the tribe (Pollard, 2011, p. 1).

An example of family involvement outside the immediate parents is found in Lakota families. This involvement begins early in life when a second set of parents are selected for newborn babies (Sandoz, 1961). Therefore, the "total" family involved in child rearing and support includes unrelated members of the Indian community (Gibbon, 2003) who assume responsibility for others' actions. Thus, individual behavior is being monitored by other Indian family members. This commitment to the extended family ideal is expressed in the native tribal language. Among the Iroquois, for example, uncles and aunts were called fathers and mothers, a naming practice that underscores that parenting is a responsibility that is shared across several family members (Machamer and Gruber, 1998). Parents in this tribe provided affection and support, while discipline and supervision were left to aunts and uncles.

Recent studies of Indigenous families have found that the traditional definition of family as the extended family group, rather than merely the parent–child dyad has been restored. Moreover, for Indigenous youth being reared in an extended family context confers a developmental advantage especially when this involves both structure (i.e., consistent family child rearing behaviors which support youth goals) and positive support (i.e., warmth and positive responses to culturally valued and other positive behaviors) (Armenta et al., 2012). Positive support and structure on the part of the extended family unit were associated with fewer deviant friends while support was linked with lower rates of oppositional defiant behaviors. With its strong focus on extended family responsibility for children's welfare, their notion of the "ideal" family is clearly different from our contemporary view.

*Family Values:* Although there are variations, several traditional North American Indigenous tribes endorse common values. One value, *respect for elders* assumes that with age comes experience that is transmitted across generations as knowledge that is essential for group survival and harmony in life. Another value, *identity with one's group* ensures that the interests of the family and tribe are the same as one's own self-interest. Other tribal values, *cooperation* and *partnership* are viewed as desirable guides for conducting tribal activities. These values are captured in a Pueblo Indian saying "Help each other so the burden won't be so heavy" (Suina and Smolkin, 1994, p. 121). In a recent study, Goins et al. (2011) found that identification with the values of traditional Native American culture was associated with a higher level of shared caregiving activity among adults. Specifically, increased cooperative caregiving was positively correlated with attending and participating in Native American events, and engaging in and endorsing traditional healing practices. This work underscores the links between native values and cross household assistance.

*Loss of Extended Family Support and Adjustment of Native American Indian Children and Youth:* Many of the problems among contemporary North American Indian youth have been attributed to the loss of extended family support and guidance that resulted from several government policies aimed at the integration of indigenous groups into European American cultural traditions. The most tragic historic public policy of both the US and Canadian governments that disrupted family ties between children and their tribal family was the use of boarding schools for children as a mechanism for the acculturation of North American Indian children (Sarche and Whitesell, 2012). This educational initiative involved removing children from their homes and educating them away from parents, their extended family and community, teaching them English and forbidding their use of their traditional language and customs (Adams, 1995). From their founding in 1879 to the present, about 100,000 children have attended these schools. Most schools have closed and children are now educated in community public schools or tribal schools which are culturally embedded in the Native American cultural values of cooperation and sharing rather than the more individualistic orientation of non Native American public schools. The long-term effects of these residential school experiences have been widely documented. Trauma and problems such as violence, drug, and alcohol abuse are more common among those who attended such boarding schools (Chansonneuve, 2007; Sarche and Whitesell, 2012). Although boarding schools are now only a historic policy tragedy, the long term consequences of this policy are still being explored.

Another trend encouraged by government incentives is the out migration from reservations to cities for vocational training and job placement in the mainstream economy (Cobb and Fowler, 2007). Today, approximately 70% of indigenous people in the United States live off reservations (Banks, 1991), mostly in urban areas, although most research focuses on those living on reservations. Due to cultural differences and discrimination, many American Indians have a difficult time adjusting to life in urban areas. For this reason, many reservation American Indians who migrate to urban areas tend to settle in cities and towns near reservations and to maintain contact with their family on the reservation (Walls and Whitbeck, 2012). Such living arrangements close to the reservation are more conducive to the development of biculturalism than when Indians live in large urban areas removed from reservations. However, these same relocation programs, which were designed to help economic progress, in fact, led instead to economic hardship and poverty. Many of the jobs consisted of seasonal, low-paying work, and minimal job placement and training, which only maintained their economic plight. Moreover, those indigenous people who were relocated experienced a variety of cultural tensions in their new urban environments:

> For those who had never been a part of city life or the American economy, the need to pay rent on time, to keep regular hours at work, and to survive in a largely impersonal situation with few friends or relatives proved difficult. Many quit the cities and fled back to reservations permanently. Others used holidays and tribal ceremonial times as excuses to leave for home, often neglecting to explain clearly to their employers and then losing their jobs (Nichols, 1998, p. 293 cited by Walls and Whitbeck, 2012).

Even children do better when their parents stay on reservations and their children are able to retain their cultural identity and attend tribal schools. Because tribal schools are embedded in a supportive cultural context, they may ameliorate the cultural conflicts in classrooms that can arise when children attend public schools where they are exposed to more mainstream societal values and prejudices. Wall and Madak (1991) found that students attending tribal schools felt that their parents and favorite teacher held higher educational aspirations for them than their peers in public schools. The greater family connectedness found on reservations is also positively associated with more favorable attitudes toward school and less risk-taking behavior among adolescents (Machamer and Gruber, 1998). Some (Zimmerman, Ramirez, Washienko et al., 1998) have proposed an "enculturation hypothesis" to explain how involvement with Native American Indian culture buffers children from the negative effects of acculturation, such as alcohol and substance abuse. In their research with Odawa and Ojibwa tribal members, Zimmerman and colleagues found that cultural affinity positively predicted youths' self-esteem. Youth with the highest levels of self-esteem and cultural identity had the lowest levels of alcohol and substance abuse, which was consistent with the enculturation hypothesis.

The long-term effect of relocation policies on subsequent generations is illustrated in a recent study of over 500 American and Canadian Indian adolescents and their mothers (Walls and Whitbeck, 2012) whose parents or grandparents had undergone relocation from a reservation to an urban setting. As several earlier studies have shown, this type of traumatic event has serious effects on physical and mental health (Fixico, 2006), in part, due to the experience of loss of community, extended family and their connection to the land. Even for the individuals in the study who currently reside on reservations, the past trauma experienced by their elders as a result of relocation reverberated across generations. Specifically, parents who had lost their extended family connections due to the displacement of their elders were more depressed, had higher rates of drug use, and were less effective parents; in turn, their own children were more likely to experience depression and engage in delinquent behavior.

As Walls and Whitbeck (2012) concluded,

> The process is the erosion of intergenerational influences. Grandparents were separated from their sons and daughters and grandchildren. They could not teach the cultural ways of parenting by providing appropriate role models of strong parents and elders. Their children, in turn, were more at risk for demoralization (depressive symptoms) and sub-

stance abuse. This eroded their abilities as parents, so that the next generation was more susceptible to substance abuse and delinquent behaviors...one of the keys to breaking the cycle set in motion by historical cultural losses is reconnecting generations, linking lives in a good way to support the healthy growth of the next generation (p. 1290).

In sum, while it is not the loss of extended families ties alone that has led to cross–generational adjustment difficulties, it seems clear that this loss of the protective effect of this social network is a contributor. In the United States, Indian Health Services and greater tribal self-determination in the areas of education (the Indian Self-Determination and Education Assistance Act of 1975), family life (The Indian Child Welfare Act of 1978), and culture (The American Indian Religious Freedom Act of 1978) have made it possible for some tribes to sustain healthy families and to recover traditional child-rearing practices. With its strong focus on extended family responsibility for children's welfare, their notion of the "ideal" family was clearly different from the contemporary view that we have been discussing. The evidence clearly suggests that adherence to traditional family values and the social support of extended family arrangements are beneficial. Perhaps we can learn from these models of alternative family forms.

## African American Families: Kin and Fictive Kin

Further historical insights come from scholarly reconstructions of African American families and the African American experience. Again these insights can contribute more general lessons for families of all ethnic and racial backgrounds. As sociologist Carol Stack (1974) reminded us in her classic volume *All Our Kin*, an ethnographic study of poor African American families in Chicago, African Americans share a long tradition of collective responsibility for the care and rearing of children. Dating back to the era of slavery, coresidential families were the norm and an adaptive strategy to aid in their survival. Nor are the lessons that we can learn from the African American experience limited to historical accounts. Contemporary scholars focus on the strengths of modern African Americanfamilies rather than on the deficits of these families (Mandara and Murray, 2002). In fact, our views of African American families have undergone significant transformation over the past several decades. Instead of conceptualizing these families as a "tangle of pathology" as Moynihan (1965) did in his controversial report on the state of the African American family, today, most scholars and policy makers focus on the adaptive value of African American family forms, especially their endorsement of extended networks of community care. In fact, approximately one in five African American families live in extended families in contrast to one in ten White families (Glick, Bean, and Van Hook, 1997). One could argue that the trends that have characterized the family forms of African Americans have, in a real sense foreshadowed changes that have taken place in the wider society. For example, as we have seen in earlier chapters, modern families of all racial and ethnic backgrounds are dealing with more separation and divorce, the increase in single mothers either through divorce or by choice and the more active participation of women in the workforce. These issues are ones that African American families have confronted first and lessons can be learned from the strategies that these families have developed in adapting to these challenges.

*What is Old is New Again: Current Trends and Lessons From the Past:*   In a prophetic statement, Maxine Baca Zinn (1994) argued as follows:

> Belinda Tucker and Angela James (2005) offered a similar analysis: More traditional constructions of the family in the United States have been primarily kin based and focused on the rearing and support of children. However as models for romantic attachments have evolved to focus more on individual interests and are less defined by the marital model and as sexual relationships are less bound by the institutionalized commitment of marriage, family constellations have changed as well. Family structures, on the whole, have become less kin-based, less specific to childrearing, less permanent, more permeable and more flexible. These trends are evident in the United States at large, though the growing separation of childbearing and childrearing from marriage has been displayed among African Americans for a longer period of time (p. 89).

> Families may respond in a like manner when impacted by larger social forces. To the extent that White families and Black families experience similar pressures, they may respond in similar ways, including the adaptation of their family structures and other behaviors. With respect to single-parent families, teenage parents, working mothers, and a host of other behaviors, Black families serve as barometers of social change and as forerunners of adaptive patterns that will be progressively experienced by the more privileged sectors of U.S. society (1994, p. 24).

The common theme of these two quotes is that as times have shifted and there is a retreat from the definition of the "ideal" family as the nuclear father–mother–child family form, we can benefit from the lessons offered by other ethnic/racial groups such as African American families. Several recent statistics support this shift. First, the proportion of women under 30 who are having children outside of marriage has increased to over 50% in recent surveys (Wildsmith, Steward-Streng, and Manlove, 2011).

> Once largely limited to poor women and minorities, motherhood without marriage has settled deeply into middle America. The fastest growth in the last two decades has occurred among White women in their 20s who have some college education but no four-year degree. The surge of births outside marriage among younger women – nearly two-thirds of children in the United States are born to mothers under 30 – is both a symbol of the transforming family and a hint of coming generational change (DeParle and Tavenise, 2012, p. A1).

The proportion of nonmarital births is highest for African American women but the proportion of non marital births has risen the most for White and Hispanic women. Several factors have contributed to this trend, including increasing economic hardship, growing barriers to marriage among members of the lower socioeconomic class, and a greater acceptance of nontraditional family forms (Wildsmith, et al., 2011). Some (e.g., Furstenberg, 2009) have argued that poor White and Hispanic women are following the same pattern of nonmarital childbearing that African American women followed in earlier years.

Although extended family residences as a family form were historically common among African American families (and more recently among Asian and Latino immigrants), the prevalence of this family form has increased among Americans regardless of race – another example of how some patterns in the African American community are becoming more common in the wider society. According to a recent survey by the Pew Research Center (Taylor et al., 2010) about 6.6 million US households in 2009 had at least three generations of family members, an increase of 30% since 2000. When "multigenerational" is more broadly defined to include at least two adult generations, a record 49 million, or one in six people, live in such households. The increase in grandparent headed households is especially dramatic with 4.9 million American children living in grandparent-headed households in 2010 compared to about 3.7 million in 2001, a rise of 26% versus a 4% increase for children living in all other type households (Johnson and Kasarda, 2011). Over half (54% or 2.6 million) were living in households headed by both grandparents. Forty percent (1.9 million) were living in households headed by grandmother only and 6% (318,000) were residing in households headed by grandfather only. Increasingly, these grandparent-led households also include one or more adult children who are parents of the grandchildren. In about two thirds of the grandparent-headed households, the grandchildren were sharing their grandparents' homes with either one or both of their parents. These demographic shifts in family composition has prompted one commentator to ask "are grandparents the new parents?" (Warnock, 2012). The rise in multigenerational households is heavily influenced by economics, with many young adults known as "boomerang kids" moving back home with their parents because of limited job prospects and the lack of inexpensive housing (Newman, 2012).

But extended life spans and increased options in home health and outpatient care rather than moving into nursing homes have also played a role. So, too, have recent waves of immigration of Hispanics and Asians; they are likely to live with extended family who have already settled in the host country and are able to provide housing, shared childcare, and economic support to the next group of new arrivals. Perhaps we are seeing a return of *The Waltons* a popular TV family from the 1970s which had three generations residing in the same household (Taylor et al., 2010). As these trends suggest, the lessons of how African American created flexible family forms in response to their economic realities that they faced can be valuable to other groups as well.

*A Closer Look at African American Extended Families:* One of the major ways in which African American families have survived and flourished over periods of hardship, discrimination, and repression from the early days of slavery to the present is by the continual endorsement of the tradition of extended family systems of kin and fictive kin. Fictive kin is a term used by anthropologists and ethnographers to describe forms of kinship or social ties that are based on neither blood ties nor "by marriage" ties, but who nonetheless share reciprocal social or economic relationships (Stack, 1974). According to Stack (1974): "Flexible expectations and the extension of kin relationships to non-kin allow for the creation of mutual aid domestic networks which are not bounded by genealogical distance or genealogical criteria" (p. 61).

As noted in the previous chapter, while Godparenthood (or coparenthood) is a common form of fictive kin relationships, in many societies people have "aunts" or "uncles" who are merely their parents' closest friends and "cousins" who are children of adult family friends. At the same time, these fictive kin play important and sustained roles which often overlap with the roles played by biological relatives (Jelm, 2010). This flexibility allows individuals to move in and out of caregiving roles across time and as family needs shift and recognizes that the same parenting functions can be effectively delivered by a variety of figures, not just the biological parents. By including a wider range of individuals beyond blood relatives in a care network, more resources are available to be shared and help ensure the well-being of children and families.

A defining feature of this extended family system is the fluidity of household boundaries and a willingness to absorb relatives and nonrelatives into the family network (McLoyd, Aikens, and Burton, 2006; Tucker and James, 2005). Here is one description of "open household boundary" residence patterns of poor African American families involving kin and nonkin in a Washington, DC neighborhood. Anthropologist Ulf Hannerz (1969) observed that

> The household composition of (Black) families is quite variable, both between households and in a single household over time. To a certain extent, this is undoubtedly due to strains arising from external pressures – the many separations and divorces, for instance, which result in husbandless households and the economic pressure which makes it more or less a necessity to take boarders even when there is hardly any extra space to spare (p. 50).

A similar profile emerges from Stack's (1974) work in Chicago regarding the cooperative care of children: "Within a network of cooperating kinsmen, there may be three or more adults with whom, in turn, a child resides. In this cycle of residence changes, the size of the dwelling, employment and other factors determine where children sleep" (p. 63). This recognition that parenting responsibility can be distributed across several individuals is in stark contrast to our views of the "ideal" family form but is, of course, similar to the patterns of many other cultures as we saw in the previous chapter (Hrdy, 2009).

Frequent family contact among extended family members, a strong sense of family and familial obligations and a system of mutual aid are also important characteristics of the African American family. Other characteristics of African American extended-kin systems include a high degree of geographical propinquity, frequent interaction with relatives and frequent extended-family get-togethers for special occasions and holidays (Harrison et al., 1990). Some may surmise that extended-kin behavior among African Americans is a response to poverty rather than an authentic cultural characteristic of the group. However, as Hatchett and colleagues (Hatchett, Cochran, and Jackson, 1991) found in their National Survey of Black Americans: "household extendedness at both the household and extra household levels appears to be characteristic of black families, regardless of socioeconomic level" (p. 81). This suggests that both higher-SES and less affluent African Americans both derive physical and psychological benefits from these relationships. What is the nature and frequency of mutual aid among kin in extended family households? According to Hatchett et al. over two thirds of the respondents reported receiving some assistance from family members such as financial aid, child care, goods and services, and assistance during illness and at death. The range of aid is well captured by one of the participants in Stack's (1974) study "They trade food stamps, rent money, a T.V., hats, dice, a car, a nickel here, a cigarette there, food, milk, grits and children" (p. 32). The type of support varied across the age of the recipients. Younger individuals received more child-care assistance and financial help while older folk received more goods and services. Boykin (1983) has traced this focus on reciprocity in African American culture to West African traditions of spirituality, harmony, affect, and communalism.

*The Effects of Extended Family on Parents and Children:*   Extended families are an important source of support for both children and adults. Considerable evidence suggests the protective effect of extended family contact (kin and fictive kin) on children's safety and the positive effects of this support for children's social as well as spiritual development (McLoyd, et al., 2006; Wilson, 1986). Well-functioning children and families are often embedded in networks of kin who are better off economically. Not only do these networks often assist their poorer kin from the ravages of life in dangerous neighborhoods (Patillo-McCoy, 1998; Stevenson, 1998) but provide material as well as access to informational and occupational resources (Jarrett, 1998). The influence of the extended family among African Americans is important because of the large number of female-headed households that require child-rearing assistance and economic support (Hatchett et al., 1991; Wilson, 1992). The proportion of African American households with elderly heads that have young family members is also high, numbering about one in three families (Pearson et al., 1990), a rate which is significantly higher than other racial groups. When coupled with the fact that many African American grandparents live in close proximity to their married children and families, African American grandparents have many opportunities to influence the development of their grandchildren. Grandmothers provide child care and child-rearing assistance as well as economic support. Pearson et al. (1990) found that in multigenerational households, mothers were the primary caregivers, followed by grandmothers and then fathers. Grandmothers also showed more supportive behaviors in mother–grandmother families than in mother–father–grandmother families. In mother-absent families, grandmothers were more involved in control and punishment of children. The involvement of grandparents is often beneficial; for example, grandparent involvement for children at risk for negative behaviors improves children's social–emotional adjustment. Lussier et al. (2002) found that grandparental closeness following divorce was related to better adjustment of single-adult mothers, while adolescent mothers who remained in the grandmother's household were more likely to complete school and were less likely to continue to receive welfare when compared to girls who set up separate households. Kellam and his associates (Kellam, Ensminger, and Turner, 1977; Kellam, Adams, Brown et al., 1982) have found long-term effects of living arrangements involving variations of extended family structure on child's achievement and social adjustment. Children from two-parent, mother/grandmother, mother/aunt, and mother/other families were all found to be achieving and adjusting at adequate rates. Moreover, Tolson and Wilson (1990) found that the presence of grandmothers in African American families increases the moral-religious emphasis in the household, an emphasis that helps to sustain the African American family and reinforce the sense of family and family solidarity. Moreover, the positive effects of grandparents as caregivers on children's adjustment is more likely when grandparents are part of a coparenting household rather than as the sole caregiver for a grandchild; children in coparenting households had fewer behavioral problems (Jooste, Hayslip, and Smith, 2008) and less grandmother–grandchild conflict than children in grandmother headed households (Goodman and Silverstein, 2002). Finally, some have questioned the adequacy and reliability of informal child care provided by relatives (Clarke-Stewart and Allhusen, 2005). Although this is often the only economically viable child-care solution available to single mothers, relative-based care is not as good for children as formal center care-based arrangements (NICHD Early Child Care Research Network, 2005).

It is critical to recognize that extended family serve not only as direct caregivers but function as supervisors and monitors on behalf of parents when children are in the community (Furstenberg et al., 1999). In one study, African American parents who resided in a poor neighborhood used kin and nonkin who lived in more resource rich neighborhoods as safe havens for their children and to provide them with opportunities to acquire new skills (i.e., music lessons) (Furstenberg, 1993). And community members often form neighborhood watch groups to monitor their children, another example of shared community responsibility for the protection of children (DeSena, 1990). Not surprisingly, children who reside in supportive neighborhoods are better socially adjusted (Wilkenfeld, Moore, and Lippman, 2008).

The role of grandfathers, great grandfathers, and uncles has also begun to receive attention. Given that two-parent households were the plurality in the African American community before 1980, many grandfathers are currently involved in the socialization of grandchildren. In her ethnographic study of a drug ridden urban African American neighborhood, Burton (1991) found that great grandfathers and uncles as well as grandmothers stepped in to protect children from the dangers of the neighborhood. In a study of the transmission of family values through the use of proverbs, McWright (2002) found that grandfathers' influence was greatest in the area of family connectedness.

More recently, the rise of kin as well as nonkin caregivers, especially in conjunction with state foster care programs provide further illustrations of alternative care arrangements among African American families (Pinderhughes and Harden, 2005). In fact, African American children (8%) are more likely to live apart from their birth parents than European American children (3%) (U.S. Census Bureau, 2002).

*A Word of Caution*: Some scholars have raised questions about the continued viability of family networks in current society. As Miller-Cribbs and Farber (2008) argued:

> Studies of kin networks among African Americans during the first several decades of the 20th century emphasized how they supported the capacities of network members to survive harsh economic and social oppression through sharing resources, often facilitating work activity and so contributing to upward mobility over generations. Subsequent changes in the structure of economic opportunity, deteriorating urban community resources, and the effect of long-term family poverty have diminished the functional capacities of some kin networks while placing greater demands on them. They also reveal that participation could exact heavy psychological and material costs from individual members. Paradoxically, then, the very conditions of poverty that motivated some individuals to participate in kin networks can militate against effective participation in them. In recent decades, those conditions have worsened among some low-income African Americans residing in more economically homogeneous, concentrated, and isolated communities – especially when family members who achieve upward economic mobility choose to remove themselves physically from the neighborhoods where many family members remain in poverty (p. 43, 45).

And there are a variety of other well-documented challenges that African American communities face such as lack of job opportunities, high rates of crime, unsafe neighborhoods, gangs and drug problems (Wilson, 2010). Our goal is not to minimize these problems, nor their consequences for children's development but to argue that these concerns do not undermine the potential value of more cooperative approaches to family organization. At the same time, these challenges do indicate that living in a poor and unsafe neighborhood can limit the effectiveness of networks of family support. Perhaps by recognizing these constraints, policies can be developed to more effectively bolster the effectiveness of these kinds of kin and nonkin networks.

## Latino Families: A Further Challenge to the "Ideal" Family Form

The United States has been and continues to be a country of immigrants. In 1980, the foreign born represented 6% (14.1 million individuals) of the total US population. By 2010, immigrants comprised 13% (40 million) of the total US population (U.S. Census Bureau, 2010a). In 2010, 47% of the immigrants were Hispanic or Latino in origin, with over 60% of these Latinos being Mexican-born immigrants, making them the largest immigrant group in the country. Other Latinos came from El Salvador, Cuba, the Dominican Republic, and Guatemala. The next largest immigrant group, comprising nearly 20%, was from Asia, led by China followed by India, the Philippines, Vietnam, and Korea. Together, Latino and Asian immigrants made up almost 60% of all foreign born residing in the United States in 2010, a sharp contrast from 50 years ago when most immigrants were from European countries. While we will focus on broad characteristics of Latino and Asian families, it is important to recognize that there are important subgroup variations in both Latino immigrants (e.g., Cuban American, Mexican American, Puerto Rican, and Central and South American) and Asian immigrants (Chinese, Filipinos, Asian Indians, Vietnamese, Korean, Japanese) due to acculturation, generation, social class, and reasons for immigrating to the United States.

These immigrant families differ in a variety of ways from our conception of the American "ideal" family form and present both a challenge to the universality of this family form and at the same time offer insights that may be of value as we examine alternatives to our traditional views about families. Recall the Dorado family who we introduced in the opening chapter. A common characteristic of Latino families (such as the Dorado family) is the embeddedness of children in a network of caregivers that includes older siblings, cousins, grandparents, aunts, uncles, and godparents who share a collective responsibility for the care and monitoring of children (Parke and Buriel, 2006). Similarly, the Chens, an immigrant Chinese family share a similar commitment to the extended family form with their social networks composed of both dense social networks of blood-related kin as well as nonkin. Moreover, these immigrant families share several other characteristics including a recognition of the value of family obligation and duty, a strong work ethic and a relatively low divorce rate. A closer examination of these aspects of immigrant families suggests that these characteristics may, in fact, have adaptive value in aiding families and children adjust to a new country.

*The Latino Extended Family as a Buffer Against Adversity:* Latino child-rearing practices encourage the development of a self-identity embedded firmly in the context of the family or *familia*; one's individual identity is therefore part of a larger identity with the family. This family focus is supported by the religious beliefs and practices of Catholicism, the religion of most Latinos. Identity with family and community is facilitated through religious practices, such as weddings and coming-of-age celebrations (such as a *quinceañera*, that marks the beginning of adulthood for a young girl on her fifteenth birthday) which help extend family networks. The focus on family as a cultural value is reflected in several ways including a high rate of two-parent families, a relatively lower divorce rate, an embrace of extended family arrangements, a focus on a sense of family duty and obligation for their children, and a strong work ethic. For many Latinos, the word "familia" refers to a combination of nuclear and extended family members, including fictive kin such as godparents. The desire to be close to the familia often results in many members of the same familia living in the same community. The familia network extends further into the community through kinships formed by intermarriage among familias. The collective responsibility for children in Mexican American culture is captured in the practice of *el compadrazgo*, which involves special but unrelated friends who become godparents of children (Ebaugh and Curry, 2000; Jelm, 2010). As one Latino mother recalled:

> Our compadres – as well as my husband – came from Mexico, and when they first got here we were their first connection to the area, and they lived with us in our home for a year. So, when they started having their children it was almost like, as my compadre Esteban said, 'Giving you my first child is more than just a thank you for what you've done for us but is a connection we will have for the rest of our lives' (Jelm, 2010, p. 7).

In addition to the bond between the child and his godparents, adults united through el compadrazgo, called compadres (cofathers) and comadres (comothers), have mutual obligations to each other similar to those of brothers and sisters (Ebaugh and Curry, 2000).

> While the child is the 'glue' holding the bond together – the object of the relationship and the reason for its existence – the bond between compadres is even stronger because it creates a special set of mutual obligations between peers which provides an important safety net of emotional and economic insurance" (Jelm, 2010, p. 6).

Compadres/comadres serve as role models for their godchildren and are potential surrogate parents as well in case of a loss of a biological parent. For example, Vidal (1988) found that Puerto Rican godparents served as role models and social supports for their godchildren and regarded themselves as potential surrogate parents in the event of the parents' death. Moreover, most expect to provide food, shelter and monetary as well as emotional support (Jelm, 2010). In one survey in California, nearly 90% of Mexican American families reported having compadres/comadres (godfather/godmother), with most living in the nearby area (Keefe and Padilla, 1987). Although Anglo American families value their ties to extended family, too, their contact with family is less frequent and also requires travel across longer distances, due to the greater mobility of their families. Latino families, in contrast, are more likely to value living near family and do, in fact, choose to live in closer physical proximity to their relatives. Manuel, a Mexican American dad, was amazed that many people do not always appreciate the importance of staying close to family.

> I don't know how people throw their parents into places where they die, says Manuel. We kept our parents with the household until they died. And they are never too old for you to listen to. You take care of your parents. You are going to support them because they raised you when you were a kid, and we never forget that (Parke, Coltrane, and Schofield, 2010, p. 114).

Given such attitudes, it not surprising that Mexican American households are less socially isolated than their Anglo American counterparts.

The role of extended families including fictive kin is especially important for the adaptation of immigrant families. Immigrants and their children are more likely to live in either extended family living arrangements or have more extended family in their social network which may serve as a buffer against the adversities of life in a new country (Van Hook and Glick, 2007). In fact, living in an extended family arrangement is more common for recent immigrants than immigrants who have resided in the host country for a substantial period (Landale, Thomas, and Van Hook, 2011). The fragmented nature of immigration, in which only some members of a family migrate such as the father as a migrant worker, the mother and father without their children, or the nuclear family group without the extended family members leads to social and geographic isolation. As a result these extended family arrangements are more likely to involve coresidence with another adult at the same life stage such as a sibling, cousin, or friend rather than adults with their parents who are often not involved in the migration from a native country (Landale et al., 2011). In these situations, converting social ties to non-relatives into strong fictive kin bonds provides economic, emotional, and social support.

> Such networks of intensified, strong tie relationships expand and strengthen the group of individuals on whom one can depend for social and economic capital (Ebaugh and Curry, 2000). Thus, these reciprocal relationships are especially valuable to immigrants as they face the trials of incorporation into a new society (Jelm, 2010, p. 3).

These social ties among unrelated individuals or fictive kin are often facilitated by chains of immigration in which waves of immigrants follow one another to a common community where they have social ties based on prior relationships in their country of origin. Sister cities develop across borders such as the community of Plymouth, Indiana which is linked with the town of Santiago Capitiro, Mexico and is the source of waves of immigrants who move to the United States. In this case, the immigrants already have social links in their new American community based on their earlier social relationships in their common home town in Mexico. This clearly eases the transition to a new country and a new community. Here is one example:

> Roberto and Juana are first generation immigrants to the United States from Mexico City and Michoacán, respectively. Roberto migrated first to California fourteen years ago, and at the suggestion of a friend, relocated to South Bend (Indiana) to find work. Juana arrived in Chicago fifteen years ago, following a brother who had migrated a few years prior. When her brother relocated to South Bend, Juana followed, hoping to find better prospects for employment (Jelm, 2010, p. 8).

There are protective effects of extended family arrangements for children. For example, while there was less substance use among Spanish-speaking youth than more accultur-ated and non-Spanish-fluent adolescents, the protective effect was due, in part, to protective Spanish language-sensitive attributes included greater numbers of extended family members in the social network, less substance use among network members, and greater perceived parental monitoring (Allen et al., 2008). However, across generations there is a decrease in extended family living arrangements and, in turn, a loss of the protective value of this type of cooperative family form. Even when extended family members such as grandmothers remain actively involved across time, the impact of grandmother support may vary as a function of acculturation. Using a Puerto Rican sample, Contreras, Lopez, Rivera-Mosquera, and colleagues (1999) examined how acculturation affected relations between grandmother involvement and adolescent mothers' adjustment. Greater grandmother support was related to less symptomatology and parenting stress among less acculturated mothers. When mothers were more unidirectionally acculturated, greater grandmother support was associated with more symptomatology and parenting distress. Presumably, attitudes about extended family member participation shift, and this type of support is less welcome if younger generations move toward more Americanization and forget their cultural roots.

As we saw in the case of African American families, single-parent Latino households are especially likely to benefit from extended family arrangements. Children in single-parent families are better off economically if they are living in an extended family household, presumably due to the pooling and sharing of income (Davidson, 2007).

> Extended-family living arrangements may compensate for some of the difficulties faced by single parents or other overburdened families. By providing child care or helping with household tasks, extended-family members may ease family stress and ensure that children's needs are met, thereby making child outcomes more positive (Landale et al., 2011, p. 47).

In contrast to the "ideal" family form endorsed by many in American society, the experiences of immigrant Latino families remind us of the value of extended family arrangements for both caregivers and children alike.

*Family Responsibility as a Protective Factor:* The values of family responsibility, obligation, and duty as well as respect for elders are shared by Mexican immigrant parents and other immigrants from collectivist cultures (Buriel, 2012). The operationalization of these values often takes the form of young children devoting time to assisting parents in their occupations. This assistance, however, is viewed not so much as helping parents as much as contributing to the welfare of the entire family. These work-related situations involve shared parent–child activities that can influence children's perceptions and values about work, family relations, and gender roles. This recognition and value of children's family work especially among immigrant families has reignited debates about the appropriate roles and responsibilities of children in the "ideal" family. As the economist Vivian Zelizer (1985) argued in her book, *Pricing the Priceless Child*, as we have moved from our agrarian past over the last two centuries, the level of work expected of children has dropped dramatically resulting in the "economically useless child." In yet another departure from the "ideal" family form, other ethnic groups expect and cherish the contributions of children's work to the family enterprise. As we will see there are clear benefits associated with family work by children, a clear challenge to dominant conceptions of children's family roles among advocates of the ideal family form.

Compared to their European American peers, Latino and Asian children and youth are higher in their endorsement and enactment of these family values. These cultural differences in family values are well illustrated in a series of studies by Andrew Fuligni and his colleagues (Fuligni, Tseng, and Lam, 1999; Fuligni, 2010). They assessed several aspects of family values among Latino and European American adolescents.

The Latino teens were higher in feelings of respect for family (i.e., make sacrifices for family; follow parental advice concerning job and educational decisions), in their attitudes toward family assistance (help around the house; help care for siblings) and in their feelings about future support of the family (i.e., help the family financially in the future, help care for siblings even if you don't live together) than their European American peers. In later studies in which adolescents kept diary records of their daily family assistance (i.e., cooking, cleaning, looking after siblings, helping with official family business), the actual level of family assistance was higher for Latino than European American adolescents as well. In fact, in Mexican immigrant families adolescents assisted twice as much as their European American peers (Hardway and Fuligni, 2006) (see Figure 7.1). Moreover, a sense of family obligation increased during the transition to young adulthood among Latino American families, which may account for their tendency to live with and contribute financially to their families (Fuligni and Pedersen, 2002). Finally, the stronger the ethnic identity, the more the youth endorsed these traditional cultural values of family obligation (Fuligni, 2010).

In addition to household chores or sibling caretaking, children in immigrant families often assume adult-like responsibilities as workers whose labor is beneficial, and sometimes essential, to the financial well-being of the family (Orellana, 2001). For many immigrant families, economic survival creates roles for children that may promote parental involvement and contribute to family cohesion and parent–child bonding in work-related settings. Many immigrants work in manual and service labor occupations where it is not unusual to "bring children along" to help with the work and make extra money. In the past, when Mexican immigrants were involved mostly in agricultural labor, children often worked in the fields with their parents. This situation still exists today, especially during summers, but at a lesser scale due to child labor laws. More typical today, however, is the situation of children working with parents in service and manual labor sectors in jobs such as masonry, gardening and landscaping, painting, construction and cleaning, or in settings such as restaurants and auto shops. Others work with their parents in cottage industries pertaining to garment work and food preparation. Children in family worker roles may have more

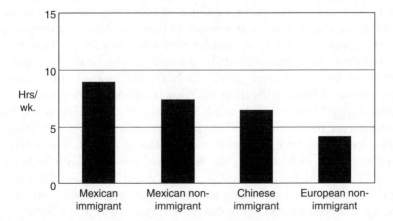

**Figure 7.1**  Ethnic differences in hours spent per week providing assistance to the family. Adapted from Hardway and Fuligni (2006).
*Source:* Andrew Fuligni.

opportunities to develop personal responsibility, autonomy, and self-efficacy by observing and modeling their parents in work-related activities.

Another form of family responsibility involves the child as a cultural or language broker on behalf of the family. Since immigrant children and adolescents often learn the language, customs, and norms of the host culture faster than their parents, they sometimes serve as cultural brokers or translators on behalf of their parents or grandparents. Children who serve as interpreters for their non-English speaking parents are referred to as "language brokers" and in their role as mediators between their parents' culture and European American society, they can also be considered "cultural brokers." It is estimated that approximately one in every five children in the United States comes from a home where at least one parent is of foreign birth (Federal Interagency Forum on Child and Family Statistics, 2002). Most of these children are the first members of their families to learn English and attend US schools. Most often it is the oldest sibling and typically girls more than boys who assume this brokering role (Villanueva and Buriel, 2010). As a result, these children are often delegated adult-like responsibilities by their parents, such as interpreting and making decisions with English-speaking agents that affect the whole family (DeMent, Buriel, and Villanueva, 2005; Orellana, Dorner, and Pulido, 2003; Valdes, 2003). Children and adolescents play a major role in helping their parents negotiate the legal maze, medical systems, and educational and workplace bureaucracies. As many as three in four immigrant children, act as language brokers for their parents (Hernandez, Denton, and Macartney, 2008).

> With responsibility as interpreters of the new culture and language, immigrant children are often in a position with no one to translate or interpret for them. Traditional intergenerational authority relationships change and the child also becomes very involved in the worries and concerns of the family, such as hassles with landlords, arranging for medical care, and dealing with the legal system (Olsen and Chen, 1988, p. 31).

While these activities clearly help the family unit thrive by aiding parents' negotiation with cultural institutions in the host country, what are the benefits and risks for children of assuming these major family responsibilities?

In our child and youth-oriented culture, skeptics may wonder whether these family obligated children suffer as a result of these burdens. Contrary to popular views that helping one's family is a burden that may lower life satisfaction, or cause anxiety and depression, providing daily assistance to the family generally was not stressful for adolescents (Fuligni, 2012). In fact, fulfilling family obligations has its benefits; a sense of family obligation was associated with more positive emotional well-being among Latin American and Filipino young adults (Fulingi and Pedersen, 2002). Adherence to traditional cultural family values was linked with lower anxiety and depression among later generation children and adolescents (Gonzales, Fabrett, and Knight, 2009), while assisting the family was associated with higher levels of happiness (Telzer and Fuligni, 2009b). Similarly, Buriel et al. (1998) found that among Latino adolescents, more language brokering was associated with more social self-efficacy. Children who broker in diverse settings such as stores, banks, hospitals, and schools have more opportunities to develop accelerated linguistic, cognitive, and interpersonal skills. Some scholars are even more bullish about the positive effects of being a cultural/language broker. Drawing on Gardner's theory of multiple intelligences, Valdes (2003) argues that competent language brokers exhibit multiple types of cognitive, social, and interpersonal intelligences and should therefore be considered "gifted." At the same time, children can use their linguistic edge to take advantage of their parents. One second generation 13-year-old Mexican American boy admitted to researchers Carola Suárez-Orozco and Marcedo Suarez-Orozco (2001) that he had told his parents that the "F" on his report card stood for "fabulous"!

These positive effects are due, in large part, to the sense of role fulfillment that family assistance provides adolescents. Family assistance serves as a meaningful activity in adolescents' lives by creating a sense of connection to the family. Being a language broker, for example, is associated with greater respect for ones' parents among Mexican youth (Villanueva and Buriel, 2010). Ethnic differences in the effects of assisting one's family actually show up in the brains of adolescents. Latino and White participants were scanned as they made decisions to contribute money to their family and themselves. Latino and White participants showed similar behavioral levels of helping but distinct patterns of neural activity within the mesolimbic reward system. Whereas Latino participants showed more reward activity when contributing to their family, White participants showed more reward activity when gaining cash for themselves. In addition, participants who felt more identified with their family and who derived greater fulfillment from helping their family two years earlier showed increased reward system activation when contributing to their family. These results suggest that family assistance may be guided, in part, by the personal rewards one attains from that assistance, and that this sense of reward may be modulated by cultural influences and prior family experiences (Telzer et al., 2010).

Academic achievement is linked with family assistance too. Immigrant Latino children who act as family cultural brokers have higher school grades (Buriel et al., 1998). Mexican and Asian youth who have a strong ethnic identity as well as clear sense of family obligation have higher motivation to succeed academically (Fuligni et al., 1999; Fuligni, 2001) which may be of great value in helping them succeed in the American educational system. As Fuligni (2010) argued:

> Perhaps because of the many challenges that Latin American, Asian and immigrant students face in their educational progress in American society, it simply takes more motivation to achieve the same level of academic success as their peers from European backgrounds (p. 110).

Several studies support this view that it simply takes more motivation to achieve for these students (Fuligni, 2010). To the extent that newly arrived immigrants adhere to these values, their children may be better behaved in school and be viewed as better socially adjusted by adults, including their teachers (Garcia and Marks, 2011).

There is a dark side to the responsibilities of fulfilling family obligations. Academic progress may suffer in some cases and parent–child authority boundaries may become blurred. As some critics fear, too much time devoted to family tasks has a downside for academic achievement. Cross time increases in the proportion of days spent helping the family were linked to declines in the GPAs of adolescents from Mexican backgrounds (Telzer and Fuligni, 2009a). In years in which they had the highest proportion of days helping their family, their grade point averages were lower. One high school student from an immigrant Mexican family captured this conflict between school and family responsibilities:

> Sometimes, I get irritated and frustrated about the fact that I have to sit late at night. Sometimes during the weekday, they (her parents) would go late at night to Wal-Mart or something, or to the market because they wouldn't have time during the day. So she (her mother) leaves it up to me to watch my little brother or sister. Sometimes I have a lot of homework and she says 'Oh you have to watch your brothers and sisters.' I wind up staying up really late or sometimes I wind up finishing it in class (Fuligni, 2010, p. 111).

There are some potential negative effects associated with the role of cultural broker as well. Child cultural brokers are unique; in addition to the stress related to their own acculturation, they experience additional stressors arising from their role as mediators between their parents and US society. In public, child cultural brokers act with adult authority on behalf of their parents, but at home they are expected to behave as children and show deference and respect to parents. Thus, as a result of the language-brokering role, there is the potential for the modification of traditional intergenerational authority relationships in immigrant families. These conflicting expectations and responsibilities represent a form of role strain that may raise children's anxiety to debilitating levels and lower their general well-being. The stress connected to language brokering may be particularly pronounced among young children because their cognitive and social capacities are still in the early stages of development (Weisskirch and Alva-Alatorre, 2002). At the same time there is evidence that the strong sense of family obligation in immigrant families and a strong affective parent–child bond may mitigate the threat to authority relationships and buffer adolescents against stress connected to language brokering (Buriel, Love, and DeMent, 2006; Fuligni et al., 1999). On balance, it seems that the benefits of assuming family responsibilities clearly outweigh the risks and argues for a rethinking of our expectations of children's family contributions in mainstream American culture.

*Marital Status as a Protective Factor:*  Immigrant families are more likely to be married or cohabitating than Mexican American families of later generations (Hummer and Hamilton, 2010).

> Although Mexican children of immigrants have a higher poverty rate than Mexican children of natives, they are more likely to live in two-parent families. Fifty-six percent of Mexican children of immigrants live with two married parents, compared with 45% of Mexican children of natives. When cohabitating parents are included, fully 75% of Mexican children of immigrants live in a two-parent family, compared with 63% of Mexican children of natives. The favorable family structures of children with foreign-born parents may reduce some of the risk factors typically associated with poverty (Landale, et al., 2011, pp. 51–52).

Cohabitating Mexican American couples are more likely to marry after the birth of a child and have a high rate of relationship stability (Landale and Oropesa, 2007). Nor is this pattern unique to Mexican immigrants; according to a recent analysis, 82% of children of immigrants of a diverse set of countries of origin live with two parents compared to 71% of children in native born families (Hernandez, Denton, Macartney et al., 2012). Moreover, compared to couples in other ethnic groups in the United States,

Mexican Americans are less likely to divorce (Landale and Oropesa, 2007). With time in the United States second and third generation immigrant families increasingly resemble native families, including the higher prevalence of single-parent families. Marital discord and divorce increase as acculturation increases (Flores et al., 2004). For example, among Mexican American families, maternal acculturation was associated with higher levels of marital problems (Parke, Coltrane, Duffy et al., 2004). The culture of divorce in American society

> conflicts with Mexican traditional values of family unity, but it is likely that more accul-
> turated Mexican Americans, especially woman, are pulled more in the direction of the
> values of their adopted country and come to see divorce as a viable option to marital
> discord (Padilla and Borrero, 2006, p. 20).

*Work Ethic as a Protective Factor:* Most Mexican immigrant children live in families with a strong work ethic (Hernandez et al., 2012). About 71% of the 10.7 million immigrants from Mexico age 16 and older were in the civilian labor force in 2009 compared to 68% of the 36.3 million immigrants age 16 and older from all countries and 64% of the 205 million native born age 16 and older (Batalova and Terrazas2010.). While Mexican immigrant fathers are more likely to work outside the home (85%) than mothers (50%), women often work in unregulated labor markets such as house-cleaning and child care and therefore may not be fully represented in official labor statistics. Moreover, about a quarter of first generation immigrant families have another adult worker who contributes to the economic capital of the family (Hernandez et al., 2012). Another index of a strong work commitment is the practice of sending funds ("remittances") back to Mexico to help other relatives improve their lives even though the wages of adults sending money are often at the poverty level (Buriel, 2012). Immigrant parents are more likely than native born parents to emphasize education for their children as a route to greater economic mobility. Immigrant parents transmit these work-related values in their children by fostering self reliance, productive use of time and early assumption of responsibility (Buriel, 1993; 2012).

## Asian American Families: Another Lesson in Interdependence

Asian American families offer further insight into how families can be organized and flourish in spite of the departure of some Asian families from the so-called "ideal" family form. As we saw in the case of Latino families, a major characteristic of Asian American families is the focus on familial interdependence by which the goals and priorities of the family group take precedence over individual personal goals. This orientation has its roots in Confucian principles concerning filial piety. Confucius developed a hierarchy defining a person's roles, duties, and moral obligations not only in the state but in the family as well, with each member's role dictated by age and gender. Typically, Asian American families are seen as patriarchal, with the father maintaining authority and emotional distance from other members (Wong, 1988; 1995). Confucian influences on family life are stronger in some Asian American populations (e.g., Chinese and Vietnamese) than others (e.g., Japanese) due to differences in immigration patterns and degree of Westernization of the country of origin. Length of US residence and acculturation also contribute to extensive within-group differences in family structure and roles. This interdependence orientation is reflected in a variety of ways. Traditionally, the family exerts major control over its members, who are taught to place family needs before individual needs. Children show obedience and loyalty to their parents and, especially male children, are expected to take care of elderly parents (filial piety). In many Asian countries, subjugation of personal will to elders is an indicator of maturity and persists in intergenerational relationships among Asian American adolescents (Ying, Coombs, and Lee, 1999). However, this parental control among Chinese American mothers for example, "reflects parents caring for their children within a highly interdependent family system" (Chao and Tseng, 2002, p. 68) and the goal of parental control is to foster relational goals such as a close and enduring parent–child relationships. In contrast, European American parents are just as caring but oriented toward more individual goals for their children such as self esteem or positive feelings about themselves as individuals (Chao and Tseng, 2002).

*Asian Extended Families:* Extended families are more prevalent among Asian immigrant families than European American families which reflects the commitment to interdependence among Asian families (Chao and Tseng, 2002). For example, in Vietnamese families, the kin group is seen as more important than the individual, a perspective that has its source in Confucian principles, especially ancestor worship (Kibria, 1993). Ancestor worship for Vietnamese Americans consists of devotion in caring for an altar containing pictures of deceased family members and praying at ritually prescribed times (Chao and Tseng, 2002). In Vietnamese families, for example, large extended families are common and enable households to connect to a variety of social and economic resources (Kibria, 1993). Moreover, large Vietnamese families varying in age and gender fared better economically than smaller nuclear families. Shared child care among parents and older relatives is a common practice among Vietnamese immigrants as well as other Asian immigrant groups such as the Hmong (Hillmer, 2010). Multigenerational and multifamily households are more common among Asian families compared to their Caucasian counterparts. Asian elders who are 60 years and older are three times as likely to live in a household with a spouse and other kin present (34 vs. 11%) than Caucasian elders (Himes, Hogan, and Eggebeen, 1996). Asian Americans are especially likely to live with family members, with relatively low rates of residing alone or with roommates (Harris and Jones, 2005). (See Figure 7.2.)

*Family Obligations:* Just as we saw in the case of Latino families, a further way in which family interdependence is reflected among Asian American families is through higher expectations for their children's obligations to their families than among European American families. "Throughout childhood and adulthood, Asian children are socialized to believe they should respect and follow the guidance of their parents as well as fulfill a range of financial, instrumental and caregiving obligations to their families" (Chao and Tseng, 2002, p. 68). And the evidence suggests that this is what happens: Asian American youth like Latino teens, are higher in their levels of family assistance than European American adolescents (Fuligni, 2010). Siblings may play an important role in Asian families as well by assisting with the care and teaching of younger siblings especially in single parent households. Sibling roles vary due to differences in rates of acculturation across siblings. For example, Pyke (2005) found that

**Figure 7.2** Extended families are a major source of support among many immigrant families. *Source*: © Catherine Yeulet/iStockphoto.

older siblings are slower to acculturate than younger siblings. This allows siblings to play different roles in the family. While older siblings help maintain ties with the traditional culture, younger ones provide a bridge to the new culture. Although conflict is possible, there may be some advantages for the Asian American family in the differential roles played by older and younger siblings.

Nor do these obligations inevitably produce stress. Neither the extent of involvement in family obligations nor the balancing of family obligations with other activities were associated with psychological distress among Chinese American adolescents (Fuligni and Hardway, 2004). However, among Asian adolescents, language brokering is associated with psychological distress such as internalizing (Chao, 2006), but not among Mexican American youth, particularly among girls (Buriel et al., 2006; Villanueva and Buriel, 2010).These ethnic differences may be due to the fact that among Mexican Americans, language brokering is viewed as normative and part of the gender role responsibilities of girls (Buriel et al., 2006). In addition, family interdependence during adolescence is linked with the delayed autonomy of Asian American adolescents from their parents compared to other ethnic groups (Chao and Tseng, 2002). For Asian American children these obligations in the form of household chores can begin as early as age five or six and are expected of both boys and girls (Phinney, Ong, and Madden, 2000). However, some report that girls devote more time each day fulfilling their family obligations than boys (Fuligni, Tseng, and Lam, 1999). Acculturation and intergenerational differences are found as well. US born adolescents disagree more with their parents regarding beliefs about family obligations than foreign born teenagers and their parents, presumably as a result of a shift to the more independent individualistic orientation of western culture (Phinney et al.,

2000). Similarly, filial obligations to elders may decrease with acculturation as well as with the economic hardship experienced by some Asian immigrants. Many Korean immigrants, for example, may have neither the time nor the money to carry out their obligations to their elders due to underemployment and work schedules (Kim and Kim, 1995).

*Marital Status:* Asians show low rates of single-mother households (9 vs. 12% nationally), whereas Pacific Islanders show relatively high rates of both single-mother (15%) and single-father (7%) living arrangements. Asian American children are more likely to live with both parents than are children of other ethnic groups. and households are more likely to include a married couple (62% for Asians and 56% for whites, respectively, vs. 53% for all households) (U.S. Census Bureau, 2003).

*Work Ethic and Asian Americans:*   Finally, Asian immigrants have a strong work ethic. Not only are they often better educated than other groups of immigrants but they view work as central to their cultural identity. As one immigrant from Hong Kong observed: "Due to the stigma attached to being unemployed in the culture, many people from Asia don't want to be on welfare and public assistance" (Lane, 2011). And another immigrant, a Vietnamese refugee, reported "that he felt looked down upon" for being unemployed. This work ethic may, in part, account for the fact that Asians have the lowest rate of unemployment compared to other racial groups in the United States.

*Summing Up:*   As we see in both Latino and Asian immigrant families, there are clear differences between these families and European American families not only in values but in family forms as well. Their endorsement of the importance of strong interdependence among immediate as well as extended family members is a major difference. Many of the features of these newcomer families may be beneficial in aiding them in their efforts to survive and flourish in their new homeland. In fact, there may be clear advantages to retaining some of these cultural traditions as they acculturate to American society. Keeping a place in both the culture of origin and the host culture may be a wise strategy.

## The Immigrant Paradox and the Bicultural Family

We often assume that immigration is a one-way process: People from other countries come to the United States to settle and work, and they routinely adopt the values, customs, and practices of the host country. This is an oversimplified view that ignores the mutual influences between cultural groups. From a systems perspective (Minuchin, 2002), the immigrant family can be thought of as an open system with both internal and external aspects of functioning. Internal aspects include the family's patterns of relationships and interactions and also the structure of the family. External aspects include the family's interactions with outside social systems including social institutions and the larger context of US society. Rueschenberg and Buriel (1989) have shown that the Mexican American family is capable of adapting to US social systems while retaining many of its internal characteristics that are cultural in nature. Many members of families that have recently immigrated from Mexico embrace a bicultural orientation, picking and choosing traits and practices of the dominant US culture that help them to survive and thrive, while still retaining distinctive aspects of their culture of origin. "We must adjust to the way of life here," observes Juan, a Mexican American father, "but it shouldn't affect [my children] speaking Spanish and learning it correctly."

But is not the goal of full acculturation desirable? Perhaps not. As the term the *immigrant paradox* so well captures, when immigrants adopt the values and customs of the host country and give up the values of their culture of origin, there is often a cost (Garcia Coll and Marks, 2011). Instead a better strategy is a bicultural orientation. Rather than a liability, a bicultural orientation comes with clear benefits. Both children and adults who straddle the cultural fence, in fact, have better physical and psychological health, including higher expectations and feelings of positive self-worth (Buriel and Vasquez, 1982). Other scholars (Gutierrez and Sameroff, 1990) find that bicultural mothers have a more sophisticated understanding of children's development than do Mexican American mothers who have become more integrated into American culture, and their children do better both academically and socially. It is often found that first generation immigrant children often outperform second and third generation children in school, despite linguistic and cultural barriers putting them at an initial disadvantage (Portes and Rumbaut, 2006; Portes and Rivas, 2011).

Moreover, first generation immigrant children are less prone to juvenile delinquency, substance use, anxiety and depression, and more likely to have a positive attitude toward their school and teachers (Fuligni and Hardway, 2004; Gonzales, Fabrett, and Knight, 2009; Pena et al., 2008). Finally, foreign-born children who immigrate to the United States typically have lower mortality and morbidity risks than children born to immigrant parents after their arrival in the United States. Over time the health advantage of immigrant children fades and by the second or third generation, health is poorer, as exemplified by increases in the number of health problems, more obesity and higher rates of asthma (Perreira and Ornelas, 2011; Singh, Kogan, and Yu, 2009). Nor can these results be attributed to different levels of poverty: these effects are found both before and after controlling for SES (Hernandez et al., 2012).

As developmental psychologist Cynthia Garcia Coll commented:

> In a time where immigrants are seen as detriments to our society and not making contributions, what this research is telling us is that the first generations come in with amazing energy and amazing capabilities of surmounting lack of education in parents, poverty, and language differences. The tragedy is that as some kids acculturate and become American, they start doing worse (September 29, 2010, p.2).

The lesson is clear: maintaining a bicultural orientation is an important factor in protecting children's academic progress, their social adjustment as well as their physical health. Retaining a commitment to shared responsibility for children among a range of family players including extended family members rather than acceptance of the "ideal" family form of mainstream American culture is a key component of this bicultural strategy. Part of the success of the Durado family was their commitment to such a strategy.

## Divided by Borders: Transnational Families as New Family Forms

> In this era of heightened globalization, transnational lifestyles may become not the exception but the rule (Levitt, 2001, p. 4).

It is misleading to think about family immigration as a unitary process. Instead it is a messy and fragmented process in which some members of the family may migrate initially while others follow to rejoin them at a later time or in some case are unable to reunite as a family. There is no single pattern of family immigration only multiple ones. Although the worldwide scope of this pattern is difficult to quantify, some suggest that approximately 25% of children in migrant-sending countries have at least one parent abroad (Mazzucato and Schans, 2011). By highlighting these "fragmented" families, we not only underscore the variability of immigrant families but also the needs and challenges faced by these families. By focusing on these transnational families, we may begin to better understand how to support these understudied but important groups of immigrant families. Finally, this work represents a further challenge to our traditional focus on the nuclear family form and forces both scholars and practitioners to expand their purview to consider the variety of family forms that arise in transnational families and recognize that new units of analysis need to be considered (Mazzucato and Schans, 2011).

The decisions to migrate are best viewed as family strategies aimed at helping their family survive economically by finding better paying jobs in another country (Stark and Bloom, 1985). For fathers who define their central family role as an economic provider, the decision is consistent with their obligation to provide for their family by gaining better wages and sending remittances back to their family members. For mothers who view themselves as caregivers first, it is a more difficult decision even though the extra income can mean better educational opportunities and increased economic security for their children in their home country.

As Dreby and Adkins (2010) note:

> Historically, it was almost always men who dominated migrant streams. Today, an increase in female migration rates worldwide means that contemporary transnational families take many forms. Some women, particularly those who are able to arrange work visas or who have family networks to facilitate their emigration, leave husbands and children behind when they come to work in the United States. Other female migrants are single and unable to find adequate employment opportunities in their countries of origin. Many women come to the United States in what scholars call a step-migration or chain-migration pattern; they join their husbands who are already abroad, leaving their children behind until they can be reunited either by sending for their children or returning home. Other parents, especially women, may migrate as older adults to help their children with child care and housework duties (p. 676).

In spite of the historical shifts, gender-linked differences in family immigration patterns persist. Although there has been an increase in female migration without their children, fathers are still more likely to leave their children and often their wives in their home countries than mothers. One study of immigrant children in Boston and San Francisco found that 79% had been separated from their fathers during migration while 55% had been separated from their mothers (Suarez-Orozco, Todorova, and

Louie, 2002). The average length of time away from their children is less for mothers than fathers. Among Mexican immigrants, mothers averaged 3.5 years away from their children whereas fathers averaged 8.3 years away (Dreby, 2010). Another gender –related difference is the time before reunification for mothers and fathers; 77% of mothers reunited with their children within two years compared to only 35% of fathers (Suarez-Orozco et al., 2002). However, many fathers make an effort to maintain ties with their children during migration-related geographic separations (Nobles, 2011) but their efforts vary by marital status. For example, married Mexican migrant fathers who are separated from their children maintain more contact with their children than divorced Mexican fathers. Finally, rather than viewing immigrant parents as uncaring, it is important to recognize the variety of mitigating factors that make it difficult for parents, especially if undocumented, to go back and visit their families including fear of job loss, danger associated with border crossings, and lack of funds (Avila, 2008; Hondagneu-Sotelo & Avila, 1997).

Another pattern emerges when both parents migrate together and later have a child. Many Asian immigrants follow a practice of sending their infants back to be cared for by their parents or other relatives in their homeland. Termed "satellite babies" by Canadian psychologist Yvonne Bohr, parents choose this arrangement due to lack of time, money and child-care options (Bohr and Tse, 2009). Similarly, as one immigrant Chinese father in Bohr's study explained:

> Because of the family financial [situation], we need to send her back to China for [our] parents to take care of her. As soon as my [visiting] parents have to go back to China, we will try to send the baby as well. If she stays here, my wife won't go to work. So I have to support the whole family myself. I have to send my child back to China, at least for a couple of years.

Another parent said,

> "I've been here for three years. I want to have my own career. I had a good job in China but here I feel like I have to start all over but because of the baby I can't go back to work. I want to work harder to get a house; the most important factor is finances" (Bohr and Tse, 2009, p. 15).

Another reason is to insure that their offspring are exposed to the language and traditions of their culture. One parent in Bohr's study reported, "I don't want my child to grow up in Canada and just talk Canadian" (Bohr and Tse, 2009, p. 14). Another parent expressed similar fears about the loss of Chinese language, "He [will not be able to] understand Chinese. That is a big problem. He [will not be able to] speak Chinese [or] read or write any Chinese. He [will not be able to] understand" (Bohr and Tse, 2009, p. 17). Among West African immigrant families in Europe or North America, children with behavior problems, which many adults view as due to lax and permissive Western approaches to discipline, may be sent back to their country of origin to live with relatives and to reconnect them to their culture and their family. Although this may involve extended separation between parents and their children, parents may view the costs as justified and as a strategy for protecting the long-term interests of their children (Dreby, 2010). In fact, parents may bring their children back to Europe or North America after the period of "resocialization" when children are better equipped to handle the risks as well as the opportunities of Western culture. Rather than viewing these "return your child" strategies as cold hearted, instead they can be thought of as long-term adaptive family strategies for maximizing good outcomes for their children.

   Less often but still worth noting are children emigrating before their parents. In the case of children and adolescents in Latino families, migration is usually due to extreme economic disadvantage or to escape violence or sexual exploitation; they move in hopes of a better life "el norte." In fact, about 150,000 minors attempt to enter the United States from Mexico each year and approximately 60,000 are returned to their home country. Another 80,000 Hondouran children attempt to cross the US border annually (Thompson, 2008). These are impressive numbers and suggest that it is not only parents and other adults who are part of the immigration flow.

*Challenges Faced by Migrant Parents:*   All members of transnational families face challenges. Parents who migrate suffer sadness and loneliness due to loss of regular contact with their children and perhaps their spouse. According to one mother, "I cried for two months after I first arrived.... I was nervous all the time and made mistakes when I first started to work" while another migrant mother recalled that "I suffered a lot in the United States without my son, especially when we first arrived. When we would go to the stores and I saw children with their parents, I would start to cry" (Dreby, 2010, p. 83). Although new technologies such as e-mail, instant messaging, and even webcams and skype allow family members to stay in touch with each other while living apart (Wilding, 2006), parents still feel deprived of regular interaction with their families. They may face difficulties finding employment, especially a steady, reliable, and well paying job. They feel obligated to work hard so that they can fulfill their obligation of sending remittances to help their children and other family members in their home country. As one father put it, "my life in the US is all work" (Dreby, 2010, p. 37) but this is part of the "migration bargain" which involves sacrifice for the hope of improving life for one's family.

*Substitute Caregivers:*   Transnational families rely on other family members to make this migration arrangement work. When men migrate, women perform both more nonfamily paid work as well as more unpaid household work and rely on a network of kin to assist them in child care and household tasks (Boehm, 2004, 2008). When women migrate either to join their husbands, prior to their husbands, or even alone, other women – kin such as grandmothers or aunts and nonkin such as other mothers, friends or fellow churchgoers in the community – share the child-care duties. Men may share in these tasks but they are much less likely to take on these responsibilities than women (Dreby, 2010; Schmalzbauer, 2005). "When migrant parents leave children with their own parents, the reciprocity in the arrangement works in two directions; not only do their children stay with loving caregivers, but migrants also provide for both their parents and their children via remittances" (Dreby and Adkins, 2010, p. 679). A reliance on nuclear family models is clearly inadequate to accommodate these other caregivers; instead to understand the range of family forms among transnational families requires models that incorporate these new actors into the family mix (Mazzucato and Schons, 2011).

*Consequences of Migration for Children Left Behind:*   There are both positive as well as negative implications of parental migration for children. Moreover, there is considerable variability in children's reactions to separation. Some may suffer, while others adapt and do well in spite of parental absence. On the positive side, children are often better off economically and have better educational opportunities when parents are able to share their improved income with their children left behind (Lahaie et al., 2009; Schmalzbauer, 2005). Interestingly, when the mother migrated, children are more likely to thrive economically than father-migrant families because of the extreme sacrifices mothers make to send remittances home (Abrego, 2009). On the downside, according to a recent survey, Mexican children who stayed behind while one or more of their parents migrated to the United States did worse than their peers in terms of frequency of illness and emotional problems, having to repeat a grade, and in reports of behavioral problems (Heymann et al. 2009). Moreover, the emotional effects on children are worse when mothers rather than fathers migrate (Parrenas, 2005; Wen and Lin, 2012). The amount of contact between the migrant parent and the child left behind matters too. For example, Nobles (2011) found a positive association between the amount of father–child contact – even though across borders – and school performance of both sons and daughters. Clearly, parental contact either at a distance or by visits home is important for these families, just as amount and quality of contact is important in nonimmigrant families (Parke and Buriel, 2006).

Children's reactions to separation vary across age. Young children sometimes express their upset by feigning indifference toward their absent parent by refusing to talk on the phone when a parent calls. Older children act out; as Dreby (2010) recounted based on her interviews with children in Mexico, 14 year old Miguel started to smoke at the age of 12 when his mother left. "I felt desperate because I lived alone with my grandmother and my brother. And I started the habit because, many times, you know, it chills you out, it calms your nerves, and all that" (Dreby, 2010, p. 120). Reunification is often difficult for both children and parents. After being away for a year one mother reported that her five-year old twins hid from her. They said "since you left, we don't know you anymore" (Dreby, 2010, p. 119). Although the effects of separation on the parent–child relationships is generally temporary, after family reunification some children of migrant parents may continue to have adjustment difficulties including dropping out of school and continuing to act out (Aguilera-Guzman et al., 2004; Suarez-Orozco et al., 2002). Even if children are united with their parents in a new country, they may experience depression and/or guilt due to separation from their interim caregiver (grandmother, aunt) with whom they may have developed close ties (Avila, 2008).

Another source of variability is country of origin. On the one hand, many of the negative effects of parental migration on children found in Mexico are repeated in poorer countries, such as India, where children show elevated levels of insecurity in reaction to their migrant fathers (Rogaly et al., 2002). In rural China, over half of junior high school students reported difficulties adapting to being left behind by their parents who migrated to urban areas to find better employment (Liang and Ma, 2004). In a recent study, "left behind" children in rural China had more substance use and lower school classroom engagement but not different levels of life satisfaction compared to children without migrant parents (Wen and Lin, 2012). On the other hand, in the Philippines, children with migrant parents are not only economically better off but also physically healthier and emotionally similar to their nonmigrant peers (Asis, 2006). Strategic long distance parenting involving regular communication between parents and children (text messaging, email and skype) and a long tradition of established care networks in which female relatives serve as caregivers while parents are away are probably responsible for the more positive outcomes among Filipino children (Asis, 2006; Parrenas, 2005).

In view of this variability, the challenge is to better understand the conditions under which a child's social, emotional, and academic problems can be minimized. For example, the quality and stability of the child–caregiver relationship in the post separation period, the length of the separation, the age of the child at the time of separation and the frequency of both long distance contact and face to face visits either in the home or host country are all important factors to consider. From our cooperative family form perspective, the most likely protective factor for minimizing child problems is the availability of sensitive and responsive alternative caregivers during the separation period. Fortunately, Asian, Mexican, and other Latino groups view families as embedded in a network of kin and nonkin caregivers and it is this cooperative social arrangement that makes transnational family migration feasible and helps many children in transnational families survive and flourish in spite of the stress associated with separation.

## The Implications of Transnational Families for Our Definition of the "Ideal" Family

What do these patterns of migration mean for our definition of family and what are the effects on the migrant who leaves as well as those left behind in the home country? First, these segmented migration patterns challenge our concept of the "ideal" family form in even more dramatic terms than in many other cases that we have discussed. In terms of our definition of "ideal" family, the family members do not share a common residence but are geographically separated as well. Depending on the arrangement one or more of the parents may be away from their children and, in turn, the children may be in the care of other adults who may or may not be relatives. In some ways, there are similarities between these transnational families and nonimmigrant incarcerated parents (Parke and Clarke-Stewart, 2003). In both cases, there is limited contact between parents and children and a shift in caregiving responsibility to others. However, the migrant parents and their children view themselves as a family unit even if separated. The commitment to the family unit is expressed by migrant parents in the long hours of work in often difficult jobs, their sending of funds back to their family and their efforts to stay in contact with their children. In one study (Dreby, 2010), most parents – mothers and fathers – reported calling home to Mexico once a week. Similarly, 61% of children in this study reported talking to their parents once a week or more. Children's drawings confirm that in spite of being apart from their parents, children view their parents as central figures in their family portrayals. When 423 Mexican children in the first to sixth grades were asked to "Draw a picture of your family," 92% of the children with both parents in the United States drew both of their parents in their picture. In contrast, only 38% of children who lived without their parents due to divorce or marital separation drew both parents in their family drawings (Dreby, 2010). International migration does not diminish children's view that parents are a central part of their family. And the caregivers, usually maternal grandmothers, who look after children in their parents' absence contribute to children's awareness of the importance of their parents in their lives. They stress the sacrifices that their parents are making on behalf of the family and differentiate their own role as temporary caregivers from the role of parents which, in turn, facilitates eventual reunification. Dreby (2010) describes the role of grandmothers as follows:

> To their grandchildren they often praise the parents' sacrifice. They constantly highlight their grandchildren's need for biological parents and acknowledge biological parents' rights to their children. Grandparents do not want to undermine migrant parents' efforts and hope to support their (own children's) endeavours to care for their family, albeit from a distance. Despite young children's practices of calling grandmothers "Mama", rarely do these women consider themselves their grandchildren's mothers (p. 176).

Just as we saw in the case of children's relationships with other adults such as teachers or child-care workers, children are capable of developing meaningful but distinct relationships with a variety of social figures while at the same time not undermining their close ties to their parents. As these transnational families illustrate, children and adults are resilient, robust, and creative in maintaining family relationships in spite of temporal and physical separation. Finally, the examination of transnational families provides another and perhaps unique window into the effects of parent–child separation on children's development.

## Lessons from Immigrant Families

There are key lessons that immigrant families might have to teach nonimmigrant families: Understanding other cultural practices, values, and beliefs may not only increase our tolerance and acceptance of differences – a lesson that is valuable for both children and adults in our increasingly multicultural society – but also contribute to our own well-being. Just as biculturalism is beneficial for Mexican American immigrants, it could benefit other families as well. Mexican American and Asian American families teach us that a renewed commitment to the centrality of the interdependent family and kin and non kin networks in our lives could provide significant social and emotional benefits, such as greater buffers against the stresses, strains, and sorrows of everyday life. Our own research suggests that the negative impacts of financial hardship and other stressful life circumstances on children are reduced in Mexican American families with high levels of family cohesion (Parke et al., 2004). From the model provided by immigrant families, we could also learn a lot about how community cohesiveness and community responsibility promote the welfare of children. The presence of many eyes and ears to monitor our children in public places would be a welcome aid for many overextended, overworked, and underavailable parents in "ideal" families.

No one is advocating an unqualified embrace of all aspects of immigrant family life. We recognize that some of the hierarchical aspects of traditional Latino and Asian family life are not desirable for many Anglo families – nor for many Latino and Asian immigrant families themselves. Modern women who are active members of the workforce are unlikely to welcome a return to patriarchal practices where husbands rule and women obey. At the same time, in fairness, the stereotype of the patriarchal Mexican American and Asian American family is outdated. Most research shows that Mexican American and Asian couples have moved toward a more equal balance of power between spouses just as their European American counterparts have. Our research, for example, shows that Mexican American couples share parenting and housework in response to the same sorts of practical pressures faced by other couples (Coltrane, Parke, and Adams, 2004).

By no means should we give up the positive gains toward more equal family roles for men and women in the United States that have been achieved over the last 40 years. But we would like to graft onto this newly emerging model some of the passionate commitment to family and community that characterizes many immigrant families. A new family form could emerge that is a fusion of an egalitarian family model but one that is better anchored by extended kin, neighbors, and communities all of whom are committed to the common good of our children. Such a synthesis may not only be possible, but may be desirable.

## Reflections

Our exploration of intracultural variations in family forms among families who are long-term inhabitants such as Native Americans and African Americans as well as among more recently arrived immigrant families yields portraits of families which clearly depart from the "ideal" family form. The thread that ties together these diverse ethnic and racial groups is their embrace of a more expansive and inclusive family form which recognizes the nuclear family as part of an extended family system. Instead of an isolated and self sufficient "ideal" nuclear family form, historically and more recently the adaptive value of defining a family form with porous boundaries and a range of kin and nonkin participants is strikingly clear. Moreover, these models underscore the degree of interchangeability across caregivers which serves to protect and insure the well-being of children, whether fictive kin in poor African American families, compadres in Latino immigrant families, or grandmothers in Chinese or Mexican transnational families. At the very least, these examples remind us of the rich diversity of family forms not just in other cultures and other countries but in our own society. And they underscore that children thrive intellectually, socially, and physically in a wide range of family forms. As the work on the benefits of biculturalism so dramatically illustrates, retaining a commitment to family forms that recognize the embeddedness of families in a social network of extended kin, neighbors, and communities may provide more protection against developmental risk for immigrant children and youth. In many ways, we have moved as a society in this direction through our joint sharing of socialization of our children with day care providers, teachers, coaches, and nonfamily mentors. The next step is to embrace explicitly these alternative forms, learn how to effectively utilize these collective approaches to family organization and child socialization and rid ourselves of the outdated and irrelevant model of the alleged "ideal" family form.

# 8

# Multiple Caregivers
## *Harmful or Helpful for Caregivers Themselves*

*Being a caregiver is not only good for children but good for caregivers too*
(Anonymous)

Is being a caregiver, either as a parent or as a secondary caregiver where the individual is one among many, harmful or helpful for the caregivers themselves? There is no simple answer. While there are joys and pleasure associated with being a parent or caregiver, there are challenges too. So while it is true that the opportunity to be a caregiver is beneficial for the caregivers themselves and not just for the children who receive care, it is also the case that at times it can be a tough task. As we have documented, many parents have opted for alternative family forms which depart from the "perfect" family ideal. Do the benefits and challenges of parenthood vary across different family forms? Do parents who adhere to the traditional nuclear family arrangement fare better than those in other family forms? Do parents benefit more and experience less stress from this caregiving experience when they are part of a cooperative or shared child rearing arrangement that is an increasingly common alternative to the "perfect" family form? And do the partners in cooperative parenting such as extended family members and nonkin such as daycare providers, mentors, and coaches benefit from their caregiving involvement. In this chapter, I critically examine the benefits as well as the risks for different caregivers – parents and nonparents. The evidence clearly indicates that on balance shared parenting is more helpful than harmful not only for parents themselves but for alternative caregivers as well.

## Is Parenting Beneficial for the Parent?
## The Impact of Being a Parent on Adult Development

In recent years, there has been a revival of interest in the effects of being a parent and/or caregiver on adult development. This focus has emerged in response to several theoretical, scholarly, and societal developments. One contributor was the theoretical advances in life span theory with its focus on the continuing changes that occur across the life course such as the onset of parenthood. Of particular importance is the timing

*Future Families: Diverse Forms, Rich Possibilities*, First Edition. Ross D. Parke.
© 2013 John Wiley & Sons, Inc. Published 2013 by John Wiley & Sons, Inc.

of these changes and their links with other events such as educational and occupational shifts in adults' lives (Elder, 1998). As we saw earlier, adolescent parenthood is an off time life event and may blunt some of the positive benefits of parenthood. This theoretical paradigm led to an examination of the ways in which adults coordinate different spheres of their adult lives including work and family life, especially as more women become full-time work force members. According to life course theory, becoming a parent can affect various aspects of family relationships, work relationships as well as individual development. A second contributor which specifically focused on the effects of becoming a parent was Erik Erikson's concept of generativity which suggested that parenting or more broadly taking responsibility for younger generations such as mentoring was linked with healthy adult development (McAdams, Hart, and Maruna, 1998). It can make you more generative, according to psychologist John Snarey (1993) and lead to more active involvement in nurturing the development of younger generations not just in your own family but in the wider community as well. Third, advances in the psychobiology of parenting and caregiving have led to new insights concerning the hormonal and neurological underpinnings of care in both animals and humans. Specifically, there are well-documented biological changes not only in response to impending parenthood but more recently discovered biological changes that accompany being a parent or caregiver. These hormonal and neurological shifts in response to the tasks of caregiving provide insight into the rewards associated with being a caregiver.

The Parenthood Paradox: Why We Believe Children Are Good for Us but May Not Be

Parenting is both a joy and a burden. Most people expect to and hope to become parents since it is assumed that parenting will bring increased satisfaction and meaning to your life. However, in spite of these expectations, parenthood is associated with decreased feelings of well-being, what psychologist Roy Baumeister (1991) termed "the parenthood paradox." Is this really the case?

According to folk wisdom – as assessed by surveys of people's attitudes about parenthood, most of us do want to have children (Hansen, 2012). Nearly everyone (90–95%) of young adults across the world plan to have children (Stanley, Edwards, and Hatch, 2003; Toulemon, 1996). Another belief is that children are a source of happiness and satisfaction. About 80–90%, and slightly more women than men, agree with this statement "watching children grow up is life's greatest joy" in virtually all parts of the world and across two decades (Halle, 2002; Koropeckyj-Cox and Pendell, 2007; NSD, 2002). Moreover, many feel that having children will be rewarding and provide, companionship and support, meaning, love, excitement, and happiness, and that having children will reduce fear of loneliness and depression in old age (e.g., Friedman, Hechter, and Kanazawa, 1994; Schoen et al., 1997). Most of us view parenthood as a positive and desirable outcome.

Nor is it just folk beliefs but also social science theories that predict positive links between parenthood and psychological satisfaction (Hansen, 2012). First, according to a needs theory of well-being, children may gratify core human needs such as meaningfulness in one's life, companionship, affiliation, respect, security, positive self-image, and self-realization. By satisfying these needs parental happiness is assumed to increase (Baumeister and Leary, 1995; Lyubomirsky and Boehm, 2010). Second, goal theories of well-being (e.g., Michalos, 1985; Michalos 1991) suggest that children bring happiness because parenthood is a widely held life goal. Moreover, achieving parenthood is a marker of personal success, may lead to social recognition and feelings of pride, increased self esteem, and greater life satisfaction. Third, as we noted earlier in Chapter 2, even our brains are organized for parenting and the reward areas of our brains are activated when we see, touch, or even smell our offspring (Seifritz et al., 2003). Fourth, the benefits of having offspring also derive from classical sociological and psychological theories. The sociologist Durkheim theorized a century ago that parenthood structures people's lives and integrates people into social networks, thereby providing them with meaning and purpose in life. As noted earlier, life course theory stresses the centrality of parenthood for generativity and adult psychosocial development (Erikson, 1975).

Although both laypeople and theorists think that becoming a parent is a good idea, the data suggests that there are real downsides to becoming a parent. Being a parent is not an easy task, nor is it inexpensive in either time or money. As any harried parent knows changing diapers, juggling family and work schedules, locating high quality but affordable day care, and finding time to relax either by yourself or with your partner can be challenging and often frustrating. And if you are a single parent, it can be even more challenging. As we have argued, parenting was never designed as a socially independent and self sufficient enterprise for either the two partner or single-parent family. In fact, the rewards associated with raising children are more likely to materialize by sharing and outsourcing some of the joy as well as some of the hard parts to others in the community.

*Parenthood Is Expensive:* On the financial side, in 2010, it cost nearly 227,000 to provide the basics of food, shelter, clothes, health care, and transportation to raise a child until age 18, an increase of over $60,000 since 2000 (U.S. Department of Agriculture, 2012a). Forget designer strollers, organic baby formula, or all the extras such as lessons, clubs, and summer camps that many parents believe their child ought to have; just providing a child with the basics has become more than most parents can afford (Dickler, 2011; Folbre, 2008) (Figure 8.1).

If your child attends a private four year college, add another $200,000 or more. Clearly, parenthood does not come cheap! As economist Nancy Folbre estimates in her book, *Valuing Children* (2008), if you had invested the $165,630 that you expected to spend on raising a child in 2000 at 5% interest, 18 years later, your nest egg would be $545,284. If you left the money until retirement, you could retire well on the accumulated $1.5 million. As Folbre notes using an agricultural metaphor "Children are an expensive crop" (2008, p. 65).

*The Psychological Costs of Parenthood:* It is not just monetary costs; parenthood has psychological costs too. On the psychological side, being a parent leads to increases in worries and anxiety which accompany the responsibility of caring for and protecting a young and dependent child (Twenge, Campbell, and Foster, 2003). Personal freedom and flexibility are reduced as well; no more spontaneous nights out to the theater, the local bar or dinner with friends without first organizing a baby sitter to care for your offspring (Stanca, 2012). And especially in the early years of parenthood, infant

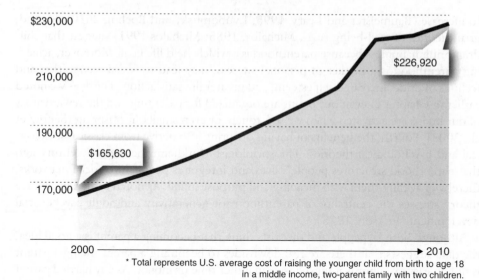

\* Total represents U.S. average cost of raising the younger child from birth to age 18
in a middle income, two-parent family with two children.

**Figure 8.1**  The rising cost of raising children.
*Source*: Department of Agriculture, 2012

demands for feeding, diaper changes, and attention mean, less sleep and higher levels
of fatigue (Cowan and Cowan, 2000) (Figure 8.2).

Some are more burdened than others: Those who assume the greater burden of
care for dependent children experience the biggest emotional toll. Women are more
negatively affected than men by becoming parents. In fact, in one recent study
(Nelson et al., 2012), fathers reported higher life satisfaction and happiness than
nonfathers while mothers did not differ from nonparents on these measures. Since
women still do more of the child care than men and the culture still views women as
primarily responsible for children's welfare and housework, this set of burdens may
offset the pleasures of parenthood (Nomaguchi and Milkie, 2003). Not surprising is
the fact that single parents report lower life satisfaction than partnered parents; single
parents encounter more challenges and greater emotional stress since they do not
have the assistance and support available to parents with partners (McLanahan and
Sandefur, 1994; Nelson et al., 2012). The timing of the onset of parenthood is
important too, and becoming a parent too early in life can be difficult (Nelson et al.,
2012). While young parents (17–25) were less satisfied with their lives than their
peers without children, more mature parents (26–62) were more satisfied than those
who did not have children. Older parents (63 and older) did not differ from their
childless peers (Nelson et al., 2012). As is so often the case, the poor who have fewer
financial resources tend to suffer more stress and lower life satisfaction by the responsibility of raising children than the more affluent (Mastekaasa, 1994; Stanca, 2012).
Finally, the country where you live matters too. In countries with low family welfare
benefits such as the United States and Eastern European countries, raising children
is related to more psychological stress and lower life satisfaction, while in countries
such as Norway and other Nordic countries with family friendly social policies having
children is positively associated with happiness and life satisfaction especially for

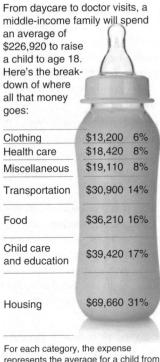

What kids cost

From daycare to doctor visits, a middle-income family will spend an average of $226,920 to raise a child to age 18. Here's the breakdown of where all that money goes:

| Clothing | $13,200 | 6% |
| Health care | $18,420 | 8% |
| Miscellaneous | $19,110 | 8% |
| Transportation | $30,900 | 14% |
| Food | $36,210 | 16% |
| Child care and education | $39,420 | 17% |
| Housing | $69,660 | 31% |

For each category, the expense represents the average for a child from age 0 to 18 in a two-child, two-parent family

**Figure 8.2** Where the money goes: The parental costs of different aspects of rearing a child. *Source*: U.S. Department of Agriculture, 2012; Source of graphic: © karandaev – Fotolia.com

women (Hansen, Slagsvold, and Moum, 2009; Myrskylä and Margolis, 2012). Similarly, in these family friendly countries where retirement benefits, health care and social services are readily available in old age, the impact of childlessness on depression and loneliness is less than in countries where children are the main source of "old age insurance" for the elderly (Dykstra and Hagestad, 2007; Hansen et al., 2009). These findings underscore the important role that government social policies play in how families cope with the challenges of combining parenthood, marriage, employment, and even old age (Hansen et al., 2009), an issue we will return to in the final chapter.

A continuing theme of this book has been the variability in how individuals in different family forms respond to the challenges of parenthood. As these factors (i.e., age, single parent status and levels of support offered by social policies in various countries) that contribute to this variability illustrate, social support for parenting is a critical determinant of how well individuals cope with the challenges of parenthood. As we saw earlier (Chapter 6), historically and cross culturally, parenting has been a cooperative enterprise which has eased the burden. A similar sentiment was captured recently by Lyubomirsky and Boehm (2010) who argued that

Our ancestors brought up very young children in the context of a larger village, clan, or tribe, which allowed childcare responsibilities to be shared across many individuals – both family members and neighbors. By contrast, the level of distress for modern-day parents is magnified when only one or two individuals are available to respond to a child's cries and needs. Thus, evolutionary explanations for why parenthood is not associated with increased happiness can be traced to the obstacles parenthood poses to other motivational needs, the long-term benefits stemming from having children, and the conflict between ancestral and modern-day environments (p. 330).

Finding ways to ease the parental burden and increase the life satisfaction and happiness of parents is an important goal since it has important effects on children's well-being. The implications for children of life satisfaction and happiness being part of the parenthood package, is summed up by Nelson et al. (2012):

Happiness is a central life goal for people around the world and has been associated with numerous positive outcomes for work, relationships, and health (Lyubomirsky, King, and Diener, 2005). Consequently, if parenthood is linked with relatively higher well-being, the resultant benefits may accrue not only to the parents themselves, but also to their children. Indeed, positive parental factors, such as emotional expression (Haviland and Lelwica, 1987), involvement and warmth (Klein and Forehand, 2000), and self regulation (Park and Peterson, 2006) have been associated with positive outcomes for children (p. 15).

*Summing Up:* There a variety of potentially positive outcomes associated with parenting and in spite of the challenges and daily hassles associated with this set of responsibilities, it is clear that adults derive satisfaction by assuming the tasks of parenthood. At the same time, a cooperative model of parenting in which parental responsibility is shared with others in the community is more likely to ensure that the joys and satisfaction of parenting will be fully realized. High levels of stress which are often prevalent in self sufficient "ideal" families in which parents assume total responsibility for child rearing not only undermines the individual's effectiveness as a parent but may reduce the benefits of parenting as well. In contrast, when parents gain assistance, guidance, and support as well as emotional and physical relief in the form of community or extended family assistance with child care and rearing, stress is lessened and both parents and children benefit. For example, social support is related to higher quality of the infant–parent attachment relationship (Crockenberg, 1981), to lower severity of postpartum depression (Logsdon, McBride, and Birkimer, 1994) and to reduced levels of child abuse (Cicchetti and Toth, 2006). Social support from kin and nonkin and competent and satisfying parenting go hand in hand.

## Beyond Parents: Do Relatives as Caregivers Benefit Too?

If a cooperative model of caregiving is viable, then we need to explore the benefits and costs experienced by nonparental alternative caregivers. In the next two sections, we examine the costs and rewards for relatives (i.e., siblings, grandparents) and nonrelatives (i.e., child care workers, mentors) of sharing some of the caregiving responsibilities.

*Sibling Caregivers:* Are there benefits of being a sibling caregiver? As we discussed in Chapter 5, in many cultures it is common for siblings to play an active role as a supervisor and caregiver of either younger siblings or even unrelated children in their community. And family historians remind us that in past times with large families in agricultural economies, children were expected to both contribute to the family chores as well as assist with the care of siblings (Pollack, 2002). Even in contemporary Midwest farm families it is expected that children will participate in family work (Elder and Conger, 2000). In past centuries when maternal death at child birth was more prevalent, older daughters were routinely recruited as substitute mothers (Mintz and Kellogg, 1988). And even in our own culture older siblings are not simply inexpensive babysitters for parent's night out, but play roles as mentors, protectors, and caregivers for their younger brothers and sisters or even for older relatives. Patricia East summed up the changing role of sibling care providers in current times as follows:

> The convergence of several demographic trends in the United States, including high divorce rate, lower marriage rates, and increasing numbers of single parents, has left fewer adults spending fewer hours in the home and, consequently, shifted a large share of family care onto children and adolescents. Family size in the United States has diminished, such that the average child has only one sibling, which effectively increases the caregiving load for each child within the family. In addition, the geographic dispersion of extended families has contributed to the fragmentation of kin ties and led to increased reliance on care by family members who are willing, present, and able (Ganong and Coleman, 1999). Collectively, these trends have created "care gaps," which are increasingly being met by today's youth. A recent national survey of young caregivers in the United States estimated that 1.4 million children and adolescents are involved in some type of family caregiving, with close to 1 million American households having a young caregiver (National Alliance for Caregiving, 2005). In the United Kingdom, approximately 50,000 children and adolescents care for an ill or disabled family member (Dearden et al., 2000). A review of American and European adolescents' time use found that, internationally, teenagers spend up to 40 min a day on family household tasks, which include caring for a family member (Larson and Verma, 1999). Most caregiving situations involve helping a grandparent (38%) or parent (34%), with the remainder caring for a sibling (11%), other relative (9%), or nonrelative (8%; National Alliance for Caregiving, 2005). When researchers asked 8- to 18-year-old caregivers how much time they spent providing care, 49% reported "a lot." Most of children's caregiving involves helping others with instrumental activities of daily living, such as shopping, household tasks, and meal preparation, but more than half of youth also perform more personal care, such as helping with bathing, dressing, and feeding (National Alliance for Caregiving, 2005) (East, 2010, p. 55).

What are the costs and benefits of assuming these caregiving responsibilities for siblings? As anthropologists have found, in settings such as Africa, Polynesia, and Mexico where siblings routinely act as caregivers, they are more responsible and selfless than siblings in cultures that do not provide these caregiving opportunities (Weisner, 1982, 1987; Whiting and Edwards, 1988). Other cross-cultural experts (Rabain-Jamin, Maynard, and Greenfield, 2003; Zukow-Goldring, 2002) report that sibling caregiving provides youth with a sense of purpose and meaning, and provides children opportunities to learn about the importance and rules governing social hierarchies. In contrast to earlier eras or in other cultures, where sibling care was viewed as normative, in the modern era children are not routinely expected to assume major caregiving roles. In fact, many parents are reluctant to publically acknowledge their use of their children as caregivers for fear of disapproval (Dodson and Dickert, 2004). This attitude is part of the current view that it is the parents' responsibility to provide for their children's care and that siblings should be shielded and protected from these "parental" responsibilities. In our contemporary society, children, especially those in the middle and upper classes are expected to have "developing space" so they can not only enjoy their childhood years but develop their social and recreational skills by spending time with peers and in cultivating their budding talents, a view that Gregory Jurkovic (1997) captures well in his book *Lost Childhoods*. The nonnormative nature of siblings as caregivers may, in part, account for the mixed benefits or "competence at a cost" (Kuperminc, Jurkovic, and Casey, 2009) associated with these family responsibilities for child and adolescent development.

On the positive side, children and adolescents who assume household responsibilities including sibling caregiving often gain a sense of maturity, increased self esteem, self reliance and empathy (East, 2010). As ethnographer Linda Burton (2007) has shown, for poor, inner city teens, family care increases self confidence and a sense of "mattering." Sibling caregivers can also develop greater perspective taking and socioemotional understanding (Bryant, 1992; Stewart and Martin, 1984). Others have found that sibling caregiving is associated with greater competence, self restraint, and self efficacy (Kuperminc et al., 2009). Although the focus is typically on the older sibling as caregiver, the role of younger siblings in assisting with the care of their adolescent sisters' infant has been explored as well (East, Weisner, and Reyes, 2006; East, Weisner, and Slonim, 2009). Younger siblings report that through these experiences they learn about children and parenting especially when an adult caregiver is present rather than when children perform these caregiving tasks alone (East et al., 2009). These experiences were linked with lower rates of school drop, a more positive school orientation, and fewer pregnancies among the involved younger siblings (East et al., 2006). The first-hand experience about the realities of parenting may have motivated these adolescents to stay in school and delay motherhood.

At the same time, there has been considerable attention given to "dark side" associated with overburdening children with caregiving roles. In fact, a variety of negative outcomes have been documented which provides some support to those social commentators (Burton, 2007; Chase, 1999; Jurkovic, 1997) who argue that we need to be careful in defining the proper role of siblings as caregivers in our society. There can be too much responsibility that may lead to negative effects on children. What are these negative consequences? Sibling care that is overly time consuming (20 or more hours per week) or extends across time (several years) has been linked with increased stress, depression, school dropout, academic difficulties, and increased rate of teen pregnancy (East, 2010; East and Jacobsen, 2001; East and Weisner, 2009; Jordan, Lara, and McPartland, 1996). Large-scale studies in the United Kingdom found higher levels of depression, stress, lower rates of school attendance, and concerns about "less time for themselves" among sibling caregivers (Becker, Aldridge, and Dearden, 1998). These effects are not surprising since the need to help with sibling care and other forms of family work can interfere with their ability to study and reduce their available time for recreational activities with peers and friends (Fuligni, Tseng, and Lam, 1999; Telzer and Fuligni, 2009b). A quote from a Mexican adolescent illustrates the conflict between school and family obligations. When asked to describe the thoughts of a girl in a picture who is holding school books while watching her parents labor in the fields, she said:

> she is watching her parents working so hard…she feels like they have a big problem. She tries to help her parents, but she also has to study. In the end, she tries to help them (Suarez-Orozco and Suarez-Orozco, 1995, p. 129).

In extreme cases, associated with parental absence (death, divorce, or abandonment) or family dysfunction due to poverty, disability, or parental drug use, "parentification" may ensue; the child or adolescent becomes the caregiver who is primarily responsible for the family caregiving needs. The effects can be devastating and long lasting. School dropout, early onset of smoking and alcohol use as well as heightened stress, depression, suicidal feelings, shame, excessive guilt, unrelenting worry, and social isolation are linked with this overburdening process (East, 2010; Jurkovic, 1997). Long-term effects include interpersonal distrust, an inability to function independently, and tendency to misuse parental authority (Jurkovic, 1997).

Not all children and youth are negatively affected nor are all circumstances equally likely to yield negative outcomes. Positive effects of sibling caregiving occur most likely when there is a moderate amount of time devoted to this set of tasks (Fuligni et al., 1999; Kuperminc et al., 2009; McMahon and Luthar, 2007). When it is too little, no benefits accrue, and when it is overwhelming, negative outcomes are found. Attitudes toward the fairness of their caregiving responsibilities may be important moderator of the effects of sibling caregiving (Kuperminc et al., 2009). African American siblings who feel coerced or "conscripted" are more likely to be resentful and angry than those that feel that their contributions are voluntary (Stack and Burton, 1993). Similarly, among Latino adolescents a high sense of felt family obligation in interaction with high caregiving was linked with poorer adjustment when compared to Latino youth who had high family caregiving but low feelings of family obligation. Thus, high-felt family obligation, even though family obligation is valued among Latino families, functioned as an additional burden for these Latino youth (East and Weisner, 2009). Moreover, as is evident in other family dyads such as parent–parent relationships (Cummings and Davies, 2010), frequent conflict surrounding caregiving was associated with increased stress and depression, and lower school grades for these Latino sibling caregivers (East and Weisner, 2009). Clearly, the opportunity to elect to engage in sibling care or at least feel that their degree of commitment is fair rather than feeling either obligated or coerced reduces the negative effects of this responsibility. The more positive effects associated with helping the family through sibling caregiving in times of family stress such as after a divorce (Hetherington, 1999) or after immigrating to a new country (Walsh et al., 2006) may, in part, be due to the perceived fairness of this contribution to the family good.

*A Word of Caution:* It is clear that it is risky to generalize from the anthropological record and the sibling caregiver experiences of children in other cultures to our own culture. In our culture with the extended nature of childhood and adolescence and the accompanying demands of educational attainment, it is unclear that clear guidelines can be set for the types and amounts of caregiving responsibility that we can expect of our children and youth. At the same time, there are clearly positive consequences that flow from the opportunities to assist with family tasks such as caring for one's siblings. However, as we have noted not only the amount but the autonomy to engage or not in these tasks are both critical in determining whether these experiences are likely to promote or impede development.

*Grandparents as Part-Time and Full-Time Caregivers:*   In the case of relatives such as grandparents who assume caregiving responsibilities for their grandchildren, there are benefits as well as downsides. Caregiving by grandparents can take a variety of forms. Traditionally, grandparents are part-time caregivers who assist their adult children by providing advice, financial assistance, and occasional direct caregiving either when the parents are present or when they are temporarily absent (i.e., out for an evening or on a more extended child free vacation). In contrast, a minority of grandparents assume a custodial caregiving role whereby they assume primary responsibility for the day to day care of their grandchildren (Smith and Drew, 2002).

On the positive side, older adults as noncustodial grandparents have the chance to develop a close bond with their own adult children and their grandchildren; they may experience appreciation, affection, love, companionship, and the sharing of mutually enjoyable activities (Smith, 2005; Smith and Drew, 2002). Many British grandparents agreed with the song:

> Granny spoils us, oh what fun, Have some sweets and a sticky bun, Don't tell mum you were up till ten, I want to come and babysit again! (Smith, 2005, p. 684).

Just as in the case of parents, involvement as mentor, advisor or confidant to grandchildren can be a generative experience which yields positive benefits such as gains in self-esteem, morale, life satisfaction, and feelings of control over the future. Roles change in positive ways too. Gerontologist Bert Hayslip (Hayslip and Patrick, 2006) argues that some see a "second chance" at parenting where they can apply their previous experiences to improve their parenting skills. Although grandmothers are generally more involved with their grandchildren than grandfathers (Dench and Ogg, 2002), grandfathers experience benefits as well. Some older caregivers, especially grandfathers, see this as an opportunity to play a major role in children's lives that they had missed in earlier phases of their life course due to work demands.

Just as in the case of the timing of the transition to parenthood, the age that adults enter grandparenthood matters too. In their interviews with African American grandparents, Burton and Bengtson (1985) found that those women who became grandmothers early (25–37 years) were discontented, feeling obligations they were not ready for: "I don't have time to do what I would like to do as a grandmother. I work everyday. I have young children. Right now I'm just too busy," said one 31-year-old grandmother (p. 67). They were also affected by the stereotypes associated with grandparenting and age: "I am just too young to be a grandmother. That's something for old folks, not for me" (p. 68).

Similarly, achieving grandparenthood later in life (in their 70s) can diminish the pleasures of this experience. Being a grandparent requires energy, stamina, and good physical health which may be lacking among older grandparents. In a British survey, on time grandparents (ages 50–65) reported more pleasure from the role than either early (before 50) or late-timed (66 or older) grandparents (Dench and Ogg, 2002).

Work in the United States confirms these findings concerning the mid 50s as optimal for the onset of grandparenthood (Tinsley and Parke, 1987). Being "on time" – even for grandparents has its advantages. Clearly, the opportunity to engage in parental activities on a part-time basis is in line with the traditional grandparental role. Providing after school or school holiday care can be beneficial and rewarding for grandparents as well as for their adult children and their grandchildren. By being part of the cooperative matrix of parenting, all participants can benefit.

Is being a custodial grandparent rewarding too? While being a custodial grandparent is sometimes viewed as rewarding and associated with increased happiness and feelings of usefulness and youthfulness (Rodgers and Jones, 1999; Waldrop, 2003) most studies find that being a full-time custodial caregiver in one's grandparent phase comes at a cost. As one observer noted:

> When someone is raising his/her grandchild, it takes away the opportunity for the grandparent to act as a grandparent. Grandparents are the people that children go to visit, get spoiled and then go home to mommy and daddy. These grandparents don't have that luxury. They must be the disciplinarian and provider in every way. The role of grandparent is meant to bring complete joy. When a grandparent has to discipline his/her grandchild, it changes the relationship between them (Hawkins, 2009, p. 2).

Being a caregiver means less time for hobbies, travel, and leisure as well as increased problems with physical as well as mental health. In terms of physical health, the added burden and stress of caregiving is linked with poorer physical outcomes (Fuller-Thomson and Minkler, 2000; Hayslip and Patrick, 2006). To illustrate grandmothers who provided moderate amounts of child care (9 or more hours per week) were 1.5 times more likely to have heart disease than those who were not providing regular care for their grandchildren (Lee, Colditz, Berkman et al., 2003). Moreover, increased smoking and alcohol use as well as less exercise has been associated with a custodial grandparenting role (Burton, 1992; Hughes, Waite, LaPierre et al., 2007). Mental health suffers too. Compared to traditional grandparents, custodial grandparents experience more stress and higher levels of depression (Fuller-Thomson and Minkler, 2000; Musil and Ahmad, 2002). Role satisfaction and the meaning of the role differ across types of grandparents too. Compared to noncustodial grandparents, those with regular caregiving responsibilities were less satisfied with the grandparental role (McGowen, Ladd, and Strom, 2006), while some felt cheated of the traditional role that they had imagined (Baird, 2003). And there is often intergenerational conflict, role strain, and role ambiguity if the custodial grandparent is coparenting with their own children (Moore and Brooks-Gunn, 2002). In contrast to the traditional grandparent role, being a custodial grandparent is a mixed blessing with some rewards but also considerable cost in terms of mental and physical health. As we documented earlier, this family form is increasingly common in our society. Recently, a better understanding of ways to make this family form work better for the sake of both caregivers themselves and the grandchildren that they are raising has emerged. Just as in the case of single mothers, social support is a key element in improving the outcomes for custodial grandparent families (Dolbin-MacNab, 2006). For example, social support from friends, relatives, and the community was related to higher morale among custodial grandmothers of a preschool age child which, in turn, was related to less grandmother stress and better child outcomes (Ramaswamy, Bhavnagri, and Barton, 2008). Other strategies such as parenting reeducation have been suggested as well to improve grandparent's understanding of current child-rearing practices and to increase their sense of parenting self efficacy (Dolbin-MacNab, 2006; Emick and Hayslip, 1999). In sum, the role of the custodial grandparent is not an easy one but a family form that needs to be recognized as part of the diversity of family forms in our contemporary society.

*Aunts and Uncles as Caregivers:*  Just as parents and grandparents experience an increased sense of generativity through their involvement in caregiving, so do aunts and uncles who are active participants in the lives of their nieces and nephews as well as in the lives of their adult siblings. Listen to Aunt Harriet's commentary on her relationship with her niece as an example of how being an active aunt can promote their own personal development as an adult:

> There is something about my niece that reflects back on how I need to understand myself. I feel that as I nurture her, I am also nurturing myself (Milardo, 2010, p. 185).

The involvement with a niece or nephew can provide the kind of parent like experience that is central to generativity that for many childless aunts and uncles might not otherwise be available. A childless aunt noted the experience with her niece provided her the opportunity "to receive and express the kind of unquestioning affection parents get to enjoy every day" (DiPerna, 1998, p. 154). Similarly, a single uncle commented: "having really good relationships with my nephews and nieces satisfied a lot of my need for generativity and seems to nullify my need for children" (Milardo, 2010, p. 60). This was good since this uncle was a priest by profession! Godparents often function as aunt like figures and often experience similar rewards from this role. This is well illustrated by the reflection of a colleague on his own adult daughter's situation.

> She is 32 and single without children. Yet she is a godmother to two children who greatly respect, love and appreciate her. I think this gives my daughter the satisfaction of being in a maternal role, thus also fulfilling for her the cultural expectation of her being a mother (Raymond Buriel, 2010, personal communication).

Aunts and uncles provide support, advice and mentoring not only for nieces and nephews but for their parents (i.e., their siblings) as well. Offering this kind of assistance often results in closer emotional bonds between themselves and their adult siblings (Milardo, 2010). Moreover, reverse mentoring is evident in the aunt/uncle–niece/nephew relationships whereby the younger generation advises the older generation. For example, on such matters as fashion, personal relationships, career decisions, or even tattoos, adult nieces may advise their aunts. Or uncles may receive advice from nieces and nephews about planning family events or selecting gifts for a family member. As aunts and uncles age, nieces and perhaps nephews may assist in caregiving of their older frail relatives, as part of their mutually beneficial relationship. This caregiving role is more likely to occur for nieces than nephews, a reminder of the still differing roles of women and men as caregivers. As Milardo (2010) found, in some cases even children can play this caregiver role.

Elena, a young girl (age 12) nursed her aunt back to health. In the young girls words "I remember nursing her wounds, and I remember that I would put salve on them and it was traumatic for me because burns are very painful....We slept together like we did when I was young...I think that was a moment of connection and healing" (2010, p. 126).

Clearly, cross-generational relationships are bidirectional and both parties benefit. At the same time as this anecdotal report of the young girl illustrates, this can be a burden and stressor for the niece just as in the case of children who act as cultural brokers for their parents.

While the qualitative work (Ellingson and Sortin, 2006; Milardo, 2010) on this issue is innovative and opens up this neglected area of inquiry, quantitative, cross-time explorations are needed to more fully understand not only the impact of these relationships on aunts and uncles but the processes that underlie these potential effects.

## Nonrelatives as Caregivers/Socializers

Many other individuals beyond relatives play important socializing roles for children including fictive kin, compadres, day care providers, teachers, coaches, and mentors who are increasingly recognized as part of the matrix of socialization players who share responsibility for our children. Do these individuals, in spite of the lack of blood ties, experience positive gains for themselves as a result of their nurturing and guiding roles? Are nonparental caregivers biologically prepared for caregiving other people's children? Is being a part of children's lives a generative experience for these individuals as we saw for relatives? The story is similar to our narrative about relatives, namely that roles such as mentoring and teaching are both rewarding and challenging. Many find the opportunity to be part of children's lives a positive and enriching experience. At the same time, nonfamily contributors face challenges including boundary ambiguity, parental resentment, and jealousy and fear of failing to fulfill their roles adequately on behalf of their child and adolescent charges. We explore each of these issues next.

*Are Nonparental Adults Biologically Prepared for Caregiving:* The biological shifts that we described for parents when exposed to infants in Chapter 2 can even occur in nonparents and nonrelatives. As we saw in earlier chapters, biologically unrelated individuals such as fictive kin often play important and active caregiving roles and there may be brain-related activation accompanying caregiving for these individuals as well. In fact, this effect is found in samples of adults who are not parents which suggests that there is a possible rewarding impact of infants on nonparental caregivers too. In support of this claim, brain activation was recorded while nonparent women watched baby faces (Glocker, Langleben, Ruparel et al., 2009). Just as ethologist Konrad Lorenz suggested, we may be hard wired as a species to respond to baby features since these nonparents showed similar neural activation patterns (i.e., brain reward system) that have been found in parents. Nor are the effects restricted to women; men may also be responsive to infants as well. Caria and her colleagues (2012) showed men and women all of whom were not parents a series of images (of puppy and kitten faces, full-grown dogs and cats, human infants and adults) while recording their brain activity. The infant images evoked more activity than any of the other images in three distinctive brain areas associated with three main functions. First, they found some of the brain activity in the premotor cortex, an area associated with caregiving actions such as picking up or talking to an infant. Second, the area of the brain associated with facial recognition – the fusiform gyrus on each side of the brain, near the ears – was activated by infant pictures which may indicate heightened attention to an infant's facial expressions. Third, the brain areas associated with emotion and reward were responsive to images of babies. When participants rated how they felt when viewing adult and infant faces, they reported feeling happier, more willing to approach, smile at, and communicate with an infant than an adult. The findings suggest a readiness to interact with and care for infants in spite of being unrelated to the infants or even being a parent. Nonparents may be better prepared for caregiving than previously thought and supports our argument for a role for nonparents in the caregiving mix. "Such brain activity in nonparents could indicate that the biological makeup of humans includes a mechanism to ensure that infants survive and receive the care they need to grow and develop" (NIH NEWS, 2012). As Glocker et al. (2009) speculate:

> From an evolutionary perspective, recruitment of "hardwired" motivational brain mechanisms in response to baby schema in nonparents could be adaptive, as human ancestors likely evolved as cooperative breeders, a social system characterized by the spread of the caretaker role to group members other than the mother (Hrdy, 2005). Baby schema could motivate caring for any infant by any potential caregiver in a group, regardless of kinship (p. 9116).

Even nonparents may be biologically prepared for executing parental tasks, a further argument for the potential benefits of rediscovering cooperative parenting in our own era.

At the same time, it is doubtful whether all nonparents are equally likely to show these neural patterns or at least the same degrees of neural activation. Perhaps nonparental adults who have had experience with infants such as child-care workers or neonatal nurses or biologically unrelated adults who play a caregiving role for others' children in the community may show heightened neural activity that is more similar to parental activation patterns than adults with less experience or involvement with children. In contrast, less experienced or unrelated nonparents may show less robust patterns of neural activity. Nor do we know whether biological ties between alternate caregivers such as older siblings, aunts, uncles, or grandparents modify the nature of the neural activation patterns in response to children. However, we do know a good deal about the social, cognitive, and physical benefits and challenges that face nonrelatives who serve as caregivers. We turn to these issues next.

*Child care providers and teachers – Caregiving others' children:*  Being a child care provider is both a labor of love and a challenging and stressful undertaking. "Rewarding" is how most child care workers describe their jobs, and the joy of helping children grow – both intellectually and emotionally – is one of its most appealing features (Princeton Review, 2012). Or as one child-care provider reflected

> I started doing daycare to be there for my own kids, and through the years I have been there for many other children as well. The kids are as good for me as I am for them. It works out well for all of us (p. 3).

A recent study of child care workers in Great Britain confirmed this impression (Gambaro, 2011). Based on interviews about their attitudes toward their jobs as child care providers, most saw their jobs as intrinsically rewarding. With only a few exceptions, all workers enjoyed working with children and expressed their passion for seeing children growing up. Their role in children's development and witnessing children's achievements were the most satisfying aspects of working in child care. Here are several testimonials from child care staff:

> It's so rewarding when you see the child progress. It is really. [Ann, nursery assistant]. It's because you can see a child that comes in not speaking, very shy, not confident or they come in as a baby and you just see them leave as a child ready for school with the tools ready to go and learn. That's what's rewarding about the job (Rose, deputy manager) (Gambaro, 2011, p. 6).

> It's the enjoyment of seeing the child go through the different stages" or "It is satisfying to see a change in a child due to something that you've done." Another said that "I felt it was the most rewarding thing I have ever done, except for parenting my own children (Cameron, Mooney, Owen et al., 2001 p. 86).

Moreover, according to British surveys, child-care workers were among those groups of workers most satisfied with their jobs, in comparison with other occupational groups (Cameron, Owen, and Moss, 2001; Cameron, Mooney et al., 2001; Rose, 1999). Similarly, a US study of job satisfaction among child-care workers concluded that "Overall it appears that the work itself is a key factor in job commitment and satisfaction. Working with children is both valued and enjoyed by child care workers. It appears that this factor overshadows the negative aspect" (Schryer, 1994, p. 44).

The rewards of being a child care provider stem, in part, from the close and intimate relationships that develop between the children in their care and their caretakers (Nelson, 1990). However, these close ties come with risks as well including balancing the intimacy with the role as objective caregiver. In a qualitative ethnographic study of child-care workers, Murray (1998) found that many saw themselves in "family-like" relationship with the families and functioning "like-moms" and "pseudo-parents" While rewarding, the closeness of these ties meant "workers continually engaged in 'emotional labor' – managing the intimacy they experienced as caregivers against the expectations placed on them as workers" (Murray, 1998, p. 149). Negotiating these multiple roles of paid providers and close "parent-like" figures and carefully defining boundaries between themselves and the children's families as can be a challenge and a potential stressor.

One of the main negative aspects is the lack of value, recognition, and status given to careers in childcare placed by society on this type of work (Cameron, Owen, et al., 2001; Hale-Jinks, Knopf, and Kemple, 2006). This perception is based on the reality of low pay, few or absent health benefits, long hours, and constant activity; it means that the intrinsic rewards are offset by reports of stress, burnout, and high turnover. This tension between intrinsic satisfaction and extrinsic dissatisfaction has been noted among child-care personnel in both Great Britain and the United States (Cameron, Owen, et al., 2001; Clarke-Stewart and Allhusen, 2005). In part, due to these attitudes, yearly national rates of turnover consistently have been found to be quite high in the United States, where the annual job turnover rate is between 30 and 40%

(Childcare.net, 2013). This is almost four or even five times greater than the 7.3% annual turnover rate among school teachers (Harris and Adams, 2007) In fact, the best predictor of job satisfaction, turnover rate and quality of care provided is pay level; while money isn't everything, it helps to be well compensated for your work even if it is intrinsically rewarding (Clarke-Stewart and Allhusen, 2005).

*Is Being a Mentor Beneficial for the Mentor?*   Mentors have clear effects on the social and emotional development of children and youth. Do the mentors themselves benefit too? Although the focus is usually on the effects of mentoring on the youth themselves, mentoring is a reciprocal relationship with both participants potentially benefiting from the arrangement (Rhodes, 2002). Individuals who volunteer as mentors have their own motivations and expectations about the benefits that will be associated with this kind of activity. A variety of motives including values (to show one's concern for youth), understanding (to learn more about youth culture), enhancement (to make a difference in another person's life), protection (to feel less selfish, guilty and disconnected) social (to live up to one's community responsibilities), and career (to explore possible roles involving working with youth) have been identified (Clary et al., 1998). Support for each of these potential benefits has been found both individually and collectively. According to a national survey of over 1500 individuals, who had mentored youth in the past five years, 73% reported that the experience was very positive (McLearn, Colasanto, and Schoen, 1998). Most mentors (83%) learned or gained something personally from their mentoring experiences, including feeling that they were a better person, increased patience, formation of friendships, a feeling of effectiveness, and the acquisition of new skills (such as listening and working with people). Most mentors said they are very likely to mentor again (54%), and more than four of five would be somewhat or very likely to mentor again (84%). Nearly all mentors (91%) stated that they are likely to recommend mentoring to a friend, with the majority stating this is very likely (59%).

Mentors gain a variety of rewards as a result of their efforts including the "sense of efficacy and pride that can come from being admired and helpful" to their protégés (Taylor and Bressler, 2000). Here is one example of the positive rewards of mentoring. In a Scottish study of 30 informal adult mentors, the adults indicated several ways in which they gained from this activity including developing a better understanding of the reality of youth's lives which, in turn, helped them better make sense of their own experiences as youth and even their own children (Philip and Hendry, 2000). The mentors valued their relationships with their charges as equals and the opportunity to redefine adult–youth relationships. The emotional meaningfulness of these relationships for mentors is illustrated by their reports of sadness if the relationship were to end (Beam, Chen, and Greenberger, 2002). Improved physical health, increased self esteem, less isolation, and loneliness as a result of new opportunities for social interactions as well as public recognition associated with doing "good works" are other benefits that mentors gain from this role (Schulz, 1995). Among older adults, volunteering as a mentor provides a sense of accomplishment, purpose, and increased life satisfaction (Freedman, 1999) as well as a greater sense of personal control and lower levels of depression (Krause, Regula, Herzog and Baker, 1992). And mentoring activity even carries over to the workplace. Seventy-five percent of insurance workers who mentored elementary school children reported improved attitudes at work (Weinberger, 2000). As Rhodes (2002) argues it has possible community wide implications as well:

> Volunteering can have the effect of creating a common fabric in a community – a breaking down of artificial we-them distinctions between more and less privileged members of society (pp. 51–52).

For example, when the members of mentoring dyads come from different ethnic groups, such as Caucasian adults mentoring Latino youth, one of the positive features is developing relationships across class and ethnicity and learning about other cultural norms and values (Diversi and Mecham, 2005). However, focusing on single benefits fails to recognize that our social actions are almost always multiply determined. In fact, volunteers who were able to fulfill several motives by the activity that they were involved in felt more satisfied, were more likely to plan to continue volunteering, and had a greater trust and sense of community than those for whom only a single motivation was fulfilled (Stukas, Worth, Clary et al., 2009). Mentoring is good for the mentors as well as the youth being helped.

Mentoring can be stressful and challenging too. Mentoring takes time, commitment and persistence in order to develop the kind of trust to make the relationship "work," especially among high-risk youth or those from another social class or a different ethnic background (Rogers and Taylor, 1997). If unsuccessful, mentors can experience disappointment, frustration, anger, and a sense of failure (Rhodes, 2002). Relationships with parents of the youth who are being mentored can sometimes be a source of stress as well. Parents may feel jealous or marginalized by the close relationship their child has developed with a nonfamily member which may negatively affect the parent's view of the mentor or may lead to an undermining of the mentor–child relationship. In view of these challenges, it is not surprising that mentors who receive social support from either other mentors or supervisors are more likely to continue their mentoring activity (Sipe and Roder, 1999). As we saw in the case of other caring roles such as parents and extended family members, being a mentor has benefits and challenges as well.

## Reflections

There are positive and negative aspects to caregiving for both biological parents as well as others in the matrix of caregivers. Parenting is a difficult task; it is expensive, labor intensive, and often psychologically challenging. At the same time, it is one of the great boosters of life satisfaction and a source of happiness for many individuals. The issue is how to maximize the positive aspects of parenting so that parents themselves experience joy and fulfillment, and in turn, ensure that their children develop well. By including others in the caregiving mix, parents are most likely to reap the positive benefits of parenting for themselves as individual adults. However, when parents view assistance from outside caregivers as a failure to manage tasks that in the ideal nuclear family are the sole responsibility of the parents, the positive aspects associated with caregiving may sometimes be diminished. Parenting can be good for us, but more often when we recognize the value of a shared view of parenting responsibility.

Nor are the benefits and drawbacks of caregiving limited to parents themselves. Siblings as well as extended family members who function as caregivers often benefit and experience generativity as a result of these opportunities. Stress and time pressures, of course, can reduce the positive aspects of these responsibilities for both siblings and grandparents alike. On balance, these caregivers not only gain from these experiences but provide often critical support for parents as well. Parents and other kin are not the only players who benefit as individuals from caregiving activities even when they are responsible for others' children. Parents who increasingly are outsourcing child care and socialization responsibilities to nonkin can be reassured by the fact that even nonparents (men and women) are biologically prepared to respond to infants and children and can reap rewards from caregiving activities. This suggests that the system of shared caregiving is not simply a cultural invention of convenience to assist overextended contemporary parents but has deeper roots in both evolution and biology, which ensures that these care activities are satisfying for a range of individuals beyond parents themselves. At the same time, mentors, child care providers, and other nonkin contributors face challenges including boundary ambiguity, parental resentment, and jealousy and fear of failing to fulfill their roles adequately on behalf of their child and adolescent charges. However, in spite of some challenges associated with cooperative caregiving, the benefits clearly outweigh the difficulties. As greater cultural acceptance and understanding of these cooperative family models as viable alternatives to the traditional ideal family form increase, it is likely that the cost-benefit ratio will increase in a positive way. In the final chapter, we explore some of the policies that can facilitate and legitimize this cultural change toward acceptance and support for cooperative caregiving.

# 9

# In Support of Alternative Family Forms

## Overcoming the Barriers to Change

*Families continue to be everyone's concern but nobody's responsibility* (Theodora Ooms, 1990)

As new family forms emerge as alternatives to the culturally ideal family form, how can we design policies to ensure that parents and children in these families function effectively so that members of all family forms can thrive? In this final chapter, I explore the barriers that need to be overcome in order to gain acceptance of alternative family forms and to identify the conditions that can improve the lives of children and parents in these families. In addition, I summarize the research gaps that have been outlined in the earlier chapters since good policy and meaningful social change are best achieved when informed by solid empirically-grounded advances in research. By identifying the missing pieces of the puzzle, a guide as well as a challenge is presented to the next generation of researchers to join in filling in the gaps in our knowledge.

One goal of this closing chapter is to recognize the fundamental unfairness of the guiding assumption of policy makers in favor of a narrow definition of family as the nuclear family ideal. Instead, a diverse set of alternative family forms which all recognize the value of a wider network of caregivers who share in the responsibility of rearing children – irrespective of caregiver's age, gender, sexual orientation or kinship status – needs to be given legitimacy by policy makers. Cultural change, especially one that challenges our deep commitment to an entrenched version of the "ideal" family is not easily achieved. Action on a variety of policy fronts is necessary including legal, economic, media, political, and even architectural domains. By confronting the ideal family form bias and by casting a wide policy net, greater acceptance and greater support for all forms of families can be achieved.

*Future Families: Diverse Forms, Rich Possibilities*, First Edition. Ross D. Parke.
© 2013 John Wiley & Sons, Inc. Published 2013 by John Wiley & Sons, Inc.

# The Legal Landscape: Treacherous Terrain for All but the "Ideal" Family Form

Legal changes in support of new social trends including new family forms often lag behind the demographic realities. Existing family law favors a traditional ideal family (married, heterosexual, two parent) such as the Evans even though this family form is no longer the dominant form in our contemporary society. As legal scholar Stephan Sugarman (2008) noted:

> Programs aimed primarily at middle-class and richer families advantage the traditionally "ideal" nuclear family in which the husband goes out to work and the wife stays at home to care for the children. (p.232)

In fact, as we have seen many policies clearly discriminate against alternative family forms such as cohabiting unmarried heterosexual couples, gay and lesbian families, single-parent families, and families that include children unrelated to their caregivers by marriage, blood, or adoption. Some government programs such as Head Start aimed at low-income families are much more expansive in the sort of families they recognize as eligible for participation. As Sugarman continued:

> However, even if programs aimed at low-income families are more inclusive of what constitutes a "family," they are not necessarily more generous to those families, as compared with financially better-off families. Indeed, "recent reforms – especially in tax and welfare – have largely moved in the opposite direction, providing more financial benefits to wealthier families while cutting back on support for poorer ones (p. 232).

This is not surprising since the goal of government policy is, of course, to promote those family forms which it values, namely the so-called "ideal" family form. Our view is that government policies need to reflect and respect a wider range of family configurations and recognize that this shift would be consistent with a widely held belief in the value of supporting young children in all families. So let us examine current US social policies with the goal of exposing implicit biases in favor of an "ideal" family form and explore ways in which policies can be modified to benefit a wider range of family forms.

*Social Security Policy:*   Preferential treatment and implicit condoning of the nuclear family form is especially evident in the areas of income tax provisions and social security (Gershoff, Aber, and Raver, 2005). Social security was originally designed in 1935 to provide a pension for men upon their retirement. Since then spouses and biological step and adopted children have been included as beneficiaries albeit often at reduced levels. "Overall, then, the initial parameters of the family benefit features of Social Security plainly favored the 'ideal' family" (Sugarman, 2008, p. 237). In spite of the increased inclusiveness of this program, diverse family forms such as Elaine Baker and John Ashe, a cohabiting couple or Janice Standish and her partner Darlene McCloud, a lesbian couple are not eligible for their partner's benefits since their relationships are not recognized legally. The Defense of Marriage Act (1996) explicitly disallowed social security benefits to a partner of a nonlegally married same sex couple even when they are recognized as legally wed in their home state (i.e., New York, Vermont, California, Washington). The 2013 Supreme Court ruling overturning the Defense of Marriage Act will create a more level financial playing field for many gay/lesbian partner families. Clearly, federal legal recognition of same-sex marriage throughout the United States would be an important step, especially in view of the patchwork of laws across different states. Short of the federal legalization of same-sex marriage, recognition of same-sex partnerships or civil unions would provide some of the benefits usually restricted to married couples (Patterson, 2007). While same sex marriages are legal in 13 states (i.e., Vermont, New Hampshire, New York, Connecticut, California, Maine, Rhode Island, Minnesota, Iowa, Washington, Delaware, Massachusetts, Maryland), these marriages are still not recognized by other states. Moreover, even divorced spouses are not eligible for benefits unless they were married for at least 10 years prior to the divorce. In the case of divorced same-sex couples, if they do not reside in a state with either legal same-sex marriage or same-sex unions, the partner is not eligible for survivor benefits. Since a majority of divorces occur in the first decade of marriage, this is a highly discriminatory rule and a clear bias in favor of long-term and stable marriages as a cultural ideal. Even the benefit structure favors a one-earner family as widow benefits have risen over the years more than survivor benefits for partners in alternative family forms, a further indication of the bias toward a more traditional family form (Liu, 1999). The Social Security Program guidelines clearly lag behind the realities of the myriad of forms that modern families assume.

*Tax Policy:* Favoritism shown to the "ideal" family form is evident in several aspects of the tax laws in the United States. First, two-earner families can choose to file joint returns which allows the couple to pool their income with the result that the tax rate is often lower than if each person filed as a single person. It is particularly helpful if the discrepancy in the couple's wages is great and less helpful if husband and wife earn roughly equal income. This situation, then favors the traditional family form in which the husband as main breadwinner makes the major contribution to the family's financial pool, while the wife either stays at home or works only part time. In an ironic twist that the designers of tax policy probably did not anticipate, not only the Evans would benefit but so would the Lewin family since Todd is a full-time dad while Mary Helen works full time as a software engineer. However, not all alternative families fare well under existing tax policies. An example is the ineligibility of unmarried but financially interdependent domestic partners for this tax-break opportunity. The tax code, in effect, punishes financially cohabitating and gay/lesbian couples such as the Baker–Ashe family and the Standish–McCloud family who do not conform to the "ideal" family concept. Even the Millers who both work full time suffer if they earn similar amounts; they pay a "marriage penalty" (i.e., more tax as "married filing jointly" than they would for the same two people "married filing separate" tax returns) if their incomes are similar. This is not surprising since the goal of government policy is, of course, to promote those family forms which it values, namely the so-called "ideal" family form in which men work outside the home and women manage the home front. Our view is that government policies need to reflect and respect a wider range of family configurations and recognize that this shift would be consistent with a widely held belief in the value of supporting young children in all families.

However, it is not bad news for all alternative family forms. For example, the tax code permits Mary Winston a single mother to file as "head of household" (unmarried parent maintaining his or her own household) which gives her a lower tax rate than single individuals who are not parents. Under US tax law, children (under age 19, under 24 and a full-time student or disabled) are more broadly recognized for purposes of being claimed as a dependent (and therefore eligible for a child tax credit) regardless of whether or not they are biologically related to their caregivers. As long as the caregiver resides with and is financially responsible for the child, he or she is able to claim the child as a dependent. This means that grandparent caregivers, as well as nonkin such as compadres who function as caregivers would be eligible for these tax breaks, a clear instance of enlightened tax policy that recognizes the role of non-parent or even unrelated others as caregivers of children. In spite of these modest glimmers of acknowledgement of the diversity of family forms, "given the continuing political strength of well-off married couples with one main breadwinner, it is not surprising to see the ongoing bias at the couple level in both the tax and Social Security programs" (Sugarman, 2008, p. 241).

*Policies Governing Access to Health Insurance:*  Few public policy issues in the United States have generated as much controversy as the rules governing who has health care coverage and who pays for it. In spite of the 2012 Supreme Court decision supporting "The Affordable Care Act," many families still left without coverage may or may not be included in the planned expansion of coverage under Medicaid. This lack of coverage is due to the lack of a Federal mandate that individual states must comply with this expansion of coverage. So some poor people including single-parent families in some states will be covered while others will be left without coverage because of their states' refusal to abide by the new federal expansion of Medicare guidelines. Second, the uneven legal recognition of partner rights in either cohabitating or same-sex couples means that many individuals – partners and children – are not covered by their partner's employer-provided medical coverage. Legal recognition of the partner-ship would allow access to two-employee plans instead of just one as is the case for married heterosexual couples (Patterson, 2007).

Another issue that has received less attention is the unequal access to alternative routes to parenthood afforded by ART programs. There is considerable variability across countries with some offering equal access regardless of marital status or sexual orientation (i.e., Great Britain, Israel) while others such as Italy and India restrict access to ART services to married heterosexual couples of childbearing age (Fenton, 2006). In the United States,

> a variety of circumstances can function to impede or deny access to ART for some individuals seeking to have children. Denials may result from providers' decisions about whom they will serve, from legal rules establishing the availability of ART and the legal treatment of participants in ART, or from disparities in insurance coverage or financial wherewithal (Crossley, 2005, p. 274).

A survey of reproduction clinics in the United States found that there is a bias against certain types of individuals and families who do not conform to the "ideal" family form of married heterosexual couples (Gurmankin, Caplan, and Braverman, 2005). Fortunately for them, the Darcys, a heterosexual married couple, had no difficulty gaining access to ART medical services in their community even though their insurance company paid only a small portion of their expenses. However, individuals who wish to parent without a partner are more likely to be denied access to ART services by insurance companies. While 20% of single women may be viewed as unsuitable candidates, 55% of single men were deemed unfit for assistance. Not only is there a clear bias against potential single parents who wish to use ART services, lesbian and gay couples who seek assistance in becoming parents through this route face discrimination as well. This may be part of the reason that Janice and Darlene Standish decided to follow the international adoption route to parenthood instead of the ART path. While 83% of programs were open to assisting lesbian couples seeking donor insemination, only 52% were willing to assist gay couples in search of a surrogate, a further confirmation of the failure of our society to confer equal access to reproductive assistance for couples in alternative family forms. As legal scholar Mary Crossley (2005) notes:

> Restrictions on access to ART create a double standard for becoming a parent. Those individuals who are able to conceive a child in the 'usual and customary manner' are not subject to scrutiny regarding their fitness to parent, while those who are infertile may be blocked in their efforts to achieve parenthood by the fitness judgments of medical providers or policy makers (p. 278).

Another barrier to equal access to ART services is their high cost. In some places such as Great Britain, Israel, and the Scandinavian countries this opportunity to become a parent through the assistance of these medical advances is available to individuals at all income levels through national health insurance. In the United States, insurance coverage is not only unequally available but generally does not cover these services. The result is that when infertility or related medical problems prevent natural conception, only the wealthy can afford to reach parenthood through the new but expensive ART alternatives (Noah, 2003; Spar, 2006). One consequence is that many individuals and couples use ART services in other countries where the costs are lower. However, the standards of care may be lower and policies which permit more liberal implanatation of fertilized eggs can increase the risk of multiple births (Hoorens, Conklin, and Tiessen, 2008; Pennings et al., 2008). The infertile as well as same-sex couples are the targets of discrimination in terms of insurance protection for their reproductive needs. In effect, we are deciding who can achieve parenthood based on income even though many would disagree with such a policy. It is evident that an equal opportunity to become a parent needs to be a goal of future policy decisions in the US.

*Legal Guidelines for the Rights of all Parties in ART-Based Families:*   Even when the problem of access is settled, there are still legal uncertainties surrounding who has access to the child and who has obligations to the child produced through these procedures. When families are formed through the help of ART, clearer guidelines concerning the rights of surrogates and egg and sperm donors are needed. In order to achieve this goal, the assumption that biological parentage is superior and more privileged than psychological or social parentage needs to be addressed. For example, are the donors or surrogate anonymous and have legal agreements been drafted in advance to protect their right to privacy? What roles should the donors or surrogate play in the life of the child? Do they have the right to be "secondary" parents with contact and visitation opportunities or can they legally apply to be an adoptive parent if the contracting parents die? As we discussed earlier in Chapter 5, these are complex issues that are only beginning to be addressed with some arguing for privacy and anonymity for the donors and surrogate and others seeing value in the active participation of these nonkin players in these ART families (Parke et al., 2012). In fact, in the future one could imagine a new form of extended family in which donors or surrogate could provide support and care for the child that they helped create in ways that historically were restricted to relatives such as aunts or grandparents. These issues are even more uncertain for single parents or unmarried heterosexual or same sex couples since most of the existing laws concerning the respective rights of donors surrogates and contracting parents apply mainly to married couples, another protective nod in the direction of the "ideal" family form.

A related issue that we addressed in Chapter 5 concerns the rights of children to know the identity of the egg and or sperm donors who made their existence a reality. Unlike Joni and Laser, the donor-conceived teenagers of lesbian couple Jules and Nic in the film *The Kids Are All Right*, very few donor-conceived people have access to their donor's information. Most donors are anonymous and wish to remain so, and most records are destroyed. Yet, an increasing number of young adults are demanding to know their origins including their biological parents, and their genetic makeup as part of defining their identity.

> Currently, in the United States, you need a license to sell a condo or cut hair in a salon, but not to broker human life. The $3 billion fertility industry goes largely unregulated, offering blank pages to those searching for information where the rest of us are free to access vital statistics of public record. 'I'm not a treatment, I'm a person, and those records belong to me,' says one young woman in search of her biological past (Rafferty, 2011).

Clearly, legal guides that would permit better access to this information while at the same time protecting the rights of donors are needed. Other countries provide blueprints for such actions. In the United Kingdom, Sweden, Norway, Germany, Italy, New Zealand, and Australia there are laws that provide for more transparency pertaining to sperm and egg donation. Unlike the United States where it is legal to sell eggs and sperm, these countries do not permit the sale of eggs and sperm, donors are not anonymous and there are central registries to oversee the donor process.

*Adoption Laws: Who Can Adopt and Who Cannot?*   Another way in which the bias of our social policies in the United States favors the "ideal" family form is reflected in the laws governing adoption, foster care and second parent adoption by gay/lesbian partners. To put this issue into perspective, in the United States there are an estimated 410,000 children in the foster care system and 107,000 awaiting adoption (U.S. Department of Health and Human Services, 2011). At the same time not enough families are available to adopt these children (Farr and Patterson, 2013a; Ryan, Pearlmutter, and Groza, 2004). Nevertheless, several states (Utah, Mississippi) continue to legally disallow gay and lesbian individuals – single or couples – to adopt minor children. Moreover, there are differences across adoption agencies in their receptivity to gay or lesbian couples as adoptive parents, although some estimate that about 60% are open to adoption by same-sex couples (Brodzinsky, 2012). To avoid these potential problems, some same-sex couples such as Janice and Darlene Standish adopted their children from China and Russia. In spite of these barriers to domestic adoption, there are approximately 33,000 adopted children being raised by gay or lesbian couples in 2009, a nearly four-fold increase from 2000 (U.S. Census Bureau, 2010a). Gay and lesbian parents are raising 4% of all adopted children in the United States. As noted earlier in Chapter 4, there is little evidence that the adjustment of adopted children is related to the sexual orientation of the parent or parents. Instead internal family processes, such as the quality of the parent–child relationship is a more important predictor of children's well-being than the sexual orientation of their parents (Farr and Patterson, 2013a; Patterson, 2009). Therefore, the legal restrictions on adoption by gay/lesbian individuals or couples have little justification (Goldberg, 2012) and are another example of the bias in favor of the "ideal" family form that merits correction.

Another aspect of this issue is the legal parental rights of the second parent/partner in either cohabiting couples or same-sex couples where only one parent is either the biological parent or the adoptive parent. In either case, both partners are involved in the care and rearing of the child but only one partner is viewed as a legal parent. To address this inequality, secondary adoption is available by which the other partner legally adopts the child in recognition of their committed parental role in the family. In 17 states and the District of Columbia, secondary adoption is legal and provides important protections for the couple such as the right to hospital visitations, the right to make medical decisions on their child's behalf and recognition by school personnel as a legitimate parent figure, privileges that heterosexual, married couples expect and take for granted. However, this opportunity for adoption by a second parent is still not available in all states and needs a consistent federal solution.

*Custody and Postdivorce Visitation Policies:*   As alternative family forms become more common and a reassessment of the centrality of the gender of parent in deciding on parental competence continues, the issue of child custody after divorce is undergoing a marked change. No longer is the "Tender Years Doctrine" according to which the mother is the presumed custodial parent in case of a marital breakup commonly and uncritically accepted. Instead, as we noted in Chapter 3, joint custody is increasingly common and even sole father custody is more prevalent if not widespread. Recall that Oscar Bailey had joint custody of his children, Melissa and Frank after his divorce. Part of the reason for this shift toward joint or sole custody for fathers is the recognition of fathers as important parents in their children's lives as well as their competence as parents. Encouraging joint custody is one of the best ways to accomplish the goal of keeping fathers involved in their children's lives and reducing the ravages of divorce on children. Men with joint custody are more likely to pay child support on time and in full and be more involved with their children after divorce (Fabricius et al., 2010). Making joint custody a rebuttable assumption in divorce cases will ensure that each parent is at least given the opportunity to spend as much time as possible with his or her children. As we noted earlier, joint custody works best when the two parents are at least civil with each other and place the child's best interests first (Clarke-Stewart and Brentano, 2006). In cases where there is a high level of couple conflict protecting the child from this conflict needs to be the first priority. In the final analysis, parental competence and mental health and the cooperativeness of the couple should be taken into account in custody decisions irrespective of parental gender.

The liberalization of custody decisions based on parental competence irrespective of gender is based on the recognition that single parent families (male or female) as well as same sex families can provide socialization contexts for the adequate development of children. In view of this evidence, one might expect that parental gender or sexual orientation would not be factors in custody decisions. However, there is no consistent set of federal legal guidelines, only a patchwork of state-based practices. As Patterson (2009) notes, "In many states parental sexual orientation is considered relevant to custody and visitation disputes only if it can be shown to have an adverse impact on the child. At the other end of the spectrum some states have in place presumptions against lesbian or gay parents" (p. 143). Since many same-sex partnerships are not legally recognized as either civil unions or marriages, this leaves many individuals without the legal protections in the aftermath of separation that is afforded to married heterosexual couples. In some states such as Ohio which does not legally recognize same-sex marriage or domestic partnerships, some couples use a cocustody agreement, which asserts the same rights and responsibilities of a natural or adoptive parent. If the birth mother dies, or if the partnership ends in a "divorce," the nonbiological coparent will maintain legal standing for custody or visitation.

However, not all nonbiological parents have legally adopted the child who they are jointly rearing with the biological parent and same-sex partner and this may under-mine the nonbiological parent's claim to custody in favor of the biological mother. A similar situation may occur in the case of unmarried but cohabiting couples where one parent is the biological parent and the other is not biologically related or has not legally adopted the child. In other cases, children are the products of earlier hetero-sexual relationships, and sometimes, courts allow a divorced man or woman who is now gay to share child custody with their ex-spouse. But not always, and courts sometimes condition custody and visitation orders on shielding the child from the homosexual relationship. In January, 2004, for instance, a Tennessee appeals court forbade an estranged husband from "exposing the child to his gay lover(s) and/or his gay lifestyle" (Belluck and Liptak, 2004). In either case, the child is potentially losing the opportunity to continue to have regular contact with a parent who was an active part of the child's life. The long term impact of this loss of a second parent in same-sex parent families is unclear but based on the evidence from children of heterosexual divorce, it is generally in the child's best interest to have a continuing relationship with both parents after divorce. A consistent Federal policy that provides clear guide-lines and recognizes the importance of considering both parents in custody and visitation decisions among same sex as well as heterosexual parent families is needed. Some are optimistic about future policy changes. "Although the pace of change may vary from state to state, the direction of movement over time during the last 50 years is clearly toward provision of greater legal recognition of the many different family types formed by lesbian and gay adults" (Patterson, 2009, p. 145).

*Other Legal Barriers Facing Alternative Families:*   New laws that support acceptance of cohabiting but unmarried heterosexual and gay/lesbian couples and parents by medical agencies, government, and insurance companies would help legitimize alternative but increasingly common nontraditional family forms. Immigration laws that support family unification policies that recognize multigenerational households by permitting the entry of grandparents into the United States could be expanded to include nonkin care-givers such as godparents (compadres) who are part of some Latino extended families.

At the political level, governmental social policies that recognize and support extended family members and other nonkin caregivers need to be crafted and enacted. Through such policies these nontraditional caregivers could be included in family welfare policies, in tax codes (permitting dependent deductions for recognized nonkin caregivers), in social security beneficiary rules and in health insurance coverage by expanding definitions of individuals who can be included in "family" policies.

## MEDICAL ESTABLISHMENT AND NEW FAMILY FORMS

Too often hospitals and doctors treat parents who are in alternative family forms as second class citizens without the rights afforded to members of traditional or "ideal" family forms (Parker-Pope, 2009). Medical personnel need to be educated about the diversity of family forms and adjust their policies regarding treatment and visitation to include alternative family forms. For example, a wider range of family members need to be recognized as central to a patient's care including custodial grandparents, same-sex partners/coparents and nonkin if these individuals are part of the primary child-care network. In the case of single parent or even two-parent families who rely on extended family or nonkin for caregiving assistance, a more flexible system of medical authorization which would allow these supplementary caregivers to accompany a sick child to medical visits would be a way of easing the family health care burden. Consultation with and inclusion of the "functional" family rather than a narrowly defined legal subset of family members will ensure that the child patient receives support and makes it more likely that after-care will be adequate and in compliance with medical directives.

Cohabitating heterosexual couples or unmarried same-sex partners should be granted hospital visitation rights to be with their partner or the child who they are jointly raising when a family member is hospitalized. While heterosexual couples typically are not required to provide marriage licenses to hospitals in order to prove they are husband and wife, same-sex couples often must document their relationship to hospital officials before being allowed to take part in a partner's care. And even then the policy of allowing hospital visitation for legally recognized partners is sometimes not followed. A woman from Washington collapsed while on vacation in Miami. Although her partner had documentation of her relationship and a power of attorney, she claims hospital officials told her she wasn't a family member under Florida law and was seriously delayed before being able to see her partner (Parker-Pope, 2009, p.1).

Here is another example of the difficulties same-sex couples can face:

> A Bakersfield, California couple rushed their child to the emergency room with a 104 degree fever. The women were registered domestic partners, but the hospital only allowed the biological mother to stay with the child. Although hospitals typically allow both parents to stay with a child during treatment, in this case, the second parent was forced to stay in the waiting room (Parker-Pope, 2009, p.1).

The situation is slowly improving and on June 4, 2010, the Joint Commission, which issues performance standards and guidelines followed by about 80% of US hospitals, released "Advancing effective communication, cultural competence, and patient- and family-centered care: A roadmap for hospitals." This document is an important step toward protecting same-sex families and cohabiting couples from discrimination by hospital personnel. In the future, perhaps Janice Standish and Darlene McCloud may not need to worry that they both will be able to be at Michele's or Eric's bedside if one of their children is hospitalized.

Furthermore, the right to make medical decisions on behalf of either a partner or a child should be granted to both parents regardless of marital status. Similarly, when families are formed through ART procedures, clearer guidelines concerning the rights of surrogates and egg and sperm donors are needed if the active participation of these players in these ART-assisted families is to be realized.

Even fathers are often treated by doctors and hospitals as individuals whose primary function is to pay the bills. Yet fathers and same-gender parental partners who are expected to play active roles in caregiving need opportunities, just as do biological mothers, to learn about the care and feeding of new babies in the hospital and to have programs available that are sensitive to their needs and roles (Parke and Brott, 1999). Tom Evans, even though he works and leaves the primary caregiving responsibilities to his wife (i.e., "ideal" family form) as well as all the other dads that we have met including Harry Darcy whose baby was an ART infant could all benefit from parenting tips and guidance. Similarly, Janice Standish and Darlene McCloud who adopted their children could profit from some lessons in parenting too. If relatives such as an aunt or grandmother are assuming responsibility for the care of an infant or child, this kind of childcare instruction should be available to them as well. Why not include some of the Dorado extended family members who could benefit from expert parenting advice, especially if they are going to be part of the child's caregiving team?

Another challenge faced by working families, especially single-parent families is balancing the need to access medical care for their children with work schedules. Many doctors' offices are open from nine to five, which doesn't accommodate working parents of either sex very well. Fathers are often affected by this schedule since employers are often reluctant to allow men to take time off to care for a sick child or take a child to a medical appointment. Instead, mothers are the ones who commonly make the appointments and accompany children to medical visits. Single parents like Jackie Fuller who often work at low paying, hourly jobs are also unlikely to persuade employers to grant them time off for children's medical needs. And without a back up partner, single parents are often left with no choice but emergency room visits which are expensive and time consuming. Taking unscheduled time off to care for an ill child, especially one with chronic problems can even lead to job loss. Creating more flexible schedules for doctor visits would be another way of solving this problem. In fact, fathers were twice as likely to bring their children to a health clinic when it offered services in the evening than when it was open only during the day (Turya and Webster, 1986). Single parents and working parents in general would likely take advantage of this expanded access to medical care and would be a sensible solution to the scheduling conflicts encountered by all but the shrinking number of "ideal" families. Even dads in traditional families might participate more in managing their children's medical needs if appointments were more flexible.

## GOVERNMENT FAMILY POLICY INITIATIVES

There are a variety of ways that government policies can better support all forms of families not just "ideal" two-parent heterosexual families. Of particular concern for families are policies aimed at reducing poverty since economic disadvantage takes a serious toll on children as well as adults (Conger and Donnellan, 2007; McLoyd, Aikens, and Burton, 2006).

*Families in Poverty: A Social Policy Challenge and Opportunity:*    Poverty varies greatly across family forms. In 2011 in the United States, among single-parent female families: 48% lived in poverty while among married couple families only 11% lived in poverty (Child Trends, 2012b). For example, while Mary Winston is single but relatively well off, many single parents such as Jackie Fuller are poor and often short of funds by the end of a pay period. Moreover, race matters. In single-parent families, 22.5% of whites were poor but 33.4% of Hispanics and 44% of Blacks were poor. Racial discrepancies are evident among two-parent married families too. While 5.4% of white two-parent families were poor, the poverty rates nearly doubles for Blacks (9.7%) and tripled for Hispanics (14.9%). In fact, the Mexican American Dorado family is struggling to make ends meet even though both Maria and Jose work full time. Finally, children suffer most with 22% of children under 18 living in families with incomes below the poverty line in 2010 (U.S. Census Bureau, 2010a). In light of the links between single parenthood and minority family status, it is clear that anti-poverty policies are important to our discussion of family forms. In fact, many have argued that the effects of single parenthood on children as well as the impact of being a member of a minority group are due, in large part, to the economic struggles and stresses associated with these demographic conditions.

A number of policies have been implemented to combat the effects of poverty on children's development. Some focus on children directly, and others increase parental income or job skills as a way of lifting families out of poverty. The Personal Responsibility and Work Opportunity Reconciliation Act (PRWORA) aimed at reducing single-parent families' long-term reliance on welfare while Temporary Assistance to Needy Families (TANF) was designed to assist single parents through block grants to the states. TANF introduced time limits on cash assistance and required recipients to be searching or preparing for a job and then engaging in full-time work within two years of receiving their first aid check and limited aid to a maximum of five years. Proponents of welfare reform argued that requiring single mothers to leave welfare for work would provide the most reliable pathway out of poverty and that work requirements would promote healthier child development by enhancing mothers' self-esteem and introducing productive daily routines into family life. Opponents argued that children's well-being would worsen as mothers became overwhelmed by the work requirements and time-limited aid. In turn, the new requirements would deepen the poverty of some families, forcing young children into unacceptable child care environments and decreasing parents' abilities to monitor their older children (Chase-Lansdale et al., 2003).

What were the effects of TANF? Parents benefited from going to work and earning money. Mothers who moved into stable employment and increased their incomes experienced improved psychological well-being and reported less domestic violence (Cheng, 2007; Coley et al., 2007; Gennetian and Miller, 2002). On the downside, many jobs pay poorly and keep families in poverty and often result in the termination of schooling for mothers as well. However, since TANF was aimed at employment for mothers, it did little to encourage father involvement with their children, or aid father's employability (Cabrera, 2010). But how did the children fare? A comprehensive evaluation found few effects on children (Administration for Children and Families, 2004). Children did benefit from increases in family income. A synthesis of a dozen TANF experiments found that welfare policies that increased parents' employment and family income did reduce children's social behavior or psychological problems (Morris, Duncan, and Clark-Kauffman, 2005) but not adolescent well-being. When parents moved from welfare to work, they were not able to provide as much supervision and monitoring for their adolescents. Clearly, intervention programs aimed at enhancing parent–child relationships and increasing parental awareness of the importance of monitoring, might enhance the overall well-being of the children and adolescents (Dishion and Stormshak, 2007).

Another challenge that needs to be acknowledged is the bias in family service and welfare agencies against fathers. "Child welfare agencies and fathers of the families they serve have an uneasy, almost underground, relationship. While the majority of caseworkers believe involving nonresident fathers enhances a child's well-being in practice, it is not a regular occurrence" (Brooks, 2010, p. 1). If fathers are part of the family unit or even in their child's life, their participation in programs aimed at improving family functioning such as parenting is needed. This "invisible father" bias is evident in other programs such as Head start, which only recently have begun to encourage father involvement in program activities (Coltrane and Behnke, 2012). Their cooperation with social service personnel is critical to the success of the programs. However, social service agencies often do not make dads feel welcome. Not only are the walls painted pink, with pictures of moms and babies, and women's magazines, but the staff are mostly women who may not fully embrace father participation. To overcome this bias, there needs to be training in father inclusion in services (expanded hours, fathers' names on case files, health visitors speaking to fathers when they visit homes etc) and incentives to use fathers as resources. Fathers are more likely to act responsibly when they are treated as an integral and valued part of the family.

## Child Care: Another Policy Challenge

One consequence of the high percentage of working families is the need to find and pay for child care for their young children. The Millers, a two-worker family spend nearly 20% of their income on child care (Lino, 2011). As more women enter the workforce and as the number of single-parent families remains high, child care is a central priority for many families. In view of the centrality of this issue, it is surprising that child care in the United States lacks unified government policy. There have been times in our history when the government was poised to step in with a comprehensive plan, but this has not happened. As a result there are no national liscensing requirements for all child-care providers and no system to ensure that all facilities provide quality care and meet adequate standards of care. The United States may never experience the level of federal involvement found in other countries. In many European countries and Japan, for example, the government makes a substantial contribution to

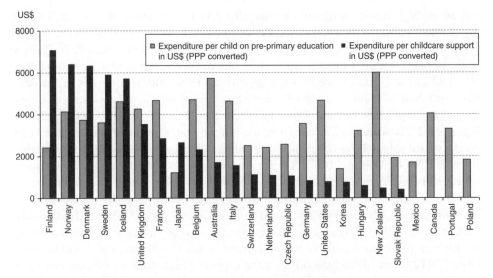

**Figure 9.1** Public expenditure on child care, per child, in 2005, converted to US dollars. *Source:* Social Expenditure Database 1980–2005; OECD Education Database; U.S. Department of Health and Human Services.

the cost of child care (see Figure 9.1; OECD, 2008). In the United States, child care is viewed as a private responsibility and parents pay for child-care costs themselves unless they are poor and receive a welfare supplement or are eligible for a government-subsidized program. Instead child care ought to be the responsibility of not just families but the community and government as well.

Nevertheless, there are a number of ways that policies could be implemented to help parents in their quest for high-quality care. The first way is by increasing the availability of high-quality care. One way to increase availability is to expand the public school system by extending school days in which before- and after-school care is provided in a safe, educational environment. Another expansion is to extend the public educational system downward to include four-year-olds. Many US states as well as several provinces in Canada have implemented or are exploring the possibility of universal preschool for four-year-olds. Universal preschool is already a feature in countries throughout Europe. In France and Italy, for example, about 95% of all three- to five-year-olds are enrolled in state-sponsored preschool.

Even if quality care is available, parents may not find it. The second way governments could help parents find high-quality care is by educating parents about care. Many parents are first-time users of child care, with little experience and may assume that they have few choices. Even if they do search, parents are not particularly astute judges of quality care. For example, parents consistently rated the quality of their children's classes higher than trained observers did (Cryer and Burchinal, 1997). Government policy could increase parents' knowledge by providing written materials, You Tube videos, and TV public service announcements focused on components of quality. Government support has already been used to create child-care resource and referral services, which are a useful starting point when parents are searching for care.

A third way that policy could help parents is by providing more money to pay for care. Affordability is a major issue for most parents. Because parents with high incomes can afford high-quality care and parents with very low incomes may be eligible for government-subsidized care, it is middle-income families who are likely to receive the poorest-quality care (NICHD Early Child Care Research Network, 1997; Phillips et al., 1994). The public investment in child care has been estimated to be about $600 per child in the United States, compared with up to $7000 in countries in Europe, where the bulk of child-care costs is covered by a combination of subsidies, tax benefits, and employer contributions (Gornick and Meyers 2003; OECD, 2008; Figure 10.1). Research indicates that in the United States, states with more generous child-care subsidy policies have child-care centers offering higher-quality care (Rigby, Ryan, and Brooks-Gunn, 2007). A recent study, however, which examined the effects of federal subsidies found that subsidy recipients use *higher* quality care compared to nonrecipients who use no other publicly funded care, but *lower* quality care compared to nonrecipients who instead use Head Start or public pre-K. While subsidies may have the potential to enhance care quality, parents who use subsidies are not accessing the highest quality care available to low-income families (Johnson, Ryan, and Brooks-Gunn, 2012). Part of the reason is that the supply of high quality care may not be as readily available to lower income parents in their neighborhoods (Loeb et al., 2004). Even if high quality care options are available, the subsidies may not be high enough to afford the highest quality care (Adams and Rohacek, 2002).

Another reason that many families cannot use higher-quality care programs which operate during normal business hours is due to scheduling problems. About 40% of the American labor force now works some form of nonstandard hours, including evenings, nights, weekends, and early mornings (Presser, 2003). Instead low-income parents may use lower quality care options such as home based care that are available in evenings and early mornings (Henly, Ananat, and Danziger, 2006; Presser, 2003). In fact, one helpful policy change would be to encourage high-quality centers to adopt more flexible schedules to accommodate the changing work schedules of families. Day care may need to become night care or round the clock care and there are indications that the market is responding to the new work schedule realities. In Ohio, the number of centers offering nighttime hours is up by more than 50% since 2003 (Tavernise, 2012). Centers with overnight hours have doubled and those open on weekends have quadrupled, though the absolute numbers remain small (Tavernise, 2012).

> On a recent day, a grandmother dropped off a first grader at 4:30 a.m. on the way to her early morning shift at Burger King. A mother picked up her three-year-old at 11:30 p.m. after getting off work at a nursing home. Another mother came for her two-year-old twins at 1:30 a.m., after her shift as a cleaner at a gym (Tavernise, 2012).

Another response to parental need for flexibility are drop-in child care centers which allow parents the option of dropping off their child for a few hours in the evening to allow them to attend a job or an education-related function (McCLure, 2010; Singler, 2011).

A fourth policy to improve child-care quality would be to increase caregivers' wages in order to reduce turnover rates which are among highest of any profession, ranging between 30 and 40% per year (Childcare.net, 2013). By comparison, the percent of public-school teachers who earn at least one third more than child-care workers leave their jobs at a 7% rate each year. Paying caregivers more would encourage them to stay longer and provide a more stable, predictable child-care environment for children. To illustrate, when the US armed services made pay for child-care workers comparable to that for other jobs on military bases that required similar levels of training, education, and responsibility, staff turnover dropped from 48 to 24% (Campbell et al., 2000).

Fifth, policies need to be implemented to regulate the quality of care. At present there are no federal standards for evaluating child-care quality only a patchwork of state regulations. When a state by state evaluation was undertaken to assess regulations addressing health, safety, and quality in child care (the National Association of Child Care Resource and Referral Agencies, 2012) most states were found to be poorly rated. Staff were being hired without background checks. Inspections were infrequent. State licensing offices had unmanageable caseloads. Child-to-staff ratios were not in line with suggested standards. The Department of Defense got the top score, but most states received a failing grade. States can solve some of these problems without huge infusions of money. For example, it requires only a modest budget increase to check employee rolls against sex-offender registries. Other factors – like child-to-staff ratios – cannot be addressed unless centers increase their tuition (which many families are already struggling to afford) or find other sources of funding to pay for more staff members. Changes in state and federal laws will be required to set minimum levels of quality and to impose penalties when centers do not comply. When states do have more stringent regulations, child-care quality is higher (Rigby et al., 2007). Finally, policies could be developed to limit the number of hours children spend in care but it is unlikely that many parents would find such policies acceptable. To allow families the flexibility to work and to guarantee a safe haven for children, the United States needs to do a better job of providing high quality, affordable child care for all families. Child care is not simply a private concern, but a community and government responsibility too.

## Family–Workplace Policies

There are several policy changes which could make the workplace more family friendly and reduce the strain between work and home demands. Unfortunately, the assumption guiding policy is still based on an outmoded view as women as caregivers and men as breadwinners rather than a dual earner/dual caregiver model for both men and women (Gornick and Meyers, 2007). Family leave policies are needed not just for mothers, but fathers, both gay and lesbian parents or coparents, heterosexual cohabitating partners, and others such as relatives (aunts, grandparents) or nonrelatives who play significant caregiving roles in the lives of infants and children. Flextime, job sharing, part-time employment, and telecommuting are all part of the package of policies that could ease the burden on families with children. In recognition of the range of family forms, these options need to be broadly available and not restricted to only traditional two-parent "ideal" families. Members of all forms of families can benefit from more family friendly workplace policies by permitting parents to be better supported by their partners and children by having their parents and other caregivers more available to nurture and guide them.

*Family Leave, Not Just Maternity Leave:*   Family leave policies need to be expanded to provide paid leave for not just women but men and domestic partners who are partners in caregiving and need time off after the birth of a child as well as the birth mother does (Heymann and Earle, 2010). Although post birth leave is no longer termed maternity leave, progress toward granting leave to both mothers and fathers has been slow and even slower for domestic partners. Even though a survey found that 76% of respondents endorsed laws that would provide paid leave for family care and childbirth (IWPR, 2010), the United States is one of the last Western countries without a paid leave policy for new parents. According to the recent report, *Failing its Families* (Walsh, 2011), at least 178 countries have national laws guaranteeing paid leave for new mothers, while the handful of exceptions include the United States, Swaziland, and Papua New Guinea. More than 50 nations, including most Western countries, also guarantee paid leave for new fathers (Heymann and Earle, 2010; Walsh, 2011). At the same time, some fathers do not take advantage of these leaves due to the lingering bias against men as caregivers and work place pressure not to take time off. As international studies show, if the programs are structured around a "use it or lose it" rule according to which unused father leave time cannot be used by a partner, fathers are more likely to participate (Moss and O'Brien, 2006).

Currently, the US Family and Medical Leave Act (1993) is the major policy guide to policies concerning family leave. Under this Act, eligible employees at companies with more than 50 employees can take up to 12 weeks of unpaid leave per year after the birth or adoption of a child or for any other personal or family problem. By excluding companies with fewer than 50 employees, it covers only about 60% of the work force. Only about 25% of US employers offer fully paid family leave of any length (Ray, Gornick, and Schmitt, 2010). There are signs of more generous family leave policies. As Coltrane and Behnke (2012) note, "More than 10 states have improved and expanded the unpaid FMLA policies, including more time off, flexibility regarding the minimum size of employer requirement, and permitting intermittent leave" (p. 431). Although some individual companies offer a paid family leave benefit, many parents end up using a combination of short-term disability, sick leave, vacation, personal days, and unpaid family leave. It is particularly challenging for single mothers to take maternity leave since the loss of wages may be economically crippling for single earner families (Lenhoff and Withers 1994). Other countries are more generous. In Canada female employees are entitled to a standard 17 weeks unpaid, job-protected maternity leave. In addition, both male and female employees are granted up to 37 weeks unpaid, job-protected parental leave (35 weeks for women if being combined with maternity leave for a total of 52 weeks) in order to care for a newborn or newly adopted child (Catalyst, 2012). In the European Union, paid parental leave varies from 14 weeks in Malta to 16 months in Sweden, which reserves at least two months of its leave exclusively for fathers.

Even though men are becoming more active participants in the care of their infants and children, such as stay at home dad Todd Lewinsky, fewer men (72%) have access to leave than women (90%) (Phillips, 2004). According to one survey of users of family leave, 76% were women in comparison to only 45% of men (Waldfogel, 2001). And when men do take a leave, they take off far less time than women do, in part, because in most countries the duration of paid leave for fathers is generally shorter (Heymann and Earle, 2010). A major reason for men's rather anemic participation in family leave is that in most cases it isn't paid time off and many families cannot afford this loss of wages. Only 11% of private-sector workers have paid family leave benefits and among the poorest paid members of the workforce, only 5% have paid family leaves (U.S. Department of Labor, 2010a). Workers in the public sector are better protected with 17% having access to paid family leave; among the poorest paid, 14% have paid leave (Houser and Vartanian, 2012). However, when men are financially well compensated during paternity leaves, nearly 90% of men in some countries (e.g., Sweden, Denmark, Norway) take some time off (Moss, 2010). Provision of adequate leave compensation can help close the gender gap in leave taking and support the trend toward more equitable roles in caregiving of males and females in contemporary families.

And there are still differences in income across gender. Even in 2012, in the United States, women's median annual earnings were 77% of men's for full-time, year-round workers, a gap which remains even when controlling for factors such as experience, education, industry, and hours (Coukos, 2012). As a result many families simply conclude that they can better survive the loss of the woman's salary than the higher salary of the male in the household. This is precisely the reason that Ellen Miller stopped working when their first child was born; her husband Tom made more money than she did. In addition, even when paid leave is available, women on post birth leave receive only 77% of their wages while men on paternity leave receive 84% of their wages. According to one survey of over 1200 worksites, 64% of those workers who were aware of their leave options and needed to take time off chose not to take it because they could not afford the loss in wages (Lenhoff and Withers, 1994). Moreover, access to family leave is not equally available for workers at all income levels. For example, the top 25% are three times more likely to be eligible for paid family leave benefits than those in the bottom quarter of wage earners (U.S. Department of Labor/Bureau of Labor Statistics, 2010a).

Immediate financial pressures as a result of leave taking are not the only consideration, however. Both men and women suffer in terms of upward occupational movement if they exercise the family leave option in spite of the illegality of discrimination based on the use of family leave. When women take leave they suffer a "motherhood penalty" which is reflected in reduced earnings due to slower wage growth after taking leave to care for a new baby. In the United States, this wage penalty is estimated to be 5–7% per child (Budig and England, 2000; Manchester, Leslie, and Park, 2008). Moreover, the effect increases over time. In a recent study of Australian mothers the initial wage–penalty effect was 7% but rose to 12% during the second and third years after returning to work (Baker, 2011). High earning women suffer even more than low earners as a result of taking leave (Kornberg, 2008). A portion of this "motherhood penalty" is likely a direct result of lost wages and lost time toward scheduled earnings increases. Another part of this effect is likely indirect due to a reduced status in the company as a result of reassignments during the employee's absence or assumptions about reduced job commitment (Houser and Vartanian, 2012). These concerns were expressed by Judith K., after taking a three month leave with no pay other than accrued sick and vacation time. She said,

My boss kept referring to this great gift [of leave] he'd given me. 'You've been off for three months,' he'd say. It was frustrating. I was an awesome employee and he knew it....

They gave pay increases to others, and felt giving three months off was enough for me. People think you're not committed to work or a dependable employee. There's so much stigma that you're not reliable because you now have a child. Taking time off, I worried from a career standpoint (Walsh, 2011, pp. 66–67).

These negative effects on women's wages are largely absent when the employer offers paid family leave, perhaps because of the investment in their employees (Houser and Vartanian, 2012).

Women are not the only ones who may encounter career obstacles after childbirth and family leave. Men who otherwise might be interested in breaking through the glass wall that separates them from their fuller participation in the care of their children are hindered by the fear that getting on the "daddy track" will hurt their careers. As one young father who elected not to take advantage of his law firm's family leave plan put it, "I wanted to take the leave but I knew I'd never make partner if I did. All the male associates knew that it would be career suicide" (Parke and Brott, 1999, p. 130). In fact, corporations often view men who want to spend time with their families as less serious and devoted than those who do not take family leave. Even a manager at a family friendly company advised an employee who sought paternity leave. "As your boss, I have to grant you this leave. But as your friend, I'm advising you not to request it. Just take vacation time if you want to be with your family. Applying for paternity leave will send the wrong message around here about your commitment to work" (Levine and Pittinsky, 1997, p. 134). And even coworkers may not be supportive of men who take paternity leave. Taunts by fellow male workers, like "Mr. Mom" and "Babysitter" reflect the attitude that a "real man" wouldn't take time off for their new infant. For women, for sure, but not for men.

How do nontraditional families fare under these leave policies? Until recently there was no protection for domestic partners who were either cohabitating or in gay/lesbian couple families. Nor did leave policies apply to other caregivers beyond parents such as members of the extended family such as aunts, uncles, grandparents, and others who are active participants in cooperative caregiving arrangements. As legal scholar Jessica Weaver (2013) argues "Amending the Family Medical Leave Act to include grandparents and expand the reasons allowed for taking a leaves of absence from work would be one way of supporting contemporary extended families who share the daily tasks of child care" (p. 73).There is some progress. In 2010, the definition of "son and daughter" under the FMLA " was expanded to ensure that an employee who assumes the role of caring for a child receives parental rights to family leave regardless of the legal or biological relationship" including "an employee who intends to share in the parenting of a child with his or her same sex partner" (U.S. Department of Labor, 2010b). This shift recognizes the diversity of family forms and to some extent, no longer privileges more traditional (i.e., "ideal") families over others. However, not completely; unmarried same-sex partners (even those in legally recognized civil unions or domestic partnerships) are still not entitled to FMLA leave to care for one another, which can be difficult for same-sex partners. As one female college professor, Amelia S., who was denied FLMA leave after her partner Maya T., gave birth lamented:

I have a tremendous sense of loss. I felt very torn…. It was horrible to go back after one week (of sick leave). I had a hard time focusing. Maya had problems, the baby had reflux.

We felt robbed and scared.... I was torn because Maya was home with our screaming kid, and I was literally down the block (Walsh, 2011, p. 41).

The counterintuitive fact is that more liberal leave policies are beneficial for families and employers too. For families, the opportunity for both partners to be able to share in the joys and burdens of caregiving and to develop a close attachment with their baby is important. Fathers or same-sex partners themselves not only benefit from this time with their infant but also can ease the load for their partner so that she can recover more quickly. As one mother, Alyssa L., who had a C section delivery said, "Having to manage two kids while recovering from major surgery was physically very difficult. If my husband could have had at least two weeks, I'd probably have felt better at four weeks.... I think it would have allowed for some basic recovery. It's major surgery, and your body is not anywhere near ready, physically or emotionally, to handle all the challenges [alone]" (Walsh, 2011, p. 40). Other benefits include lower rates of postpartum depression (Chatterji and Markowitz, 2005), lower infant and child mortality (Han, Ruhm, and Waldfogel, 2009), especially when paid leave is provided (Tanaka, 2005), and better compliance with immunization schedules for infant and well baby check ups (Berger, Hill, and Waldfogel, 2005). Another benefit of family leave is that mothers are likely to breast feed for longer while no leaves or very short ones decrease even the initiation of breast feeding. This is significant since breast feeding is linked with positive outcomes for both mother (reduced postpartum bleeding, decreased risk of breast and ovarian cancer) and baby (reduced mortality, fewer infections and even enhanced cognitive development) (American Academy of Pediatrics, 2005; Caspi, William, Kim-Cohen et al., 2007). Another consequence of a limited leave policy is that families who take unpaid leave often suffer financially and some even face bankruptcy. For example, nearly 9% of families who slip into poverty do so when a child is born and nearly 20% suffer temporary poverty around this time in their lives (Rynell, 2008). For some the birth of a child is not a bundle of joy but a bundle of debt. Listen to Christina S., a mother without paid leave: "It was very stressful. We used a food bank when we had my third son.... [Paid leave] would have reduced my worry about finances, and whether we were going to make it. It would have given some security, emotional and financial" (Walsh, 2011, p. 58). Lack of paid leave is even worse for single parents. "Juliana E., a single mother of an infant had an eight-week leave with partial pay. She said, "I did the math to see [if I could take a longer leave]. I could only do eight weeks because I couldn't pay the bills" (Walsh, 2011, p. 59). Losing some of her income during this period forced her to seek financial help from family and friends, and she was late on car payments. She went on food stamps and welfare for a few months. Having consistent pay during maternity leave would have helped her avoid falling behind financially.

Work-family supports like paid family leave can benefit employers as well. Employees who are paid during family leave are more likely return to the same employer: Ninety-four percent of leave-takers who received full pay during family leave returned to the same employer, compared to 76% of employees who took unpaid leave (Bell and Newman, 2003). A study of U.S. women workers found that lengthier childbearing leave (combined paid and unpaid leave) had a strong deterrent effect against women quitting the labor force or changing jobs postpartum (Glass and Riley, 1998). Employers can also avoid recruitment and training expenses by reducing turnover (Dube and Ethan

Kaplan, 2002). Finally, worker loyalty and productivity is higher under paid leave policies than under unpaid ones (Bassanini and Venn, 2008). As one commentator summed up

> The US is actually missing out by failing to ensure that all workers have access to paid family leave. Countries that have these programs show productivity gains, reduced turnover costs, and health care savings. Around the world, policymakers understand that helping workers meet their work and family obligations is good public policy. It's good for business, for the economy, for public health, and for families (Walsh, 2011, p. 60).

*Making the Workplace More Family Flexible:*   Although family leave is one of the most widely recognized family friendly policies, it is not the only one that counts. Caregiving responsibilities do not end in infancy and children need parental attention when they are older too. As we know the popular notion of critical periods for cognitive and social development has been largely debunked. Instead, caregivers play a continuing and influential role in shaping their children's development throughout childhood and adolescence. Even after the leaves are over, many parents and other caregivers do not have the opportunity to spend enough time with their children due to insensitive and inflexible work place policies. To be a successful parent or caregiver requires more than a few days or even a few weeks of family leave.

Flextime, an employer sanctioned program which allows flexibility in employee work schedules, is an option that can allow those who are responsible for the care of children more time with their families. While the focus was once simply on new moms, as economist Tom Beers of the Bureau of Labor Statistics states, "The overall idea of flextime is becoming less tied to an option for new mothers and parents to take care of their children and more of a benefit that can be enjoyed by everyone." And many need it. One study found that 54% of employed parents felt that they spent too little time with their youngest child (Milkie et al., 2010). Others report that the option has high desirability among the overwhelming majority of employees (Rocereto, Forquer Gupta, and Mosca, 2011; Saltzstein, Ting, and Saltzstein, 2001). A father who can start his workday a few hours later can get his children ready for school. Or if he goes in a few hours early, he can spend some of the after school time with his children. As family trends chronicler, James Levine wrote over a decade ago,

> Flexible use of time is the single most important element in creating a workplace that is friendly to fathers, mothers and all employees regardless of parental status. This does not mean asking employees to work less, but giving them more control over when and where they get their jobs done (Levine and Pittinsky, 1997, p. 69).

This is still the case today. Recently, Phyllis Moen and her colleagues examined the effects of an organizational shift aimed at moving away from standard time practices to focus on results rather than time spent at work (ROWE – Results Only Work Environment) among white-collar salaried workers at the headquarters of a US Fortune 500 company. They found several benefits including lower commuting times, more schedule control, more and higher quality sleep, more energy, and lowered work-family conflict in the ROWE groups than in the control groups (Moen, Kelly, and Chermack, 2009; Moen, Kelly, and Hill, 2011). Turnover rates were lower for the employees in the ROWE program as well (Moen et al., 2011). Whether these policy shifts could be implemented for hourly workers remains an open question (Lambert, 2009), but stag-gering work shifts for teenagers to accommodate their school schedules suggests that it may apply to hourly workers too. Does flextime increase time with children? In a German study where workers in the former DGR were assigned to positions with either flexible or nonflexible working schedules, Scheffel (2011) found that mothers who work flextime spend about 32% more time with their children overall and fathers spend more time with their kids during weekends. Even corporations benefit since flextime employees are more committed to the organization (Thompson, Beauvais, and Lyness, 1999), work more hours overall and work longer before the onset of work–family conflict (Hill, Hawkins, Ferris & Weitzman, 2001).

Other options are possible to accommodate families need to balance work and family life. Part-time work is another way to create more family time. But how many are interested in shifting to part time? In one study, fewer than 20% of the women and 2% of the men who claimed to be interested in part-time work actually made the change (Hochschild, 1997). In a 1990 study of manufacturing firms, although 88% informally offered employees the chance to do part-time work, only 3–5% of them switched. Clearly having one parent working part time is not an option every family can afford. This is especially true for single-parents such as Jackie Fuller who are often struggling to make ends meet.

Cutting back on work hours leads to other fears. Perhaps employers will not view you as committed as full time employees which can lead to fewer promotions and raises. Another problem is more work for less pay. For too many people – especially for a job without a clearly defined structure – part-time work often turns into full time work for part-time wages. As Arlie Hochschild wrote, "The only way to keep a part-time schedule without violating the unspoken rules of the workplace was, in effect, to work full time" (1997, p. 77).

What about job sharing as a solution? In this version of part-time work in which two employees share a single job, employees are simply colleagues or in some cases, particularly in academia, they are married to each other or unmarried couples. Erik Grønseth (1975), a Norwegian researcher found that couples who either shared a job or worked part time divided child care more equally. Mothers enjoyed their children more while fathers felt closer to their children, and understood them better. Marital relationships improved as well, which is related to better children's development.

Telecommuting, which involves working out of one's home and communicating with the workplace through technology, is one of the other ways that caregivers can better connect with their families. Currently, there are nearly three million workers who work at least part of their week at home and are connected electronically to their workplace (Lister and Harnish, 2011). Based on current trends, regular telecommuters will increase by 69% to 4.9 million by 2016 (Lister and Harnish, 2011). In spite of this progress, in 2010, only 5% of companies offered their employees a telecommuting option (Bureau of Labor Statistics, 2010) even though over 50% were interested in this possibility. Thirty-seven percent were even willing to take a small pay cut in exchange for being able to work at home two days a week (Telework Trendlines, 2009).

Are there benefits of telecommuting? A meta-analysis of telecommuting studies involving 12,833 employees (Gajendran and Harrison, 2007) found that telecom-muting has modest but mainly positive consequences for employees and employers. Employees' job satisfaction, autonomy, and manager-rated performance were higher and stress and work-family conflict were lower. For example, a study of nearly 25,000 IBM workers found that work-family conflict kicks in around 38 hours a week for office workers, but not until about 57 hours for telecommuters while quality of work-place relationships and career outcomes were unaffected (Hill, Erickson, Holmes Holmes, & Ferris, 2010). Moreover, this option saves time (almost a week of free time per year) and money ($2000–$6700/year), in part, by reducing the fuel costs of commuting (Lister and Harnish, 2011) as well as the amount of child care needed. Reducing child care costs would be appealing to single-parent (and often poor) families as well as dual-earner couples. As one satisfied telecommter said, "I can take care of the sick child and get my work done. A win-win situation." Unfortunately, the average teleworker is older, better educated and better paid than the average worker, which suggests that workers with young families or single parents who could most benefit from this flexibility are less likely to be teleworkers. We need to make these opportunities available for individuals in all kinds of families and determine whether cultural biases, beyond income, limit access to flexible work place options. Clearly, telecommuting is not for every family. But in the struggle to give mothers, fathers, and partners more time with their families, every hour is important. And telework certainly gives caregivers the power to spend less of their day at work (or getting there and back) and more at home.

*The Child-Care Challenge as An Opportunity for Employers:*   Companies can help families spend more time with their children by providing on-site child care, an option that is usually only offered by fairly large employers. The federal government provides child care at many offices and so do such private employers as Ben and Jerry's Homemade, John Hancock, Nike, Afflac and the Men's Wearhouse. It is more common in European countries (i.e. Denmark and Sweden) due to government subsidies (Hjern et al., 2000). In the United States, less than 10% (80,000–90,000) of companies offer on-site child care, but it may be catching on. A 2012 survey of the best 100 US companies to work for found that a third of these companies offered on-site child care (Fortune, 2012). Although white collar workers are twice as likely to have on-site care than blue collar workers, one innovative Alabama company even designed mobile childcare facilities so workers could bring their children to the construction site with them (Employee Benefit Plan Review, 1994), a reminder that on-site care need not be restricted to high tech companies with well-paid employees. One US study of on-site child care with hourly blue collar factory workers found wide support among employees and financial savings ($150,000–$250,000 in wages) for the company. Most workers were willing to pay between $125 and $225 per year to subsidize on-site daycare – whether or not they had young children (Connolly, DeGraff, and Willis, 2004). And the parents who use on-site child care were less stressed and more comfortable being close by their children. As one mother who used on-site care said "It makes it easier to do my job. It gives me peace of mind." while another said. "If something happens, if he gets sick. I can be there instantly" (Hixson-Somanchi, 2010, p. 67). Moreover, commuting time is reduced by avoiding the need to drop off children at non work- site care facilities. Fathers with their children in on-site care echoed these sentiments. Seventy-four percent were less anxious about their children and often visited them at lunchtime two or three times a week, which increased the time they get with their kids by approximately fifty hours a year (Employee Benefit Plan Review, 1994).

Employers can assist with parental child care needs in other ways such as referrals and subsidies to help defray the costs of child care. According to a 2003 Work/Life Benefits report, "child care assistance remains the most prevalent work/life program, with 95% of employers today offering some kind of assistance to their employees (up from 87% in 1998)" (Hewitt Associates, 2003, p. 1). However, most of the assistance takes the form of no-cost child care options – such as Dependent Care Assistance Plans (45%) which allows an employee to contribute, tax free, part of their salary into a flexible spending account which can be used to pay for child care expenses. Another option favored by 34% of employers is the Child Care Resource and Referral Program which provides information for parents who are seeking child-care services (Bond et al., 2005). This referral service will steer you in the right direction, help you contribute to a plan to pay for it but provide little in the way of direct subsidies. Those who need the assistance most, such as poor and/or single-parent families rely on Government programs for assistance.

## Depictions of Family in the Media: Beyond the "Ideal" Family form

One of the ways in which outdated representations of family forms are maintained in the culture is through the mass media. As Signorielli (2001) observed, television has become the "nation's primary story-teller" (p. 36). In this role, the mass media could play a significant role by increasing awareness of the social, emotional, and economic benefits of diverse family forms through more accurate portrayals of a wider range of families. The image of the nuclear family such as the Evans continues to dominate the TV landscape out of proportion to their prevalence in US society. As we noted earlier, there are still stereotyped images of the contemporary family, outdated roles of mothers and fathers in families, and too few portrayals of alternative family forms. By watching TV and the movies one rarely sees stay at home dads, lesbian-parent families, ART families or Asian, Latino or even African American families. While some progress has been made in correcting stereotypic portrayals of fathers and mothers in the media, alternative family forms such as extended families or children in a nonrelative family configuration are seldom presented (Comstock and Scharrer, 2006). Programs that feature the participation of a wider range of individuals as caregivers could move us toward greater understanding and greater cultural acceptance of these alternative family forms. Yes, there have been some exceptions over the last few decades and some recent progress. Besides *Murphy Brown* about single motherhood by choice or the *Cosby* show about an African American family, recent programs such as *Up All Night* about a stay at home dad, *Parenthood* featuring a three generational family, and *Modern Family* with a family of two gay-fathers are taking clear steps toward correcting the imbalance. Yet, other contemporary TV shows such as *Two and a Half Men* continue to depict men as incompetent parents or even portray the children as parental figures. Another limitation of current media offerings is the serious underrepresentation on TV programs of Hispanic and Asian American families who are more likely than Caucasian families to practice cooperative parenting arrangements (Armstrong and Watson, 2008). The media needs to do a better job of highlighting not just the diversity of family forms but showcasing successful alternative living arrangements involving multiple caregivers and erasing the stereotypes of alternative families.

*Mothers in the Media:*  Contemporary TV portrayals of women in families are no longer restricted to the 1950s stereotypes of women as housewives and men as breadwinners found in classic shows such as *All in the Family* and *Leave it to Beaver*. Although the shift toward casting women as employed outside the home has increased, women are still more likely to be portrayed as stay-at-home caregivers than males (Coltrane and Adams, 2008; Heintz-Knowles, 2001). Even recent shows such as *Modern Family*, which set out to embrace diversity in family forms, ended up continuing to stereotype women as stay at home mothers. In a critique of *Modern Family*, Lehmann (2011) notes "New family visions are never fully embraced, but instead altered to fit into a common family ideology. In contrast to its title, *Modern Family* promotes traditional gender roles and stereotypes of women, which result in the portrayal of an inaccurate image of the female" (p.2). Nor do women fare much better in TV commercials; they are more often depicted as consumers who express interest in products than as the spokespersons who extol the virtues of a product. When they are cast as the expert, they are usually promoting food products, laundry soap and beauty aids which underscores their homemaker role and their focus on appearance rather than more serious issues (Coltrane and Adams, 2008). The plethora of ads directed toward women has led to a comedy correction. For example, in the Current TV InfoMania segment "Target Women", comedian Sarah Haskins commented on products, advertising, and media aimed at women in a mocking way that exposed the stereotypical underpinnings of these advertising messages. In spite of the fact that a large percentage of women are actively engaged in both the world of work and the caregiving arena, outdated media stereotypes of maternal roles as unidimensional rather than multidimensional still persist.

*Fathers in the Media:*  Although fathers are increasingly active caregivers who competently execute their domestic responsibilities as nurturers of children, fathers are still portrayed in a majority of television programs and movies as inept, uninvolved or unimportant. From the venerable *Homer Simpson* to more recent TV dads such as Jay Pritchett in *Modern Family*, fathers continue to be outwitted or shown up by their wives, ridiculed by their children and often portrayed as parentally challenged. A future goal of the media ought to be to promote contemporary, realistic, and appropriate images of fatherhood so that the media becomes a vehicle for supporting new views of responsible fathering. Movies and television can help shape our vision of men as partners for their wives and as involved and equal contributors to the care and upbringing of their children. Nor is it just movies and TV programs. Books need to more realistically portray men as involved and competent fathers. Young adult novels often focus on boys and men in action but rarely do they feature plots that highlight the impact of involved fathering on the story's characters (Parke and Brott, 1999). Instead you have to turn to historical or political books or memoirs to read about fathers. We need more books to inspire boys to want to be involved and responsible fathers and to show them that fatherhood is not incompatible with being successful, exciting, and adventuresome. Fiction for girls needs to convey a similar message so their expectations for their future partners are in line with contemporary egalitarian roles for both parents.

*Media Portrayals of Single Parents:*  Several themes are evident in the portrayal of single parents in the media. The diversity of single parents is inadequately represented.

Instead of recognizing that there are a wide range of single mothers including widows, divorcees, teenage mothers, and single mothers by choice, they share the fact that they are all raising a child without a partner but in stereotypic fashion. When single mothers are portrayed they are either successful career women or young welfare check dependent mothers. Little attention is paid to ways that single mothers lives can be improved by community support from friends and extended family members or to the coping strategies used by single but poor mothers to manage their lives successfully (e.g., Furstenberg, Brooks-Gunn, and Morgan,1987; Leadbeater and Way, 2001). While Mary Winston could easily relate to Candice Bergen (of *Murphy Brown* fame) since both were single mothers by choice, Jackie Fuller is unlikely to easily relate to any of the poor single mothers who she sees on TV. Single dads have perhaps provided more inspirational models than single moms, going back to Andy Griffith's homey advice to Opie and Fred McMurray's care of *My Three Sons*. Today's shows, including *Castle*, *Raising Hope*, *Louie*, *Touch*, and *Suburgatory*, also featuring single dads, suggesting there continues to be a place on TV for this family form.

*Stepparents and Custodial Grandparents in the Media:* In general, stepfamilies are underrepresented or misrepresented in the media (Leon and Angst, 2005). Successful and harmonious stepfamilies like the Tremblay–Bailey family are seldom found. Conflict and dysfunction apparently attracts more viewers. Outside of *The Brady Bunch*, stepfamilies are portrayed as conflicted and unstable with a weak spousal relationship. A new TV show, *Reed Between the Lines*, however, depicts a well-functioning African American stepfamily, which helps dispel some of the negative stereotypes and at the same time reminds viewers that stepfamilies come from all racial/ethnic parts of society. It is difficult to find custodial grandparents on television, but in *Raising Hope*, the grandparents are active participants helping the single dad raise his daughter. They provide a loving child-rearing environment, albeit not exemplary role models. In light of the growing number of custodial grandparents in this country, this family form needs more air time and offers rich material for screenwriters.

*Same-Sex Parents in the Media:* Portrayals of same-sex parent families are still rare, but they are increasing. *Will and Grace* was the first prime time TV show showing such a couple, albeit briefly: at the end of the show, two gay men have married and apparently successfully reared a son together. Since then other TV shows, such as *Modern Family*, and films, such as *The Kids Are All Right*, portray same-sex parents in the process of successfully rearing children. As portrayals of such diverse family forms increase, public acceptance of these family forms will likely rise as well.

*Nongenetic Parents in the Media:* Adoption and surrogacy, in which parents raise nongenetically related children, are beginning to receive overdue media attention. In both *Modern Family* and *Parenthood* adoption is featured as an alternative route to parenthood. Even surrogacy is being recognized in media offerings with the presence of a surrogate mom in the TV show *The New Normal*. In fact their multifaceted characters and their normalness are major steps toward reducing negative stereotypes about adoption and surrogacy.

*Racial/Ethnic Families in the Media:* Although the percentage of ethnic families is growing, with over a third of the population belonging to an ethnic/racial minority, white families still dominate TV programs, advertising, and movies while other ethnic groups are underrepresented. For minority children who see mainly white families on TV, the message is "You are irrelevant. You don't matter." (Slattery, 2012). Black characters comprise only 16% of prime time roles on television (Monk-Turner et al., 2010). Even though the *Cosby Show*, *Fresh Prince of Bel Air*, and *Family Matters* were staples of TV in the 1980s and 1990s, few African American families are currently on TV. The exception is the Fox channel's *The Cleveland Show*, about an animated cartoon family who happen to live next door to a family of Bears – not exactly a fair representation of the modern Black family. Things are a little better if you examine other offerings beyond the major networks. TBS's *Are We There Yet?* and *House of Payne*, along with BET's *Reed Between the Lines* and *The Game*, are examples of the few shows that currently feature primarily African American casts. Moreover, many programs continue to present stereotypic portrayals of African American families, although there are some programs such as *Little Bill*, a children's TV show, which do depict Africa American families not as stereotypically dysfunctional but as loving families (Hurtado and Silva, 2008).

Latino and Asian families are almost invisible, with Latinos appearing in 5% of prime time roles and Asians in fewer than 2% (Monk-Turner et al., 2010). Of course, there are Spanish and Asian language networks devoted to specific ethnic groups. However, few viewers outside the targeted audience watch these programs, so their role in dispelling ethnic and racial stereotypes among nonminority individuals is limited. Although *Ugly Betty* and *The George Lopez Show* were a corrective to the startling underrepresentation of Latinos on TV, few new shows featuring Latino characters have replaced them. And the ones that have, often make fun of the Latino characters rather than embracing their strengths. In the program *Rob*, in which the Caucasian lead marries into a Latino family, the cultural differences are lamented not celebrated, while in *Modern Family*, Gloria's Columbian accent is a regular source of humor. In fact, Latino characters are more often depicted with heavy accents and as being less articulate than TV characters of other races (Monk-Turner et al., 2010). Little attention is paid to Latino family values or their involvement with extended family, which means an opportunity is lost to educate the wider TV audience about the admirable aspects of Latino family life. It is doubtful if Maria and Jose Dorado, our representative Latino family, would recognize themselves or their extended family from current TV shows.

Asians in search of families like theirs in the mass media do not fare too well either. As one commentator recently said,

> If you're Asian, yeah, you can pretty much forget about getting any semblance of a representation of your family life on TV. Lost's Sun and Jin gave TV viewers the story of a South Korean family for six seasons, but now all we've got are brief glimpses of Mike Chang's parents, who showed up for an episode or two of Glee to perpetuate a few Tiger Dad stereotypes before disappearing into the ether (Slattery, 2012).

So much for models of alternative family forms in which relatives across generations cooperatively share responsibility for the health and safety of children.

Clearly, there is a serious cultural lag between the rich diversity of forms of modern families and the fictional families that we routinely watch on TV or even see at the movies. As a profound influence on the ways in which we form attitudes and gain information about families in our society, the mass media needs to catch up and provide more realistic and up-to-date portrayals of the full range of contemporary families.

## Harnessing Innovations in Communication Technology to Reduce Distance between Families

The new ways of communication such as the social networking, cell phones, instant messaging, and Skype are complements to the old standby, email, as ways of keeping in touch with family members even when they are on a different coast or a different continent. With the increasing separation of families from their extended kin, these technologies offer social support and advice for isolated and separated families such as immigrant families, single-parent families, or divorced families. Even the Evans family, our example of the ideal family, benefit by being able to keep in touch with their distant extended family as well. A friend indicated that he talks and "sees" members of his extended family almost daily through Skype which allows him to remain connected to other family members in spite of living vast distances apart. At the same time, as Rochel Berman, author of *Oceans Apart: A Guide to Maintaining Family Ties at a Distance* (2010) cautions "Skype does help but you can't hug a Skype and you can't hug a jpeg." Others have created family websites, family listservs, and Webbased family magazines as a way to share photos and updates among far flung family members. While it is not the same as residing in the same house, in the same neighborhood, or even in the same city, it is a strategy that overcomes, in part, the problem of limited face-to-face contact between distant family members. In other cases, new technologies allow parents to monitor and keep in touch with their children's whereabouts and activities. Moreover, a frequently traveling parent or partner can maintain contact during an out of town trip. Both custodial and noncustodial divorced parents can maintain ties with their child during times when the child is with the other parent. Moreover, the communication innovations allow for "lost" family members to reconnect after periods of no contact due to moving. The Internet is used by adopted or ART offspring who are searching for their biological family members. However, the new communication opportunities are not without some downsides. For example, longitudinal findings from a large national panel of Americans suggest that using the Internet may lead to declines in visiting with friends and family. This effect is largest for those who initially had most social contact, that is, the extroverts (Shklovski, Kraut, and Rainie, 2004). Moreover, smartphone and twitter contacts with friends sometimes replace family interaction and conversation among family members even during dinner time. While new technology enabled modes of communication may be helpful in maintaining ties with family, it is not a substitute for visiting. Finally, affluent and two-parent, especially the two-earner, families are more likely to have access to these technologies than the poor single mothers who are struggling to make ends meet.

## Can We Design More Family Friendly Communities?

Architects and urban designers can play a role in this move toward increasing the viability of alternative family forms. Unfortunately, housing designers have not kept pace with the changing demographics of Western society. As architects Kathryn McCamant and Charles Durrett (2011) remind us,

The modern single family detached home which makes up 69 percent of the American housing stock, was designed for a nuclear family consisting of a breadwinning father, a homemaking mother and two to four children. Today this family type is in the minority. In fact even the family with two working parents is no longer predominant. The single parent household is the fastest growing family form in American history and for the first time ever more than half of the women over eighteen in this country do not live with a husband. Well over one quarter of the population lives alone and this proportion will grow as the number of Americans over 60 years old increases. Traditional forms of housing no longer address the needs of many people. Things that people once took for granted – family, community, a sense of belonging – must now be actively sought out. Cohousing re-establishes many of the advantages of traditional villages within the context of modern life (p. 4).

Another trend is that more members of elderly generations are moving in with their adult children which has resulted in approximately 50 million (nearly one in six) Americans living in households with at least two adult generations, and sometimes three generations (Taylor et al., 2010). In light of these shifts, we need to rethink how we design houses and organize communities to better accommodate the needs of children, parents, and senior citizens in a society with an increasing diversity of family forms. By designing communities and housing units more thoughtfully, we can increase social capital so that alternative family forms receive the social support needed to flourish.

The design of houses and the organization of communities can be modified to make it more feasible for multiple caregiver families to physically cohabitate or to be in close proximity. In Europe, intergenerational cohousing which began in Denmark in the early 1970s is an innovative example of how communities can be planned to support and facilitate more shared cross-generation responsibility for the care and rearing of children (Fromm and de Jong, 2009; Scanzoni, 2000). The cohousing movement was inspired by early pioneers such as author Bodil Graae who argued in her 1967 article, "Children Should Have a Hundred Parents," that children's needs are being neglected in modern society and that neighborhood design gave greater consideration to cars and parking than children. She advocated a different kind of environment where children can "go in and out of the homes around us...crawl under hedges...feel like they belong" (cited in McCamant and Durrett, 1994, p. 137). She envisioned a community in which all the adults would share responsibility for the care of all the children. In Denmark, over 700 cohousing projects have been designed and developed in response to Graae's early call for alternatives to traditional communities of single family houses (McCamant and Durrett, 2011). These planned communities include private dwellings as well as communal spaces and facilities which by design foster a sense of community. These experiments in community design are not limited to Denmark; there are hundreds of cohousing communities in the United States, Canada, Australia, New Zealand, the Netherlands, Sweden, Germany, France, Belgium, Austria and elsewhere (McCamant and Durrett, 2011). Several projects across the United States from California and Colorado to Texas, Delaware, and New York have been developed guided by similar principles. Approximately 120 cohousing projects are currently active in the United States and another 50 are in the planning stage (Margolis and Entin, 2011; McCamant and

Durrett, 2011). The early established community of Trudeslund just north of Copenhagen in Denmark illustrates this alternative approach to housing. In this community 33 families, each with their own private dwelling, share laundry facilities, a workshop, a darkroom, and a music room for teens; they often eat meals together in a communal dining room and keep a watch on other people's children in the community. There is no lack of playmates with nearly 50 children living in the community and cars park on the periphery so the pedestrian area is safe for children and adults. "The community serves as a large extended family – children have many people besides their parents to look after them and to whom they can turn for assistance, or just talk to. It becomes second nature for the older kids to keep an eye on the smaller ones, and the adults know every child by name" (McCamant and Durrett, 1994, p. 27). One of the goals was to provide a wider network of support for the nuclear family, and through this cooperative design the Trudeslund community has achieved this goal. In a similar vein, others report social support for parents, especially new parents as a clear benefit of living in a multigenerational community. And seniors benefit as well by staying actively involved with members of the younger generations. According to a recent survey of U.S. based cohousing communities, 73% of the communities reported providing meals for new parents (Figure 9.2). Respondents also cited the presence of "great mentors for new parents" as one of the attractions of cohousing (Margolis and Entin, 2011, p. 7). It is important to underscore that these housing arrangements can accommodate a rich array of family forms, not just couples with children. In several other Danish cohousing projects some own their houses and others rent, which allows families and individuals across the economic spectrum to be part of the residential mix. In many cohousing developments, single parents, couples with children, older couples who are empty nesters, and single individuals without children are all part of the

**Figure 9.2**   A cohousing project *Heartstone* in Colorado consists of 33 homes with 75 residents, including 32 children.
*Source:* Co-Housing Communities: A Life Shared, January 14, 2011 by Heather Clisby in Life ClizBiz Blog.

community. This combination of multiple generations and diverse family forms provides community support for single parents, opportunities for older residents to remain involved as mentors and support figures for younger generations and single individuals to enjoy contact with children and families. In fact, some cohousing projects such as the Family Support Center's Life Start Village in Utah have been developed specifically to support low income single-parent families in recognition of the need for alternative housing options for this increasingly common family form (Graber and Wolfe, 2004). While older adults may serve as mentors for parents and children, seniors themselves benefit not only from remaining actively engaged but from help and care when they need it. According to a survey of US cohousing communities (Margolis and Entin, 2011), 94% of the communities either occasionally or frequently provided assistance for a sick or injured neighbor while 34% provided long-term care for their elderly residents. Nor is it just parents and seniors who benefit. A central feature of these settings is their focus on the care and supervision of children. In the cohousing survey, 84% of the communities reported that they engaged in occasional or frequent child-care exchange or cooperative arrangements (Margolis and Entin, 2011). One resident, Frede Dublijaer, a mother of three children in a Danish cohousing project noted the community support for children: "We never worry about finding a baby sitter because we know we can depend on one of our neighbors – and the kids are comfortable staying with them. The older kids can just stay home because they have neighbors to call if they have any problems" (McCamant and Durrett, 1994, p. 88). The residents of the Santa Rosa Creek commons project in California which was completed in 1982 reported similar positive benefits for the children in cohousing communities. One father told an interviewer, "The neighbors had a daughter the same age as mine, and they were like 'sisters.' When they have a problem, they have a choice of people to turn to for assistance." (Fromm, 1991, p. 103; cited by Scanzoni, 2000, p. 83). In another case one member took care of an eight-year-old in the afternoon while her father, a single-parent worked. "I watch her when she comes home from school and if I'm busy, the neighbors take turns keeping an eye" (Fromm, 1991, p. 104; cited by Sconzoni, 2000, p. 83). In another cohousing project, Great Oak Cohousing Community in Ann Arbor, Michigan, one parent noted that "Other parents sometimes take over when we can't take it anymore, which can be very helpful." (Cohousing, 2010). Some projects solve the issue of child care by developing community child care programs which are staffed by hired teachers but supplemented by the residents.

Moreover, parents felt that the high number of children and adults surrounding their children improved the child's social and conflict resolution skills, and helped to foster a respect for individual differences (Margolis and Entin, 2011). Many parents feel the community takes an active role in supervising children, freeing up time for parents, and reducing worry about a child's safety (Cohousing, 2010). Children also benefit from exposure to diverse family configurations and expand their sense of the concept of the normal family. As one parent put it, "My kids love it and are learning so much from being in community with a variety of people" (Margolis and Entin, 2011). One index of how much these communities value their children is that according to a recent survey four-fifths of the nearly 90 US based cohousing communities have constructed playgrounds for their children (Margolis and Entin, 2011).

Even cohousing communities just as in the case of more isolated families have issues and disputes. There are problems such as some members of the community not doing their share of the community wide tasks and long meetings to settle disputes and agree on plans for renovations or rule changes (Fromm, 1991; Margolis and Entin, 2011). Even unruly children sometimes become an issue for some residents who feel that their parents should exercise better control over their offspring. At the same time many of the problems such as after school care, safe places for children to interact and someone to help out during an illness faced by parents even in ideal family forms are less likely in these types of communities.

While the cohousing examples that we have outlined offer the promise of better environments for raising children and supporting diverse family forms, to date few data are available beyond qualitative reports and some surveys documenting the pros and cons of these alternative communities. Perhaps well-adjusted individuals simply choose to join these types of cohousing entities.

Findings from a new project – Hope Meadows – in which residents in a cohousing project adopt foster children provides stronger evidence for the possible positive effects of this arrangement especially for the academic achievement of the children. This innovative multigenerational community, a highly regarded model for intergenerational life in the United States, illustrates the feasibility of this alternative family living arrangement and the mutual benefits experienced by different generations who are members of this community (Eheart, Hopping, Power et al., 2009). Built on the site of an old Air Force base in Rantoul, Illinois, Hope Meadows is a multigenerational, residential community who feel and act like an extended family. Parents such as the Winfields who we met earlier adopted three or four children and are compensated with an annual salary, health benefits, and free housing. Older residents such as the Benningtons serve at least six hours a week as mentors, tutors, companions and surrogate "grandparents" for the children and, in turn, receive reduced rent on spacious three-bedroom apartments. To facilitate social interaction there is an Intergenerational Center which serves as the hub of social, cultural, and educational activity for Hope Meadows. It houses a children's library, a computer room, several rooms for individual tutoring, a kitchen and a large multipurpose space. At the Center seniors help kids with homework, read aloud to young children, or help older ones to read, play cards, or board games, or gather a group to go outside for soccer or basketball. Other features of the physical design encourage cross generational contact. Since all buildings are geographically contiguous, this provides the context for the formation and development of the social dimensions of a caring community. In addition, the flow of foot, car, and bicycle traffic through the neighborhood increases the odds of residents encountering one another. The informal relationships that take root in this way constitute the social core of the community. The physical design which facilitates relationships and engagement among the members of this multigenerational community is good for the children, the parents as well as the seniors. Hope Meadows has three older adult households for every adoptive family, and every young person who has stayed at Hope Meadows until their late teens has either graduated from high school or received a GED (a high school equivalent certificate). In contrast, the high school graduation rate for children in the general foster care system was 50% and in the general population 70% (Legislative Analyst's Office, 2009). Clearly, the support provided by the program increased the achievement of the youth at Hope Meadows. As one long time adoptive parent said

> Being out here, with the seniors and staff involved, we've got constant support. They've raised their own kids and give us some hindsight about what might work. The support makes a lot of difference in the closeness out here, because everyone is looking at what's good for the children, and it's not just us by ourselves (Eheart et al, 2009, p.49).

And the seniors enjoy the intergenerational contact too, not just the reduced rent. As one observer of the program noted "seniors at Hope generally feel a sense of continued purpose because of the impact they can have on young lives, and the relationships they build provide meaningful interaction. As seniors grow older, they can rely on community members to look after them" (Power, Eheart, Racine et al., 2007, p. 20). Older couples as well as their younger neighbors, benefit from the shared caregiving across the generations that is common at Hope Meadows. Although this community was designed to serve families of children adopted from the foster care system, it is a model that has more general relevance for guiding the development of similar multigenerational communities that can bring unrelated generations together as cooperative caregivers. As family mobility increases and opportunities for extended family members to engage in face to face sharing in the care of children decrease, these communities can function as "surrogate extended families" to the benefit of individuals across several generations. Both the Winfields from the child rearing generation and the Benningtons from the grandparent generation and, of course, the children all benefit in this type of community.

*Implications of the Cohousing Model for Wider Housing Policy:*   Cohousing represents a tiny fraction of housing options worldwide but other less radical and more modest innovations flow from the insights offered by cohousing. Several steps could be taken. First, reversing the trend toward age segregated (adults only) communities and housing projects by embracing mixed-age communities in which multiple generations reside together in the same community would be a major step forward. The opportunities for older adults to interact with younger parents and children could be potentially beneficial for the older adults, and offer support for parents and children as well. Surely, social interactions with adults and children of the younger generation are as beneficial for seniors as taking responsibility for pets and plants! Second, a simple but meaningful change would be to build more houses with "in-law" apartments as part of the original design to encourage the inclusion of multiple generations in a household. Many families with young children would welcome the availability and assistance of either their own parents or even an unrelated older caregiver. With so much geographic dispersion of family members in our mobile society, this change would improve the lives of struggling families, especially single-parent families such as Jackie Fuller's. An innovative approach to providing low-cost housing for extended families was undertaken in New Zealand where housing officials and architects collaborated on the design of a house which can accommodate several sets of families (Housing New Zealand, 2007; Productivity Commission, 2012). It includes a communal eating area, a play area for children and private sleeping quarters. This innovative design is cost effective, accommodates multiple families and avoids overcrowding. It is important to design houses which can adequately accommodate multifamily groups since overcrowding may offset some of the social and economic advantages and lead to heightened conflict, poorer health, or even reduced cognitive performance (Evans, 2006). Clearly, housing designs in support of extended, multigenerational or multifamily dwellings are feasible and warrant consideration by policy makers.

A related solution would be to liberalize current housing restrictions to allow existing houses to be renovated to accommodate grandparents. Since many adults with children live far from their biological extended family the expanded space allows the addition of "surrogate" or nonkin "aunts, uncles, or grandparents" to join the household as potential co-caregivers. From an economic perspective, multigenerational households may be a more viable future economic housing model than single family, single dwelling arrangements for some older individuals or couples as well as younger individuals and their families. Although reverse mortgages have gained in popularity among seniors as a solution to allow them to afford to remain in their homes, another option is to encourage older adults to rent extra space in their "empty nest" houses to younger families. This would reduce the isolation of older generation individuals as well as provide some economic support. In turn, younger tenant families would have access to potentially more affordable housing as well as provide the opportunities for informal interaction with older parental figures who could offer advice and support and possibly even share some of the child-care responsibilities. Especially in uncertain economic times, multifamily and/or multigenerational households may be a more sustainable economic strategy and permit more young families to enter not just the housing market but to enjoy the benefits of assistance in child rearing as well. In fact, in 2010 there was a spike in multigenerational households due, in part, to the economic recession (Taylor et al., 2010). As generations of immigrant families as well as some African American families have demonstrated, multifamily, cross-generation housing arrangements are adaptive strategies for many poor families. In other countries, groups such as the Maori of New Zealand use a strategy of pooling funds while sharing a residence to permit families to enter the housing market, stay in a house or move up to a better one (Productivity Commission, 2012; Reimers, 2006). According to one study, single parents are particularly likely to benefit from pooling arrangements with other extended family members in a household (Dunifon and Kowaleski-Jones, 2002). Moreover, these living arrangements often include cooperative caregiving, which can be a further economic advantage (reducing expenses of child care) as well as social support for many families, especially single parent families. As this excursion into the arena of housing and architecture illustrates, solutions to the problems facing contemporary families will come from scholars and practitioners from many disciplines who by working together can help various family forms thrive.

## Final Reflections

The cultural changes that are necessary to overcome the barriers and resistance to modifications in the ideal family model will be slow in coming and will require effort on many fronts. As in the case of any social paradigm change, there is no silver bullet; only through dialogue at many levels, among many change agents, and in many arenas will progress be achieved. By imagining and critically examining alternatives to the "ideal" family form, greater acceptance as well as heightened interest in new and nontraditional family arrangements will ensue. The resistance to change lies not only in our institutions (government, workplace, medical, and social service delivery systems, etc) but also in all of us who continue to endorse the ideal family form as the favored cultural model. There needs to be a change of hearts and minds at all levels of society from citizens to legislators. By challenging researchers as well as policy makers to jointly embrace this agenda, better knowledge about family forms and their effects on children's outcomes will become available and provide a better basis for developing future social policies on behalf of families and children. A common theme across many alternative forms is the recognition of the value of a cooperative approach to child care, a lesson from our past and a useful guide for our future. Finally, it is both important and reassuring to remember that the family processes within these various alternative family forms remain the most important determinant of children's developmental outcomes.

There is no single "ideal" family form, only many variations of family form. In fact, these alternative family forms are becoming the new norm in many Western societies. This diverse array of family forms deserves recognition, acceptance, and support as alternatives to traditional "ideal" families such as the Evans. In the long run, children, families, and our society can potentially benefit from the embrace of a wider range of family forms. Harnessing support from many parts of our society – informal and formal – for all forms of families is our best hope for optimizing the functioning of these varied family types.

# References

Abrego, L. (2009). Economic well-being in Salvadoran transnational families: How gender affects remittances practices. *Journal of Marriage and Family, 71*, 1070–1085.

Acs, G., & Nelson, S. (2002). *The kids are alright? Children's well-being and the rise in cohabitation*. New Federalism B-48: National Survey of America's Families. Washington, DC: The Urban Institute.

Adams, D. W. (1995). *Education for extinction: American Indians and the boarding school experience 1875–1928*. Lawrence, KS: University Press of Kansas.

Adams, G., & Rohacek, M. (2002). More than a work support? Issues around integrating child development goals into the child care subsidy system. *Early Childhood Research Quarterly, 17*, 418–440.

Administration for Children and Families. (2004). *Temporary Assistance for Needy Families (TANF), Sixth Annual Report to Congress. TANF research and evaluation*. Washington, DC: U.S. Department of Health and Human Services.

After School Alliance. (2009). *Afterschool essentials: Research and polling. Report on the afterschool hours in America*. Washington, DC: After School Alliance. Retrieved April 29, 2013 from http://www.afterschoolalliance.org/documents/2012/Essentials_4_20_12_FINAL.pdf

Aguilera-Guzman, R. M., Salgado De Snyder, V. N., Romero, M., & Medina-Mora, M. E. (2004). Paternal absence and international migration: Stressors and compensators associated with the mental health of Mexican teenagers of rural origin. *Adolescence, 39*, 711–723.

Allen, J., Mohatt, G. V., Markstrom, C., Novins, D., & Byers, L. (2012). Oh no, we are just getting to know you: The relationship in research with children and youth in indigenous communities. *Child Development Perspectives, 6*, 55–60.

Allen, M. L., Elliot, M. N., Fuligni, A. J., Morales, L. S., Hambarsoomian, K., & Schuster, M. A. (2008). The relationship between Spanish language use and substance use behaviors among Latino youth: A social network approach. *Journal of Adolescent Health, 43*, 372–379.

Almack, K. (2006). Seeking sperm: Accounts of lesbian couples' reproductive decision making and understandings of the needs of the child. *International Journal of Law, Policy, and the Family, 20*, 1–22.

Alvergne, A., Faurie, C., & Raymond, M. (2009). Variation in testosterone levels and male reproductive effort: Insight from a polygynous human population. *Hormonal Behavior, 56*, 491–497.

*Future Families: Diverse Forms, Rich Possibilities*, First Edition. Ross D. Parke.
© 2013 John Wiley & Sons, Inc. Published 2013 by John Wiley & Sons, Inc.

Amato, P. L., Loomis, L. S., & Booth, A. (1995). Parental divorce, parental marital conflict, and offspring well-being during early adulthood. *Social Forces, 73*, 895–915.

Amato, P. R. (2000). Consequences of divorce for adults and children. *Journal of Marriage and Family, 62*, 1269–1287.

Amato, P. R. (2001). Children of divorce in the 1990s: An update of the Amato and Keith (1991) meta-analysis. *Journal of Family Psychology, 15*, 355–370.

Amato, P. R. (2005). The impact of family formation change on the cognitive, social, and emotional well-being of the next generation. *Future of Children, 15*, 75–96.

Amato, P. R. (2006). Marital discord, divorce, and children's well-being: Results from a 20 year long study of two generations. In A. Clarke-Stewart & J. Dunn (Eds.), *Families count: Effects on child and adolescent development* (pp. 179–202). New York: Cambridge University Press.

Amato, P. R. (2010). Research on divorce: Continuing trends and new developments. *Journal of Marriage and Family, 72*, 650–666.

Amato, P. R., & Dorius, C. (2010). Fathers, children, and divorce. In M. Lamb (Ed.), *The role of the father in child development* (5th ed., pp. 177–200). Hoboken, NJ: Wiley.

American Academy of *Pediatrics*. (2005). Policy statement: Breastfeeding and the use of human milk. *Pediatrics, 115*, 499.

American Society for Reproductive Medicine. (2010). *Oversight of assisted reproductive technology*. Retrieved April 29, 2013 from http://www.asrm.org/Oversight_of_ART/

Argys, L. M., Peters, E., Cook, S., Garasky, S., Nepomnyaschy, L., & Sorenson, E. (2007). Measuring contact between children and nonresident fathers. In S. L. Hofferth & L. M. Casper (Eds.), *Handbook of measurement issues in family research* (pp. 375–398). Mahwah, NJ: Erlbaum.

Armenta, B. E., Whitbeck, L. B., Martinez, M. M., & Walls, M. L. (2012, October). *Child-rearing in context: Validation of the family parenting practices measure for indigenous youths*. Paper presented at the meeting of the Native Children's Research Exchange, Denver, CO.

Armstrong, J., & Watson, M. (2008, June 13). *Diversity in entertainment: Why is TV so white?* Retrieved April 29, 2013 from http://www.ew.com/ew/article/0,,20206185,00.html

Artis, J. E. (2007). Maternal cohabitation and child well-being among kindergarten children. *Journal of Marriage and Family, 69*, 222–236.

Asis, M. (2006). Living with migration: Experiences of children left behind in the Philippines. *Asian Population Studies, 2*, 45–67.

Avila, E. (2008). *Transnational motherhood and fatherhood: Gendered challenges and coping*. Unpublished doctoral dissertation, University of Southern California, Los Angeles.

Baca-Zinn, M., & Wells, B. (2000). Diversity within Latino families: New lessons for family social science. In D. H. Demo, K. R. Allen, & M. A. Fine (Eds.), *Handbook of family diversity* (pp. 252–273). New York: Oxford University Press.

Baird, A. (2003). Through my eyes: Service needs of grandparents who raise their grandchildren, from the perspective of a custodial grandmother. In B. Hayslip & J. Patrick (Eds.), *Working with custodial grandparents* (pp. 59–68). New York: Springer.

Baker, D. (2011). Maternity leave and reduced future earning capacity. *Family Matters: Australian Institute of Family Studies Journal, 89*, 25–89.

Banks, J. A. (1991). *Teaching strategies for ethnic studies* (5th ed.). Boston: Allyn & Bacon.

Barnas, M. V., & Cummings, E. M. (1994). Caregiver stability and toddlers' attachment-related behavior towards caregivers in day care. *Infant Behavior and Development, 17*, 141–147.

Barnes, J., Sutcliffe, A. G., Kristoffersen, I., Loft, A., Wennerholm, U., Tarlatzis, B. C., et al. (2004). The influence of assisted reproduction on family functioning and children's socio-emotional development: Results from a European study. *Human Reproduction, 19*, 1480–1487.

Barnett, R. C., & Hyde, J. S. (2001). Women, men, work, and family: A new theoretical view. *American Psychologist, 56,* 781–796.

Barret, R., & Robinson, B. (1990). *Gay fathers.* New York: The Free Press.

Barrett, H., & Tasker, F. (2001). Growing up with a gay parent: Views of 101 gay fathers on their sons' and daughters' experiences. *Educational and Child Psychology, 18,* 62–77.

Barry, H. I., & Paxton, L. (1971). Infancy and early childhood: Cross-cultural codes 2. *Ethnology, 10,* 466–508.

Bassanini, A., & Venn, D. (2008). The impact of labour market policies on productivity in OECD countries. *International Productivity Monitor, 17,* 11.

Batalova, J., & Terrazas, A. (2010). *Migration information source – Frequently requested statistics on immigrants and immigration in the United States.* Retrieved April 29, 2013 from http://www.migrationinformation.org/USfocus/display.cfm?id=818

Bauman, J. H. (2001). Discovering donors: Legal rights to access information about anonymous sperm donors given to children of artificial insemination. *Johnson v. Superior Court of Los Angeles County. Golden Gate University Law Review, 31,* 193–217.

Baumeister, R. F. (1991). *Meanings of life.* New York: Guilford Press.

Baumeister, R. F., & Leary, M. R. (1995). The need to belong: Desire for interpersonal attachments as a fundamental human motivation. *Psychological Bulletin, 117,* 497–529.

Baumrind, D. (1991). Effective parenting during the early adolescent transition. In P. A. Cowan & E. M. Hetherington (Eds.), *Family transitions* (pp. 111–164). Hillsdale, NJ: Erlbaum.

Bauserman, R. (2002). Child adjustment in joint-custody versus sole-custody arrangements: A meta-analytic review. *Journal of Family Psychology, 16,* 91–102.

Beam, M. R., Chen, C., & Greenberger, E. (2002). The nature of the relationships between adolescents and their "very important" nonparental adults. *American Journal of Community Psychology, 30,* 305–325.

Becker, B. S., Aldridge, J., & Dearden, C. (1998). *Young carers and their families.* Oxford, UK: Blackwell Science.

Beckerman, S., Lizarralde, R., Lizarralde, M., Bie, J., Ballew, C., Schroeder, S., et al. (2002). The Barí partible paternity project: Phase 1. In S. Beckerman & P. Valentine (Eds.), *Cultures of multiple fathers: The theory and practice of partible paternity in South America* (pp. 27–41). Gainesville, FL: University of Florida Press.

Beckerman, S., & Valentine, P. (Eds.). (2002). *Cultures of multiple fathers: The theory and practice of partible paternity in South America.* Gainesville, FL: University of Florida Press.

Bell, L., & Newman, S. (2003, September). Paid family & medical leave: Why we need it, how we can get it (policy brief). *Family Caregiver Alliance, 4.*

Belle, D. (1999). *The after-school lives of children.* Mahwah, NJ: Erlbaum.

Belluck, P., & Liptak, A. (2004, March 24). Split gay couples face custody hurdles. *New York Times.* Retrieved April 29, 2013 from http://www.nytimes.com/2004/03/24/us/split-gay-couples-face-custody-hurdles.html?pagewanted=all&src=pm

Bem, S. L. (1973). The measurement of psychological androgyny. *Journal of Consulting and Clinical Psychology, 42,* 155–162.

Bem, S. L. (1993). *The lenses of gender: Transforming the debate on sexual inequality.* New Haven, CT: Yale University Press.

Bender, H. L., Allen, J. P., McElhaney, K. B., Antonishak, J., Moore, C. M., Kelly, H. O., et al. (2007). Use of harsh physical discipline and developmental outcomes in adolescence. *Development and Psychopathology, 19,* 227–242.

Benson, A. L., Silverstein, L. B., & Auerbach, C. F. (2005). From the margins to the center: Gay fathers reconstruct the fathering role. *Journal of GLBT Family Studies, 1,* 1–31.

Benson, P. L., & Roehlkepartain, E. C. (1993). *Youth in single-parent families: Risk and resiliency.* Minneapolis, MN: Search Institute.

Berger, L., Hill, J., & Waldfogel, J. (2005). Maternity leave, early maternal employment and child health and development in the US. *Economic Journal, 115*, F39–F40.

Berkowitz, D., & Marsiglio, W. (2007). Gay men negotiating procreative, father, and family identities. *Journal of Marriage and Family, 69*, 366–381.

Berman, P. W. (1980). Are women more responsive than men to the young? A review of developmental and situational variables. *Psychological Bulletin, 88*, 668–695.

Berman, R. (2010). *Oceans apart: A guide to maintaining family ties at a distance.* Jersey City, NJ: KTAV Publishing House.

Bernstein, A., & Cowan, P. A. (1975). Children's concepts of how people get babies. *Child Development, 46*, 77–91.

Bianchi, S. M. (2006). Mothers and daughters do, fathers don't do family: Gender and generational bonds. *Journal of Marriage and Family, 68*, 812–816.

Bianchi, S. M. (2009). What gives' when mothers are employed? Parental time allocation in dual- and single-earner two-parent families. In D. R Crane & E. J. Hill (Eds.), *Handbook of families and work* (pp. 305–330). Lanham, MD: University Press of America.

Biblarz, T. J., & Stacey, J. (2010). How does the gender of parents matter? *Journal of Marriage and Family, 72*, 3–22.

Bigner, J. J. (1999). Raising our sons: Gay men as fathers. *Journal of Gay and Lesbian Social Services, 10*, 61–77.

Bigner, J. J., & Jacobsen, R. B. (1989). Parenting behaviors of homosexual and heterosexual fathers. *Journal of Homosexuality, 18*, 73–186.

Bjorklund, D. F., & Pellegrini, A. D. (2000). Child development and evolutionary psychology. *Child Development, 71*, 1687–1708.

Black, D. S., Grenard, J. L., Sussman, S., & Rohrbach, L. A. (2010). The influence of school-based natural mentoring relationships on school attachment and subsequent adolescent risk behaviors. *Health Education Research, 25*, 892–902.

Blake, L., Casey, P., Readings, J., Jadva, V., & Golombok, S. (2010). "Daddy ran out of tadpoles": How parents tell their children that they are donor conceived, and what their 7 year olds understand. *Human Reproduction, 25*, 2527–2534.

Blankenhorn, D. (1995). *Fatherless America.* New York: Basic Books.

Bock, J. D. (2000). Doing the right thing? Single mothers by choice and the struggle for legitimacy. *Gender and Society, 14*, 62–86.

Boehm, D. (2004). *Gender(ed) migrations: Shifting gender subjectivities in a transnational Mexican community.* (Working Paper No. 100 in Center for Comparative Immigration Studies.) San Diego, CA: University of California.

Boehm, D. A. (2008). For my children: Constructing family and navigating the state in the U.S.-Mexico transnation. *Anthropological Quarterly, 81*, 777–802.

Bohr, Y., & Tse, C. (2009). Satellite babies in transnational families: A study of parents' decision to separate from their infants. *Infant Mental Health Journal, 30*, 1–22.

Bond, J., Galinsky, E., Kim, S., & Brownfield, E. (2005). *National study of employers.* New York: Families and Work Institute.

Bonkowski, S. E., Boomhower, S. J., & Bequette, S. Q. (1985). What you don't know can hurt you: Unexpressed fears and feelings of children from divorced families. *Journal of Divorce, 9*, 33–45.

Booth, A. (1999). Causes and consequences of divorce: Reflections on recent research. In R. A. Thompson & P. R. Amato (Eds.), *The postdivorce family: Children, parenting and society* (pp. 29–48). Thousand Oaks, CA: Sage.

Booth, C. A., Clarke-Stewart, K. A., Vandell, D. L., McCartney, K., & Owen, M. T. (2002). Child-care usage and mother-infant "quality time." *Journal of Marriage and Family, 64*, 16–26.

Borgerhoff Mulder, M. (1998). The demographic transition: Are we any closer to an evolutionary explanation? *Trends in Ecology and Evolution, 13*, 266–270.

Borgerhoff Mulder, M. (2007). Hamilton's rule and kin competition: The Kipsigis case. *Evolution and Human Behavior, 28*, 299–312.

Bornstein, M. H., & Putnick, D. L. (2007). Chronological age, cognitions, and practices in European American mothers: A multivariate study of parenting. *Developmental Psychology, 43*, 850–864.

Bos, H. M. W., van Balen, F., & van den Boom, D. C. (2004). Experience of parenthood, couple relationship, social support, and child-rearing goals in planned lesbian mother families. *Journal of Child Psychology and Psychiatry, 45*, 755–764.

Bos, H. M. W., van Balen, F., & van den Boom, D. C. (2007). Child adjustment and parenting in planned lesbian-parent families. *American Journal of Orthopsychiatry, 77*, 38–48.

Bos, H. M. W., & Hakvoort, E. M. (2007). Child adjustment and parenting in planned lesbian families with known and as-yet-unknown donors. *Journal of Psychosomatic Obstetrics & Gynecology, 28*, 121–129.

Bos, H. M. W., & van Rooij, F. B. (2007). The influence of social and cultural factors on infertility and new reproductive technologies. *Journal of Psychosomatic Obstetrics & Gynecology, 28*, 65–68.

Botcheva, L. B., & Feldman, S. S. (2004). Grandparents as family stabilizers during economic hardship in Bulgaria. *International Journal of Psychology, 39*, 157–168.

Bourçois, V. (1997). *Modalités de présence du père et développement social de l'enfant d'âge préscolaire* [Forms of father involvement and social development in preschoolers]. *Enfance, 3*, 389–399.

Bowen, J., Gibson, F., Leslie, G., & Saunders, D. (1998). Medical and developmental outcome at 1 year for children conceived by intracytoplasmic sperm injection. *Lancet, 351*, 1529–1534.

Bowlby, J. (1969). *Attachment and loss: Vol. 1. Attachment.* New York: Basic Books.

Boykin, A. W. (1983). The academic performance of Afro-American children. In J. Spence (Ed.), *Achievement and achievement motives* (pp. 321–371). San Francisco: W. Freeman.

Braver, S. L., Griffin, W. A., & Cookston, J. T. (2005). Prevention programs for divorced nonresident fathers. *Family Court Review, 43*, 81–96.

Brewaeys, A. (1996). Donor insemination, the impact on family and child development. *Journal of Psychosomatic Obstetrics and Gynecology, 17*, 1–13.

Brewaeys, A. (2001). Review: Parent–child relationships and child development in donor insemination families. *Human Reproduction Update, 7*, 38–46.

Brodzinsky, D. M. (2012). Adoption by lesbians and gay men. In D. M. Brodzinsky & A. Pertman (Eds.), *Adoption by lesbians and gay men* (pp. 62–84). New York: Oxford University Press.

Brodzinsky, D. M., & Pinderhughes, E. (2002). Parenting and child development in adoptive families. In M. Bornstein (Ed.), *Handbook of parenting* (2nd ed., Vol. *1*, pp. 279–312). Mahwah, NJ: Erlbaum.

Bronfenbrenner, U., & Morris, P. (2006). The ecology of developmental processes. In W. Damon & R. M. Lerner (Series Eds.) & R. M. Lerner (Vol. Ed.), *Handbook of child psychology: Vol. 1. Theoretical models of human development* (6th ed., pp. 793–828). Hoboken, NJ: Wiley.

Brooks, S. (2010). *Exploring the bias against fathers in the child welfare system: Current issues for welfare practices in rural communities.* Davis, CA: Northern California Training Academy, Center for Human Services, UC Davis Extension.

Brown, S. (2004). Family structure and child well-being: The significance of parental cohabitation. *Journal of Marriage and Family, 66*, 351–367.

Brown, S. (2010). Marriage and child well-being: Research and policy perspectives. *Journal of Marriage and Family, 72*, 1059–1077.

Brown, S. L. (2006). Family structure transitions and adolescent well-being. *Demography, 43*, 447–461.

Brown, S. L., & Rinelli, L. N. (2010). Family structure, family processes, and adolescent smoking and drinking. *Journal of Research on Adolescence, 20,* 259–273.

Bryant, B. K. (1992). Sibling caretaking: Providing emotional support during middle childhood. In F. Boer & J. Dunn (Eds.), *Children's sibling relationships* (pp. 55–70). Hillsdale, NJ: Erlbaum.

Buchanan, C. M., & Heiges, K. L. (2001). When conflict continues after the marriage ends: Effects of post-divorce conflict on children. In J. H. Grych & F. D. Fincham (Eds.), *Interparental conflict and child development* (pp. 337–362). Cambridge, MA: Cambridge University Press.

Buchanan, C. M., Maccoby, E. E., & Dornbusch, S. M. (1991). Caught between parents: Adolescents' experience in divorced homes. *Child Development, 62,* 1008–1029.

Budig, M., & England, P. (2000). The wage penalty for motherhood. *American Sociological Review, 66,* 204–225.

Bulanda, R. E., & Manning, W. D. (2008). Parental cohabitation experiences and adolescent behavioral outcomes. *Population Research and Policy Review, 27,* 593–618.

Burchinal, M. R., & Clarke-Stewart, K. A. (2007). Maternal employment and child cognitive outcomes: The importance of analytic approach. *Developmental Psychology, 43,* 1140–1155.

Bureau of Labor Statistics. (2010). *Annual benefits survey.* Washington, DC: Bureau of Labor.

Burgess, B. J. (1980). Parenting in the Native American community. In M. D. Fantini & R. Cardenas (Eds.), *Parenting in a multicultural society: Practice and policy* (pp. 63–73). New York: Longman.

Buriel, R. (1993). Childrearing orientations in Mexican American families: The influence of generation and sociocultural factors. *Journal of Marriage and Family, 55,* 987–1000.

Buriel, R. (2012). Historical origins of the immigrant paradox for Mexican American students: The cultural integration hypothesis. In C. Garcia Coll & A. Marks (Eds.), *The immigrant paradox in children and adolescents: Is becoming American a developmental risk?* (pp. 37–60). Washington, DC: American Psychological Association.

Buriel, R., Love, J. A., & DeMent, T. L. (2006). The relationship of language brokering to depression and parent–child bonding among Latino adolescents. In M. H. Bornstein & L. R. Cote (Eds.), *Acculturation and parent–child relationships.* Mahwah, NJ: Lawrence Erlbaum.

Buriel, R., Perez, W., DeMent, T. L., Chavez, D. V., & Moran, V. R. (1998). The relationship of language brokering to academic performance, biculturations, and self-efficacy among Latino adolescents. *Hispanic Journal of Behavioral Sciences, 20,* 283–297.

Buriel, R., & Vasquez, R. (1982). Stereotypes of Mexican descent persons: Attitudes of three generations of Mexican Americans and Anglo American adolescents. *Journal of Cross-Cultural Psychology, 13,* 59–70.

Burrell, N. (2002). How spouses seek social support. In M. Allen et al. (Eds.), *Interpersonal communication research: Advances through meta-analysis* (pp. 247–262). Mahwah, NJ: Erlbaum.

Burton, L. M. (1991). Caring for children: Drug shifts and impact on families. *American Enterprise, 2,* 34–37.

Burton, L. M. (1992). Black grandparents rearing children of drug-addicted parents: Stressors, outcomes, and social service needs. *The Gerontologist, 32,* 744–751.

Burton, L. M. (2007). Child adultification in economically disadvantaged families: A conceptual model. *Family Relations, 56,* 329–345.

Burton, L. M., & Bengtson, V. L. (1985). Black grandmothers: Issues of timing and continuity of roles. In V. L. Bengtson & J. F. Robertson (Eds.), *Grandparenthood* (pp. 61–77). Beverley Hills, CA: Sage.

Cabrera, N. (2010). Father involvement and public policies. In M. Lamb (Ed.), *The role of the father in child development* (5th ed., pp. 517–550). Hoboken, NJ: Wiley.

Cabrera, N., Shannon, J., & Tamis-LaMonda, C. (2007). Fathers' influence on their children's cognitive and emotional development: From toddlers to pre-K. *Applied Developmental Science, 11,* 208–213.

Cameron, C., Mooney, A., Owen, C., & Moss, P. (2001). *Childcare students and nursery workers: Follow-up surveys and in-depth interviews* (DfES Research Report No. 322). London: Department for Education and Skills, Thomas Coram Research Unit, Institute of Education, University of London.

Cameron, C., Owen, C., & Moss P. (2001). *Entry, retention and loss: A study of childcare students and workers* (DfES Research Report No. 275). London: Department for Education and Skills, Thomas Coram Research Unit, Institute of Education, University of London.

Campbell, N. D., Appelbaum, J. C., Martinson, K., & Martin, E. (2000). *Be all that we can be: Lessons from the military for improving our nation's child care system.* Washington, DC: National Women's Causes Center.

Caria, A., de Falco, S., Venuti, P., Lee, S., Esposito, G., Rigo, P., et al. (2012). Species-specific response to human infant faces in the premotor cortex. *NeuroImage, 60,* 884–893.

Carlson, M. J. (2006). Family structure, father involvement, and adolescent behavioral outcomes. *Journal of Marriage and Family, 68,* 137–154.

Carlson, M., & McLanahan, S. (2006). Strengthening unmarried families: Could enhancing couple relationships also improve parenting? *Social Service Review, 80,* 297–321.

Carlson, M., & McLanahan, S. (2010). Fathers in fragile families. In M. Lamb (Ed.), *The role of the father in child development* (5th ed., pp. 241–269). Hoboken, NJ: Wiley.

Carlson, M., McLanahan, S., & England, P. (2004). Union formation in fragile families. *Demography, 41,* 237–261.

Carrington, C. (2002). *No place like home: Relationships and family life among lesbians and gay men.* Chicago: University of Chicago Press.

Carroll, L. (2011, March 15). *Gay families more accepted than single moms.* Retrieved April 29, 2013 from http://www.msnbc.msn.com/id/42078511/ns/health-childrens_health/t/gay-families-more-accepted-single-moms/#.UF6YTURXCCM

Carter, C. S., & Altemus, M. (1997). Integrative functions of lactational hormones in social behavior and stress management. *Annals of the New York Academy of Sciences, 807,* 164–174.

Caspi, A., Williams, B., Kim-Cohen, J., Craig, I. W., Milne, B. J., Poulton, R., et al. (2007). Moderation of breastfeeding effects on the IQ by genetic variation in fatty acid metabolism. *Proceedings of the National Academy of Sciences of the United States of America, 104,* 18860–18865.

Catalyst. (2012). *Catalyst quick take: Family leave – U.S., Canada, and Global.* New York: Catalyst.

Catalyst and Brandeis University. (2006). *After-school worries: Tough on parents, bad for business.* Retrieved April 29, 2013 from http://www.catalyst.org/knowledge

Cavanagh, S., & Huston, A. (2008). The timing of family instability and children's social development. *Journal of Marriage and Family, 70,* 1258–1269.

Centers for Disease Control and Prevention. (2003). *2001 Assisted reproductive technology success rates: National summary and fertility.* Atlanta, GA: CDC.

Centers for Disease Control and Prevention. (2011a). *2009 Assisted Reproductive Technology Success Rates: National Summary and Fertility Clinic Reports.* Atlanta, GA: CDC.

Centers for Disease Control and Prevention. (2011b). *Multiple births.* Retrieved April 29, 2013 from http://science.howstuffworks.com/environmental/life/human-biology/human-reproduction13.htm

Centers for Disease Control and Prevention. (2012a, August 1). *Assisted Reproductive Technology (ART).* Retrieved April 29, 2013 from http://www.cdc.gov/art/index.htm

Centers for Disease Control and Prevention. (2012b, November 2). Assisted reproductive technology surveillance – United States, 2009. *Surveillance Summaries, 61*(SS7), 1–23. Atlanta, GA: U.S. Department of Health and Human Services.

Chambers, G. M., Sullivan, E. A., Ishihara, O., Chapman, M. G., & Adamson, G. D. (2009). The economic impact of assisted reproductive technology: A review of selected developed countries. *Fertility and Sterility, 91*, 2281–2294.

Chan, R. W., Brooks, R. C., Raboy, B., & Patterson, C. (1998). Division of labor among lesbian and heterosexual parents: Associations with children's adjustment. *Journal of Family Psychology, 12*, 402–419.

Chan, R. W., Raboy, B., & Patterson, C. J. (1998). Psychosocial adjustment among children conceived via donor insemination by lesbian and heterosexual mothers. *Child Development, 69*, 443–457.

Chandra, A., Martinez, G. M., Mosher, W. D., Abma, J. C., & Jones, J. (2005). *Fertility, family planning, and reproductive health of U. S. women: Data from the 2002 National Survey of Family Growth.* Hyattsville, MD: National Center for Health Statistics.

Chansonneuve, D. (2007). *Addictive behaviours among aboriginal people in Canada.* Ottawa, Ontario, Canada: Aboriginal Healing Foundation.

Chao, R. (2006). The prevalence and consequences of adolescents' language brokering for their immigrant parents. In M. Bornstein & L. R. Cote (Eds.), *Acculturation and parent–child relationships: Measurement and development* (pp. 271–296). Mahwah, NJ: Lawrence Erlbaum.

Chao, R. K., & Tseng, V. (2002). Parenting of Asians. In M. H. Bornstein (Ed.), *Handbook of parenting: Vol. 4: Social conditions and applied parenting* (2nd ed., pp. 59–93). Mahwah, NJ: Erlbaum.

Chase, N. D. (Ed.) (1999). *Burdened children: Theory, research and treatment of parentification.* Thousand Oaks, CA: Sage.

Chase-Lansdale, P. L., Moffitt, R. A., Lohman, B. J., Cherlin, A. J., Coley, R. L., Pittman, L. D., et al. (2003). How are children affected by employment and welfare transitions? *JCPR Policy Brief, 5*(3). Chicago: Northwestern University/University of Chicago.

Chatterji, P., & Markowitz, S. (2005). Does the length of maternity leave affect maternal health?, *Southern Economic Journal, 72*, 38.

Cheng, T. C. (2007). Impact of work requirements on the psychological well-being of TANF recipients. *Health & Social Work, 32*, 41–48.

Cherlin, A. J. (2009). *The marriage-go-round: The state of marriage and the family today.* New York: Knopf.

Cherlin, A. J., Cross-Barnet, C., Burton, L. M., & Garrett-Peters, R. (2008). Promises they can keep: Low-income women's attitudes toward motherhood, marriage, and divorce. *Journal of Marriage and Family, 70*, 919–933.

Cherlin, A. J., & Furstenberg, F. F. (1994). Stepfamilies in the United States. *Annual Review of Sociology, 20*, 259–281.

ChildCare.net. (2013). *Caregiver turnover.* Retrieved April 29, 2013 from http://www.childcare.net/library/caregiverturnover.shtml

Children's Defense Fund. (2004). *The state of America's children.* Washington, DC: Children's Defense Fund.

Child Trends. (2012a). *Births to unmarried women.* Retrieved April 29, 2013 from www.childtrendsdatabank.org/?q=node/196

Child Trends. (2012b). *Children in poverty.* Retrieved April 29, 2013 from www.childtrendsdatabank.org/?q=node/221.

Ciano-Boyce, C., & Shelly-Sireci, L. (2002). Who is mommy tonight? Lesbian parenting issues. *Journal of Homosexuality, 43*, 1–13.

Cicchetti, D., & Toth, S. L. (2006). Developmental psychopathology and preventive intervention. In A. Renninger & I. Sigel (Eds.), *Handbook of child psychology* (6th ed., pp. 497–547). Hoboken, NJ: Wiley.

Clark, R., & Nelson, S. (2000, March). *Beyond the two-parent family.* Paper presented at the annual meeting of the Population Association of America, Los Angeles, CA.

Clarke, V., & Kitziner, C. (2005). "We're not living on a lesbian planet": Constructions of male role models in debates about lesbian families. *Sexualities, 8,* 137–152.

Clarke-Stewart, K. A. (1980). The father's contribution to children's cognitive and social development in early childhood. In F. A. Pedersen (Ed.), *The father-infant relationship: Observational studies in the family setting* (pp. 111–146). New York: Praeger.

Clarke-Stewart, K. A., & Allhusen, V. (2005). *What we know about child care.* Cambridge, MA: Harvard University Press.

Clarke-Stewart, K. A., & Brentano, C. (2005). *Divorce lessons: Real-life stories and what you can learn from them.* Charleston, SC: BookSurge Publishing.

Clarke-Stewart, K. A., & Brentano, C. (2006). *Divorce: Causes and consequences.* New Haven, CT: Yale University Press.

Clarke-Stewart, K. A., & Hayward, C. (1996). Advantages of father custody and contact for the psychological well-being of school-age children. *Journal of Applied Developmental Psychology, 17,* 239–270.

Clarke-Stewart, K. A., Vandell, D. L., McCartney, K., Owen, M. T., & Booth, C. (2000). Effects of parental separation and divorce on very young children. *Journal of Family Psychology, 14,* 304–326.

Clary, E. G., Snyder, M., Ridge, R. D., Copeland, J., Stukas, A. A., Haugen, J., et al. (1998). Understanding and assessing the motivations of volunteers: A functional approach. *Journal of Personality and Social Psychology, 74,* 1516–1530.

Coall, D. A., & Hertwig, R. (2010). Grandparental investment: Past, present and future. *Behavioral and Brain Sciences, 33,* 1–5.

Coall, D. A., & Hertwig, R. (2011). Grandparental investment: A relic of the past or a resource for the future? *Current Directions in Psychological Science, 20,* 93–98.

Cobb, D. M., & Fowler, L. (2007). *Beyond red power: American Indian politics and activism since 1900.* Santa Fe, NM: School for Advanced Research.

Cochran, M., & Niego. S. (2002). Parenting and social networks. In M. Bornstein (Ed.), *Handbook of parenting* (2nd ed., pp. 123–147). Mahwah, NJ: Erlbaum.

Cohousing. (2010). *Advantages and disadvantages of co-housing for families.* Retrieved April 29, 2013 from http://co-housing.wikidot.com/parent-s-perspective

Coleman, H., Unau, Y. A., & Manyfingers, B. (2001). Revamping family preservation services for native families. *Journal of Cultural and Ethnic Diversity in Social Work, 10,* 49–65.

Coleman, J. S. (1988). Social capital in the creation of human capital. *American Journal of Sociology, 94,* 95–120.

Coley, R. L., Lohman, B. J., Votruba-Drzal, E., Pittman, L. D., & Chase-Lansdale, P. L. (2007). Maternal functioning, time, and money: The world of work and welfare. *Children and Youth Services Review, 29,* 721–741.

Colpin, H., & Bossaert, G. (2008). Adolescents conceived by IVF: Parenting and psychosocial adjustment. *Human Reproduction, 23,* 2724–2730.

Colpin, H., Demyttenaere, K., & Vandemeulebroecke, L. (1995). New reproductive technology and the family: The parent–child relationship following in vitro fertilisation. *Journal of Child Psychology and Psychiatry, 36,* 1429–1441.

Coltrane, S. (2009). Fatherhood, gender and work-family policies. In J. C. Gornick, M. K. Meyers, & E. O. Wright (Eds.), *Gender equality* (pp. 385–409). New York: Verso.

Coltrane, S., & Adams, M. (2008). *Gender and families* (Gender Lens Series, 2nd ed.). Lanham, MD: Rowman & Littlefield.

Coltrane, S., & Behnke, A. (2012). Fatherhood and family policies. In N. J. Cabrera & C. S. Tamis LeMonda (Eds.), *Handbook of father involvement: Multidisciplinary perspectives* (2nd ed., pp. 419–437). New York: Psychology Press.

Coltrane, S., & Collins, R. (2001). *Sociology of marriage and the family: Gender, love and property* (5th ed.). Belmont, CA: Wadsworth/ITP.

Coltrane, S., Parke, R. D., & Adams, M. (2004). Complexity of father involvement in low-income Mexican American families. *Family Relations: Interdisciplinary Journal of Applied Family Studies, 53,* 179–189.

Comstock, G., & Scharrer, E. (2006). Media and pop culture. In W. Damon & R. M. Lerner (Series Eds.), & K. A. Renninger & I. Sigel (Vol. Eds.), *Handbook of child psychology: Vol. 4. Child psychology in practice* (6th ed., pp. 817–863). Hoboken, NJ: Wiley.

Conger, K. J., & Conger, R. D. (1996). Sibling relationships. In R. L. Simons (Ed.), *Understanding differences between divorced and intact families: Stress, interaction, and child outcome* (pp. 104–121). Thousand Oaks, CA: Sage.

Conger, R. D., & Donnellan, M. B. (2007). An interactionist perspective on the socioeconomic context of human development. *Annual Review of Psychology, 58,* 175–199.

Conger, R. D., Ebert-Wallace, L., Sun, Y., Simons, R. L., McLoyd, V. C., & Brody, G. H. (2002). Economic pressure in African American families: A replication and extension of the family stress model. *Developmental Psychology, 38,* 179–193.

Connolly, R., DeGraff, D., & Willis, R. (2004). *Kids at work: The value of employer-sponsored on-site child care centers.* Kalamazoo, MI: W.E. Upjohn Institute for Employment Research.

Contreras, J. M., Lopez, I. R., Rivera-Mosquera, E. T., Raymond-Smith, L., & Rothstein, K. (1999). Social support and adjustment among Puerto Rican adolescent mothers: The moderating effect of acculturation. *Journal of Family Psychology, 13,* 228–243.

Cooke, I. (1991). *My story.* England: Jessop Hospital for Women.

Coontz, S. (1992). *The way we never were: American families and the nostalgia trap.* New York: Basic Books.

Coontz, S. (2010). The evolution of American families. In B. J. Risman (Ed.), *Families as they really are* (pp. 30–47). New York: Norton.

Corter, C., & Fleming, A. S. (2002). Psychobiology of maternal behavior in human beings. In M. Bornstein (Ed.), *Handbook of parenting* (2nd ed., Vol. 2, pp. 141–182). Mahwah, NJ: Erlbaum.

Coukos, P. (2012). *Myth busting the pay gap.* Washington, DC: Department of Labor Office of Federal Contract Compliance Programs/U.S. Department of Labor.

Cowan, P., & Cowan, C. (2000). *When partners become parents: The big life change for couples.* Mahwah, NJ: Erlbaum.

Cowen, E. L., & Pedro-Carroll, J. L., & Alpert-Gillis, L. J. (1990). Relationships between support and adjustment among children of divorce. *Journal of Child Psychology and Psychiatry, 31,* 727–735.

Cox, D. (2007). Biological basics and the economics of the family. *Journal of Economic Perspectives, 21,* 91–108.

Craig, L., & Powell, A. (2011). Non-standard work schedules, work-family balance and the gendered division of childcare. *Work Employment & Society, 25,* 274–291.

Crawley, S. B., & Sherrod, K. B. (1984). Parent-infant play during the first year of life. *Infant Behavior and Development, 7,* 65–75.

Crockenberg, S. B. (1981). Infant irritability, mother responsiveness and social support influences in the security of infant-mother attachment. *Child Development, 52,* 857–865.

Crocker, W. H., & Crocker, J. G. (2004). *The Canela: Kinship, ritual, and sex in an Amazonian tribe* (2nd ed.). Toronto, Ontario, Canada: Wadsworth.

Crognier, E., Villena, M., & Vargas, E. (2002). Helping patterns and reproductive success in Aymara communities. *American Journal of Human Biology, 14,* 372–379.

Crossley, M. (2005). Dimensions of equality in regulating assisted reproductive technologies. *The Journal of Gender, Race & Justice, 9,* 273–289.

Crouter, A. C., Bumpus, M. F., Maguire, M. C., & McHale, S. (1999). Linking parents' work pressure and adolescents' well-being: Insights into dynamics in dual-earner families. *Developmental Psychology, 35,* 1453–1461.

Cryer, D., & Burchinal, M. (1997). Parents as child care consumers. *Early Childhood Research Quarterly, 12*, 35–58.

Cultural Cognition Project. (2009). *Gay & lesbian parenting: Perceptions and policy preferences.* Retrieved April 29, 2013 from http://www.culturalcognition.net/browse-papers/first-report-on-gay-and-lesbian-parenting.html

Cummings, E. M., & Davies, P. T. (2010). *Marital conflict and children: An emotional security perspective.* New York and London: The Guilford Press.

Current Population Survey. (2002). *Labor force participation of families with children.* Annual Demographic Supplement to the March 2002 Current Population Survey. Washington, DC: U.S. Census Bureau.

Daly, M., & Kwok, J. (2009, August 3) Does welfare reform work for everyone? A look at young single mothers. *FRBSF Economic Letter, 24* San Francisco: Federal Reserve Bank of San Francisco.

David, A., & Avidan, D. (1976). Artificial insemination donor: Clinical and psychological aspects. *Fertility and Sterility, 27*, 528–532.

Davidson, P. R. (2007). Diversity in living arrangements and children's economic well-being in single-mother households. In B. A. Arrighi & D. J. Maume (Eds.), *Child poverty in America today.* Westport, CT: Praeger Publishers.

DeGarmo, D. S., Patras, J., & Eap, S. (2008). Social support for divorced fathers' parenting: Testing a stress-buffering model. *Family Relations, 57*, 35–48.

Deleire, T., & Kalil, A. (2002). Good things come in threes: Single-parent multigenerational family structure and adolescent adjustment. *Demography, 39*, 393–413.

DeMaris, A., & Greif, G. L. (1992). The relationship between family structure and parent–child relationship problems in single father households. *Journal of Divorce and Remarriage, 18*, 55–77.

DeMent, T., Buriel, R., & Villanueva, C. (2005). Children as language brokers: Recollections of college students. In S. Farideh (Ed.), *Language in multicultural education* (pp. 255–272). Greenwich, CT: Information Age Publishing.

Dench, G., & Ogg, J. (2002). *Grandparenting in Britain.* London: Institute of Community Studies.

Denham, S. A. (1998). *Emotional development in young children.* New York: Guilford Press.

DeParle, J., & Tavernise, S. (2012, February 17). For women under 30, most births occur outside marriage. *New York Times, A1.*

Derosas, R. (2002). Fatherless families in 19th century Venice. In R. Derosas & M. Oris (Eds.), *When dad died: Individuals and families coping with distress in past societies* (pp. 421–452). Bern, Switzerland: Peter Lang.

DeSena, J. N. (1990). *Protecting one's turf: Social strategies for maintaining urban neighborhoods.* New York: University Press of America.

Deutsch, F. (1999). *Halving it all: How equally shared parenting works.* Cambridge, MA: Harvard University Press.

DeVita, C. J. (1996). The United States at mid-decade. *Population Bulletin, 50*(4), 1–48.

Dickler, J. (2011, September 21). *The rising cost of raising a child.* Retrieved April 29, 2013 from http://money.cnn.com/2011/09/21/pf/cost_raising_child/index.htm

Dickstein, S., & Parke, R. D. (1988). Social referencing: A glance at fathers and marriage. *Child Development, 59*, 506–511.

DiPerna, P. (1998). Becoming Aunt Paula. *Parents, 73*, 152–154.

Dishion, T., & Stormshak, E. (2007). *Intervening in children's lives: An ecological, family-centered approach to mental health care.* Washington, DC: American Psychological Association.

Diversi, M., & Mecham, C. (2005). Latino(a) students and Caucasian mentors in a rural afterschool program: Towards empowering the adult-youth relationship. *Journal of Community Psychology, 33*, 31–40.

Djerassi, C. (1999). Sex in an age of mechanical reproduction. *Science, 285,* 53–54.

Dobson, J. C. (2004). *Marriage under fire: Why we must win this war.* Sisters, OR: Multnomah Publishers.

Dodson, L., & Dickert, J. (2004). Girls' family labor in low-income households: A decade of qualitative research. *Journal of Marriage and Family, 66,* 318–332.

Dolbin-MacNab, M. L. (2006). Just like raising your own? Grandmothers' perceptions of parenting a second time around. *Family Relations, 55,* 564–575.

Dolgin, J. L. (1997). *Defining the family: Law, technology, and reproduction in an uneasy age.* New York: New York University Press.

Donor Sibling Registry(2012, January 1) "https://www.donorsiblingregistry.com/blog 2011 Year End Update from the Donor Sibling Registry. Retrieved July 12, 2013.

Doucet, A. (2004). "It's almost like I have a job, but I don't get paid": Fathers at home reconfiguring work, care, and masculinity. *Fathering, 2,* 277–302.

Doucet, A. (2006). *Do men mother?* Toronto, Ontario, Canada: University of Toronto Press.

Dreby, J. (2010). *Divided by borders: Mexican migrants and their children.* Berkeley, CA: University of California Press.

Dreby, J., & Adkins,T. (2010). Inequalities in transnational families. *Sociology Compass, 4,* 673–689.

Dubas, J. S. (2001). How gender moderates the grandparent-grandchild relationship: A comparison of kin-keeper and kin-selector theories. *Journal of Family Issues, 22,* 478–492.

Dube, A., & Ethan Kaplan, E. (2002, June). *Paid family leave in California: An analysis of costs and benefits.* Unpublished manuscript. Retrieved April 29, 2013 from http://www.paidfamilyleave.org/pdf/dube.pdf

DuBois, D. L., Portillo, N., Rhodes, J. E., Silverthorn, N., & Valentine, J. C. (2011). How effective are mentoring programs for youth? A systematic assessment of the evidence. *Psychological Science in the Public Interest, 12,* 57–91.

DuBois, D. L., & Silverthorn, N. (2005). Natural mentoring relationships and adolescent health: Evidence from a national study. *American Journal of Public Health, 95,* 518–524.

Duncan, G. (2012). Give us this day our daily breadth. *Child Development, 83,* 6–15.

Dunifon, R., Kalil, A., & Danziger, S. K. (2003). Maternal work behavior under welfare reform: How does the transition from welfare to work affect child development? *Children and Youth Services Review, 25,* 55–82.

Dunifon, R. E., & Kowaleski-Jones, L. (2002). Who's in the house? Race differences in cohabitation, single-parenthood and child development. *Child Development, 73,* 1249–1264.

Dunn, J., Cheng, H., O'Connor, T. G., & Bridges, L. (2004). Children's perspectives on their relationships with their non-resident fathers: Influences, outcomes, and implications. *Journal of Child Psychology and Psychiatry, 45,* 553–566.

Dunn, J., & Davies, L. C. (2001). Sibling relationships and inter-parental conflict. In J. Grych & F. D. Fincham (Eds.), *Child development and interparental conflict* (pp. 273–290). New York: Cambridge University Press.

Dunn, J., Davies, L. C., O'Connor, T. G., & Sturgess, W. (2000). Parents' and partners' life course and family experiences: Links with parent–child relationships in different family settings. *Journal of Child Psychology and Psychiatry, 41,* 955–968.

Dunn, J., Fergusson, E., & Maughan, B. (2006). Grandparents, grandchildren and family change in contemporary Britain. In A. Clarke-Stewart & J. Dunn (Eds.), *Families count: Effects on child and adolescent development* (pp. 299–320). New York: Cambridge University Press.

Dye, J. L. (2010). *Fertility of American women: 2008* (Current Population Reports, P20-563). Washington, DC: U.S. Census Bureau.

Dykstra, P. A., & Hagestad, G. O. (2007). Roads less taken. Developing a nuanced view of older adults without children. *Journal of Family Issues, 28,* 1275–1310.

East, P. L. (2010). Children's provision of family caregiving: Benefit or burden? *Child Development Perspectives, 4*, 55–61.

East, P. L., & Jacobson, L. J. (2001). The younger siblings of teenage mothers: A follow-up of their pregnancy risk. *Developmental Psychology, 37*, 254–264.

East, P. L., & Weisner, T. S. (2009). Mexican-American adolescents' family caregiving: Selection effects and longitudinal associations with adjustment. *Family Relations, 58*, 562–577.

East, P. L., Weisner, T. S., & Reyes, B. T. (2006). Youths' caretaking of their adolescent sisters' children: Its costs and benefits for youths' development. *Applied Developmental Science, 10*, 86–95.

East, P. L., Weisner, T. S., & Slonim, A. (2009). Youths' caretaking of their adolescent sisters' children: Results from two longitudinal studies. *Journal of Family Issues, 30*, 1671–1697.

Ebaugh, H. R., & Curry, M. (2000). Fictive kin as social capital in new immigrant communities. *Sociological Perspectives, 43*, 189–209.

Edin, K., & Kefalas, M. J. (2005). *Promises I can keep: Why poor women put motherhood before marriage*. Berkeley, CA: University of California Press.

Eheart, B. K., Hopping, D., Power, M. B., Mitchell, E., & Racine, D. (2009). Generations of Hope Communities: An intergenerational neighborhood model of support and service. *Children and Youth Services Review, 31*, 47–52.

Elder, G. H., Jr. (1998). The life course as developmental theory. *Child Development, 69*, 1–12.

Elder, G. H., & Conger, R. D. (2000). *Children of the land: Adversity and success in rural America*. Chicago: University of Chicago Press.

Ellingson, L. L., & Sotirin, P. J. (2006). Exploring young adults' perspectives on communication with aunts. *Journal of Social and Personal Relationships, 23*, 483–501.

Emery, R. E. (2011). *Renegotiating family relationships: Divorce, child custody, and mediation* (2nd ed.). New York: Guilford.

Emick, M. A., & Hayslip, B. (1999). Custodial grandparenting: Stresses, coping skills, and relationships with grandchildren. *International Journal of Aging and Human Development, 48*, 35–61.

Employee Benefit Plan Review. (1994, August). Corporate centers important to working dads. *Employee Benefit Plan Review, 49*, 38.

Erickson, L. D., McDonald, S., & Elder, G. H. (2009). Informal mentors and education: Complementary or compensatory resources? *Sociology of Education, 82*, 344–367.

Erikson, E. (1975). *Life history and the historical moment*. New York: Norton.

Evans, G. W. (2006). Child development and the physical environment. *Annual Review of Psychology, 57*, 423–451.

Fabricius W. V., Braver, S. L., Diaz, P., & Velez, C. E. (2010). Custody and parenting time: Links to family relationships and well-being after divorce. In M. E. Lamb (Ed.), *The role of the father in child development* (5th ed., pp. 201–240). Hoboken, NJ: Wiley.

Fabricius, W. V., & Luecken, L. J. (2007). Post-divorce living arrangements, parent conflict, and long-term physical health correlates for children of divorce. *Journal of Family Psychology, 21*, 195–205.

Fagan, J., & Lee, Y. (2012). Effects of fathers' and mothers' cognitive stimulation and household income on toddlers' cognition: Variations by family structure and child risk. *Fathering, 10*, 140–158.

Falicov, C. J. (1998). *Latino families in therapy: A guide to multicultural practice*. New York: Guilford Press.

Farr, R. H., Forssell, S. L., & Patterson, C. J. (2010a). Lesbian, gay, and heterosexual adoptive parents: Couple and relationship issues. *Journal of GLBT Family Studies, 6*, 199–213.

Farr, R. H., Forssell, S. L., & Patterson, C. J. (2010b). Parenting and child development in adoptive families: Does parental sexual orientation matter? *Applied Developmental Science, 14*, 164–178.

Farr, R. H., & Patterson, C. J. (2009). Transracial adoption by lesbian, gay, and heterosexual couples: Who completes transracial adoptions, and with what results? *Adoption Quarterly, 12,* 187–204.

Farr, R. H., & Patterson, C. J. (2013a). Lesbian and gay adoptive parents and their children. In A. E. Goldberg & K. R. Allen (Eds.), *LGBT-parent families: Innovations in research and implications for practice.* New York: Springer.

Farr, R. H., & Patterson, C. J. (2013b). Coparenting among lesbian, gay, and heterosexual couples: Associations with adopted children's outcomes. *Child Development, 84, 1226–1240.*

Farrell, W. (1993). *The myth of male power: Why men are the disposable sex.* New York: Berkeley Books.

Federal Interagency Forum on Child and Family Statistics. (2002). *America's children: Key national indicators of well-being.* Washington, DC: Author.

Feldman, R., Eidelman, A. I., & Rotenberg, N. (2004). Parenting stress, infant emotion regulation, maternal sensitivity, and the cognitive development of triplets: A model for parent and child influences in a unique ecology. *Child Development, 75,* 1774–1791.

Feldman, R., Gordon, I., Schneiderman, I., Weisman, O., & Zagoory-Sharon, O. (2010). Natural variations in maternal and paternal care are associated with systematic changes in oxytocin following parent-infant contact. *Psychoneuroendocrinology, 35,* 1133–1141.

Feldman, R., Weller, A., Zagoory-Sharon, O., & Levine, A. (2007). Evidence for a neuroendocrinological foundation of human affiliation: Plasma oxytocin levels across pregnancy and the postpartum period predict mother-infant bonding. *Psychological Science, 18,* 965–970.

Fenton, R. A. (2006). Catholic doctrine versus women's rights: The new Italian law on assisted reproduction. *Medical Law Review, 14,* 73–107.

Fenton, L., & Fenton, A. (October 25, 2011). *The changing landscape of second-parent adoptions.* Section on Child Litigation, American Bar Association. Retrieved May 6, 2013, from apps.americanbar.org

Ferree, M. M. (2010). Filling the glass: Gender perspectives on families. *Journal of Marriage and Family, 72,* 420–439.

Field, T. M. (1978). Interaction behaviors of primary versus secondary caretaker fathers. *Developmental Psychology, 14,* 183–185.

Fingerman, K. L., & Hay, E. L. (2002). Searching under the streetlight? Age biases in the personal and family relationships literature. *Personal Relationships, 9,* 415–433.

Fixico, D. L. (2006). *Daily life of Native Americans in the twentieth century.* New York: Greenwood Press.

Flaks, D. K., Ficher, I., Masterpasqua, F., & Joseph, G. (1995). Lesbians choosing motherhood: A comparative study of lesbian and heterosexual parents and their children. *Developmental Psychology, 31,* 105–114.

Fleming, A. S., Corter, C., Stallings, J., & Steiner, M. (2002). Testosterone and prolactin are associated with emotional response to infant cries in new fathers. *Hormones and Behavior, 42,* 399–413.

Fleming, A. S., & Li, M. (2002). Psychobiology of maternal behavior and its early determinants in nonhuman mammals. In M. Bornstein (Ed.), *Handbook of parenting* (2nd ed., Vol. 2, pp. 62–98). Mahwah, NJ: Erlbaum.

Fleming, A. S., Steiner, M., & Corter, C. (1997). Cortisol, hedonics, and maternal responsiveness in human mothers. *Hormones and Behavior, 32,* 85–98.

Flinn, M. V., Duncan, C., Ponzi, D., Quinlan, R. L., Decker, S. A., & Leone, D. V. (2011). Hormones in the wild: Monitoring the endocrinology of family relationships. *Parenting: Science and Practice, 12,* 124–133.

Flinn, M. V., Quinlan, R. J., Decker, S. A., Turner, M. T., & England, B. G. (1996). Male–female differences in effects of parental absence on glucocorticoid stress response. *Human Nature, 7,* 125–162.

Flores, E., Tschann, J., Marin, B., & Pantoja, P. (2004). Marital conflict and acculturation among Mexican American husbands and wives. *Cultural Diversity and Ethnic Minority Psychology, 10*, 39–52.

Folbre, N. (2008). *Valuing children: Rethinking the economics of the family.* Boston: Harvard University Press.

Fomby, P., & Cherlin, A. J. (2007). Family instability and child well-being. *American Sociological Review, 72*, 181–204.

Fomby, P., & Estacion, A. (2011). Cohabitation and children's externalizing behavior in low-income Latino families. *Journal of Marriage and Family, 73*, 46–66.

Fortune. (2012, February 6). *Fortune survey of 100 best companies 2012.* Retrieved April 29, 2013 from http://money.cnn.com/magazines/fortune/best-companies/2012/snapshots/1.html

Freedman, M. (1999). *Prime time: How baby boomers will revolutionize retirement and transform America.* New York: Public Affairs.

Freeman, T., Jadva, V., Kramer, W., & Golombok, S. (2009). Gamete donation: Parents experiences of searching for their child's donor siblings and donor. *Human Reproduction, 24*, 505–516.

Friedman, D., Hechter, M., & Kanazawa, S. (1994). A theory of the value of children. *Demography, 31*, 375–401.

Friedman, H., & Martin, L. (2012). *The longevity project: Surprising discoveries for health and long life from the landmark eight-decade study.* New York: Plume.

Frodi, A. M., Lamb, M., Leavitt, L. A., & Donovan, W. L. (1978). Fathers' and mothers' responses to infant smiles and cries. *Infant Behavior & Development, 1*, 187–198.

Fromm, D. (1991). *Collaborative communities: Cohousing, central living, and other new forms of housing with shared facilities.* New York: Van Nostrand Reinhold.

Fromm, D., & de Jong, E. (2009). Community and health: Immigrant senior cohousing in the Netherlands. *Communities: Life in Cooperative Culture, 145*, 50–53.

Fry, R., & Cohn, D. (June 27, 2011). *Living together: The economics of cohabitation.* Washington, DC: Pew Research Center.

Fulcher, M., Sutfin, E. L., & Patterson, C. J. (2008). Individual differences in gender development: Associations with parental sexual orientation, attitudes, and division of labor. *Sex Roles, 58*, 330–341.

Fuligni, A. J. (2010). The academic desire of students from Latin American backgrounds. In N. Landale, S. McHale, & A. Booth (Eds.), *Growing up Hispanic: Health and development of children of immigrants.* Washington, DC: Urban Institute Press.

Fuligni, A. J. (2012). The intersection of aspirations and resources in the development of children from immigrant families. In C. García Coll & A. Marks (Eds.), *The immigrant paradox in children and adolescents: Is becoming American a developmental risk?* (pp. 299–308). Washington, DC: American Psychological Association.

Fuligni, A., & Hardway, C. (2004). Preparing diverse adolescents for the transition to adulthood. *Future of Children: Children of Immigrant Families, 14*, 99–119.

Fuligni, A. J., & Pedersen, S. (2002). Family obligation and the transition to young adulthood. *Developmental Psychology, 38*, 856–868.

Fuligni, A. J., Tseng, V., & Lam, M. (1999). Attitudes toward family obligations among American adolescents with Asian, Latin American, and European backgrounds. *Child Development, 70*, 1030–1044.

Fuller-Thomson, E., & Minkler, M. (2000). America's grandparent caregivers: Who are they? In B. Hayslip & R. Goldberg-Glen (Eds.), *Grandparents raising grandchildren: Theoretical, empirical, and clinical perspectives* (pp. 3–21). New York: Springer.

Fundación BBVA. (2008, December 17). *Attitudes towards assisted reproduction and preimplantation genetic diagnosis.* Madrid, Spain: Fundación BBVA.

Furstenberg, F. F. (1993). How families manage risk and opportunity in dangerous neighborhoods. In W. J. Wilson (Ed.), *Sociology and the public agenda* (pp. 231–258). Newbury Park, CA: Sage.

Furstenberg, F. F. (2009). If Moynihan had only known: Race, class, and family change in the late twentieth century. *The Annals of the American Academy of Political and Social Science, 621,* 94–110.

Furstenberg, F. F., Jr., Brooks-Gunn, J., & Chase-Lansdale, L. (1989). Teenage pregnancy and childbearing. *American Psychologist, 44,* 313–320.

Furstenberg, F. F., Brooks-Gunn, J., & Morgan, S. P. (1987). *Adolescent mothers in later life.* New York: Cambridge University Press.

Furstenberg, F. F., Cook, T. D., Eccles, J., Elder, G. H., Jr., & Sameroff, A. (1999). *Managing to make it: Urban families and adolescent success.* Chicago: University of Chicago Press.

Gailey, C. W. (2004). Adoptive families in the United States. In S. Coltrane (Ed.), *Families and society* (pp. 277–289). Belmont, CA: Thompson/Wadsworth.

Gailey, C. W. (2010). *Blue ribbon babies and labors of love: Race, class, and gender in US adoption practice.* Austin, TX: University of Texas Press.

Gajendran, R., & Harrison, D. A. (2007). The good, the bad, and the unknown about telecommuting: Meta-analysis of psychological mediators and individual consequences. *Journal of Applied Psychology, 92,* 1524–1541.

Gambaro, L. (2011). *For love and for money: Work motivations among childcare workers in the UK.* Retrieved April 29, 2013 from http://www.google.com/url

Gameiro, S., Moura-Ramos, M., Canavarro, M. C., & Soares, I. (2011). Network support and parenting in mothers and fathers who conceived spontaneously or through assisted reproduction. *Journal of Reproductive and Infant Psychology, 29,* 170–182.

Gameiro, S., Nazaré, B., Fonseca, A., Moura-Ramos, M., & Canavarro, M. C. (2011). Changes in marital congruence and quality of life across the transition to parenthood in couples who conceived spontaneously or with assisted reproductive technologies. *Fertility and Sterility, 96,* 1457–1462.

Ganong, L., & Coleman, M. (1999). *Changing families, changing responsibilities: Family obligations following divorce and remarriage.* Hillsdale, NJ: Erlbaum.

Garcia Coll, C. (2010, September 29). *The immigrant paradox – NYTimes.com. Interview for New York Times.* Retrieved April 29, 2013 from http://schott.blogs.nytimes.com/2010/09/29/the-immigrant-paradox/

García Coll, C., & Magnuson, K. (1999). Cultural influences on child development: Are we ready for a paradigm shift? In A. Masten (Ed.), *Minnesota symposium on child psychology, Vol. 29.* Mahwah, NJ: Lawrence Erlbaum Associates.

Garcia Coll, C., & Marks, A. K. (Eds.). (2011). *The immigrant paradox in children and adolescents: Is becoming American a developmental risk?* Washington, DC: American Psychological Association.

Gartrell, N., Banks, A., Hamilton, J., Reed, N., Bishop, H., & Rodas, C. (1999). The national lesbian family study: II. Interviews with mothers of toddlers. *American Journal of Orthopsychiatry, 69,* 362–369.

Gartrell, N., Banks, A., Reed, N., Hamilton, J., Rodas, C., & Deck, A. (2000). The national lesbian family study: 3. *Interviews with mothers of five-year-olds. American Journal of Orthopsychiatry, 70,* 542–548.

Gartrell, N., Deck, A., Rodas, C., Peyser, H., & Banks, A. (2005). The national lesbian family study: 4. Interviews with the 10-year-old children. *American Journal of Orthopsychiatry, 75,* 518–524.

Gartrell, N., Rodas, C., Deck, A., Peyser, H., & Banks A. (2006). The USA national lesbian family study: 5. Interviews with mothers of ten-year-olds. *Feminism and Psychology, 16,* 175–192.

Gates, G. J. (2012, April). *Same-sex couples in census 2010: Race and ethnicity.* Los Angeles: UCLA Williams Institute.

Gates, G. J. (2013, February). *Same sex and different sex couples in the American community survey: 2005–2011.* Los Angeles: UCLA Williams Institute.

Gates, G. J., Badgett, M. V. L., Chambers, K., & Macomber, J. (2007). *Adoption and foster care by gay and lesbian parents in the United States.* Washington, DC: The Urban Institute.

Gates, G. J., & Cooke, A., M. (2011). *United States census snapshot: 2010.* Los Angeles: UCLA Williams Institute.

Gaulin, S. J. C., McBurney, D. H., & Brakeman-Wartell, S. L. (1997). Matrilateral biases in the investment of aunts and uncles: A consequence and measure of paternity uncertainty. *Human Nature, 8,* 139–152.

Genetics and IVF. (2006, May 1). Advertisement.). *American Way Magazine, 92.*

Gennetian, L. A., & Miller, C. (2002). Children and welfare reform: A view from an experimental welfare program in Minnesota. *Child Development, 73,* 601–620.

Gershoff, E. T. (2002). Corporal punishment by parents and associated child behaviors and experiences: A meta-analytic and theoretical review. *Psychological Bulletin, 128,* 539–579.

Gershoff, E. T., Aber, J. L., & Raver, C. C. (2005). Child poverty in the United States: An evidence based conceptual framework for programs and policies. In R. M. Lerner, F. Jacobs, & D. Wertlieb (Eds.), *Applied developmental science* (pp. 269–324). Thousand Oaks, CA: Sage Publications.

Gerson, K. (2010). *The unfinished revolution.* New York: Oxford University Press.

Gettler, L. T., McDade, T. W., Feranil, A. B., & Kuzawa, C. W. (2011). Longitudinal evidence that fatherhood decreases testosterone in human males. *Proceedings of the National Academy of Sciences, 108,* 16194–16199.

Gibson, F. L., Ungerer, J. A., Tennant, C. C., & Saunders, D. M. (2000). Parental adjustment and attitudes to parenting after in vitro fertilization. *Fertility and Sterility, 73,* 565–574.

Gibson-Davis, C. M. (2008). Family structure effects on maternal and paternal parenting in low-income families. *Journal of Marriage and Family, 70,* 452–465.

Glass, J., & Riley, L. (1998). Family responsive policies and employee retention following childbirth. *Social Forces, 76,* 1426.

Glazebrook, C., Sheard, C., Cox, S., Oates, M., & Ndukwe, G. (2004). Parenting stress in first-time mothers of twins and triplets conceived after in vitro fertilization. *Fertility and Sterility, 81,* 505–511.

Glick, J. E., Bean, F. D., & Van Hook, J. V. (1997). Immigration and changing patterns of extended family household structure in the United States: 1970–1990. *Journal of Marriage and the Family, 59,* 177–191.

Glocker, M. L., Langleben, D. D., Ruparel, K., Loughead, J. W., Val-dez, J. N., Griffin, M. D., et al. (2009). Baby schema modulates the brain reward system in nulliparous women. *Proceedings of the National Academy of Sciences, 106,* 9115–9119.

Goins, R. T., Spencer, S. M., McGuire, L. C., Goldberg, J., & Henderson, J. A. (2011). Adult caregiving among American Indians: The role of cultural factors. *The Gerontologist, 51,* 310–320.

Goldberg, A. E. (2006). The transition to parenthood for lesbian couples. *Journal of GLBT Family Studies, 2,* 13–42.

Goldberg, A. E. (2007). (How) does it make a difference? Perspectives of adults with lesbian, gay, and bisexual parents. *American Journal of Orthopsychiatry, 77,* 550–562.

Goldberg, A. E. (2010). *Lesbian and gay parents and their children: Research on the family life cycle.* Washington, DC: American Psychological Association Press.

Goldberg, A. E. (2012). *Gay dads: Transitions to adoptive fatherhood.* New York: New York University Press.

Goldberg, A. E., & Allen, K. R. (2007). Imagining men: Lesbian mothers' ideas and intentions about male involvement across the transition to parenthood. *Journal of Marriage and Family, 69,* 352–365.

Goldberg, A. E., Downing, J. B., & Sauck, C. C. (2008). Perceptions of children's parental preferences in lesbian two-mother households. *Journal of Marriage and Family, 70,* 419–434.

Goldberg, A. E., & Smith, J. Z. (2008). Social support and psychological well-being in lesbian and heterosexual preadoptive couples. *Family Relations, 57,* 281–294.

Goldberg, W. A., Prause, J., Lucas-Thompson, R., & Himsel, A. (2008). Maternal employment and children's achievement in context: A meta-analysis of four decades of research. *Psychological Bulletin, 134,* 77–108.

Golinkoff, R. M., & Ames, G. (1979). A comparison of fathers' and mothers' speech to their young children. *Child Development, 50,* 28–32.

Golombok, S. (2000). *Parenting: What really counts?* London: Routledge.

Golombok, S. (2002). Parenting and contemporary reproductive technologies. In M. Bornstein (Ed.), *Handbook of parenting* (2nd ed., pp. 339–361). Mahwah, NJ: Erlbaum.

Golombok, S. (2006). New family forms. In A. Clarke-Stewart & J. Dunn (Eds.), *Families count: Effects on child and adolescent development.* New York: Cambridge University Press.

Golombok, S., & Badger, S. (2010). Children raised in fatherless families from infancy: A follow-up of children of lesbian and single heterosexual mothers in early adulthood. *Human Reproduction, 25,* 150–157.

Golombok, S., Brewaeys, A., Cook, R., Giavazzi, M. T., Guerra, D., Mantovani, A., et al. (1996). The European study of assisted reproduction families: Family functioning and child development. *Human Reproduction, 11,* 2324–2331.

Golombok, S., Brewaeys, A., Giavazzi, M. T., Guerra, D., MacCallum, F., & Rust, J. (2002). The European study of assisted reproduction families: The transition to adolescence. *Human Reproduction, 17,* 830–840.

Golombok, S., Cook, R., Bish, A., & Murray, C. (1995). Families created by the new reproductive technologies: Quality of parenting and social and emotional development of the children. *Child Development, 66,* 285–298.

Golombok, S., Cook, R., Bish, A., & Murray, C. (1997). Families created by the new reproductive technologies: Quality of parenting and social and emotional development of the children. In M. Hertzig & E. Farber (Eds.), *Annual progress in child psychiatry and child development 1996* (pp. 529–550). New York: Brunner Mazel.

Golombok, S., MacCallum, F., & Goodman, E. (2001). The "test-tube" generation: Parent–child relationships and the psychological well-being of in vitro fertilization children at adolescence. *Child Development, 72,* 599–608.

Golombok, S., Murray, C., Brinsden, P., & Abdalla, H. (1999). Social versus biological parenting: Family functioning and the socioemotional development of children conceived by egg or sperm donation. *Journal of Child Psychology and Psychiatry, 40,* 519–527.

Golombok, S., Murray, C., Jadva, V., MacCallum, F., & Lycett, E. (2004). Families created through surrogacy arrangement: Parent–child relationships in the 1st year of life. *Developmental Psychology, 40,* 400–411.

Golombok, S., Owen, L., Blake, L., Murray, C., & Jadva, V. (2009). Parent–child relationships and the psychological well-being of 18-year-old adolescents conceived by in vitro fertilisation. *Human Fertility, 12,* 63–72.

Golombok, S., Perry, B., Burston, A., Murray, C., Mooney-Somers, J., Stevens, M., et al. (2003). Children with lesbian parents: A community study. *Developmental Psychology, 39,* 20–33.

Golombok, S., Readings, J., Blake, L., Casey, P., Marks, A., & Jadva, V. (2011a). Families created through surrogacy: Mother–child relationships and children's psychological adjustment at age 7. *Developmental Psychology, 47*(6), 1579–1588.

Golombok, S., Readings, J., Blake, L., Casey, P., Mellish, L., Marks, A., et al. (2011b). Children conceived by gamete donation: The impact of openness about donor conception on psychological adjustment and parent–child relationships at age 7. *Journal of Family Psychology, 25,* 230–239.

Golombok, S., Spencer, A., & Rutter, M. (1983). Children in lesbian and single parent households: Psychosexual and psychiatric appraisal. *Journal of Child Psychology & Psychiatry, 24*, 551–572.

Golombok, S. E., & Tasker, F. (2010). Gay fathers. In M. E. Lamb (Ed.), *The role of the father in child development*. Hoboken, NJ: Wiley.

Gonzales, N., Fabrett, F., & Knight, G. (2009). Acculturation, enculturation, and the psychological adaptation of Latino youth. In F. A. Villarruel, G. Carlo, J. M. Grau, M. Azmitia, N. J. Cabrera, & T. J. Chahin (Eds.), *Handbook of U.S. Latino psychology* (pp. 115–134). Thousand Oaks, CA: Sage Publications.

Goodman, C., & Silverstein, M. (2002). Grandmothers raising grandchildren: Family structure and well-being in culturally diverse families. *The Gerontologist, 42*, 676–689.

Gordon, I., Zagoory-Sharon, O., Leckman, J. F., & Feldman, R. (2010). Oxytocin and the development of parenting in humans. *Biological Psychiatry, 68*, 377–382.

Gornick, J. C., & Meyers, M. K. (2003). *Families that work: Policies for reconciling parenthood and employment*. New York: Russell Sage Foundation.

Gornick, J. C., & Meyers, M. (2007). *Institutions for gender egalitarianism*. New York: Verso.

Gottfried, A. E., Gottfried, A. W., & Bathurst, K. (2002). Maternal and dual-earner employment status and parenting. In M. H. Bornstein (Ed.), *Handbook of parenting: Biology and ecology of parenting* (2nd ed., Vol. 2, pp. 207–230). Mahwah, NJ: Erlbaum.

Gottfried, A. W., Gottfried, A. E., & Guerin, D. W. (2006). The Fullerton Longitudinal Study: A long-term investigation of intellectual and motivational giftedness. *Journal for the Education of the Gifted, 29*, 430–450.

Graae, B. (1967, April). Børn skal have Hundrede Foraeldre. *Politiken* [Copenhagen].

Graber, H. V., & Wolfe, J. L. (2004). Family support center village: A unique approach for low-income single women with children. *Journal of Family Social Work, 8*, 61–73.

Gray, P. B., & Anderson, K. G. (2010). *Fatherhood: Evolution and human paternal behavior*. Cambridge, MA: Harvard University Press.

Greenberger, E., Chen, C., & Beam, M. (1998). The role of "very important" nonparental adults in adolescent development. *Journal of Youth and Adolescence, 27*, 321–343.

Greenberger, E., O'Neill, R., & Nagel, S. K. (1994). Linking workplace and homeplace: Relations between the nature of adults' work and their parenting behaviors. *Developmental Psychology, 30*, 990–1002.

Grief, G. (1985). Single fathers rearing children. *Journal of Marriage and Family, 47*, 185–191.

Grimm-Thomas, K., & Perry-Jenkins, M. (1994). All in a day's work: Job experiences, self-esteem, and fathering in working-class families. *Family Relations, 43*, 174–181.

Gringlas, M., & Weinraub, M. (1995). The more things change: Single parenting revisited. *Journal of Family Issues, 16*, 29–52.

Griswold, R. (1993). *Fatherhood in America: A history*. New York: Basic Books.

Grønseth, E. (1975). Work sharing families. *Acta Sociologica, 18*, 202–221.

Grossman, F. K., Pollack, W. S., & Golding, E. (1988). Fathers and children: Predicting the quality and quantity of fathering. *Developmental Psychology, 24*, 82–91.

Grossmann, K., Grossmann, K. E., Fremmer-Bombik, E., Kindler, H., Scheuerer-Englisch, H., & Zimmerman, P. (2002). The uniqueness of the child-father attachment relationship: Fathers' sensitive and challenging play as a pivotal variable in a 16-year longitudinal study. *Social Development, 11*, 301–337.

Grotevant, H. D. (2007). Openness in adoption: Re-thinking "family" in the United States. In M. C. Inhorn (Ed.), *Reproductive disruptions: Gender, technology, and biopolitics in the new millennium* (pp. 122–143). New York: Berghahn Books.

Grotevant, H. D., & McRoy, R. G. (1998). *Openness in adoption: Connecting families of birth and adoption*. Thousand Oaks, CA: Sage.

Guastello, D. D., & Guastello, S. J. (2003). Androgyny, gender role behavior, and emotional intelligence among college students and their parents. *Sex Roles, 49*, 663–673.

Gubernskaya, Z. (2010). Changing attitudes toward marriage and children in six countries. *Sociological Perspectives, 53,* 179–200.

Guichon, J. (2010, November 22). Don't let market forces govern human procreation. *BioNews.* Retrieved April 29, 2013 from http://www.bionews.org.uk/page_81679.asp

Gurmankin, A. D., Caplan, A. L., & Braverman, A. M. (2005). Screening practices and beliefs of assisted reproductive technology programs. *Fertility & Sterility, 83,* 61–67.

Gutierrez, J., & Sameroff, A. (1990). Determinants of complexity in Mexican-American and Anglo-American mothers' conceptions of child development. *Child Development, 61,* 384–394.

Haddad, E., Chen, C., & Greenberger, E. (2011). The role of important non-parental adults (VIPs) in the lives of older adolescents: A comparison of three ethnic groups. *Journal of Youth and Adolescence, 40,* 310–319.

Hahn, C. -S., & DiPietro, J. A. (2001). In vitro fertilization and the family: Quality of parenting, family functioning, and child psychological adjustment. *Developmental Psychology, 37,* 37–48.

Hale-Jinks, C., Knopf, H., & Kemple, K. (2006). Tackling teacher turnover in child care: Understanding causes and consequences, identifying solutions. *Childhood Education, 82,* 219–226.

Halle, T. (2002). *Charting parenthood: A statistical portrait of fathers and mothers in America.* Washington, DC: Child Trends.

Han, W. -J. (2005). Maternal nonstandard work schedules and child cognitive outcomes. *Child Development, 76,* 137–154.

Han, W. -J., Ruhm, C., & Waldfogel, J. (2009). Parental leave policies and parents' employment and leave-taking. *Journal of Policy Analysis and Management, 28,* 29–54.

Han, W. -J., Waldfogel, J., & Brooks-Gunn, J. (2001). The effects of early maternal employment on later cognitive and behavioral outcomes. *Journal of Marriage and Family, 63,* 336–354.

Hannerz, U. (1969). *Soul side: Inquiries into ghetto culture and community.* New York: Columbia University Press.

Hansen, M., Bower, C., Milne, E., de Klerk, N., & Kurinczuk, J. J. (2005). Assisted reproductive technologies and the risk of birth defects: A systematic review. *Human Reproduction, 20,* 328–338.

Hansen, T. (2012). Parenthood and happiness: A review of folk theories versus empirical evidence. *Social Indicators Research, 108,* 29–64.

Hansen, T., Slagsvold, B., & Moum, T. (2009). Childlessness and psychological well-being in midlife and old age: An examination of parental status effects across a range of outcomes. *Social Indicators Research, 94,* 343–362.

Hanson, T. L. (1999). Does parental conflict explain why divorce is negatively associated with child welfare? *Journal of Marriage and Family, 61,* 451–464.

Hao, L. (1996). Family structure, private transfers, and the economic well-being of families with children. *Social Forces, 75,* 269–292.

Hardway, C., & Fuligni. A. J. (2006). Dimensions of family connectedness among adolescents with Mexican, Chinese, and European backgrounds. *Developmental Psychology, 42,* 1246–1258.

Harlow, H. F. (1958). The nature of love. *American Psychologist, 13,* 673–676.

Harris, D. N., & Adams, S. J. (2007). Understanding the level and causes of teacher turnover: A comparison with other professions. *Economics of Education Review, 26,* 325–337.

Harris, P. M., & Jones, N. A. (2005). *We the people: Pacific Islanders in the United States* (Census 2000 1244–1257. Special Report No. CENSR-26). Washington, DC: U.S. Census Bureau. Retrieved April 29, 2013 from http://www.census.gov/prod/2005pubs/censr-26.pdf

Harrison, A. O., Wilson, M. N., Pine, C. J., Chan, S. Q., & Buriel, R. (1990). Family ecologies of ethnic minority children. *Child Development, 61,* 347–362.

Harvey, E. (1999). Short-term and long-term effects of early parental employment on children of the national longitudinal survey of youth. *Developmental Psychology, 35*, 445–459.

Hatchett, S., Cochran, D., & Jackson, J. (1991). Family life. In J. Jackson (Ed.), *Life in black America* (pp. 103–116). Newbury Park, CA: Sage Publications.

Haviland, J., & Lelwica, M. (1987). The induced affect response: 10-week-old infants' responses to three emotional expressions. *Developmental Psychology, 23*, 97–104.

Hawkes, K., O'Connell, J. F., Blurton Jones, N. G., Alvarez, H., & Charnov, E. (1998). Grandmothering, menopause and the evolution of human life histories. *Proceedings of the National Academy of Sciences of the United States of America, 95*, 1336–1339.

Hawkins, D. (2009, June 5). The effects of grandparents parenting their grandchildren. *Raising Your Grandchildren. Yahoo! Contributor Network.* Retrieved April 29, 2013 from http://voices.yahoo.com/the-effects-grandparents-parenting-their-grandchildren-3437402.html?cat=25

Hayslip, B., Jr., & Patrick, J. H. (Eds.). (2006). *Custodial grandparenting: Individual, cultural and ethnic diversity.* New York: Springer.

Heard, H. E. (2007). The family structure trajectory and adolescent school performance. *Journal of Family Issues, 28*, 319–354.

Heath, K. M. (2003). The effects of kin propinquity on infant mortality. *Social Biology, 50*, 270–280.

Heiland, F., & Liu, S. H. (2006). Family structure and wellbeing of out-of-wedlock children: The significance of the biological parents' relationship. *Demographic Research, 15*, 61–104.

Heintz-Knowles, K. E. (2001). Balancing acts: Work-family issues on prime-time TV. In J. Bryant & J. A. Bryant (Eds.), *Television and the American family* (2nd ed., pp. 177–206). Hillsdale, NJ: Erlbaum.

Henly, J. R., Ananat, E. O., & Danziger, S. K. (2006). *Nonstandard work, schedules, child care subsidies, and child care arrangements.* Chicago: University of Chicago.

Hequembourg, A., & Farrell, M. (1999). Lesbian motherhood: Negotiating marginal-mainstream identities. *Gender & Society, 13*, 540–557.

Herek, G. M. (2007). Confronting sexual stigma and prejudice: Theory and practice. *Journal of Social Issues, 63*, 905–925.

Hernandez, D. J., Denton, N. A., & Macartney, S. E. (2008). Children in immigrant families: Looking to America's future. *Social Policy Report, 22*, 3–22.

Hernandez, D. J., Denton, N. A., Macartney, S., & Blanchard, V. L. (2012). Children in immigrant families: Demography, policy, and evidence for the immigrant paradox. In C. Garcia Coll & A. Marks (Eds.), *The immigrant paradox in children and adolescents: Is becoming American a developmental risk?* (pp. 17–36). Washington, DC: American Psychological Association.

Herrera, C., Grossman, J. B., Kauh, T. J., Feldman, A. F., & McMaken, J. (2007). *Making a difference in schools: The Big Brothers Big Sisters school-based mentoring impact study.* Philadelphia: Public/ Private Ventures.

Hertz, R. (2006). *Single by chance, mothers by choice.* New York: Oxford University Press.

Hetherington, E. M. (1999). Should we stay together for the sake of the children? In E. M. Hetherington (Ed.), *Coping with divorce, single parenting, and remarriage: A risk and resiliency perspective* (pp. 93–116). Mahwah, NJ: Erlbaum.

Hetherington, E. M. (2006). The influence of conflict, marital problem-solving and parenting on children's adjustment in non-divorced, divorced, and remarried families. In A. Clarke-Stewart & J. Dunn (Eds.), *Families count: Effects on child and adolescent development* (pp. 203–237). New York: Cambridge University Press.

Hetherington, E. M., Bridges, M., & Insabella, G. M. (1998). What matters? What does not? Five perspectives on the association between marital transitions and children's adjustment. *American Psychologist, 53*, 167–184.

Hetherington, E. M., & Jodl, K. (1994). Stepfamilies as settings for development. In A. Booth & J. Dunn (Eds.), *Stepfamilies* (pp. 55–80). Cambridge, MA: Harvard University Press.

Hetherington, E. M., & Kelly, J. (2002). *For better or worse: Divorce reconsidered*. New York: Norton & Co.

Hetherington, E. M., & Stanley-Hagan, M. (2002). Parenting in divorced and remarried families. In M. Bornstein (Ed.), *Handbook of parenting* (2nd ed., pp. 287–316). Mahwah, NJ: Erlbaum.

Heuveline, P., Timberlake, J. M., & Furstenberg, F. F., Jr. (2003). Shifting childrearing to single mothers: Results from 17 western countries. *Population and Development Review, 29,* 47–71.

Hewitt Associates. (2003). *Spec summary: United States salaried work/life benefits, 2003–2004*. Lincolnshire, IL: Author.

Hewlett, B. S., & Lamb, M. E. (2005). *Hunter-gatherer childhoods: Evolutionary, developmental and cultural perspectives*. New Brunswick, NJ: Transaction Publishers.

Heymann, J., & Earle, A. (2010). *Raising the global floor: Dismantling the myth that we can't afford good working conditions for everyone*. Stanford, CA: Stanford University Press.

Heymann, J., Flores-Macias, F., Hayes, J. A., Kennedy, M., Lahaie, C., & Earle, A. (2009). The impact of migration on the well-being of transnational families: New data from sending communities in Mexico. *Community, Work & Family, 12,* 91–103.

Hill, E. J., Erickson, J. J., Holmes, E. K., & Ferris, M. (2010). Workplace flexibility, work hours, and work-life conflict: Finding an extra day or two. *Journal of Family Psychology, 24,* 349–358.

Hill, E. J., Hawkins, A. J., Ferris, M., & Weitzman, M. (2001). Finding an extra day a week: The positive effect of job flexibility on work and family life balance. *Family Relations, 50,* 49–58.

Hill, K., & Hurtado, A. M. (1996). *Ache life history: The ecology and demography of a foraging people*. New York: Aldine de Gruyter.

Hillmer, P. (2010). *A people's history of the Hmong*. Minneapolis, MN: Minnesota Historical Society Press.

Himes, C. L., Hogan, D. P., & Eggebeen, D. J. (1996). Living arrangements of minority elders. *Journal of Gerontology: Social Sciences, 51b,* S42–S48.

Hixson-Somanchi, S. L. (2010). *Working mothers' decisions, experiences and feelings about using on-site childcare*. Unpublished doctoral dissertation, Portland State University, Portland.

Hjelmstedt, A., WidstrÖm, A. M., & Collins, A. (2006). Psychological correlates of prenatal attachment in women who conceived after in vitro fertilization and women who conceived naturally. *Birth, 33,* 303–310.

Hjern, A., Haglund, B., Rasmussen, F., & Rosen, M. (2000). Socio-economic differences in daycare arrangements in Swedish preschool children. *Acta Paediatrica, 89,* 1250–1256.

Hochschild, A. R. (1989). *The second shift: Working parents and the revolution at home* (with Anne Machung). New York: Viking Penguin.

Hochschild, A. R. (1997). *The time bind: When work becomes home and home becomes work*. New York: Metropolitan/Holt.

Hochschild, A. R. (2012). *The outsourced self: Intimate life in market times*. New York: Metropolitan Books.

Hock, E. (1978). Working and nonworking mothers with infants: Perceptions of their careers, their infants' needs, and satisfaction with mothering. *Developmental Psychology, 14,* 37–43.

Hock, E., & DeMeis, D. K. (1990). Depression in mothers of infants: The role of maternal employment. *Developmental Psychology, 26,* 285–291.

Hoeffer, B. (1981). Children's acquisition of sex-role behavior in lesbian-mother families. *American Journal of Orthopsychiatry, 51,* 536–544.

Hoffman, L. W. (2000). Maternal employment: Effects of social context. In R. D. Taylor & M. C. Wang (Eds.), *Resilience across contexts: Family, work, culture and community* (pp. 147–176). Mahwah, NJ: Erlbaum.

Holden, G. (1988). Adults' thinking about a child-rearing problem: Effects of experience, parental status, and gender. *Child Development, 59*, 1623–1632.

Holden, G. W. (2010). *Parenting: A dynamic perspective.* Thousand Oaks, CA: Sage.

Hole, J., & Levine, E. (1971). *Rebirth of feminism.* New York: Quadrangle Books.

Hondagneu-Sotelo, P., & Avila, E. (1997). "I'm here, but I'm there": The meanings of Latina transnational motherhood. *Gender and Society, 11*, 548–571.

Hoorens, S., Conklin, A., & Tiessen, J. (2008). *Between politics and clinics: The many faces of biomedical policy in Europe: Analysis of drivers and outcomes of assisted reproductive technologies policy.* Santa Monica, CA: RAND Corporation.

Horwitz, S. M., Klerman, L. V., Kuo, H. S., & Jekel, J. F. (1991). Intergenerational transmission of school-age parenthood. *Family Planning Perspectives, 23*, 162–172.

Houser, L., & Vartanian, T. P. (2012). *Pay matters: The positive economic impacts of paid family leave for families, businesses.* New Brunswick, NJ: The Public Center for Women and Work, Rutgers, The State University of New Jersey School of Management and Labor Relations.

Housing New Zealand. (2007). *The healthy housing programme outcomes evaluation.* Wellington, New Zealand: Housing New Zealand.

Howe, T. (2012). *Marriage and families in the 21st century.* Malden, MA: Wiley-Blackwell.

Howes, C., Rodning, C., Galluzzo, D. C., & Myers, L. (1988). Attachment and child care: Relationships with mother and caregiver. *Early Childhood Research Quarterly, 3*, 403–416.

Howes, C., & Spieker, S. (2008). Attachment relationships in the context of multiple caregivers. In J. Cassidy & P. Shaver (Eds.), *Handbook of attachment: Theory, research, and clinical applications* (2nd ed., pp. 317–332). New York: Guilford.

Hrdy, S. B. (2005). Evolutionary context of human development: The cooperative breeding model. In C. S. Carter, L. Ahnert, K. E. Grossmann, S. B. Hrdy, M. E. Lamb, S. W. Porges, & N. Sachser (Eds.), *Attachment and bonding* (pp. 9–32). Cambridge, MA: MIT Press.

Hrdy, S. B. (2009). *Mothers and others: The evolutionary origins of mutual understanding.* Cambridge, MA: Harvard University Press.

Hua, C. (2002). *A society without fathers or husbands: The Na of China.* New York: Zone Press.

Huggins, S. L. (1989). A comparative study of self-esteem of adolescent children of divorced lesbian mothers and divorced heterosexual mothers. *Journal of Homosexuality, 18*, 123–135.

Hughes, F. P. (1999). *Children, play and development* (2nd ed.). Boston: Allyn & Bacon.

Hughes, M. E., Waite, L. J., LaPierre, T. A., & Luo, Y. (2007). All in the family: The impact of caring for grandchildren on grandparents' health. *Journals of Gerontology Series B—Social Sciences, 62*, S108–S119.

Hummer, R. A., & Hamilton, E. R. (2010). Race and ethnicity in fragile families. *The Future of Children, 20*, 113–131.

Hurtado, A., & Silva, J. M. (2008). Creating new social identities in children through critical multicultural media: The case of Little Bill. *New Directions for Child and Adolescent Development, 120*, 17–30.

Huston, A. C., & Rosencrantz Aronson, S. (2005). Mothers time with infant and time in employment as predictors of mother-child relationships and children's early development. *Child Development, 76*, 467–482.

Hwang, P. (1987). The changing role of Swedish fathers. In M. E. Lamb (Ed.), *The father's role: Cross-cultural perspectives* (pp. 115–138). Hillsdale, NJ: Lawrence Erlbaum.

Hyde, J. S. (2007). *Half the human experience: The psychology of women* (7th ed.). Boston: Houghton-Mifflin.

International Committee for Monitoring Assisted Reproductive Technologies. (2012, July). *The world's number of IVF and ICSI babies has now reached a calculated total of 5 million.* Paper presented at 28th annual meeting of ESHRE (European Society of Human Reproduction and Embryology), Istanbul, Turkey.

Ipsos Reid Poll. (2010, Thursday, September 30). How Canadians see the family. Conducted for *Postmedia News*. Retrieved April 29, 2013 from www2.canada.com/story

Ivey, P. K. (2000). Cooperative reproduction in Ituri Forest hunter-gatherers: Who cares for Efe infants. *Current Anthropology, 41*, 856–866.

Ivey Henry, P. K., Morelli, G. A., & Tronick, E. Z. (2005). Child caretakers among Efe foragers of the Ituri Forest. In B. S. Hewlett & M. E. Lamb (Eds.), *Hunter-gatherer childhoods: Evolutionary, developmental and cultural perspectives* (pp. 191–213). New Brunswick, NJ: Aldine Transaction.

IWPR. (2010, October 29). *Majority of voters support workplace flexibility, job quality, and family support policies*. Retrieved April 29, 2013 from http://www.iwpr.org/pdf/Press ReleaseRock_WorkFam_28Oct2010.pdf

Jackson, R. A., Gibson, K. A., Wu, Y. W., & Croughan, M. S. (2004). Perinatal outcomes in singletons following in vitro fertilization: A meta-analysis. *Obstetrics & Gynecology, 103*, 551–563.

Jadva, V., Blake, L., Casey, P., & Golombok, S. (2012). Surrogacy families 10 years on: Relationship with the surrogate, decisions over disclosure and children's understanding of their surrogacy origins. *Human Reproduction, 27*, 3008–3014.

Jadva, V., Casey, P., Readings, J., Blake, L., & Golombok, S. (2011). A longitudinal study of recipients' views and experiences of intra-family egg donation. *Human Reproduction, 10*, 2777–2782.

Jadva, V., Freeman, T., Kramer, W., & Golombok, S. (2010). Experiences of offspring searching for and contacting their donor siblings and donor. *Reproductive BioMedicine Online, 20*, 523–532.

Jadva, V., & Imrie, S. (2013). The significance of relatedness for surrogates and their families. In M. Richards, T. Freeman, F. Ebtehaj, & S. Graham (Eds.), *We are family?* Cambridge: Cambridge University Press.

Jadva, V., Murray, C., Lycett, E., MacCallum, F., & Golombok, S. (2003). Surrogacy: The experiences of surrogate mothers. *Human Reproduction, 18*, 2196–2204.

Jarrett, R. L. (1998). African American children, families, and neighborhoods: Qualitative contributions to understanding developmental pathways. *Applied Developmental Science, 2*, 2–16.

Jelm, E. (2010, Spring). *Fictive kinship and acquaintance networks as sources of support and social capital for Mexican transmigrants in South Bend*. Notre Dame, IN: Institute for Latino Studies, University of Notre Dame.

Johnson, A. D., Ryan, R. M., & Brooks-Gunn, J. (2012). Child-care subsidies: Do they impact the quality of care children experience? *Child Development, 83*(4), 1444–1461.

Johnson, J. H., & Kasarda, J. D. (2011). *Six disruptive demographic trends: What census 2010 will reveal*. Chapel Hill, NC: The Frank Hawkins Kenan Institute of Private Enterprise at the University of North Carolina.

Johnson, S. M., & O'Connor, E. (2002). *The Gay baby boom: The psychology of gay parenthood*. New York: New York University Press.

Jooste, J., Hayslip, B., & Smith, G. (2008). The adjustment of children and grandparent caregivers in grandparent-headed families. In B. Hayslip & P. A. Kaminski (Eds.), *Parenting the custodial grandchild: Implications for clinical practice* (pp. 17–39). New York: Springer.

Jordan, W. J., Lara, J., & McPartland, J. M. (1996). Exploring the causes of early dropout among race-ethnic and gender groups. *Youth & Society, 28*, 62–94.

Jurkovic, G. J. (1997). *Lost childhoods: The plight of the parentified child*. Philadelphia: Brunner/ Mazel.

Kaitz, M., Shiri, S., Danzinger, S., Hershko, Z., & Eidelman, A. I. (1994). Fathers can also recognize their newborns by touch. *Infant Behavior & Development, 17*, 205–207.

Kane, E. W. (2006). Parents' responses to children's gender nonconformity. *Gender & Society, 20*, 149–176.

Katz Rothman, B. (2002). *The book of life: A personal and ethical guide to race, normality and the implications of the Human Genome Project.* Boston: Beacon.

Keefe, S. E., & Padilla, A. M. (1987). *Chicano ethnicity.* Albuquerque, NM: University of New Mexico Press.

Kellam, S. G., Adams, R. G., Brown, C. H., & Ensminger, M. E. (1982). The long-term evolution of the family structure of teenage and older mothers. *Journal of Marriage and Family, 46*, 539–554.

Kellam, S. G., Ensminger, M. A., & Turner, J. T. (1977). Family structure and the mental health of children. *Archives of General Psychiatry, 34*, 1012–1022.

Kelly, R., Redenbach, L., & Rinaman, W. (2005). Determinants of custody arrangements in a national sample. *American Journal of Family Law, 19*, 25–43.

Kendler, K. S., Myers, J., & Prescott, C. A. (2005). Sex differences in the relationship between social support and risk for major depression: A longitudinal study of opposite-sex twin pairs. *The American Journal of Psychiatry, 162*, 2250–2256.

Kennedy, S., & Bumpass, L. (2011, April). *Cohabitation and trends in the structure and stability of children's family lives.* Paper presented at the annual meeting of the Population Association of America, Washington, DC.

Kensinger, K. M. (2002). The dilemmas of co-paternity in Cashinahua society. In S. Beckerman & P. Valentine (Eds.), *Cultures of multiple fathers: The theory and practice of partible paternity in lowland South America* (pp. 14–26). Gainesville, FL: University Press of Florida.

Kibria, N. (1993) *Family tightrope: The changing lives of Vietnamese Americans.* Princeton, NJ: Princeton University Press.

Kiernan, K. E. (2001). The rise of cohabitation and childbearing outside of marriage in Western Europe. *International Journal of Law, Policy and the Family, 15*, 1–21.

Kiernan, K. E., & Smith, K. (2003). Unmarried parenthood: New insights from the Millennium Cohort Study. *Population Trends, (114)*, 26–33.

Kim, H. S. (2011). Consequences of parental divorce for child development. *American Sociological Review, 76*, 487–511.

Kim, K., & Kim, S. (1995). Family and work roles of Korean immigrants in the United States. In E. McCubbin, A. Thompson, & J. Fromer (Eds.), *Resiliency in ethnic minority families. Vol. 1: Native and immigrant American families* (pp. 225–242). Madison, WI: University of Wisconsin Press.

Kindle, P. A., & Erich, S. (2005). Perceptions of social support among heterosexual and homosexual adopters. *Families in Society, 86*, 541–546.

Kirkpatrick, M., Smith, C., & Roy, R. (1981). Lesbian mothers and their children: A comparative survey. *American Journal of Orthopsychiatry, 51*, 545–551.

Klein, K., & Forehand, R. (2000). Family processes as resources for African American children exposed to a constellation of sociodemographic risk factors. *Journal of Clinical Psychology, 29*, 53–65.

Klipstein, S., Regan, M., Ryley, D. A., Goldman, M. B., Alper, M. M., & Reindollar, R. H. (2005). One last chance for pregnancy: A review of 2,705 in vitro fertilization cycles initiated in women age 40 years and above. *Fertility and Sterililty, 84*, 435–445.

Konigsberg, R. D. (2011, August 8). *Chore wars. Time*, 45–48.

Konner, M. J. (2005). Hunter-gatherer infancy and childhood: The Kung and others. In B. S. Hewlett & M. E. Lamb (Eds.), *Hunter-gatherer childhoods: Evolutionary, developmental and cultural perspectives* (pp. 19–64). New Brunswick, NJ: Aldine Transaction.

Kornberg, J. C. (2008). Jumping on the mommy track: A tax for working mothers. *UCLA Women's Law Journal, 17*, 187.

Koropeckyj-Cox, T., & Pendell, G. (2007). The gender gap in attitudes about childlessness in the United States. *Journal of Marriage and Family, 69*, 899–915.

Kosciw, J. G., & Diaz, E. M. (2008). *Involved, invisible, ignored: The experiences of lesbian, gay, bisexual and transgender parents and their children in our nation's K-12 schools.* New York: GLSEN.

Kovacs, G. T., Morgan, G., Wood, E. C., Forbes, C., & Howlett, D. (2003). Community attitudes to assisted reproductive technology: A 20-year trend. *Medical Journal of Australia, 179*, 536–538.

Kramer, K. L. (2002). Variation in juvenile dependence: Helping behavior among Maya children. *Human Nature, 13*, 299–325.

Krause, N., Regula Herzog, A., & Baker, E. (1992). Providing support to others and well-being in later life. *Journal of Gerontology, 47*, 300–311.

Kreider, R. (2008). *Improvements to demographic household data in the current population survey.* Housing and Household Economic Statistics Division Working Paper. Retrieved April 29, 2013 from http://www.census.gov/population/www/documentation/twps08/twps08. pdf

Kreider, R. M. (2005). *Timing, and duration of marriages and divorces: 2001 (Population Reports, P70-97).* Washington, DC: Census Bureau.

Kuperminc, G. P., Jurkovic, G. J., & Casey, S. (2009). Relation of filial responsibility to the personal and social adjustment of Latino adolescents from immigrant families. *Journal of Family Psychology, 23*, 14–22.

Lahaie, C., Hayes, J. A., Markham Piper, T., & Heymann, J. (2009). Work and family divided across borders: The impact of parental migration on Mexican children in transnational families. *Community, Work & Family, 12*, 299–312.

Lamb, M. E. (1975). Physiological mechanisms in the control of maternal behavior in rats: A review. *Psychological Bulletin, 82*, 104–119.

Lamb, M. E. (1976). Effects of stress and cohort on mother and father-infant interaction. *Developmental Psychology, 12*, 435–443.

Lamb, M. E., & Lewis, C. (2010). In M. E. Lamb (Ed.). *The role of the father in child development* (5th ed.). Hoboken, NJ: Wiley.

Lambert, S. J. (2009). Making a difference for hourly employees. In A. C. Crouter & A. Booth (Eds.), *Work-life policies that make a real difference for individuals, families, and organizations.* Washington, DC: Urban Institute Press.

Landale, N. S., & Oropesa, R. S. (2007). Hispanic families: Stability and change. *Annual Review of Sociology, 33*, 381–405.

Landale, N. S., Thomas, K., & Van Hook, J. (2011). The living arrangements of the children of immigrants. *The Future of Children, 21*, 43–70.

Lane, T. (2011). *Being unemployed and Asian is rare and, among some, a point of shame.* Chicago: Northwestern University Medill Reports.

Lareau, A. (2011). *Unequal childhoods: Class, race and family life* (updated edition). Berkeley, CA: University of California Press.

Larson, R., & Richards, M. (1994). *Divergent realities.* New York: Basic Books.

Larson, R. W., & Verma, S. (1999). How children and adolescents around the world spend time: Work, play, and developmental opportunities. *Psychological Bulletin, 125*, 701–736.

Le Camus, J. (1995). *Pères et bébés.* Paris: L. Harmattan.

Leadbeater, B., & Way, N. (2001). *Growing up fast: Transitions to early adulthood of inner-city adolescent mothers.* New York: Psychology Press.

Lee, M. L., & Mather, M. (2008). U.S. labor force trends. *Population Bulletin, 63*, 1–16.

Lee, S., Colditz, G., Berkman, L., & Kawachi, I. (2003). Caregiving and risk of coronary heart disease in U.S. women: A prospective study. *American Journal of Preventive Medicine, 24*, 113–119.

Lee-St. John J. (2007, April 19). *Outsourcing breast milk. Time Magazine.* Retrieved April 29, 2013 from: http://www.time.com/time/magazine/article/0,9171,1612710,00.html

Leger Marketing Survey for the BMO Financial Group (2011, June) *BMO father's day study: More dads staying at home with the kids.* Toronto, Ontario, Canada: BMO Financial Group. Retrieved April 29, 2013 from newsroom.bmo.com

Legislative Analyst's Office. (2009). *Education of foster youth in California.* Retrieved April 29, 2013 from http://www.lao.ca.gov/2009/edu/ foster_children/foster_ed_052809.pdf

Lehmann, C. (2011). *How "modern" is 'modern family'? A critical review on the U.S. sitcom regarding gender roles and hegemonic ideologies.* Retrieved April 29, 2013 from http://rug.academia.edu/CarolinLehmann/Papers/1340944/

Leidy, M., Schofield, T., Miller, M., Parke, R. D., Coltrane, S., Cookston, J., et al. (2011). Fathering and adolescent adjustment: Variations by family structure and ethnic background. *Fathering, 9,* 44–68.

Lende, D. (2011, December). *On testosterone and real men: An interview with Lee Gettler. Plos Blogs: Neuroanthropology.* Retrieved April 29, 2013 from http://blogs.plos.org/ neuroanthropology/2011/12/14/

Lengua, L. J., Wolchick, S. A., & Braver, S. (1995). Understanding children's divorce adjustment from an ecological perspective. *Journal of Divorce and Remarriage, 22,* 25–53.

Lenhoff, D., & Withers, C. (1994). Implementation of the Family and Medical Leave Act: Toward the family-friendly workplace. *American University Journal of Gender and Law, 3,* 39.

Leon, I. (2008). *Psychology of reproduction: Pregnancy, parenthood, and parental ties.* Global Library of Women's Medicine. Philadelphia: Lippincott.

Leon, K., & Angst, E. (2005). Portrayals of stepfamilies in film: Using media images in remarriage education. *Family Relations, 54,* 3–23.

Lev, A. I. (2004). *The complete lesbian and gay parenting guide.* New York/Berkley: Penguin Press.

Levine, J. A. (1976). *Who will raise the children? New options for fathers (and mothers).* New York: Lippincott.

Levine, J. A., & Pittinsky, T. L. (1997). *Working fathers: New strategies for balancing work and family.* Cambridge, MA: Da Capo Press.

Levine, R. (2003). *Childhood socialization: Comparative studies of parenting, learning and educational change.* Hong Kong: University of Hong Kong Press.

Levitt, P. (2001). *The transnational villagers.* Berkeley, CA: University of California Press.

Levy-Shiff, R., Vakil, E., Dimitrovsky, L., Abramovitz, M., Shahar, N., Har-Even, D., et al. (1998). Medical, cognitive, emotional, and behavioural outcomes in school-age children conceived by in-vitro fertilization. *Journal of Clinical Child Psychology, 27*(3), 320–329.

Liang, Z., & Ma, Z. (2004). China's floating population: New evidence from the 2000 census. *Population and Development Review, 30,* 467–488.

Lick, D. J., Tornello, S. L., Riskind, R. G., Schmidt, K. M., & Patterson, C. J. (2012). Social climate for sexual minorities predicts well-being among heterosexual offspring of lesbian or gay parents. *Sexuality Research and Social Policy, 9,* 99–112.

Light, H. K., & Martin, R. E. (1996). American Indian families. *Journal of American Indian Education, 26,* 1–5.

Lino, M. (2011). *Expenditures on children by families, 2010.* (U.S. Department of Agriculture, Center for Nutrition Policy and Promotion. Miscellaneous Publication No. 1528–2010). Washington, DC: U.S. Government Printing Office.

Lipman, E. L., Boyle, M. H., Dooley, M. D., & Offord, D. R. (2002). Child well-being in single-mother families. *Journal of the American Academy of Child & Adolescent Psychiatry, 41,* 75–82.

Lister, K., & Harnish, T. (2011, June). *The state of telework in the US: How individuals, business, and government benefit.* San Diego, CA: Telework Research Network.

Little, L. (2010, October 28). *How stay-at-home dads bounce back from career hiatus.* Retrieved April 29, 2013 from http://article.wn.com/view/2010/10/28/How_StayatHome_Dads_Bounce_Back_From_Career_Hiatus/

Liu, G. (1999). Social security and the treatment of marriage: Spousal benefits, earnings sharing, and the challenge of reform. *Wisconsin Law Review, 1,* 61.

Loeb, S., Fuller, B., Kagan, S. L., & Carrol, B. (2004). Child care in poor communities: Early learning effects by type, quality, and stability. *Child Development, 75,* 47–65.

Logan, T., Walker, R., Horvath, L., & Leukefeld, C. (2003). Divorce, custody, and spousal violence: A random sample of docket records in a circuit court. *Journal of Family Violence, 18,* 269–279.

Logsdon, M. C., McBride, A. B., & Birkimer, J. C. (1994). Social support and postpartum depression. *Research in Nursing & Health, 17,* 449–457.

Loury, L. D. (2006). All in the extended family: Effects of grandparents, aunts, and uncles on educational attainment. *American Economic Review, 96,* 275–278.

Loury, L. D. (2008). *All in the extended family: Grandparents and college attendance (Working Paper).* Medford, MA: Department of Economics, Tufts University.

Lum, D. (1986). *Social work practice and people of color: A process-stage approach.* Monterey, CA: Brooks/Cole.

Lussier, G., Deater-Deckard, K., Dunn, J., & Davies, L. (2002). Support across two generations: Children's closeness to grandparents following parental divorce and remarriage. *Journal of Family Psychology, 16,* 363–376.

Lycett, E., Daniels, K., Curson, R., & Golombok, S. (2005). School-age children conceived by donor insemination: A study of parents' disclosure patterns. *Human Reproduction, 20,* 810–819.

Lynch, J. M., & Murray, K. (2000). For the love of the children: The coming out process for lesbian and gay parents and stepparents. *Journal of Homosexuality, 39,* 1–24.

Lyubomirsky, S., & Boehm, J. K. (2010). Human motives, happiness, and the puzzle of parenthood. *Perspectives on Psychological Science, 5,* 327–334.

Lyubomirsky, S., King, L., & Diener, E. (2005). The benefits of frequent positive affect: Does happiness lead to success? *Psychological Bulletin, 131,* 803–855.

Macaluso, M., Wright-Schnapp, T. J., Chandra, A., Johnson, R., Satterwhite, C. L., Pulver, A., et al. (2010). A public health focus on infertility prevention, detection and management. *Fertility and Sterility, 93,* 16.e1–16.e10.

MacCallum, F., & Golombok, S. (2004). Children raised in fatherless families from infancy: A follow-up of children of lesbian and single heterosexual mothers at early adolescence. *Journal of Child Psychology and Psychiatry, 45,* 1407–1419.

MacCallum, F., Lycett, E., Murray, C., Jadva, V., & Golombok, S. (2003). Surrogacy: The experience of commissioning couples. *Human Reproduction, 18,* 1334–1342.

Maccoby, E. E., & Mnookin, R. H. (1992). *Dividing the child: Social and legal dilemmas of custody.* Cambridge, MA: Harvard University Press.

MacDonald, K., & Parke, R. D. (1986). Parent–child physical play: The effects of sex and age of children and parents. *Sex Roles, 78,* 367–379.

Machamer, A. M., & Gruber, E. (1998). Secondary school, family, and educational risk: Comparing American Indian adolescents and their peers. *Journal of Educational Research, 91,* 357–369.

Mahoney, A., Pargament, K. I., Tarakeshwar, N., & Swank, A. B. (2001). Religion in the home in the 1980s and 90s: A meta-analytic review and conceptual analyses of links between religion, marriage and parenting. *Journal of Family Psychology, 15,* 559–596.

Mahoney, J. L., Parente, M. E., & Lord, H. (2007). After-school program engagement: Developmental consequences and links to program quality and content. *The Elementary School Journal, 107,* 385–404.

Mahoney, J. L., Vandell, D. L., Simpkins, S., & Zarrett, N. (2009). Adolescent out-of-school activities. In R. M. Lerner & L. Steinberg (Eds.), *Handbook of adolescent psychology* (3rd ed.). New York: Wiley.

Main, M., & Weston, D. (1981). The quality of the toddler's relationship to mother and father: Related to conflict behavior and readiness to establish new relationships. *Child Development, 52*, 932–940.

Mallon, G. P. (2004). *Gay men choosing parenthood.* New York: Columbia University Press.

Manchester, C., Leslie, L., & Park, T.-Y. (2008). *Screening for commitment: The effect of maternity leave usage on wages* (Technical Report). Minneapolis, MD: University of Minnesota.

Mandara, J., & Murray, C. B. (2002). Development of an empirical typology of African American family functioning. *Journal of Family Psychology, 16*, 318–337.

Manning, W., & Lamb, K. A. (2003). Adolescent well-being in cohabiting, married, and single-parent families. *Journal of Marriage and Family, 65*, 876–893.

Manning, W. D. (2002). The implications of cohabitation for children's well-being. In A. Booth & A. C. Crouter (Eds.), *Just living together: Implications for children, families, and public policy* (pp. 121–152). Mahwah, NJ: Lawrence Erlbaum.

Manning, W. D., & Brown, S. L. (2006). Children's economic well-being in marriage and cohabiting parent families. *Journal of Marriage and Family, 68*, 345–362.

Manning, W. D., & Brown, S. L. (2012). Cohabitation and parenting. In N. J. Cabrera & C. S. LeMonda (Eds.), *Handbook of father involvement: Multidisciplinary perspectives* (2nd ed., pp. 281–296). New York: Psychology Press.

Manning, W. D., Brown, S. L., & Stykes, J. K. (2012). *Father involvement in cohabiting and married families.* Paper presented at the annual meeting of the American Sociological Association, Denver, CO.

Manning, W. D., & Cohen, J. A. (2012). Premarital cohabitation and marital dissolution: An examination of recent marriages. *Journal of Marriage and Family, 74*, 377–387.

Margolis, D., & Entin, D. (2011). *Report on survey of co-housing communities 2011 cohousing association of America.* Retrieved April 29, 2013 from http://www.google.com/url

Marks, N. F., & McLanahan, S. S. (1993). Gender, family structure and social support among parents. *Journal of Marriage and Family, 55*, 481–493.

Marquardt, E. ( 2011). *One parent or five: A global look at today's new intentional families.* New York: Institute for American Values.

Marquardt, E., Norval D., Glenn, N. D., & Clark, K. (2010). *My daddy's name is donor: A new study of young adults conceived through sperm donation. Commission on Parenthood's Future.* New York: Institute for American Values.

Martin, A., Ryan, R. M., & Brooks-Gunn, J. (2007). The joint influence of mother and father parenting on child cognitive outcomes at age 5. *Early Childhood Research Quarterly, 22*, 423–439.

Martini, M., & Kirkpatrick, J. (1992). Parenting in polynesia: A view from the Marquesas Islands. In J. L. Roopnarine & D. B. Carter (Eds.), *Parent–child socialization in diverse cultures: Vol. 5. Annual advances in applied developmental psychology* (pp. 199–222). Norwood, NJ: Ablex.

Mastekaasa, A. (1994). Marital status, distress, and well-being: An international comparison. *Journal of Comparative Family Studies, 25*, 183–205.

Mather, M. (2010, May). *U.S. children in single-mother families.* Washington, DC: Population Reference Bureau.

Mavoa, H., Park, J., & Pryce, C. (1997). Social interaction in Tongan and European families in New Zealand: Implications for health care. *Pacific Health Dialog, 4*, 33–37.

Mayes, L. C., & Leckman, J. F. (2007). Parental representations and subclinical changes in postpartum mood. *Infant Mental Health Journal, 28*, 281–295.

Mazzucato, V., & Schans, D. (2011). Transnational families and the well-being of children: Conceptual and methodological challenges. *Journal of Marriage and Family, 73,*704–712.

McAdams, D., Hart, H., & Maruna, S. (1998). The anatomy of generativity. In D. McAdams & E. St. Aubin (Eds.), *Generativity and adult development. How and why we care for the next generation.* Washington, DC: American Psychological Association.

McBurney, D. H., Simon J., Gaulin, S. J. C., & Geliebter, A. (2002). Matrilateral biases in the investment of aunts and uncles replication in a population presumed to have high paternity certainty. *Human Nature, 13,* 391–402.

McCamant, K., & Durrett, C. (1994). *Cohousing: A contemporary approach to housing ourselves* (2nd ed.). Berkeley, CA: Ten Speed Press.

McCamant, K., & Durrett, C. (2011). *Creating cohousing: Building sustainable communities.* Gabriola Island, British Columbia, Canada: New Society Publishers.

McCloskey, W. (2010, May 21). *Adventures in (single male) parenting. New York Times.* Retrieved April 29, 2013 from http://parenting.blogs.nytimes.com/2010/05/21/single-dads-are-different/

McClure, R. (2010). *Top 12 trends in child care: As lifestyles change, so do child care offerings.* Retrieved April 29, 2013 from http://childcare.about.com/od/evaluations/tp/trends.htm

McGowen, M. R., Ladd, L., & Strom, R. D. (2006). On-line assessment of grandmother experience in raising grandchildren. *Educational Gerontology, 32,* 669–684.

McHale, J. P., & Lindahl, K. M. (Eds.) (2011). *Coparenting: A conceptual and clinical examination of family systems.* Washington, DC: American Psychological Association.

McKay, S. (2010). *The effects of twins and multiple births on families and their living standards.* Retrieved April 29, 2013 from http://www.tamba.org.uk/Document.Doc?id=268

McLanahan, S. (2004). Diverging destinies: How children fare under the second demographic transition. *Demography, 41,* 607–627.

McLanahan, S. (2011). Family instability and complexity after a nonmarital birth: Outcomes for children in fragile families. In M. J. Carlson & P. England (Eds.), *Social class and changing families in an unequal America.* Stanford, CA: Stanford University Press.

McLanahan, S., & Percheski, C. (2008). Family structure and the reproduction of inequalities. *Annual Review of Sociology, 34,* 257–276.

McLanahan, S., & Sandefur, G. (1994). *Growing up with a single parent: What hurts, what helps.* Cambridge, MA: Harvard University Press.

McLearn, K. T., Colasanto, D., & Schoen, C. (1998). *Mentoring makes a difference: Findings from the Commonwealth Fund 1998 survey of adults mentoring young people.* New York: The Commonwealth Fund.

McLoyd, V. C., Aikens, N., & Burton, L. (2006). Childhood poverty, policy, and practice. In W. Damon, R. Lerner, A. Renninger, & I. Sigel (Eds.), *Handbook of child psychology: Vol. 4. Child psychology in practice* (6th ed., pp. 700–775). Hoboken, NJ: Wiley.

McLoyd, V. C., Jayaratne, T. E., Ceballo, R., & Borquez, J. (1994). Unemployment and work interruption among African American single mothers: Effects on parenting and adolescent socioemotional functioning. *Child Development, 65,* 562–589.

McMahon C. A., & Gibson F. L. (2002). A special path to parenthood: Parent–child relationships in families giving birth to singleton infants through IVF. *Reproductive Biomedicine Online, 5,* 179–186.

McMahon, C. A., Ungerer, J. A., Beaurepaire, J. C., Tennant, C., & Saunders, D. (1995). Psychosocial outcomes for parents and children after in vitro fertilization: A review. *Journal of Reproductive and Infant Psychology, 13,* 1–16.

McMahon, T. J., & Luthar, S. S. (2007). Defining characteristics and potential consequences of caretaking burden among children living in urban poverty. *American Journal of Orthopsychiatry, 77,* 267–281.

McPheeters, A., Carmi, M., & Goldberg, A. E. (2008, August). *Gay men's experiences of sexism and heterosexism in the adoption process*. Poster presented at the American Psychological Association annual conference, Boston, MA.

McWright, L. (2002). African American grandmothers' and grandfathers' influence in the value socialization of grandchildren. In H. P. McAdoo (Ed.), *Black children: Social, educational, and parental environments* (2nd ed., pp. 27–44). Thousand Oaks, CA: Sage.

Meehan, C. L. (2005). The effects of residential locality on parental and alloparental investment among the Aka foragers of the Central African Republic. *Human Nature, 16*, 58–80.

Mendes, H. A. (1976). Single fathers. *The Family Coordinator, 25*, 439–444.

Mentor. (2006). *Mentoring in America 2005: A snapshot of the current state of mentoring*. Retrieved April 29, 2013 from http://www.mentoring.org/downloads/mentoring_333.pdf

Michalos, A. C. (1985). Multiple discrepancies theory (MDT). *Social Indicators Research, 16*, 347–413.

Michalos, A. C. (1991). *Global report on student well-being: Life satisfaction and happiness*. New York: Springer.

Milardo, R. (2010). *The forgotten kin: Aunts and uncles*. New York: Cambridge University Press.

Milkie, M. A., Kendig, S. M., Nomaguchi, K. M., & Denny, K. E. (2010). Time with children, children's well-being, and work-family balance among employed parents. *Journal of Marriage and Family, 72*, 1329–1343.

Miller-Cribbs, J. E., & Farber, N. B. (2008). Kin networks and poverty among African Americans: Past and present. *Social Work, 53*, 43–51.

Mintz, S., & Kellogg, S. (1988). *Domestic revolutions: A social history of American family life*. New York: Free Press.

Minuchin, P. (1985). Families and individual development: Provocations from the field of family therapy. *Child Development, 56*, 289–302.

Minuchin, P. (2002). Looking toward the horizon: Present and future in the study of family systems. In J. P. McHale & W. S. Grolnick (Eds.), *Retrospect and prospect in the psychological study of families* (pp. 259–278). Mahwah, NJ: Erlbaum.

Moen, P., Kelly, E., & Chermack, K. (2009). Learning from a natural experiment: Studying a corporate work-time policy initiative. In A. C. Crouter & A. Booth (Eds.), *Work-life policies* (pp. 97–132). Washington, DC: Urban Institute Press.

Moen, P., Kelly, E., & Hill, R. (2011). Does enhancing work-time control and flexibility reduce turnover ? A naturally occurring experiment. *Social Problems, 58*, 69–98.

Moffitt, T. (2002). Teen-aged mothers in contemporary Britain. *Journal of Child Psychology and Psychiatry, 43*, 727–742.

Monk-Turner, E., Heiserman, M., Johnson, C., Cotton, V., & Jackson, M. (2010). The portrayal of racial minorities on prime time television: A replication of the Mastro and Greenberg Study a decade later. *Studies in Popular Culture, 32*, 101–114.

Montgomery, T. R., Aiello, F., Adelman, R. D., Wasylyshyn, N., Andrews, M. C., Brazelton, T. B., et al. (1999). The psychological status at school age of children conceived by in vitro fertilization. *Human Reproduction, 14*, 2162–2165.

Moore, M. R. (2011). *Invisible families*. Berkeley, CA: University of California Press.

Moore, M. R., & Brooks-Gunn, J. (2002). Adolescent parenthood. In M. Bornstein (Ed.), *Handbook of parenting: Vol. 3. Being and becoming a parent* (2nd ed., pp. 173–214). Mahwah, NJ: Erlbaum.

Morin, R. (2011, February 16). *The public renders a split verdict on changes in family structure*. Pew Research Center. Retrieved April 29, 2013 from http://pewsocialtrends. org/2011/02/16/the-public-renders-a-split-verdict-on-changes-in-family- structure/1

Morris, J. F., Balsam, K. F., & Rothblum, E. D. (2002). Lesbian and bisexual mothers and non-mothers: Demographics and the coming out process. *Journal of Family Psychology, 16*, 144–156.

Morris, P., Duncan, G. J., & Clark-Kauffman, E. (2005). Child well-being in an era of welfare reform: The sensitivity of transitions in development to policy change. *Developmental Psychology, 41*, 919–932.

Morrison, D. R., & Coiro, M. J. (1999). Parental conflict and marital disruption: Do children benefit when high-conflict marriages are dissolved? *Journal of Marriage and Family, 61*, 626–637.

Morton, H. (1996). *Becoming Tongan: An ethnography of childhood.* Honolulu, HI: University of Hawaii Press.

Moss, P. (Ed.). (2010). *International review of leave policies and related research 2010. Employment relations research series 115.* London: BIS Department for Business Innovation & Skills.

Moss, P., & O'Brien, M. (2006). *International review of leave policies and related research* (Employment Relations Research Series No. 57). London: Department of Trade and Industry. Retrieved April 29, 2013 from http://www.berr.gov.uk/files/file31948.pdf

Mounts, N. S. (2002). Parental management of adolescent peer relationships in context: The role of parenting style. *Journal of Family Psychology, 16*, 58–69.

Moura-Ramos, M., Gameiro, S., Soares, I., Santos, T. A., & Canavarro, M. C. (2010). Psychosocial adjustment in infertility: A comparison study of infertile couples, couples undergoing assisted reproductive technologies and presumed fertile couples. *Psicologia Saúde & Doenças, 11*(2), 297–318.

de Mouzon, J., Goossens, V., Bhattacharya, S., Castilla, J. A., Ferraretti, A. P., Korsak, V., et al. (2010). Assisted reproductive technology in Europe, 2006: Results generated from European registers by ESHRE. *Human Reproduction, 25*, 1851–1862.

Moynihan, D. (1965). *The negro family: The case for national action.* Washington, DC: U.S. Department of Labor.

Mroz, J. (2011, September 6). One sperm donor, 150 offspring. *New York Times.*

Muller, M. N., Marlowe, F. W., Bugumba, R., & Ellison, P. T. (2009). Testosterone and paternal care in East African foragers and pastoralists. *Proceedings of Biological Sciences, 276*, 347–354.

Mundy, L. (2007). *Everything conceivable: How assisted reproduction is changing our world.* New York: Knopf.

Murphy, M. J., & Grundy, E. (2003). Mothers with living children and children with living mothers: The role of fertility and mortality in the period 1911–2050. *Population Trends, 112*, 36–44.

Murray, S. B. (1998). Child care work: Intimacy in the shadows of family-life. *Qualitative Sociology, 21*, 149–168.

Murray, T. H. (1996). *The worth of a child.* Berkeley, CA: University of California.

Musil, C., & Ahmad, M. (2002). Health of grandmothers: A comparison by caregiver status. *Journal of Aging and Health, 14*, 96–121.

Myrskylä, M., & Margolis, R. (2012, November). *Happiness: Before and after the kids.* (Max Planck Institute for Demographic Research Working Paper 2012–013 Rostock, Germany.) Retrieved April 29, 2013 from http://www.demogr.mpg.de/papers/working/wp-2012-013.pdf

Nadel, C. (2007). *Mommy, was your tummy big?* Arlington, VA: Mookind Press.

National Alliance for Caregiving. (2005). *Young caregivers in the U.S.* Retrieved April 29, 2013 from http://www.caregiving.org/data/youngcaregivers.pdf

National Association of Child Care Resource and Referral Agencies. (2012). *Child care in America: 2012 state fact sheets.* Arlington, VA: NACCRRA.

National Council of State Legislators. (2012). *State laws related to insurance coverage for infertility treatment.* Washington, DC: National Council of State Legislators.

Nelson, M. K. (1990). Mothering others' children: The experiences of family day-care providers. *Signs, 15*, 586–605.

Nelson, S. K., Kushlev, K., English, T., Dunn, E. W., & Lyubomirsky, S. (2012). In defense of parenthood: Children are associated with more joy than misery. *Psychological Science Online First*. Retrieved April 29, 2013 from http://pss.sagepub.com/content/early/2012/11/30/0956797612447798.full.pdf+html

New, R., & Benigini, L. (1987). Italian fathers and infants: Cultural constraints on paternal behavior. In M. E. Lamb (Ed.), *The father's role: Cross-cultural perspectives*. Hillsdale, NJ: Lawrence Erlbaum.

Newman, K. S. (2012). *The accordion family*. New York: Beacon Press.

NICHD Early Child Care Research Network. (1997). The effects of infant child care on infant-mother attachment security: Results of the NICHD Study of Early Child Care. *Child Development, 68*, 860–879.

NICHD Early Child Care Research Network. (2005). *Child care and child development: Results from the NICHD study of early child care and youth development*. New York: Guilford Press.

Nichols, R. (1998). *Indians in the United States and Canada: A comparative history*. Lincoln, NE: University of Nebraska Press.

NIH NEWS. (2012, March 16). *NIH brain imaging study finds evidence of basis for caregiving impulse*. Washington, DC: NIH.

Nixon, E., Greene, S., & Hogan, D. M. (2012). Negotiating relationships in single-mother households: Perspectives of children and mothers. *Family Relations, 61*, 142–156.

Noah, L. (2003). Assisted reproductive technologies and the pitfalls of unregulated biomedical Innovation. *Florida Law Review*, Vol. 55, April.

Nobles, J. (2011). Parenting from abroad: Migration, nonresident father involvement, and children's education in Mexico. *Journal of Marriage and Family, 73*, 729–746.

Nomaguchi, K. M., & Milkie, M. A. (2003). Costs and rewards of children: The effects of becoming a parent on adults' lives. *Journal of Marriage and Family, 65*, 356–374.

Notaro, P. C., & Volling, B. L. (1999). Parental responsiveness and infant-parent attachment: A replication study with fathers and mothers. *Infant Behaviour and Development, 22*, 345–352.

Nsamenang, A. B. (2004). *Cultures of human development and education: Challenge to growing up African*. New York: Nova Science Publishers.

NSD. (2002). *Spørreundersøkelse om familie og kjønnsroller [ISSP survey on family and gender roles]*. Retrieved April 29, 2013 from http://tinyurl.com/ydadt4h

Nyboe Andersen, A., Gianaroli L., Nygren KG. 2004 Assisted reproductive technology in Europe, 2000. Results generated from European registers by ESHRE. *Human Reproduction, 19*, 490–503.

Nyboe Andersen, A., Goossens, V., Ferraretti, A. P., Bhattacharya, S., Felberbaum, R., de Mouzon, J., K.G. Nygren, The European IVF-monitoring (EIM) Consortium, for the European Society of Human Reproduction and Embryology (ESHRE). (2008). Assisted reproductive technology in Europe, 2004: Results generated from European registers by ESHRE. *Human Reproduction, 23*, 756–771.

Oberlander, S. E., Black, M. M., & Starr, R. H., Jr. (2007). African American adolescent mothers and grandmothers: A multigenerational approach to parenting. *American Journal of Community Psychology, 39*, 37–46.

OECD Family Database. (2008). *Public spending on childcare and early education*. Retrieved April 29, 2013 from http://www.oecd.org/dataoecd/45/27/37864512.pdf

Ogilvie, M. (2009, November 22). *The search for a sperm-donor father*. Toronto, Ontario, Canada: Toronto Star.

Olsen, L., & Chen, M. T. (1988). *Crossing the schoolhouse border: Immigrant students and the California public schools*. San Francisco: California Tomorrow Policy Research Report.

Ooms, T. (1990, March 16). *Implementation of P.L. 99–457: Parent/professional partnership in early intervention. Background briefing report and meeting highlights*. Washington, DC: American Association for Marriage and Family Therapy.

Orellana, M. F. (2001). The work kids do: Mexican and Central American children's contributions to households and schools in California. *Harvard Educational Review, 71*, 366–389.

Orellana, M. F., Dorner, L., & Pulido, L. (2003). Accessing assets: Immigrant youth's work as family translators or "para-phrasers." *Social Problems, 50*, 505–524.

Osborne, C., & McLanahan, S. (2007). Partnership instability and child well-being. *Journal of Marriage and Family, 69*, 1065–1083.

Owen, L., & Golombok, S. (2009). Families created by assisted reproduction: Parent–child relationships in late adolescence. *Journal of Adolescence, 32*, 835–848.

Padilla, A. M., & Borrero, N. (2006). Effects of acculturative stress on the Hispanic family. In P. T. P. Wong & L. C. J. Wong (Eds.), *Handbook of multicultural perspectives on stress and coping.* New York: Kluwer Academic Press.

Paquette, D. (2004). Theorizing the father-child relationship: Mechanisms and developmental outcomes. *Human Development, 47*, 193–219.

Pargament, K. I. (1997). *The psychology of religion and coping: Theory, research, practice.* New York: Guilford.

Park, N., & Peterson, C. (2006). Character strengths and happiness among young children: Content analysis of parental descriptions. *Journal of Happiness, 7*, 323–341.

Parke, R. D. (1981). *Fathers.* Cambridge, MA: Harvard University Press.

Parke, R. D. (1988). Families in life-span perspective: A multi-level developmental approach. In E. M. Hetherington, R. M. Lerner, & M. Perlmutter (Eds.), *Child development in life span perspective* (pp. 159–190). Hillsdale NJ: Erlbaum.

Parke, R. D. (1996). *Fatherhood.* Cambridge, MA: Harvard University Press.

Parke, R. D. (2002a). Fathers and families. In M. Bornstein (Ed.), *Handbook of parenting* (2nd ed., Vol. 3, pp. 27–73). Mahwah, NJ: Erlbaum.

Parke, R. D. (2002b). Parenting in the new millennium: Prospects, promises, and pitfalls. In J. P. McHale & W. S. Grolnick (Eds.), *Retrospect and prospect in the psychological study of families* (pp. 65–93). Mahwah, NJ: Erlbaum.

Parke, R. D. (2004). The Society for Research in Child Development at 70: Progress and promise. *Child Development, 75*, 1–24.

Parke, R. D. (2013). Gender differences and similarities in parenting. In K. K. Kline & W. B. Wilcox (Eds.), *Gender and parenthood: Natural and social scientific perspectives.* New York: Columbia University Press.

Parke, R. D., & Brott, A. (1999). *Throwaway dads.* Boston: Houghton-Mifflin.

Parke, R. D., & Buriel, R. (2006). Socialization in the family: Ethnic and ecological perspectives. In W. Damon & R. M. Lerner (Series Eds.) & N. Eisenberg (Vol. Ed.), *Handbook of child psychology* (6th ed., Vol. 3, pp. 429–504). Hoboken, NJ: Wiley.

Parke, R. D., & Clarke-Stewart, K. A. (2003). Effects of parental incarceration on children: Perspectives, promises and polices. In J. Travis & M. Waul (Eds.), *Prisoners once removed.* Washington, DC: Urban Institute Press.

Parke, R. D., Coltrane, S., Borthwick-Duffy, S., Powers, J., Adams, M., Fabricius, W., et al. (2003). Assessing father involvement in Mexican-American families. In R. Day & M. E. Lamb (Eds.), *Conceptualizing and measuring paternal involvement* (pp. 17–38). Mahwah, NJ: Erlbaum.

Parke, R. D., Coltrane, S., & Schofield, T. (2010). The bicultural advantage. In J. Marsh, R. Mendoza-Denton, & J. A. Smith (Eds.), *Are we racist? New insights from neuroscience and positive psychology.* Boston: Beacon Press.

Parke, R. D., Coltrane, S., Duffy, S., Buriel, R., Dennis, J., Powers, J., et al. (2004). Economic stress, parenting and child adjustment in Mexican American and European American families. *Child Development, 75*, 1632–1656.

Parke, R. D., Gailey C., Coltrane, S., & DiMatteo, R. (2012). The pursuit of perfection: Transforming our construction of parenthood and family in the age of new reproductive technologies. In P. Essed & D. T. Goldberg (Eds.), *Clones, fakes and posthumans: Cultures of replication*. Amsterdam: Rodopi.

Parke, R. D., Kim, M., Flyr, M., McDowell, D. J., Simpkins, D. S., Killian, C. M., et al. (2001). Managing marital conflict: Links with children's peer relationships. In J. Grych & F. Fincham (Eds.), *Child development and interparental conflict*. New York: Cambridge University Press.

Parke, R. D., & O'Leary, S. (1976). Family interaction in the newborn period: Some findings, some observations, and some unresolved issues. In K. Riegel & J. Meacham (Eds.), *The developing individual in a changing world: Social and environmental issues* (pp. 653–663). The Hague: Mouton.

Parke, R. D., & Sawin, D. B. (1980). The family in early infancy: Social, interactional, and attitudinal analyses. In F. A. Pedersen (Ed.), *The father-infant relationship: Observational studies in a family context* (pp. 44–70). New York: Praeger.

Parker, K. (2009, October 1). *The harried life of the working mother*. Washington, DC: Pew Research Center.

Parker, K. (2012, April). *Women, work and motherhood: A sampler of recent Pew research survey findings*. Washington, DC: Pew Research Center.

Parker-Pope, T. (2009, May 12). How hospitals treat same-sex couples. *New York Times*. Retrieved April 29, 2013 from http://well.blogs.nytimes.com/2009/05/12/how-hospitals-treat-same-sex-couples/

Parrenas, R. S. (2005). *Children of global migration: Transnational families and gendered woes*. Stanford, CA: Stanford University Press.

Pashos, A. (2000). Does paternity uncertainty explain discriminative grandparental solicitude? A cross-cultural study in Greece and Germany. *Evolution and Human Behavior, 21*, 97–109.

Patillo-McCoy, M. (1998). Sweet mothers and gangbangers: Managing crime in a Black middle-class neighborhood. *Social Forces, 76*, 747–774.

Patterson, C. J. (1995). Gay and lesbian parents. In M. Bornstein (Ed.), *Handbook of parenting* (Vol. 3, pp. 255–274). Mahwah, NJ: Erlbaum.

Patterson, C. J. (2006). Children of lesbian and gay parents. *Current Directions in Psychological Science, 15*, 241–244.

Patterson, C. J. (2007). Lesbian and gay family issues in the context of changing legal and social policy environments. In K. J. Bieschke, R. M. Perez, & K. A. DeBord (Eds.), *Handbook of counseling and psychotherapy with lesbian, gay, bisexual and transgender clients* (2nd ed.). Washington, DC: American Psychological Association.

Patterson, C. J. (2009). Lesbian and gay parents and their children: A social science perspective. In D. A. Hope (Ed.), *Contemporary perspectives on lesbian, gay and bisexual identities: Vol. 54. The Nebraska symposium on motivation* (pp. 141–182). New York: Springer.

Patterson, C. J., & Farr, R. H. (2011). Coparenting among lesbian and gay couples. In J. P. McHale & K. M. Lindahl (Eds.), *Coparenting: A conceptual and clinical examination of family systems*. Washington, DC: American Psychological Association.

Patterson, C. J., Hurt, S., & Mason, C. D. (1998). Families of the lesbian baby boom: Children's contacts with grandparents and other adults. *American Journal of Orthopsychiatry, 68*, 390–399.

Patterson, C. J., & Riskind, R. G. (2010). To be a parent: Issues in family formation among gay and lesbian adults. *Journal of GLBT Family Studies, 6*, 326–340.

Patterson, C. J., Sutfin, E. L., & Fulcher, M. (2004). Division of labor among lesbian and heterosexual parenting couples: Correlates of specialized versus shared patterns. *Journal of Adult Development, 11*, 179–189.

Paulson, R. J., & Sachs, J. (1999). *Rewinding your biological clock: Motherhood late in life: Options, issues, and emotions*. San Francisco: Freeman.

Pearson, J. L., Hunter A. G., Ensminger, M. E., & Kellam, S. G. (1990). Black grandmothers in multigenerational households: Diversity in family structure and parenting involvement in the Woodlawn community. *Child Development, 61,* 434–442.

Peisner-Feinberg, E. S., Burchinal, M. R., Clifford, R. M., Culkin, M. L., Howes, C., Kagan, S. L., et al. (2001). The relation of preschool child-care quality to children's cognitive and social developmental trajectories through second grade. *Child Development, 72,* 1534–1553.

Pellet, S. P. (2006). *The kangaroo pouch: A story about gestational surrogacy for young children.* Bloomington, IN: Trafford Publishing.

Pena, J., Wyman, P. A., Hendricks Brown, C., Matthieu, M. M., Olivares, T. E., Hartel, D., et al. (2008). Immigration generation status and its association with suicide attempts, substance use, and depressive symptoms among Latino adolescents in the USA. *Prevention Science, 9,* 299–310.

Pennings, G., de Wert, G., Shenfield, F., Cohen, J., Tarlatzis, B., & Devroey, P. (2008). ESHRE task force on ethics and law 15: Cross-border reproductive care. *Human Reproduction, 23,* 2182–2184.

Perreira, K. M., & Ornelas, I. J. (2011). The physical and psychological well-being of immigrant children. *The Future of Children, 21,* 195–218.

Perry-Jenkins, M., Repetti, R., & Crouter, A. C. (2000). Work and family in the 1990s. *Journal of Marriage and Family, 62,* 981–998.

Peterson, J. L., & Zill, N. (1986). Marital disruption, parent–child relationships, and behavioral problems in children. *Journal of Marriage and Family, 48,* 295–307.

Pew Charitable Trust. (2011, November 18). *The decline of marriage and rise of new families.* Washington, DC: Pew Research Social & Demographic Trends Project.

Pew Research Center. (2010). *Since the start of the Great Recession, more children raised by grandparents.* Washington, DC: Pew Research Center.

Pew Research Center. (2011). *Most say homosexuality should be accepted by society.* Washington, DC: Pew Research Center

Philip, K., & Hendry, L. B. (2000). Making sense of mentoring or mentoring making sense? Reflections on the mentoring process by adult mentors with young people. *Journal of Community and Applied Psychology, 10,* 211–223.

Phillips, D. A., Voran, M., Kister, E., Howes, C., & Whitebook, M. (1994). Child care for children in poverty: Opportunity or inequity. *Child Development, 65,* 472–492.

Phillips, K. R. (2004, April). Getting time off: Access to leave among working parents. *Urban Institute, 2.*

Phinney, J. S., Ong, A., & Madden, T. (2000). Cultural values and intergenerational value discrepancies in immigrant and non-immigrant families. *Child Development, 71,* 528–539.

Pinderhughes, E. E., & Harden, B. J. (2005). Beyond the birth family: African American children reared by alternate caregivers. In V. C. McLoyd, N. E. Hill, & K. A. Dodge (Eds.), *African American family life: Ecological and cultural diversity* (pp. 285–310). New York: Guilford Press.

Plattner, S., & Minturn, L. (1975). A comparative and longitudinal study of the behavior of communally-raised children. *Ethos, 3,* 469–480.

Pleck, J. H. (2010). A revised conceptualization of paternal involvement. In M. E. Lamb (Ed.), *The role of the father in child development* (5th ed.). Hoboken, NJ: Wiley.

Pollack, E. G. (2002). The childhood we have lost: When siblings were caregivers, 1900–1970. *Journal of Social History, 36,* 31–61.

Pollard, S. L. (2011). *Native Americans: What we want others to know about us.* Retrieved April 29, 2013 from http://www.empowermentzone.com/ind_know.txt

Pollet, T. V., Nelissen, M., & Nettle, D. (2009). Lineage based differences in grandparental investment: Evidence from a large British cohort study. *Journal of Biosocial Science, 41,* 355–379.

Popenoe, D. (1996). *Life without father: Compelling new evidence that fatherhood and marriage are indispensable for the good of children and society*. New York: The Free Press.

Portes, A., & Rivas, A. (2011). The adaptation of migrant children. *The Future of Children, 21*, 219–246.

Portes, A., & Rumbaut, R. G. (2006). *Immigrant America* (3rd ed.). Berkeley, CA: University of California Press.

Powell, B., Bolzendahl, C., Geist, C., & Steelman, L. C. (2010). *Counted out: Same-sex relations and American's definitions of family*. New York: Russell Sage Foundation.

Power, M. B., Eheart, B. K., Racine, D., & Karnik, N. S. (2007). Aging well in an intentional intergenerational community: Meaningful relationships and purposeful engagement. *Journal of Intergenerational Relationships: Programs, Policy and Research, 5*, 7–25.

Power, T. G., & Parke, R. D. (1982). Play as a context for early learning: Lab and home analyses. In I. E. Sigel & L. M. Laosa (Eds.), *The family as a learning environment*. New York: Plenum.

Presser, H. B. (2003). *Working in a 24/7 economy: Challenges for American families*. New York: Russell Sage Foundation.

Princeton Review. (2012). *Career: Child care worker*. Princeton, NJ: TPR Education, LLC.

Productivity Commission. (April, 2012). *Affordable housing: A focus on Māori issues*. Auckland, New Zealand: New Zealand Government.

Pruettt, K. (1987). *The nurturing father*. New York: Warner Books.

Pruett, K. D. (2000). *Fatherneed: Why father care is essential as mother care for your child*. New York: Free Press.

Pryor, J. (Ed.) (2008). *The international handbook of stepfamilies: Policy and practice in legal, research, and clinical environments*. Hoboken, NJ: Wiley.

Putnam, R. D. (2000). *Bowling alone: The collapse and revival of American community*. New York: Simon & Schuster.

Pyke, K. (2005). Generational deserters and "black sheep": Acculturative differences among siblings in Asian immigrant families. *Journal of Family Issues, 26*, 491–517.

Rabain-Jamin, J., Maynard, A. E., & Greenfield, P. (2003). Implications of sibling caregiving for sibling relations and teaching interactions in two cultures. *Ethos, 31*, 204–231.

Radin, N. (1982). Primary caregiving and role sharing fathers. In M. E. Lamb (Ed.), *Non-traditional families: Parenting and child development* (pp. 173–204). Hillsdale, NJ: Erlbaum.

Radin, N. (1994). Primary caregiving fathers in intact families. In A. E. Gottfried & A. W. Gottfried (Eds.), *Redefining families* (pp. 11–54). New York: Plenum Press.

Rafferty, A. (2011, February 25). Donor-conceived and out of the closet. *Newsweek*. Retrieved April 29, 2013 from http://www.thedailybeast.com/newsweek/2011/02/25/donor-conceived-and-out-of-the-closet.html

Raising Children Network. (2011). *Raising twins and multiples*. Retrieved April 29, 2013 from http://raisingchildren.net.au/articles/raising_multiples.html

Ramaswamy, V., Bhavnagri, N., & Barton, E. (2008). Social support and parenting behaviors influence grandchildren's social competence. In B. Hayslip Jr. & P. Kaminski (Eds.), *Parenting the custodial grandchild: Implications for clinical practice* (pp. 165–178). New York: Springer.

Rampell, C. (2009, February 6). As layoffs surge, women may pass men in job force. *The New York Times*, A1.

Rand, C., Graham, D. L. R., & Rawlings, E. I. (1982). Psychological health and factors the court seeks to control in lesbian mother custody trials. *Journal of Homosexuality, 8*, 27–39.

Rankin, J. L. (2005). *Parenting experts: Their advice, their research & getting it right*. New York: Praeger.

Ray, R., Gornick, J. C., & Schmitt, J. (2010). Who cares? Assessing generosity and gender equality in parental leave policy designs in 21 countries. *Journal of European Social Policy, 20*, 196–216.

Ray, V., & Gregory, R. (2001). School experiences of the children of lesbian and gay parents. *Family Matters, 59*, 28–34.

Readings, J., Blake, L., Casey, P. Jadva, V., & Golombok, S. (2011). Secrecy, openness and everything in between: Decisions of parents of children conceived by donor insemination, egg donation and surrogacy. *Reproductive Biomedicine Online, 22*, 485–495.

Ricaud, H. (1998). "Influence de l'Implication Diférenciée du Couple Parental sur les Modalités de Resolution des Conflits Interpersonnels des Enfants de 3 à 5 Ans en Milieu Scolaire." Thèse de Doctorat Nouveau Régime. Université Toulouse II, France.

Reimers, C. (2006). Economic well-being Hispanics and the future of America. In M. Tienda & F. Mitchell (Eds.), *National Research Council (US) panel on Hispanics in the United States*. Washington, DC: National Academies Press.

Repetti, R. L. (1994). Short-term and long-term processes linking job stressors to father-child interaction. *Social Development, 3*, 1–15.

Repetti, R. L, & Wood, J. (1997). The effects of stress and work on mothers' interactions with preschoolers. *Journal of Family Psychology, 1*, 90–108.

Rhodes, J. E. (2002). *Stand by me: The risks and rewards of mentoring today's youth*. Cambridge, MA: Harvard University Press.

Rhodes, J. E, & DuBois, D. (2008). Mentoring relationships and programs for youth. *Current Directions in Psychological Science, 17*, 254–258.

Ricaud, H. (1998). "Influence de l'Implication Diférenciée du Couple Parental sur les Modalités de Resolution des Conflits Interpersonnels des Enfants de 3 à 5 Ans en Milieu Scolaire." Thèse de Doctorat Nouveau Régime. Université Toulouse II, France.

Rigby, E., Ryan, R. M., & Brooks-Gunn, J. (2007). Child care quality in various state policy contexts. *Journal of Policy Analysis and Management, 26*, 887–907.

Riley, D., & Cochran, M. (1987). Children's relationships with non-parental adults: Sex specific connections to early school success. *Sex Roles, 17*, 637–655.

Riskind, R. G., & Patterson, C. J. (2010). Parenting intentions and desires among lesbian, gay, and heterosexual individuals. *Journal of Family Psychology, 24*, 78–81.

Rivers, I., Poteat, V. P., & Noret, N. (2008). Victimization, social support, and psychosocial functioning among children of same-sex and opposite-sex couples in the United Kingdom. *Developmental Psychology, 44*, 127–134.

Rocereto, J. F., Forquer Gupta, S., & Mosca, J. B. (2011). The role of flextime appeal on family and work outcomes among active and non-active flextime users: A between groups and within groups analysis. *Journal of Business & Economics Research, 9*, 57–65.

Rochlen, A. B., Suizzo, M., McKelley, R. A., & Scaringi, V. (2008). I'm just providing for my family: A qualitative study of stay-at-home fathers. *Psychology of Men & Masculinity, 9*, 193–206.

Rochlen, A. R., McKelley, R. A., Suizzo, M., & Scaringi, V. (2008). Predictors of relationship satisfaction, psychological well-being, and life satisfaction among an internet sample of stay-at-home fathers. *Psychology of Men & Masculinity, 9*, 17–28.

Rochman, B. (2011, July 11). Unemployed men are more likely to divorce. *Time*.

Rodgers, A. Y., & Jones, R. L. (1999). Grandmothers who are caregivers: An overlooked population. *Child & Adolescent Social Work Journal, 16*, 455–467.

Rodgers, K. B., & Rose, H. A. (2002). Risk and resiliency factors among adolescents who experience marital transitions. *Journal of Marriage and Family, 64*, 1024–1037.

Rogaly, B., Coppard, D., Rafique, A., Rana, K., Sengupta, A., & Biswas, J. (2002). Seasonal migration and welfare/illfare in Eastern India: A social analysis. *Journal of Development Studies, 38*, 89–114.

Rogers, A. M., & Taylor, A. S. (1997). Intergenerational mentoring: A viable strategy for meeting the needs of vulnerable youth. *Journal of Gerontological Social Work, 28*, 125–140.

Rogoff, B. (2003). *The cultural nature of human development*. New York: Oxford University Press.

Ron-El, R., Lahat, E., Golan, A., Lerman, M., Bukovsky, I., & Herman, A. (1994). Development of children born after ovarian superovulation induced by long-acting gonadotropin-releasing hormone agonist and menotropins, and by in vitro fertilization. *Journal of Pediatrics, 125,* 734–737.

Roopnarine, J. (2004). African American and African Caribbean fathers: Level, quality, and meaning involvement. In M. E. Lamb (Ed.), *The role of the father in child development* (4th ed., pp. 58–97). Hoboken, NJ: Wiley.

Rose, M. (1999). *Explaining and forecasting job satisfaction: The contribution of occupational profiling.* Bath, UK: University of Bath.

Rosenblatt, J. (2002). Hormonal basis of parenting in mammals. In M. Bornstein (Ed.), *Handbook of parenting* (2nd ed., Vol. 2, pp. 3–25). Mahwah, NJ: Erlbaum.

Rosenfeld, M. J. (2010). Nontraditional families and childhood progress through school. *Demography, 47,* 755–775.

Ross, H., & Taylor, H. (1989). Do boys prefer daddy or his physical style of play? *Sex Roles, 20,* 23–33.

Ross, J. A., & Corcoran, J. (1996). *Joint custody with a jerk: Raising a child with an uncooperative ex, a hands on, practical guide to coping with custody issues that arise with an uncooperative ex-spouse.* New York: St. Martin's Griffin.

Rubin, B. M. (2007, March 4). The incredible, sellable egg: What was once a personal journey has become a booming business for donors and recruiters. *Chicago Tribune.*

Rubin, K. H., Bukowski, W. M., & Parker, J. G. (2006). Peer interactions, relationships, and groups. In W. Damon & R. M. Lerner (Series Eds.) & N. Eisenberg (Vol. Ed.), *Handbook of child psychology: Social, emotional, and personality development* (6th ed., Vol. 3, pp. 571–645). Hoboken, NJ: Wiley.

Rueschenberg, E. J., & Buriel, R. (1989). Mexican American family functioning and acculturation: A family systems perspective. *Hispanic Journal of Behavioral Sciences, 11,* 232–244.

Rumball, A., & Adair, V. (1999). Telling the story: Parents' scripts for donor offspring. *Human Reproduction, 14,* 1392–1399.

Russell, G. (1983). *The changing role of fathers.* St. Lucia, Australia: University of Queensland Press.

Russell, G., & Russell, A. (1987). Mother-child and father-child relationships in middle childhood. *Child Development, 158,* 1573–1585.

Rutter, M. (2006). *Genes and behavior.* Oxford, UK: Blackwell.

Ryan, M. (2010, May 26). Stay-at-home dads. *Woman's day.* Retrieved April 29, 2013 from http://womansday.ninemsn.com.au/lifestyle/family/995336/stay-at-home-dads

Ryan, R. M., Martin, A., & Brooks-Gunn, J. (2006). Is one good parent good enough? Patterns of mother and father parenting and child cognitive outcomes at 24 and 36 months. *Parenting: Science and Practice, 6,* 211–228.

Ryan, S. D., Pearlmutter, S., & Groza, V. (2004). Coming out of the closet: Opening agencies to gay and lesbian adoptive parents. *Social Work, 49,* 85–95.

Rynell, A. (2008, October). Causes of poverty: Findings from recent research. *Heartland Alliance Mid-America Institute on Poverty, 13.*

Sagi, A. (1982). Antecedents and consequences of various degrees of paternal involvement in childrearing: The Israeli project. In M. E. Lamb (Ed.), *Nontraditional families: Parenting and child development* (pp. 205–232). Hillsdale, NJ: Erlbaum.

Sagi, A., Koren, N., & Weinberg, M. (1987). Fathers role in Israel. In M. Lamb (Ed.), *The fathers's role: Cross-cultural perspectives* (pp. 197–226). Hillsdale, NJ: Lawrence Erlbaum.

Sagi, A., Van IJzendoorn, M. H., Aviezer, O., Donnell, F., & Mayseless. (1994). Sleeping out of home in a Kibbutz communal arrangement: It makes a difference for infant-mother attachment. *Child Development, 65,* 992–1004.

Sagi-Schwartz, A., & Aviezer, O. (2005). Correlates of attachment to multiple caregivers in Kibbutz children from birth to emerging adulthood: The Haifa longitudinal study.

In K. E. Grossmann, K. Grossmann, & E. Waters (Eds.), *Attachment from infancy to adulthood* (pp. 165–197). New York: Guilford.

Saltzstein, A. L., Ting, Y., & Saltzstein, G. H. (2001). Work-family balance and job satisfaction: The impact of family-friendly policies on attitudes of federal government employees. *Public Administration Review, 61*, 452–467.

Sandel, M. J. (2004). The case against perfection: What's wrong with designer children, bionic athletes, and genetic engineering. *The Atlantic Monthly, 293*(3), 51–62.

Sandler, I., Miles, J., Cookston, J. T., & Braver, S. L. (2008). Effects of father and mother parenting on children's mental health in high- and low-conflict divorces. *Family Court Review, 46*, 282–296.

Sandoz, M. (1961). *Crazy horse: The strange man of the Oglalas.* Lincoln, NE: University of Nebraska Press.

Sarche, M. C., & Whitesell, N. R. (2012). Child development research in North American native communities-looking back and moving forward: Introduction. *Child Development Perspectives, 6*, 42–48.

Sayer, L., England, P., Allison, P., & Kangas, N. (2011). She left, he left: How employment and satisfaction affect men's and women's decisions to leave marriages. *American Journal of Sociology, 116*, 1972–2018.

Scanzoni, J. (2000). Cohousing as family reform. In *Designing families: The search for self and community in the information age* (pp. 73–101). Thousand Oaks, CA: Sage Publications.

Scaramella, L. V., & Conger, R. D. (2003). Intergenerational continuity of hostile parenting and its consequences: The moderating influence of children's negative emotional reactivity. *Social Development, 12*, 420–439.

Schacher, J. S., Auerbach, C. F., & Silverstein, L. B. (2005). Gay fathers expanding the possibilities for us all. *Journal of GLBT Family Studies, 1*, 31–52.

Schaffer, H. R., & Emerson, P. E. (1964). The development of social attachments in infancy. *Monographs of the Society for Research in Child Development, 29*(3, Serial No. 94), 1–77.

Schaffer, P. (1988). *How babies & families are made (there is more than one way).* Berkeley, CA: Tabor Sarah.

Scheffel, J. (2011, June 16–18). *Identifying the effect of temporal work flexibility on parental time with children.* Presented at the annual conference of the European Society for Population Economics, Hangzhou, China.

Schieve, L. A., Rasmussen, S. A., & Reefhuis, J. (2005). Risk of birth defects among children conceived with assisted reproductive technology: Providing an epidemiologic context to the data. *Fertility and Sterility, 84*, 1320–1324.

Schmalzbauer, L. (2005). Searching for wages and mothering from afar: The case of Honduran transnational families. *Journal of Marriage and Family, 66*, 1317–1331.

Schoen, R., Kim, Y. J., Nathanson, C. A., Fields, J., & Astone, N. M. (1997). Why do Americans want children? *Population and Development Review, 23*, 333.

Schryer, M. (1994). *The relationship between centre size and child care workers' level of job satisfaction.* Master of Education thesis, National College of Education, National Louise University, Chicago.

Schulz, M. S., Cowan, P. A., Cowan, C. P., & Brennan, R. T. (2004). Coming home upset: Gender, marital satisfaction and the daily spillover of workday experience into couple interactions. *Journal of Family Psychology, 18*, 250–263.

Schulz, S. E. (1995). The benefits of mentoring. *New Directions for Adult and Continuing Education, 1995*, 57–67.

Sear, R., & Mace, R. (2008). Who keeps children alive? A review of the effects of kin on child survival. *Evolution and Human Behavior, 29*, 1–18.

Sears, R. B., Gates, G. J., & Rubenstein, W. B. (2005). *Same-sex couples and same-sex couples raising children in the United States: Data from census 2000.* Los Angeles: The Williams Institute.

Segal, N. (2007). *Indivisible by two: Lives of extraordinary twins.* Cambridge, MA: Harvard University Press.

Seifritz, E., Esposito, F., Neuhoff, J. G., Luthi, A., Mustovic, H., Dammann, G., et al. (2003). Differential sex-independent amygdale response to infant crying and laughing in parents versus nonparents. *Biological Psychiatry, 54,* 1367–1375.

Shaver, K. (2007, June 17). *Stay-at-home dads forge new identities, roles.* Retrieved April 29, 2013 from http://www.washingtonpost.com/wp-dyn/content/article/2007/06/16/AR2007061601289.html

Sheehan, N. W., & Petrovic, K. (2008). Grandparents and their adult grandchildren: Recurring themes from the literature. *Marriage & Family Review, 44,* 99–124.

Shelton, K. H., Boivin, J., Hay, D., van den Bree, M. B. M., Rice, F. J., Harold, G. T., et al. (2009). Examining differences in psychological adjustment problems among children conceived by assisted reproductive technologies. *International Journal of Behavioral Development, 33,* 385–392.

Shih, C. -K. (2010). *Quest for harmony: The Moso traditions of sexual union & family life.* Stanford, CA: Stanford University Press.

Shimonaka, Y., Nakazato, K., Kawaai, C., & Sato, S. (1997). Androgyny and successful adaptation across the life span among Japanese adults. *Journal of Genetic Psychology, 158,* 389–400.

Shklovski, I., Kraut, R. E., & Rainie, L. (2004). The Internet and social participation: Contrasting cross-sectional and longitudinal analyses. *Journal of Computer-Mediated Communication, 10.* Retrieved April 29, 2013 from http://jcmc.indiana.edu/vol10/issue1/shklovski_kraut.html

Shulman, S., & Klein, M. M. (1993). Distinctive role of the father in adolescent separation-individuation. In S. Shulman & A. W. Collins (Eds.), *Father-adolescent relationships: New directions for child development* (pp. 41–57). San Francisco: Jossey-Bass.

Signorielli, N. (2001). The picture in the nineties. *Generations, 25,* 34–38.

Silverstein, L. B., & Auerbach, C. F. (1999). Deconstructing the essential father. *American Psychologist, 54,* 397–407.

Silverstein, L. B., Auerbach, C. F., & Levant, R. F. (2002). Contemporary fathers reconstructing masculinity: Clinical implications of gender role strain. *Professional Psychology, Research and Practice, 33,* 361–369.

Silverstein, M., & Ruiz, S. (2006). Breaking the chain: How grandparents moderate the transmission of maternal depression to their grandchildren. *Family Relations, 55,* 601–612.

Simon, S. (2011, September). *Fatherhood, not testosterone, makes the man* (NPR report). Retrieved April 29, 2013 from http://www.npr.org/2011/09/17/140557571/fatherhood-not-testosterone-makes-the-man

Simoneau, D. K. (2006). *We're having a Tuesday.* Colorado: AC Publications Group LLC.

Singh, G. K., Kogan, M. D., & Yu, S. M. (2009). Disparities in obesity and overweight prevalence among U.S. immigrant children and adolescents by generational status. *Journal of Community Health, 34,* 271–281.

Singler, R. (2011). *Open all hours? Flexible childcare in the 24/7 era.* Retrieved April 29, 2013 from www.daycaretrust.org.uk

Sipe, C. L., & Roder, A. E. (1999). *Mentoring school-age children: A classification of programs.* Philadelphia: Public/Private Ventures.

Slade, P., O'Neill, C., Simpson, A. J., & Lashen, H. (2007). The relationship between perceived stigma, disclosure patterns, support and distress in new attendees at an infertility clinic. *Human Reproduction, 22,* 2309–2317.

Slattery, J. (2012, January 6). *Diversity drought: Why is TV so white?* Retrieved April 29, 2013 from http://www.zimbio.com/Malcolm-Jamal+Warner/articles/daPuZG7klod/ Diversity+Drought+TV+White

Small, M. F. (1998). *Our babies, ourselves: How biology and culture shape the way we parent.* New York: Anchor Books (Doubleday).

Small, M. F. (2001). *Kids: How biology and culture shape the way we raise our children.* New York: Anchor Books (Doubleday).

Small, M. F. (2003, April 1). How many fathers are best for a child? New York: Discover Magazine.

Small, M. F. (2008, December 5). The perfect family is a myth. *Live Science.* Retrieved April 29, 2013 from http://www.livescience.com/3113-perfect-family-myth.html

Smith, J. A. (2009). *The daddy shift.* Boston: Beacon Press.

Smith, P. (2011). *Stay at home dads' views.* Retrieved April 29, 2013 from http://www.stayathomedads.co.uk/dadsviews.html

Smith, P. K. (2005). Grandparents and grandchildren. *The Psychologist, 18,* 684–687.

Smith, P. K., & Drew, L. M. (2002). Grandparenthood. In M. Bornstein (Ed.), *Handbook of parenting* (2nd ed., Vol. 3, pp. 141–172). Mahwah, NJ: Erlbaum.

Smock, P. J. (2000). Cohabitation in the United States: An appraisal of research themes, findings, and implications. *Annual Review of Sociology, 26,* 1–20.

Snarey, J. (1993). *How fathers care for the next generation.* Cambridge, MA: Harvard University Press.

Snowden, R. (1988). The family and artificial reproduction. In D. R. Bromham, M. E. Dalton, & J. C. Jackson (Eds.), *Philosophical ethics in reproductive medicine.* Manchester, UK: Manchester University Press.

Solomon, J., & George, C. (1999). *Attachment disorganization.* New York: Guilford Publications.

Spar, D. L. (2006). *The baby business: How money, science, and politics drive the commerce of conception.* Cambridge, MA: Harvard University Press.

Stacey, J. (2006). Gay parenthood and the decline of paternity as we knew it. *Sexualities, 9,* 27–55.

Stacey, J. (2011). *Unhitched: Love, marriage and family values from West Hollywood to Western China.* New York: New York University Press.

Stacey, J., & Biblarz, T. J. (2001). (How) does sexual orientation of parents matter? *American Sociological Review, 65,*159–183.

Stack, C. (1974). *All our kin: Strategies for survival in a black community.* New York: Harper and Row.

Stack, C. B., & Burton, L. M. (1993). Kinscripts. *Journal of Comparative Family Studies, 24,* 157–170.

Stallings, J., Fleming, A. S., Corter, C., Worthman, C., & Steiner, M. (2001). The effects of infant cries and odors on sympathy, cortisol, and autonomic responses in new mothers and nonpostpartum women. *Parenting: Science and Practice, 1,* 71–100.

Stanca, L. (2012). Suffer the little children: Measuring the effects of parenthood on well-being worldwide. *Journal of Economic Behavior & Organization, 81,* 742–750.

Stanley, K., Edwards, L., & Hatch, B. (2003). *The family report 2003: Choosing happiness?.* London: Institute for Public Policy Research.

Stark, O., & Bloom, D. E. (1985). The new economics of labor migration. *American Economic Review, 75,* 173–178.

Statistics Canada. (2010). *On shifts in rates of stay at home fathers.* Ottawa, Ontario, Canada: Statistics Canada.

Steinem, G. (1971, August 26). *A new egalitarian life style.* New York: New York Times.

Stevenson, H. C. (1998). Raising safe villages: Cultural-ecological factors that influence the emotional adjustment of adolescents. *Journal of Black Psychology, 24,* 44–59.

Stewart, R., & Martin, R. (1984). Sibling relations: The role of conceptual perspective-taking in the ontogeny of sibling caregiving. *Child Development, 55*, 1322–1332.

Storey, A. E., & Walsh, C. J. (2012). The biological basis of mammalian paternal behavior. In N. J. Cabrera & C. S. Tamis-Lemonda (Eds.), *Handbook of father involvement: Multidisciplinary perspectives.* New York: Taylor & Francis.

Storey, A. E., Walsh, C. J., Quinton, R. L., & Wynne-Edwards, D. E. (2000). Hormonal correlates of paternal responsiveness in new and expectant fathers. *Evolution and Human Behavior, 21,* 79–95.

Story, L. B., & Repetti, R. (2006). Daily occupational stressors and marital behavior. *Journal of Family Psychology, 20,* 690–700.

Strazdins, L., Korda, R. J., Lim, L. L., Broom, D. H., & D'Souza, R. M. (2004). Around-the-clock: Parent work schedules and children's well-being in a 24-hour economy. *Social Science & Medicine, 59,* 1517–1527.

Stubben, J. D. (2001). Working with and conducting research among American Indian families. *American Behavioral Scientist, 44,* 1466–1481.

Stukas, A. A., Worth, K. A., Clary, E. G., & Snyder, M. (2009). The matching of motivations to affordances in the volunteer environment. *Nonprofit and Voluntary Sector Quarterly, 38,* 5–28.

Suarez-Orozco, C., & Suarez-Orozco, M. (1995). *Transformations: Migration, family life, and achievement motivation among Latino adolescents.* Stanford, CA: Stanford University Press.

Suárez-Orozco, C., & Suárez-Orozco, M. M. (2001). *Children of immigration.* Cambridge, MA: Harvard University Press.

Suarez-Orozco, C., Todorova, I., & Louie, J. (2002). Making up for lost time: The experience of separation and reunification among immigrant families. *Family Processes, 41,* 625–643.

Sugarman, S. D. (2008). What is a "family"? Conflicting messages from our public programs. *Family Law Quarterly, 42,* 231–261.

Suina, J. H., & Smolkin, L. B. (1994). From natal culture to school culture to dominant society culture: Supporting transitions for Pueblo Indian students. In P. M. Greenfield & R. R. Cocking (Eds.), *Cross-cultural roots of minority child development* (pp. 115–130). Hillsdale, NJ: Erlbaum.

Sun, Y., & Li, Y. (2002). Children's well-being during parents' marital disruption process? A pooled time-series analysis. *Journal of Marriage and Family, 64,* 894–909.

Sutfin, E. L., Fulcher, M., Bowles, R. P., & Patterson, C. J. (2008). How lesbian and heterosexual parents convey attitudes about gender to their children: The role of gendered environments. *Sex Roles, 58,* 501–513.

Suttor, M. (2008, February 10). Why grandparents should not interfere with parenting their grandchildren. *Helium.* Retrieved April 29, 2013 from http://www.helium.com/items/859255-why-grandparents-should-not-interfere-with-parenting-their-grandchildren

Swain, J. E., & Lorberbaum, J. P. (2008). Imaging the human parental brain. In R. S. Bridges (Ed.), *The neurobiology of the parental brain* (pp. 83–100). New York: Academic Press.

Swain, J. E., Lorberbaum, J. P., Kose, S., & Strathearn, L. (2007). Brain basis of early parent–infant interactions: Psychology, physiology, and in vivo functional neuroimaging studies. *Journal of Child Psychology and Psychiatry, 48,* 262–287.

Taht, K., & Mills, M. (2008, April). *Out of sight, out of mind? Nonstandard work schedules and parent child interaction.* Paper presented at the annual meeting of the Population Association of America meetings, New Orleans, LA.

Tamis-LeMonda, C. S., Bornstein, M. H., & Baumwell, L. (2001). Maternal responsiveness and children's achievement of language milestones. *Child Development, 72,* 748–767.

Tamis-LeMonda, C. S., Shannon, J. D., & Cabrera, N. (2004). Fathers and mothers at play with their 2- and 3-year-olds: Contributions to language and cognitive development. *Child Development, 75,* 1806–1820.

Tanaka, S. (2005). Parental leave and child health across OECD countries. *Economic Journal, 115*, F26.

Tasker, F., & Barrett, H. (2004, May 14). *The sexual identity of young adult sons and daughters of gay fathers.* Paper presented at the 7th Congress of the European Federation of Sexology, Brighton, UK.

Tasker, F., & Golombok, S. (1997). Young people's attitudes towards living in a lesbian stepfamily: A longitudinal study of children raised by lesbian mothers. *Journal of Divorce and Remarriage, 26*, 183–202.

Tavernise, S. (2012, January 15). Day care centers adapt to round-the-clock demand. *New York Times.* Retrieved April 29, 2013 from http://www.nytimes.com/2012/01/16/us/day-care-centers-adapt-to-round-the-clock-demands

Taylor, A., & Bressler, J. (2000). *Mentoring across generations: Partnerships for positive youth development.* New York: Kluwer Academic/Plenum.

Taylor, P., Passel, J., Fry, R., Morin, R., Wang, W., Velasco, G., et al. (2010). *The return of the multi-generational family household.* Washington, DC: Pew Research Center.

Teachman, J. (2008). Complex life course patterns and the risk of divorce in second marriages. *Journal of Marriage and Family, 70*, 294–305.

Telework Trendlines. (2009). *Survey brief by world at work.* Data collected by The Dieringer Research Group Inc. Retrieved April 29, 2013 from http://www.worldatwork.org/waw/adimLink?id=31115

Telzer, E. H., & Fuligni, A. J. (2009a). A longitudinal daily diary study of family assistance and academic achievement among adolescents from Mexican, Chinese, and European backgrounds. *Journal of Youth and Adolescence, 38*, 560–571.

Telzer, E. H., & Fuligni, A. J. (2009b). Daily family assistance and the psychological well-being of adolescents from Latin American, Asian, and European backgrounds. *Developmental Psychology, 45*, 1177–1189.

Telzer, E. H., Masten C. L., Berkman, E. T., Lieberman M. D., & Fuligni A. J. (2010). Gaining while giving: An fMRI study of the rewards of family assistance among white and Latino youth. *Social Neuroscience, 5*, 508–518.

The Joint Commission. (2010, June). *Advancing effective communication, cultural competence, and patient- and family-centered care: A roadmap for hospitals.* Oakbrook Terrace, IL: The Joint Commission.

Thompson, A. (2008). *A child alone and without papers: A report on the return and repatriation of unaccompanied undocumented children by the United States.* Austin, TX: Center for Public Policy Priorities.

Thompson, C. A., Beauvais, L. L., & Lyness, K. S. (1999). When work-family benefits are not enough: The influence of work-family culture on benefit utilization, organizational attachment, and work-family conflict. *Journal of Vocational Behavior, 54*, 392–415.

Thompson, R. A. (2006). The development of the person, social understanding, relationships, conscience, self. In W. Damon & R. M. Lerner (Series Eds.), & N. Eisenberg (Vol. Ed.), *Handbook of child psychology* (pp. 24–98). Hoboken, NJ: Wiley.

Tinsley, B. J., & Parke, R. D. (1987). Grandparents as interactive and social support agents for families with young infants. *International Journal of Aging and Human Development, 25*, 259–277.

Tinsley, B. R., & Parke, R. D. (1984). Grandparents as support and socialization agents. In M. Lewis (Ed.), *Beyond the dyad.* New York: Plenum.

Tolson, T. E. J., & Wilson, M. N. (1990). The impact of two- and three-generational Black family structure on perceived family climate. *Child Development, 61*, 416–428.

Tornello, S. L., Farr, R. H., & Patterson, C. J. (2011). Predictors of parenting stress among gay fathers. *Journal of Family Psychology, 25*, 591–600.

Tornello, S. L., & Patterson, C. J. (2010). *Gay fathers' pathways to parenthood: Has there been a generational shift?* Unpublished manuscript. Charlottesville, VA: University of Virginia.

Toulemon, L. (1996). Very few couples remain voluntarily childless. *Population, 8,* 1–27.

Touroni, E., & Coyle, A. (2002). Decision-making in planned lesbian parenting: An interpretative phenomenological analysis. *Journal of Community Applied Social Psychology, 12,* 194–209.

Trimble, J. E., & Medicine, B. (1993). Diversification of American Indians: Forming an indigenous perspective. In U. Kim & J. W. Berry (Eds.), *Indigenous psychologies: Research and experience in cultural context* (pp. 133–151). Thousand Oaks, CA: Sage.

Tronick, E. Z., Morelli, G. A., & Ivey, P. K. (1992). The Efe forager infant and toddler's pattern of social relationships: Multiple and simultaneous. *Developmental Psychology, 28,* 568–577.

Tronick, E. Z., Morelli, G. A., & Winn, S. (1987). Multiple caretaking of Efe (Pygmy) infants. *American Anthropologist, 89,* 96–106.

Tucker, M., & James, A. D. (2005). New families, new functions: Postmodern African American families in context. In V. C. McLoyd, N. E. Hill, & K. A. Dodge (Eds.), *African American family life ecological and cultural diversity* (pp. 86–108). New York: Guilford.

Turya, E. B., & Webster, J. N. (1986). Acceptability of and need for evening community child health clinics. *Child Care, Health, & Development, 12,* 93–98.

Twenge, J. M., Campbell, W. K., & Foster, C. A. (2003). Parenthood and marital satisfaction: A meta-analytic review. *Journal of Marriage and Family, 65,* 574–583.

Twine, F. W. (2011). *Outsourcing the womb: Race, class and gestational surrogacy in a global market.* New York: Routledge.

U.S. Bureau of Labor Statistics. (2011, July). *American time use survey.* Washington, DC: U.S. Bureau of Labor Statistics.

U.S. Census Bureau. (2002). *Census 2000, summary file 1.* Retrieved April 29, 2013 from http://www.census.gov/population/cen2000/Phc-TQ8

U.S. Census Bureau. (2003). *Population in the United States: Population characteristics, June, 2002.* Washington, DC: U.S. Government Printing Office.

U.S. Census Bureau. (2008). *Current population survey. People in families by family structure, age, and sex, iterated by income-to-poverty ratio and race: 2007.* Washington, DC: U.S. Government Printing Office.

U.S. Census Bureau. (2009). *Father's day: June 21, 2009.* Retrieved April 29, 2013 from www.census.gov/newsroom/releases/pdf/cb09-ff10.pdf

U. S. Census Bureau. (2010a). *America's families and living arrangements: 2010.* Washington, DC: U.S. Census Bureau, Housing and Household Economic Statistics Division, Fertility & Family Statistics Branch. Retrieved April 29, 2013 from http://www.census.gov/population/www/socdemo/hh-fam/cps2010.html

U.S. Census Bureau. (2010b). *Current Population Survey (CPS).* Retrieved April 29, 2013 from http://www.census.gov/population/www/cps/cpsdef.html

U.S. Census Bureau. (2010c). *Who's minding the kids? Child care arrangements: Spring 2005/ Summer 2006.* Retrieved April 29, 2013 from https://www.census.gov/prod/2010pubs/p70-121.pdf

U.S. Census Bureau. (2011). *Annual social and economic supplement (Table PoV03).* Retrieved April 29, 2013 from http://www.census.gov/hhes/www/cpstables/032011/pov/new03_100_01.htm

U.S. Department of Agriculture (USDA). (2012, June). *Expenditures on children by families: Current annual report 2011.* Washington DC: USDA. Retrieved April 29, 2013 from http://www.usda.gov/wps/portal/usda/usdahome

U.S. Department of Health and Human Services. (2011). *The AFCARS report preliminary FY 2010 estimates as of June 2011.* Retrieved April 29, 2013 from www.acf.hhs.gov/programs/cb

U.S. Department of Interior. (2007). *Indian entities recognized and eligible to receive service from the United States Bureau of Indian Affairs,* 72 Fed. Reg. 13648.

U.S. Department of Labor. (2009). *Quick stats on women workers, 2008.* Washington, DC: U.S. Bureau of Labor.

U.S. Department of Labor. (2010a). *Fact sheet # 28: The Family and Medical Leave Act of 1993.* Retrieved April 29, 2013 from http://www.dol.gov/whd/regs/compliance/whdfs28.htm

U.S. Department of Labor. (2010b). *US Department of Labor clarifies FMLA definition of 'son and daughter.* Retrieved April 29, 2013 from http://www.dol.gov/opa/media/press/WHD/WHD20100877.htm

U.S. Department of Labor. (2012). *Employment characteristics of families summary.* Retrieved April 29, 2013 from http://www.bls.gov/news.release/famee.nr0.htm

Valdes, G. (2003). *Expanding definitions of giftedness: The case of young interpreters from immigrant communities.* Mahwah, NJ: Erlbaum.

Valeggia, C. R. (2009). Flexible caretakers: Responses of Toba families in transition. In G. Bentley & R. Mace (Eds.), *Substitute parents: Biological and social perspectives on alloparenting in human societies* (pp. 100–115). New York: Berghahn Press.

Van Balen, F. (1998). Development of IVF children. *Developmental Review, 18,* 30–46.

Van Hook, J., & Glick, J. E. (2007). Immigration and living arrangements: Moving beyond economic need versus acculturation. *Demography, 44,* 225–249.

Van Ijzendoorn, M. H., Sagi, A., & Lambermon, M. W. E. (1992). The multiple caretaker paradox: Data from Holland and Israel. *New Directions for Child Development, 75,* 5–24.

Van Ijzendoorn, M. H., & Sagi-Schwartz, A. (2008). Cross-cultural patterns of attachment: Universal and contextual dimensions. In J. Cassidy & P. Shaver (Eds.), *Handbook of attachment* (2nd ed., pp. 880–905). New York: Guilford.

Van Voorhis, B. J. (2006). Outcomes from assisted reproductive technology. *Obstetrics and Gynecology, 107,* 183–200.

Vandell, D. L., Belsky, J., Burchinal, M., Steinberg, L., Vandergrift, N., & NICHD Early Child Care Research Network. (2010). Do effects of early child care extend to age 15 years? Results from the NICHD study of early child care and youth development. *Child Development, 81,* 737–756.

Vandell, D. L., Pierce, K. M., & Dadisman, K. (2005). Out-of-school settings as a developmental context for children and youth. In R. V. Kail (Ed.), *Advances in child development and behavior* (Vol. *33,* pp. 43–77). New York: Academic Press.

Vanfraussen, K., Ponjaert-Kristoffersen, I., & Brewaeys, A. (2002). What does it mean for a youngster to grow up in a lesbian family created by means of donor insemination? *Journal of Reproductive and Infant Psychology, 20,* 237–252.

Vidal, C. (1988). Godparenting among Hispanic Americans. *Child Welfare, 67,* 453–459.

Villanueva, C. M., & Buriel, R. (2010). Speaking on behalf of others: A qualitative study of the perceptions and feelings of adolescent Latina language brokers. *Journal of Social Issues, 66,* 197–210.

Vilska, S., Unkila-Kallio, L., Punamäki, R. -L., Poikkeus, P., Repokari, L., Sinkkonen, J., et al. (2009). Mental health of mothers and fathers of twins conceived via assisted reproduction treatment: A 1-year prospective study. *Human Reproduction, 24,* 367–377.

Vyncke, J. D., & Julien, D. (2007). Social support, coming out, and adjustment of lesbian mothers in Canada and France: An exploratory study. *Journal of GLTB Family Studies, 3,* 397–424.

Wainright, J. L., & Patterson, C. J. (2006). Delinquency, victimization, and substance use among adolescents with female same-sex parents. *Journal of Family Psychology*, *20*, 526–530.

Wainright, J. L., & Patterson, C. J. (2008). Peer relations among adolescents with female same-sex parents. *Developmental Psychology*, *44*, 117–126.

Wainright, J. L., Russell, S. T., & Patterson, C. J. (2004). Psychosocial adjustment and school outcomes of adolescents with same-sex parents. *Child Development*, *75*, 1886–1898.

Waldfogel, J. (2001, September). Family and medical leave: Evidence from the 2000 surveys. *Monthly Labor Review*, *21*.

Waldrop, D. P. (2003). Caregiving issues for grandmothers raising their grandchildren. *Journal of Human Behavior in the Social Environment*, *7*, 201–223.

Walker, R. S., Flinn, M. V., & Hill, K. R. (2010). Evolutionary history of partible paternity in lowland South America. *Proceedings of the National Academy of Sciences*, *107*, 19195–19200.

Wall, C. S., & Madak, P. R. (1991). Indian students academic self concept and their perceptions of teacher and parent aspirations for them in a band-controlled school and a provincial school. *Canadian Journal of Native Education*, *18*, 43–51.

Walls, M. L., & Whitbeck, L. B. (2012). The intergenerational effects of relocation policies on indigenous families. *Journal of Family Issues*, *33*, 1272–1293.

Walsh, F. (2006). *Strengthening family resilience* (2nd ed.). New York: Guilford Press.

Walsh, J. (2011). *Failing its families: Lack of paid leave and work-family supports in the US*. New York: Human Rights Watch.

Walsh, S., Schulman, S., Bar-On, Z., & Tsur, A. (2006). The role of parentification and family climate in adaptation among immigrant adolescents in Israel. *Journal of Research on Adolescence*, *16*, 321–350.

Wardle, L. D. (1997). The potential impact of homosexual parenting on children. *University of Illinois Law Review*, *833*, 335–340.

Warnock, C. (2012, February 29). *Dramatic trends churches are ignoring*. Retrieved April 29, 2013 from chuckwarnockblog.wordpress.com/

Warnock, M. (1987). Ethics, decision-making and social policy. *Community Care*, *685*, 18–23.

Warnock, M. (2002). *Making babies: Is there a right to have children?* Oxford, UK: Oxford University Press.

Warshak, R., & Santrock, J. W. (1983). The impact of divorce in father-custody and mother-custody: The child's perspective. In L. A. Kurdek (Ed.), *Children and divorce* (pp. 29–46). San Francisco: Jossey-Bass.

Weaver, J. D. (2013). Grandma in the White House: Legal support for intergenerational caregiving. *Seton Hall Law Review*, *43*, 1–74.

Weinberger, S. (2000). *The Allstate work-based mentoring project*. Norwalk, CT: Mentor Consulting Group.

Weinraub, B. (1998, June 18). *Dousing the glow of TV's first family; time for the truth about Ozzie and Harriet*. New York Times.

Weinraub, M., Horvath, D. L., & Gringlas, M. B. (2002). Single parenthood. In M. H. Bornstein (Ed.), *Handbook of parenting: Being and becoming a parent* (2nd ed., Vol. 3, pp. 109–140). Mahwah, NJ: Erlbaum.

Weisenfeld, A., Zander-Malatesta, C., & DeLoach, L. (1981). Differential parental responses to familiar and unfamiliar infant distress signals. *Infant Behavior and Development*, *4*, 281–295.

Weisfeld, G. E., Czilli, T., Phillips, K. A., Gall, J. A., &. Lichtman, C. M. (2003). Possible olfaction-based mechanisms on human kin recognition and inbreeding avoidance. *Journal of Experimental Child Psychology*, *85*, 279–295.

Weisner, T. S. (1982). Sibling interdependence and child caretaking: A cross-cultural view. In M. Lamb & B. Sutton-Smith (Eds.), *Sibling relationships: Their nature and significance* (pp. 305–327). Hillsdale, NJ: Erlbaum.

Weisner, T. S. (1986). Implementing new relationship styles in conventional and nonconventional American families. In W. Hartup & Z. Rubin (Eds.), *Relationships and development* (pp. 185–206). Mahwah, NJ: Erlbaum.

Weisner, T. S. (1987). Socialization for parenthood in sibling caretaking societies. In J. B. Lancaster, J. Altman, A. Rossi, & L. Sherrod (Eds.), *Parenting across the life span* (pp. 237–270). New York: Aldine de Gruyter.

Weisner, T. S. (2008). African childhood. In R. A. Shweder, T. R. Bidell, A. C. Dailey, S. D. Dixon, P. J. Miller, & J. Modell (Eds.), *The child: An encylopedic companion* (pp. 43–46). Chicago: University of Chicago Press.

Weissenberg, R., Landau, R., & Madgar, I. (2007). Older single mothers assisted by sperm donation and their children. *Human Reproduction, 22,* 2784–2791.

Weisskirch, R. S., & Alva-Alatorre, S. (2002). Language brokering and acculturation of Latino children. *Hispanic Journal of Behavioral Sciences, 24,* 369–378.

Wen, M., & Lin, D. (2012). Child development in rural China: Children left behind by their migrant parents and children of nonmigrant families. *Child Development, 83,* 120–136.

Weyer, M., & Sandler, I. N. (1998). Stress and coping as predictors of children's divorce-related ruminations. *Journal of Clinical Child Psychology, 27,* 78–86.

Whitbeck, L. B., Sittener Hartshorn, K. J., & Walls, M. L. (2013) *Historical and social contexts of indigenous adolescent development.* Unpublished manuscript, University of Nebraska, Lincoln, NE.

Whiting, B., & Edwards, C. P. (1988). *Children of different worlds: The formation of social behavior.* Cambridge, MA: Harvard University Press.

Whitman, T. L., Borkowski, J. G., Keogh, D., & Weed, K. (2001). *Interwoven lives: Adolescent mothers and their children.* Mahwah, NJ: Erlbaum.

Wilding, R. (2006). 'Virtual' intimacies? Families communicating across transnational contexts. *Global Networks, 6,* 125–142.

Wilkenfeld, B., Moore, K. A., & Lippman, L. (2008). *Neighborhood support and children's connectedness.* Child Trends Fact Sheet.

Williams, E., Radin, N., & Allegro, T. (1992). Sex role attitudes of adolescents reared primarily by their fathers: An 11-year follow-up. *Merrill-Palmer Quarterly, 38,* 457–476.

Williams, J. C. (2010). *Reshaping the family-work debate.* Cambridge, MA: Harvard University Press.

Wilson, M. N. (1986). The black extended family: An analytical consideration. *Developmental Psychology, 22,* 246–258.

Wilson, M. N. (1992). Perceived parental activity of mothers, fathers, and grandmothers in three-generational black families. In A. K. H. Burlew, W. D. Banks, H. P. McAdoo, & D. A. Azibo (Eds.), *African American psychology: Theory, research, and practice* (pp. 87–104). Thousand Oaks, CA: Sage Publications.

Wilson, W. J. (2010). Why both social structure and culture matter in a holistic analysis of inner-city poverty. *Annals of the American Academy of Political and Social Science, 629,* 200–219.

Wolchik, S., West, S., Sandler, I., Tein, J., Coatsworth, D., Lengua, L., et al. (2000). An experimental evaluation of theory-based mother and mother-child programs for children of divorce. *Journal of Consulting and Clinical Psychology, 68,* 843–856.

Wolchik, S. A., Sandler, I. N., Millsap, R. E., Plummer, B. A., Greene, S. M., Anderson, E. R., et al. (2002). Six-year follow-up of preventive interventions for children of divorce: A randomized controlled trial. *Journal of the American Medical Association, 288,* 1874–1881.

Wong, M. G. (1988). The Chinese-American family. In C. H. Mindel & R. W. Haberstein (Eds.), *Ethnic families in America* (pp. 230–257). New York: Elsevier.

Wong, M. G. (1995). Chinese Americans. In P. G. Min (Ed.), *Asian Americans: Contemporary trends and issues* (p. 58–94). Thousand Oaks, CA: Sage Publications.

Wu, Z., Hou, F., & Schimmele, C. M. (2008). Family structure and children's psychosocial outcomes. *Journal of Family Issues, 29*, 1625–1649.

Yeung, W. J., Sandberg, J. F., Davis-Kean, P. E., & Hofferth, S. L. (2001). Children's time with fathers in infant families. *Journal of Marriage and Family, 63*, 136–154.

Ying, Y. -W., Coombs, M., & Lee, P. A. (1999). Family intergenerational relationship of Asian American adolescents. *Cultural Diversity and Ethnic Minority Psychology, 5*, 350–363.

Zaslow, M., Jekielek, S., & Gallagher, M. (2005). Work-family mismatch through a child developmental lens. In S. M. Bianchi, L. M. Casper, & B. R., King (Eds.), *Work, family, health, and well-being* (pp. 259–278). Mahwah, NJ: Erlbaum.

Zegers-Hochschild, F. (2002). The Latin American registry of assisted reproduction. In E. Vayena, P. Rowe, & P. Griffin (Eds.), *Current practices and controversies in assisted reproduction. Report of a WHO Meeting.* Geneva: World Health Organization.

Zelizer, V. (1985). *Pricing the priceless child.* New York: Basic Books.

Zimmerman, M. A., Ramirez, J., Washienko, K. M., Walter, B., & Dyer, S. (1998). Enculturation hypothesis: Exploring direct and protective effects among Native American youth. In H. I. McCubbins, E. A. Thompson, A. I. Thompson, & J. E. Fromer (Eds.), *Resiliency in Native American and immigrant families* (Vol. 2, pp. 199–220). Thousand Oaks, CA: Sage.

Zinn, M. B. (1994). Feminist rethinking from racial-ethnic families. In M. B. Zinn & B. T. Dill (Eds.), *Women of color in U. S. society.* Philadelphia: Temple University.

Zukow-Goldring, P. (2002). Sibling caregiving. In M. H. Bornstein (Ed.), *Handbook of parenting* (2nd ed., Vol. 3, pp. 253–286). Mahwah, NJ: Erlbaum.

# Index

*Future Families: Diverse Forms, Rich Possibilities*, First Edition. Ross D. Parke.
© 2013 John Wiley & Sons, Inc. Published 2013 by John Wiley & Sons, Inc.